GLADIATOR

FRANCESCO TOTTI

GLADIATOR

FRANCESCO TOTTI

WITH PAOLO CONDO

Translated from the Italian
by Anthony Wright

English translation copyright © De Coubertin Books Ltd 2021.

First published as a hardback by deCoubertin Books Ltd in 2021.

First Edition

deCoubertin Books, 49 Jamaica Street, Baltic Triangle, Liverpool, L1 0AH.

www.decoubertin.co.uk

ISBN: 978-1-9162784-9-3

Copyright © 2018 Mondadori Libri S. p. A., Milano

A CIP catalogue record for this book is available from the British Library.

Translation: Anthony Wright

English editor: James Corbett

Cover design by Thomas Regan/MilkyOne.

Photographs: Luciano e Fabio Rossi / Roma Photo / AS Roma / Alamy / Imago

Typeset by Leslie Priestley.

Printed and bound by Standart Impressa

Contents

To Ilary, Fiorella, Chanel and Isabel
my girls.
To Enzo, Riccardo and Cristian
my boys

Introduction

THE YOUNGSTER SAT IN THE SECOND ROW IS VERY AGITATED. I don't think he'd listened to the warden's speech, and I don't think he's following mine now either. Not that it's anything unforgettable, but, well, I'd done a bit of work on it. Forget it. He's bouncing impatiently on that chair, and you know that the moment he's anticipating the most is yet to come. The photo, of course. The usual stage has been erected in the corner of the Rebibbia hall, and when the award ceremony for the *calcetto* tournament has finished, I'll head over there for a photo with anyone who wants one. That's what he's waiting for.

'Hey, I'm first,' he's saying, laughing with excited joy, over the top, which intrigues me. First for what? I finish my talk and look at him again, still bouncing excitedly over there. He must be twenty, twenty-two at most, and he's dressed a little better than the other inmates.

'I'm getting a photo first,' he repeats, and this time he turns to me, giving me a thumbs-up, as if he were communicating an organisational matter to me that I should know about.

Awards are handed over, hands are shaken, and glances, like those of fans but a bit more intense, are exchanged. It's not the first time I've been to Rebibbia, and I've visited Regina Coeli too. They were touching experiences. From outside, you can't imagine what prison means.

'Me, me, me first.'

The general movement towards the photo area, where some guards are regulating the traffic towards me in a friendly but firm way, is preceded by my 'friend' taking a step forward. Now I'm curious: what's the difference for him if he has a photo first, or tenth, or a hundredth? I've already told everyone that I'm staying until I've posed for the last one. But this guy is walking faster than the others, cutting the queue by jumping in here and there, without arrogance but with determination, and the great thing is that he's allowed to do it. He doesn't have an intimidating physical presence; he's slender, very skinny, and yet the others are treating him with a combination of respect and amusement. He's still bouncing up and down, like a boxer who's working out his opponent.

'I'm here, me now,' he says, while we're still about three metres apart and there are another two inmates between us. He looks at them with a slightly toothless smile, and they move aside to let him past. Who is he? Is he already a boss? So young?

I call him over next to me in a falsely gruff tone – 'Come on, over here, just calm down' – and he slides over to my side, wraps his arm around my waist while I put my arm around his shoulders, one, two, three, click, thumbs up, all proud. He has the bright eyes of those fans who couldn't love me more, and his joy is contagious because everyone's laughing just looking at him. As he's about to go, I put an arm out to stop him. I'm too curious. I have to know. Why absolutely first?

'Captain, I should have got out a week ago, finished, sentence served. But when I found out you were coming, I said to myself, "When will I have another chance to pose for a photo with the captain? Never, even if I lived for a hundred years..." So I asked to speak with the warden and I begged him to stay until today. But because the regulations didn't allow it, I played my joker: "Look, if you let me out, I'll do something stupid to be sent straight back here, and that's no good for either of us," and he understood. But now I want to get out of here, my girl's been waiting for me for three years...'

I hope that that girl's patience lasted that extra week, especially if the guy told her about his stunt. Seven days in jail for nothing, just to have a photo with me.

*   *   *

It's a funny story, I know. When friends come round for dinner, first their eyes go wide, then they think that I've made it up and have a big old laugh. But after having said goodbye to them and closed the front door behind me, sometimes I think about it again before going to sleep. What have I done to be worthy of such crazy, such absolute, such excessive love? I've never asked for it, and if I say that, it's not to reject the responsibilities it entails, which I've never run away from. No, I've never asked for it because I'm shy.

There. I've said it. I know it didn't seem that way on the pitch, but you mustn't rely on that alone because the football pitch is a jungle. If you don't grow up quick you don't have a chance. The pitch is above all a question of survival. I'm talking about the private Francesco, of the child who at home – when his mother went out to do the shopping, leaving him alone for half an hour – would curl up under the covers in fear, and to avoid hearing the strange noises he imagined in other rooms, he turned up the volume of *CHiPs*, the two policemen on motorcycles on the streets of California, his first childhood friends.

I was shy as a child and I still am now. I'm embarrassed in front of expressions of affection that flatter me beyond all limits, but which demand something of me too. It still happens today: when I walk with the team into a stadium, an airport, a hotel, everyone runs up to me. In those moments, I want to dig myself a hole and disappear. I'm not playing anymore, now others are the protagonists, go up to them and shower them with love just as you did for me for twenty-five years. Go up to Daniele, he's our captain now.

Not a chance.

I try to comfort myself by thinking that I'm taking pressure off the players this way, making sure that they're calmer, that they're conserving their nervous energy for the game. But I don't like it. I don't like it at all.

It's always been like this, practically from day one. Roman and Romanista, I'm considered one of the family. All the fans want to invite me to their children's communion. And maybe this is the real difference with the others: the talented footballer, the best in the team, is usually an idol, a role model, a poster boy. They're beautiful things, but different from being one of the family. I'm something more, the son and the brother.

Wonderful, but a little stressful. Idols pass, posters tear. Sons and brothers, though, never betray, or at least, no one thinks they can. This feeling, so special and so widespread, has made me the symbol of *romanità* – 'Romanness' – for many. That's another great honour. But I didn't ask for that either.

Once, after its win at the Oscars, I decided to watch *La Grande Bellezza*, which I knew was a bit demanding. After sixty seconds, maybe less, I was right in the middle of it. I'm not even joking. No one had noticed it, or at least, no one had told me, but I noticed it straight away. The opening scene is shot on the Janiculum, next to the statue of Garibaldi, and the first words you read in the film are 'Rome or death.' Then the camera moves into the gardens, framing a couple of strange faces between the busts of the patriots, and stops on a lady, no longer young but all dressed up, with a cigarette dangling from her lips. She's holding a newspaper, reading it – it's a *Gazzetta*. Well, the headline on the page in view is the second text you see in the film: 'Alarm over Totti.' My heart skipped a beat. Under the headline, you can make out a photo taken while I'm on the ground in pain. I guess the article talked about one of my injuries, and the alarm had to be related to my involvement in the next game. Trifles, but even so, the film that the whole world has seen because they're in love with this city opens with my name.

Rome is a mother, we all know that. To be her favourite child is a beautiful thing, and yet sometimes frightening too. Here's that question again: what have I done to be worthy of such crazy, such absolute, such excessive love?

1.

The Chosen One

MY COUSIN ANGELO GESTURED IMPATIENTLY. 'GO! GO!' HIS voice was a whisper, but his face was that of someone screaming. I was totally paralysed, I'd got chills, and I wanted to hide from the embarrassment.

My name had just been called over the loudspeakers for the tournament's top scorer award. It was a beautiful summer evening and the whole stand at Fortitudo's pitch had started to applaud, there must have been two thousand people there. I was just six years old.

'Totti. Francesco.' The manager paused for a moment. 'Where's he gone? Francesco?'

Angelo clapped his hands in front of my face, as if to say, *Hey, wake up, it's you.* I answered him with a scowl, one that caused my forehead to wrinkle up. It was easy for him, my dearest childhood friend, my mother's brother's son: he'd always had courage, especially around adults, and not just because he's ten months older.

'Francesco!' In the end, the manager saw me, and he called to me in a loud voice, gesturing at me with his big hand, 'Come, come!' It seemed as if everyone was repeating each word twice, as if I were slow to understand, whereas actually I was just shy. Very shy. I took a deep breath and forced myself to climb the steps to get to the top of the stand, where the awards were given out.

I'd been playing at Fortitudo for about a year, the pitch is close to home, in the heart of the neighbourhood. All the kids from Porta Metronia are registered, and a tournament is organised every summer, twelve teams of eight players. Our team was Botafogo, and we'd beaten Flamengo in the final: someone else was the captain, so that evening I was feeling relaxed, as it was up to him to go and get the cup. I hadn't known there would be individual trophies too. The manager handed me the award, Mum and Dad were around somewhere as well, though I didn't see them, while Angelo – who was obviously in the team with me – smiled happily because he thought I'd beaten my shyness. Not at all. I still wanted to be swallowed up, but once two thousand pairs of eyes have identified you, you can't ignore them anymore. I confusedly thought it would be polite to say some thanks, but the idea of speaking into the microphone absolutely wasn't an option. I kept my gaze fixed on the ground, and as soon as I felt the manager's handshake loosen a little, I slipped away, hoping that people were already focused on the next award. I quickly went down the steps and got back onto the pitch and into the protective embrace of my teammates – one of them wanted to look at the award – and I placed myself right in the centre of the group, perfectly hidden.

A whistle signalled that the microphone is about to be used again. The manager's voice was monotonous, seemingly not taking in what he was saying: 'Player of the tournament: Totti, Francesco.'

Oh no.

Shy, sure. Quiet, absolutely. It took me a long time to speak properly, almost five years. I struggled to put syllables together, so much so that Mum regularly took me to a speech therapist to find out if there was anything seriously wrong with my larynx. 'Don't worry,' he reassured her after carrying out various tests. 'Francesco just needs to "start." He's like a car with the handbrake on. You just have to get him going.' He was right. As with all children, once I'd started, I didn't think about it anymore.

Thinking back on that reluctance to express myself, it's likely that there was an impact from my heartache for my grandfather Costante, Mum's father, who had come to live with us after he had had a leg amputated, and he wasn't well. He'd worked his whole life maintaining cold storage rooms, and the constant fluctuations between heat and cold had brought him gangrene. We slept in the same room, and every evening, pretending to be asleep already, I watched with increasing shock as my mother went to remove his prosthesis and put it next to the radiator. To my eyes, she was pulling his leg off, and it frightened me a lot. One night, after waiting for my grandfather to start snoring, I got up and quietly went to touch the prosthesis, and found out that it was made of wood. I ran back to bed, risking waking him up, and hid my head under the pillow. Later on, by the time I was going to school, his condition had worsened, and Mum asked a neighbour, Mrs Schibba, if I could stay with her for a while: Dad took a foldout bed and set it up in her house, I went to school with Flavia and Roberta, her daughters, so things were good for me. When grandfather Costante passed away, Mum, while sorting through his things, showed me his Roma lifetime membership card. He was very proud of it.

I was often in the house alone. And I was a bit of a coward. In the mornings, Dad would go to the bank to work, my brother Riccardo – six years older than me – was at school, and Mum had to go shopping. She wrote down all sorts of suggestions and then went out. I was still in bed, and two minutes after hearing the door close and her footsteps go down the stairs, the fears crept in. I could feel a presence in the other rooms, strange noises, creaking, something rubbing on the ground, a muffled sound, maybe metallic. Then I curled up under the covers pretending to be dead, and I thought that when the thief – because there was definitely a thief out there – came to look in my room, he'd be shocked and saddened by the sight of a dead child, and would go away.

As a strategy it's a bit grim, but it worked because no one ever came in to check, or at least no one ever lifted up the covers. What's more, when I'd convinced myself that I'd escaped them once again, I would turn on the TV – Dad bought a second one, smaller than the one we had in the living room, and put it in my room: a big gift – and look for *CHiPs*, which was my favourite show, and I turned it up to maximum volume so as not to hear any worrying sounds. Some time later, Mum burst into the room out of breath – I'd not heard her come back – and turned the volume right down: 'Are you crazy? You'll go deaf like that!' I would go into a bit of a sulk, but actually I was happy that I'd passed another test of solitude, and especially that she was back. (Between you and me, the fear has never completely gone away: even today, at home, if the alarm goes off at night, I pretend to sleep and let Ilary get up to check…)

I liked *CHiPs* because it reflected the dreams of the time: two American policemen patrolling the California highways on their motorbikes. What more could you want than one of their Kawasakis? In the afternoon there was *Magnum, P.I.* and then, of course, *Captain Tsubasa*: I don't know any players from my generation who didn't devour the cartoons of the young Japanese footballers as children. But those were years when the street had a very strong attraction, because everyone in the neighbourhood knew each other and mothers felt comfortable about letting you out, as there were dozens of eyes to watch over you. Those of the shopkeepers of Via Vetulonia, for example, who wouldn't stay behind their counters if they didn't have any customers, as happens today, but stood in the doorway or right outside, on the pavement, where they would chat with each other, with passers-by, and even with us children. All their children were my friends. There was Antonio, called *il Morto* because he was always pale, Bambino, the two Giancarlos, Pantano and Ciccacci, then Marco and Sonia, the barman's children, as well as my inseparable cousin Angelo, obviously. A real gang, but good guys.

Once, I must have been twelve, Angelo, Bambino and I were going down the street and saw two brothers playing with a ball inside the schoolyard. They weren't fully part of our group because they only appeared from time to time; they must have had parents who were very strict about their studies. But we knew each other, so we took it for granted that we could join them. Then we'd only need one more for a nice three on three. But they didn't pass the ball, thinking they owned it: 'It's our ball and you're not playing with it.' The more we insisted, the more they moved away, always passing the ball carefully between them to keep it away from us.

Bambino was the most irritable of us, the one who acts first in certain situations: he retrieved a chain, the sort used to lock a bike to a post, and started to run it along the school gates, making a sinister sound. But the two were really stubborn and didn't have any intention of giving in, and in the end the shoving started. There was no contest, at that age what matters is how big you are, as well as how much time you've spent on the street. The brothers ran away, leaving the ball there, free for us to use.

We started playing, happy about winning that tug of war, and the fight was soon forgotten. By us. Too bad that, at the end of the afternoon, when we got back home, we found our mothers waiting for us outside the front door. More furious than they'd ever been before. They'd just come back from the police station in Via Cilicia. In short, the brothers' parents had filed a complaint about the fight and the theft of the ball, and the police officers – who knew us – had called our mothers to settle the issue without further action. It was agreed that, in addition to the cost of the ball, there should be a promise of a serious punishment, and for a few days we had to forget about our afternoons wandering around the neighbourhood.

And it didn't end there, the rest was waiting for us at school the next day. I was in class when there was a knock on the door. It was Mrs Paracallo – a real big woman, who taught music – who stuck her head in, apologised to the teacher, and turned to me with suspicious sweetness: 'Francesco, could you come out here for a moment, please?' I couldn't not go, even though I could smell a rat.

Sure enough, as soon as I went out, she – lightning-quick – caught my ear in a two-finger grip; she was holding Angelo in the same way, deaf to his protests, in her other hand. She led us like this, literally carried by the ears, around the entire building, without sparing us a single floor. In the meantime, the bell had gone and all the kids who were coming out of their classrooms saw us and laughed. Those two damned brothers must have been there too, sneering somewhere in the middle. Absolute, total shame.

Of course, it's no coincidence that the worst of my 'exploits' involved a football. Dad told me that when I was just eight months old, on holiday in the Tuscan seaside town of Porto Santo Stefano, I put on a show, the first of many, pushing the orange Super Santos ball he'd given me with my feet along the pebble beach. Not to sound like a hotshot, but usually children can't even walk at eight months. I, on the other hand, took the ball for a walk, on an uneven surface too. I even slept with it, I've been told: no toys, not even a Jeeg Robot, which was flying off the shelves at the time. Only the Super Santos. You can tell that I sensed the influence it would have on my life.

I went out on the streets every day. I came back from school – which just meant crossing the street, because Manzoni was right there, in front of the house – ate something and sat on the balcony to study, not to enjoy the fresh air but because as soon as I saw a familiar face, I would rush down, shouting to Mum that everyone was waiting for me. 'Have you studied?' was the precursor to her surrender, because no sooner had I shouted back three yeses than I was too far away to hear any more replies.

There were around thirty kids in our group, and we looked at our neighbourhood as if it were the most beautiful in Rome: working-class but not poor, full of courtyards in which to play, and above all brought to life by people on the street at all hours. My family was very large. On Sundays we often went to visit relatives in Trastevere or Testaccio. They were nice trips, but I only truly felt at home in Porta Metronia. Lots of football, lots of running about, lots of innocent jokes: for a time, the thing to do was to ring intercoms and, instead of running away, the fun consisted of answering using a famous name. I was obsessed with the TV host Gerry Scotti. 'Who is it?' 'Gerry Scotti!' And then I ran away.

We played football in the courtyards as well as in the street, because the shops weren't open all day and, at 2pm, they lowered their shutters, giving us, sometimes until five, the best goals we could have wished for. People weren't happy about it, because every ball kicked hard against the shutters brought a loud noise and protests, but none of us cared. We played 'German-style', that is, with short passes in the air, a classic pavement exercise to stop the ball from rolling into the street. As a professional we scored a goal like this in the title season against Perugia: lots of touches in front of goal without the ball ever touching the ground.

The most serious problem we had was when the schoolyard was closed and the ball ended up inside it. We had to call the caretaker, who was a bit of a gruff sort, over the intercom, hoping it would be answered by his son Gigi, who was the same age as us: he was a boy who almost never went out, very solitary, but good and kind at heart, unlike the two complaining brothers. He was always burdened with the hassle of getting the ball back, once, twice, three times an afternoon. I loved him for that.

It's not easy to identify the precise moment of my childhood when I became aware of my talent because it had always been there, ever since Porto Santo Stefano. What I mean is that it's not a question of a superpower that came to me by some quirk of fate, as happens in comics, but an innate ability.

Perhaps an early form of awareness came from Ducks, the game of precision you learn as a child. A line of kids arrange themselves at the top of a set of steps – we had our fun out the front of Manzoni – and at first they move horizontally, then diagonally, going down the steps, down to the bottom. About ten metres away, the shooter has some balls in front of him, which he has to use to hit the 'ducks' before they've completed the course. It's a simple exercise only in appearance, because you have to hit a series of moving targets while keeping calm as they approach the end of their path and as time begins to run out. The balls available to a group of kids are also different from one another: there's the leather one full of air, the deflated one, the plastic one, the volleyball... You have to hit each one with the right force, which is never the same. Well, the first time I tried it – I must have been five or six – I hit all the targets.

Looking back on it now, I remember the disbelief on the faces of Angelo and the others. 'Do it again,' someone said, and I repeated the exercise, but this time I missed a shot. I felt anger growing inside me, because I'm very competitive and, if I don't win, even a bit of a sore loser. I felt that that mistake, the only one of a dozen shots between the first and second attempts, risked tarnishing the performance in some way. It was the expression on Angelo's face, as always, that told me that the amazement hadn't watered down even a little. Then I felt an emotion between happiness and disbelief: it seemed too good to be true, but I had the feeling that I knew how to be good at the game I love most.

Over the course of my career, I've been told many times that fortune kissed me on the forehead. But when Mum gets friendly with someone, she's compelled to recount the story of a different kiss, and I have to say that even I would hardly believe her if her story weren't supported by a photo. The story dates back to the first grade, when the whole school was admitted to a papal audience in the Vatican, in the famous Sala Nervi. By pushing and elbowing, Mum managed to get through to the front, where she was certain she'd be only one step away from John Paul II. When the Pope set down a path that would lead him right past her, she took me in her arms.

I was dressed in an outfit that was so yellow it looked like the Vatican sports uniform, and I was very blond: a real little angel. When the Pope, who was caressing the children stretched out from their mothers' arms, passed me by, he lightly touched my hair with his hand, and that already seemed like so much to me. He walked on for another couple of metres and then, suddenly, he stopped. Mum, who was about to put me back on the ground, paused too. John Paul II turned around, took two steps back, bent over and kissed me on the forehead. I don't know how she managed it, but luckily my mother didn't faint and I didn't fall to the ground.

Her friend who was with her started to shout: 'Fiorella! The Pope has chosen Francesco! He turned around to kiss him!', and as chaos broke out among the mothers of my class, someone slipped her purse out of her bag. The collective attention quickly shifted to the theft, which was discovered almost immediately, and it was just as well because the Pope's about-turn had caused Mum a real shock.

Even today, when we go back to the subject, she believes in the idea that on that day I in some way became the Chosen One, just as they call LeBron James in America. My career is there to prove it. The story is supported by the photo that was taken at that moment, but the Lord has more important things to concern himself with than spreading football talent around. John Paul II kissed me on the forehead because I was blond and wore a nice yellow outfit. End of story.

I quickly became unbeatable at Ducks. I never missed a shot, so to have fun we had to play in teams with the weakest always on my side so that I'd have to worry not only about hitting my targets but also about righting their mistakes. Yet I'd still win, eliminating my targets before they'd even got halfway and then focusing on the others. My expertise was down to two factors. The first was a clean strike: the ball would remain connected to my instep for only a fraction of a second, immediately starting on a very accurate and fast trajectory, and even if the target had wanted to dodge it, they wouldn't have had time. I scored a goal like that against Inter at the San Siro a few years ago off a pass from Gervinho: a very clean strike into the corner from the edge of the penalty area, one of my last really nice goals, the first in a 3-0 win. The second factor was the ability to instantly control the balls that would arrive from whoever had to collect them and throw them into the shooting area. Almost everyone wasted time running after them because they'd miscontrolled the ball and it ran away. That didn't happen to me, thanks to my technique, and in team games, seconds won like this are decisive.

Winning is great, but what I really like is feeling the confidence of my teammates, certain of the result when they're in a team with me. Responsibility has never been a source of stress, ever since the days of Ducks, and there were a few penalties in big games when, before taking the kick, my thoughts went back to the schoolyard. But I'll tell you about that later. I swear that even in the days on Via Vetulonia, there was excitement. Excitement, and the prospect of financial gain: every day, Dad gave me a thousand lire (€0.50) for a snack, but I saved the money up because I always won whenever we played for ice cream. It was such a sentence that when I happened to lose once, I spent a fortune because everyone took advantage of it: no Arcobaleno, the cheaper ice lolly, but lots of Twisters, cream and chocolate, stuff for the rich. And when the opportunity next presented itself…

I think the first to have realised the extent of my talent was my father, Enzo. It's short for Lorenzo, but people called him 'Sheriff' because he loved to keep everything under control, and whatever anyone might need, give him half an hour and he'd have it. He always insisted on taking me to Piazza Epiro, where the market is, because older boys played there, so the test was harder. He'd accompany me to the piazza and, knowing that I was shy, would ask himself if I could join in. At first there was a bit of reticence, they saw I was small and were worried about hurting me, but it's difficult to say no to an adult. So I was added to a team and before long, in front of Dad's seemingly benevolent and satisfied smile, the game had to be stopped because my entrance had unbalanced it. 'Let's remake the teams,' and inevitably the first one to be picked was me.

They called me Gnomo, my nickname at the time, because I just wasn't growing. Mum, after taking me to the doctor and asking him with some determination – as if it were his fault – why the hell I was still so small, started to feed me Royal Jelly. At the time it was all the rage, a magical potion like the druid's in Asterix, but on the palate it was a truly disgusting thing. Carnitine was better, another growth supplement that at least had the merit of a sour cherry taste. When I read about the problems that Messi overcame as a child in Argentina, I empathised greatly. I 'set off' at twelve years old, and Gnomo quickly ended up in the bin of forgotten nicknames.

When you spend so many hours on the street, you inevitably become a son of the neighbourhood, in the sense that everyone knows you, forgives your nonsense – like the water balloons at the Atac drivers, who didn't have air conditioning and travelled with their windows down in summer – makes sure you don't get into trouble and treats you with affection. For example, the upholsterer who had the shop next door to us, Mr Corazza, when we were all a little older, began to interrupt our games to offer us some fairly well-paid jobs: five hundred lire to bring an armchair down to the ground floor, a thousand for a sofa to the second floor, and he made sure that there was something for everyone because we would all snatch at these chores.

The money started to come in useful. I spent mine mainly on pinball machines and in Mr Lustri's bar. I was the record-holder on all the machines: a string of FRA filled the leaderboards, and when someone else dared to enter them – I remember a PAO frequently appearing – I had to remove them at the cost of playing until evening. That was how I spent my first earnings, while some took their girlfriends out and others bought cigarettes. Since I was one of the first to get a moped, I'd often gather the collective funds to go to the stalls at the Maestoso cinema to buy liquorice. Or water from the Fonte Egeria, because the water from the supermarket tasted like plastic.

Playing on the streets is a great loss for today's young footballers, and you don't need to go any further to understand why previous generations were bursting with talented players while it seems so difficult to find one now. We'd spend five hours a day, ten in summer, passing and shooting or playing games, which, said like that, sounds like the height of carelessness – and maybe it is – but it's still an incomparable way of developing technique, instinct and survival skills on the pitch. Playing with a ball is prohibited everywhere now, except in sports centres, where you immediately become part of a club and fun becomes training. Sometimes I want to spring on those coaches who order their teams of kids to do drills, but I understand that this is how it works everywhere now, physical development is prevalent, and it would seem odd to do something different.

My son Cristian is privileged because he has a *calcetto* pitch in the garden, and when he doesn't have to study I encourage him to invite his friends to do what we used to do: half an hour of passing and shooting to warm up, then a game. This is the football you fall in love with, the rest is necessary work when you're approaching the age of possibly becoming professional, not when you're ten years old. When you're ten, you must strive to prevail with technique, such as by dribbling, against an opponent who is bigger and nastier than you. It's simple: people like me, Del Piero, Baggio, Mancini spent hours as a child practising free kicks, hammering at garage shutters with balls, running away if we'd broken a windowpane of the sacristy, chased by a priest who even if he'd grabbed hold of you wouldn't then actually do anything.

For me, this was what Via Vetulonia was: my wonderful playground. Precious and protected. Because the truth is that we stayed there until I was 24, the season before the *scudetto*, by which time going out without disguises had become impossible because the local roads, especially after a good win, filled with fans who wanted to see me, touch me, hug me. In the early phase of my popularity, Porta Metronia would close up like a hedgehog to let me disappear down secret paths, if I needed to. I was already Roma's captain, yet I spent my free time playing cards – *briscola* was our regular game – with old friends in the garage. When I had to go out, a group of young girls would be waiting for my Mercedes, so the coachbuilder Catalani lent me a battered car to avoid attracting attention. And in fact, no one ever glanced at that stripped-down Fiat 500 or the Golf with a dent in the side as they slowly came up the garage ramp.

The idyll of Via Vetelonia, however, ends here. There wasn't a particular day when we realised we had to leave, or perhaps there was. I remember my mother's outstretched arms, as if to say 'What can I do?', when a neighbour pointed out that the front doormat had been stolen for the third time in a week. Fans' fetishism can go a lot further than that, but I didn't know that at the time: three doormats – being 'Totti's doormats' – in a week tacitly equated to an eviction sentence, albeit a reluctant one because everyone liked us. But in the condominium assemblies, the subject of graffiti being sprayed on the walls of the building (most of them affectionate and supportive, but there were my first Laziali insults too) had become a common one. Before the neighbours' understanding turned into hostility, we decided to move house, looking for a quiet villa in Casal Palocco, not far from Trigoria, on the sea road. Although it was born out of love, the pressure from the people had become too much to bear.

2.

Off the Charts

AS A YOUNGSTER, I SCORED A TON OF GOALS BECAUSE I COULD place the ball more or less where I wanted to, and because I did it in a clever way: the goalkeepers were short, often not able to touch the crossbar even when they jumped, so all I had to do was place my shot just below it and that was that.

I stayed at my junior club Fortitudo for two years and learned the basics, or rather, I started to refine something that I evidently had inside me. The use of my body, for example. Depending on what you're doing with the ball – running, passing, shooting – the body has to accompany it, protect it, move it. I only needed to listen to the explanation once to do the training drills well, and from day one the coaches were struck by the ease of my ball control. They said it guaranteed me more composure to make the right choice. In modern football terms you'd say 'to win some time'. The secret is an old one, one which I don't tire of recommending, even if I fear it's disappeared from today's football schools: the wall. The wall is the fairest teammate that you can find. If you give it a good pass it'll give you a good one back, but if you give it a bad one it'll give you a bad one back. Talent and a lot of the wall – ever since I was a child, the one in the Manzoni courtyard – teach ball control. And ball control is the gateway to real football.

One day, Fortitudo's technical director, Armando Trillò, asked me to sign the card that certified my registration with the club. When I got back home I told Mum about it, and she got more than a little upset. 'What have you signed? You're six years old!', and she tore it up. In reality, there was nothing to worry about. The signature obviously didn't have any legal value, it was just a custom to emotionally bind youngsters to the club at which they were growing up. But Mr Trillò didn't want to hold me back, and when my mother went to him to complain, he told her in a low voice, in conspiratorial tones, 'Mrs Totti, there's something special about your son. When he plays football, he isn't like the other kids. He's not just better, it's something else entirely.' His advice was to move me to a more competitive club, as Fortitudo were only a local side.

My chance came when SMIT (Santa Maria in Trastevere) organised a trial for boys of my age. It was October 1985, I'd just turned nine years old and had progressed to the Esordienti, a level normally reserved for 11- and 12-year-olds, and I was invited to the trial together with Angelo (who was also still playing for Fortitudo). We remained on the bench in the first half, and I was asking myself why we'd come. We came on in the second half and I immediately started racking up the goals, aware that time was limited. Angelo, playing centre forward, was also getting on well. At the end of the game, the man overseeing the trial ran up to us. He had the face of a boy who had found the present he was hoping for underneath the Christmas tree: 'We'll take you. Both of you.'

My enthusiasm skyrocketed, Angelo's less so. We went for a shower and I pointed out to him that the lockers and clothes hooks were made out of metal rather than wood, like at Fortitudo, trying to find a pretext to make him say yes, but in the end he turned it down. SMIT's training pitch was at 65 San Tarcisio, under the Marconi bridge, which was actually a long way from our house, but for me that trial was enough to realise that I needed to take the next step forward. If Angelo didn't want to come, I'd have to leave him behind. Only as far as the team was concerned, of course, we'd otherwise continue to be inseparable, but it's important to note how, for the first time, the appeal that football exerts on me overcame the restraints of my shyness. Having Angelo next to me was reassuring, but giving my passion prospects mattered more. At nine years old I was still a child, but for the first time I realised that my dream of becoming a footballer when I grew up could actually come true. Or at least that a lot would be down to me.

I stayed at SMIT for less than a year, but it was a valuable experience because it introduced me to competition. I remember everything. The first game against Spes OMI, 0-0; the first win, against Tre Fontane; the first goal against Ina Casa in the pouring rain, a shot from my teammate Scano was parried by the keeper and I was the quickest to pounce on the rebound; the first compliments from opponents for a goal against Agip Petroli, round three defenders and the keeper beaten as he came out. Simply put, the growth was fast and furious. And talk about my name began to spread.

That year I also entered Trigoria for the first time, and for a young Romanista, the Giallorossi headquarters is a very exciting thing. SMIT were invited to play in the Primi Calci tournament, we won two games and lost the final, but more importantly I took the chance to explore every corner of the sports complex that was open to visitors. Another tournament worth mentioning is the Maccarese one, because we won it and I was named best player. That was the last thing I celebrated with SMIT, as Lodigiani were already making advances, but I remember the party with our coach, Carlo Barigelli, a friend of Dad's. He was the one who had organised the trial with SMIT.

Lodigiani is Rome's third club after the two major ones, and the list of players who have come out of their youth ranks and arrived in Serie A is a very long one. Everyone told me that this was the main road to breaking through. I didn't play a single minute at the trial. There was no need. They told me to freestyle with the ball to warm up, they watched me for a bit, then stopped me: 'That's great, Francesco, you are what they told us, we'll take you.'

The key director was Rinaldo Sagramola, who I would run into again as an adult when he was a director at numerous clubs in Serie A. He entrusted me to the care of two coaches, Emidio Neroni and Fernando Mastropietro. I played with the Esordienti first (Under-11s) and then with the Giovanissimi (Under-13s), waiting to properly develop physically – I was still the Gnomo – Neroni played me in front of the defence, a deep-lying playmaker, essentially a little Pirlo. I enjoyed the role a lot, because I had the feet to play long, precise passes, and I set up ten goals a game like that. But when I finally began to grow, Mastropietro took me aside with the air of someone who's telling you that playtime is over. Centre forward: I scored 40 goals that season (and by then the goalkeepers could touch their crossbar…) and I sensed I'd soon have to leave Lodigiani as well. I was off the charts there, too.

It wasn't by chance that neither Neroni nor Mastropietro ever gave me the number 10 shirt, despite knowing that I wanted it. Always and only number 8. Their reasoning, I discovered later, was that the pressure on me was increasing at such a dizzying pace that it made the danger of it going to my head very real: the number 10 shirt risked finishing the job. Neroni also frequently insisted on the need to learn how to endure being fouled, because in his opinion I was destined to suffer a lot of them. Never has there been a more accurate prophecy. Sometimes we argued, because it seemed to me that the kicks were starting to arrive almost scientifically, but he was right: that was how I cleaned up my act in terms of my behaviour on the pitch. I became less fractious. In simple terms, I began to live with my talent.

At that age, pressure is essentially a matter of expectations, but I'd learned to manage it since school tournaments, when the motto of the teacher-selectors was 'give the ball to Totti and get forward.' Of course, after a few games, you notice both the different marking setup – I always had two players on me, and in those days there was always the *libero* too, ready in case I got away from both of the others – and especially the frowns on the faces of the opposing parents: a mix between the satisfaction of seeing high-level pieces of skill in their son's game and the anger of those pieces of skill not being his or even a teammate's, but those of an opponent. Then there were our parents, who made a real noise. Not so much mine, quiet and reserved, as the others: the father of David Giubilato – a teammate at the time who later turned professional – went crazy over my performances. He was all that you could hear, and it brought me joy.

Incidentally, in January 1988, Lodigiani won the Lenzini Trophy against Lazio: it finished 2-0, and I had a good game. Our opponents' captain was called Alessandro Nesta, and his name will come up again.

That was also the time when I started attending the Olimpico. The first time I joined the members of my family who sat in the Tribuna Tevere, the stand opposite the dugouts, I was nine years old: between uncles, cousins and Dad there were around ten of us, we needed two cars, and even though it was a squeeze, I was a happy child. Backpacks could be taken in without a problem. So, at 10 in the morning, because you had to be settled in your seat three hours before kick-off – I never understood why – Mum filled mine with provisions: *panino con la frittata*, irremediably hot Coca-Cola, banana, *scopa* and *tressette* cards, a portable radio to listen to the other games. When the players went onto the pitch for the warm-up, I felt like I was on cloud nine. When Sebastiano Nela and Bruno Conti came and ran under the Tevere, so close you could almost touch them, I felt proud to be there, to support Roma. Bruno was a world champion: being able to watch such an important figure in the flesh seemed incredible to me.

Another thing I liked a lot about the stadium is the contact with people you don't know – those who were sitting next to you – and who said things you didn't expect, both about the team and about life. Sometimes I asked Dad what they meant, sometimes I didn't listen to them, especially when they criticised the players.

A couple of years later, with my Lodigiani registration card in my pocket to give me free access, I went to the Curva Sud for the first time with my brother Riccardo and two cousins. It's a different experience there because the support is a lot more belligerent. There are no families there, just very tough guys. I looked at the Capos with a mixture of admiration and fear. They were people who have since been handed a stadium ban, ended up in jail, even died; we're not talking about an easy environment. But I remember one thing about that generation: they didn't care about politics – as is the case today – they only went there to support.

I finished with the *curva* a few years later, when I was on Roma's books, on the day of a game against Napoli. I went to the Olimpico with Riccardo, we both had mopeds and parked them outside the Curva Nord in our usual place. But that afternoon there were some clashes, and as we left the stadium we suddenly found ourselves caught between a crowd of Neapolitan ultras and a battalion of cops. It was an ugly business. Molotovs on one side, tear gas on the other, impossible to escape. I had the feeling it could really end badly. Then the battle split into numerous melees, but when we got back to our mopeds we found them completely smashed up, and we returned home dejectedly three hours late. Our mistake was telling our parents why. From then on, I was banned from the stadium unless I was one of the ball boys.

There were three times in my career when there was a real possibility of me leaving Rome. I'll tell you about each of them, starting with the first, which occurred one day in the summer of '88, when Ariedo Braida knocked on our door in Via Vetulonia.

The visit, preannounced by a phone call only a few hours earlier, turned the whole family upside down. Braida was the general manager of the Italian champions AC Milan: Adriano Galliani's right-hand man, the football expert of the formidable organisational machine set up two years before by Silvio Berlusconi to relaunch the Rossoneri. The fact that he wanted to see us was obviously a testament to his interest in me. He was sat in the living room, Mum and Dad sat opposite him, Riccardo next to them, and I was in one corner of the room, as if none of this concerned me. And in fact, I realised that I didn't have a vote in this. I was a bit young for it, being only 12.

The gist of Braida's speech, who never stopped fiddling with the knot of his tie, was this: 'Mr and Mrs Totti, president Berlusconi is making some serious investments to make Milan one of the best teams in the world again. In the first two years we've signed numerous stars from both Italy and abroad, but our tradition is also to look after our youth system to nurture the stars of tomorrow: think of Paolo Maldini, the symbol of our policy. Milan have a lot of scouts in Rome, and they've all pointed out the great qualities of your son Francesco. We'd be happy if he joined us, if he moved to Milan. He's very young, of course, but from the people who will follow him and take care of him, to the schools we'll choose together, to Milanello sports centre, which will be his new home, I personally guarantee you that he'll have the best possible conditions for both his personal and sporting growth. I wouldn't be here to propose this to you if I had even a single doubt. Francesco has enormous potential: no club will be able to help him develop better than Milan.'

His speech concluded with a final flourish. Braida reached into the briefcase he had brought with him and pulled out a Rossoneri shirt in my size and gestured at me to take it. I waited for a nod from Mum, then I got up and took it from his hands. Braida also suggested that I didn't necessarily have to move straight away. If my family still considered me to be too young – and that was definitely the case – Milan wouldn't have a problem with leaving me at Lodigiani for another year or two; the important thing was to sign an agreement that would cut off the other big clubs that – in his words – 'will inevitably be knocking on your door. We at Milan got here first thanks to our organisation, but if Francesco keeps improving like this, you'll soon have a queue outside.'

Braida was a real gentleman. He didn't try to take me away by saying that his would be the only train passing by, but that it would be the best one. He barely touched on the fact that money would be there to allow my family to travel to see me, but the figure left us speechless: 150 million lire (around €75,000), which I later learned was the same offered by Milan to Lodigiani. When I shook his hand to say goodbye, he invited me to raise my gaze because it was still fixed on the ground: 'One day your eyes could rule San Siro. Keep them up, son.'

I'm not saying this because their general director had the perception to come and talk to me, but that Milan side are the only Italian team that I've had feelings for other than Roma. Let me explain. I've supported Roma ever since I can remember, there was never any other choice, and the fact that I've become their symbol is the greatest pride I feel. Having said that, Braida came to find us immediately after Sacchi's title win, and at that age my football tastes had already evolved enough for me to appreciate the quality of the game, so understand me when I say that Sacchi's Milan were the most exciting team I'd ever seen, the only one I fantasised about playing in. We're talking about a technical passion, not a sentimental one as in Roma's case, but it was there, and the prospect of becoming part of that institution touched some hidden chord in me. Having said goodbye to Mr Braida, I looked at my parents to find out how they'd taken it, and I couldn't say for sure what I wanted to see.

The answer, however, was no, and it was given a couple of days later: 'We're a very close family, splitting ourselves up isn't on the cards. Not this soon, at least.' I was too young and I would still be too young in two years, the deadline by which Milan wanted me to move north. 'Have another season at Lodigiani without making any commitments, then we'll see,' Dad said. His calculation was clear: if Braida was right, then other offers could arrive within the year, including the one we were all waiting for.

I'd only find out later, but in those turbulent days, my parents went to ask for advice from Stefano Caira, an executive who worked in the Italian Football Federation and the son of a very close friend of Mum's. He listened to the figures, which had understandably put my parents in a flutter, and replied with great confidence: 'Enzo, Fiorella... it's a lot of money, but trust me, soon that will be small change for Francesco. Don't send him away from home, and let me just try out an option.' That option was called Raffaele Ranucci, vice-president of Roma and head of the Giallorossi's youth programme.

It was a year of changes because I'd finished primary school, and at Pascoli, secondary school, my studies were starting to become more demanding. And every day Mum would come to pick me up in her Fiat 126, hand me a container of cold pasta, a ham sandwich and some juice, and we'd set off for the Campo Francesca Gianni in San Basilio, where Lodigiani trained. At that time it took 45 minutes by car, I'd arrive and sprint into the dressing room, and I'd finish at 17.30. The problem was that the 'cost' of the return journey, with it now being rush hour, was much worse: two hours by car, which I spent doing my homework and repeating my history and geography lessons that Mum had memorised while she'd been waiting for me and that she'd recite to me to speed up my learning. I'd eat another *panino*, and not infrequently I'd fall asleep midway through the journey from tiredness. I came home exhausted, and the most entertainment I'd allow myself was a game of pinball in the bar, where high scores without the tag FRA had begun to abound.

At Pascoli, the teacher with whom I found it easiest to build a relationship was my PE teacher. Mr Scala was very young, a freshly graduated 24-year-old. We'd already met each other because he oversaw the strength and conditioning training of Romulea, who are one of the biggest amateur clubs in the city. My friend Giancarlo Pantano played there, and when I went to see him once, it was he who introduced us, and his is a name that will come up often in this story. Ah, I forgot: Mr Scala's first name is Vito.

One spring day, Sagramola called my parents and Riccardo to his office. The moment had arrived, but this time I didn't take part. Lodigiani had received offers from Lazio and Roma, and Milan's money was still on the table in case we changed our minds from the previous summer. 'You need to choose,' Sagramola said, making it clear that as far as the club was concerned, Lazio's proposal was the preferred one. It's easy to understand why: theirs was a cash offer, while Roma don't pay for youngsters on principle, so they had included a couple of players from their youth team who could be very useful at Lodigiani in the negotiations.

I'll tell you something now that's well known but which always brings a laugh every time I recount it. My mother has always been a Laziale. Even though my preference for Roma was a given, Riccardo was struck by a sudden fear that Mum would make the opposite choice. Looking at her with an expression of silent intimidation, he gave her a kick under the table, and even though it only glanced off her, it was enough to give her the message. It must have been like a scene from a great comedy, a shame I missed it. 'Mr Sagramola, Francesco wants to go to Roma and we're here to indulge his wishes.' When Riccardo heard these words from Mum, he put his feet back under his chair.

Everything was settled in June: I collected my things from Lodigiani and said goodbye to my friends because at the end of August, when things started up again, I'd have to go to the Stadio Tre Fontane, the sports facility off the Via Cristoforo Colombo where the Roma youth teams trained.

*   *   *

Let's stop here for a moment because at almost 13 years old, and about to make the critical choice in my life, some aspects of my character began to form in parallel with my growth as a player. In fact, I think the two are connected. I was no longer the naïve child who dreamed of being a petrol pump attendant because the bundle of banknotes rolled up in their pockets seemed like all the money in the world. No, I understood all too well that my future was at stake on the football fields, and the certainty of my talent – increasingly solid – shaped my character day by day as a hint of leadership was added. Simply put, my teammates started to look at me questioningly at times when they didn't know what to do, and I, quite naturally, would tell one to stay back, another to stay close to me to play a one-two, a third to sprint forward quickly when he saw that I was preparing to make a pass. These are instructions given by coaches before a game, of course, but on the field the strongest player becomes the reference point. And you'll never be the strongest if you don't take on the related responsibilities.

My transformation, as I said, not only took place on the pitch but also off it. I was still shy around adults, that was something I still had to work on, but around others I was building relationships, my voice was being heard, my personality was developing. The summer of 1989 was a very special one because the fact that I'd signed for Roma obviously gave me fresh self-confidence. Not presumption, I've never had that, but rather confidence in my abilities.

My first coach at Roma was Franco Superchi, who as a goalkeeper won a *scudetto* as a regular for Fiorentina and another as a reserve for Roma. This gave him a lot of charisma. He was the coach of the Giovanissimi Provinciali (Under-15s) and had clear ideas about my role and my shirt number. He played me as a *trequartista* behind two strikers and gave me the number 10. I know that the club wanted to see me as a pure attacker, but in Superchi's view it didn't make sense to make me wait up front for the ball to arrive – I always needed to be at the centre of the play. The directors complied with him, and even when I went up an age category, to the Giovanissimi Regionali, my role and shirt number stayed the same.

With Mario Carnevale on the bench, and being watched over by Gildo Giannini – the father of my idol Giuseppe, who looked after the Giallorossi youth sector together with Giuseppe Lupi – my growth continued. Giannini had been keeping an eye on me for years. 'Until the ball goes in, you haven't done anything' was his motto, which illustrates his pragmatism. He doted on me because I reminded him of his son: Il Principe, the captain of Roma.

On Sundays I was a ball boy for Serie A games. That season would finish with the 1990 World Cup, and the Olimpico was closed for increasingly frenetic work. Roma played their home games at the Flaminio instead, where the supporters are very close to the pitch because there's no athletics track. These were immensely satisfying days in a number of ways. At the time the Italian league was unrivalled anywhere in the world, so from the sidelines I could admire a long series of superstars, learning from their expertise. Furthermore, since the team wasn't doing that well that year, the fans got angry and threw a hail of coins at them, which the ball boys would collect and pocket. A bad game could be worth a lot. We all cheered for Roma, but if they played badly and lost, then there was this small consolation.

The ball boy experience opened the door to the World Cup for me. Thirty of us were selected, 15 boys from Roma and 15 from Lazio, and on the evening of the final between Germany and Argentina, the trophy was carried around on a golf cart like a relic. When it stopped next to my position, I couldn't resist: I took courage and reached out a hand to touch it. The feeling was almost electric, I was thrilled at the very idea of having just lightly brushed it, and the other young boys were the same, among whom was Davide Lippi. If only we knew then that, 16 years later, his father and I would be lifting it up into the Berlin sky together...

Mum took me to Tre Fontane every day, maintaining her habit of studying my lessons in the car and then giving me a summary of them on the way back. Her commitment was touching, and that was why I was furious when, aged 13, I faced a failure that was totally undeserved. What happened was this: in May, my team had to go to Sardinia for a few days for a tournament. The problem was that I wasn't the only footballer in the class – there were another four, split between Romulea, Almas, and other clubs – and it was the tournament period. All five of us were absent, which meant there were fewer than the minimum number of students for the scheduled school tour to Naples, and the trip was cancelled. There was uproar, the class teacher called the players' parents to tell them bluntly that school must come before football. The music, English and maths teachers planned their revenge: we'd all agreed on the topics for the exams, but when we got to the orals we discovered that the questions were about other things entirely. Zero. I couldn't speak. The Italian and PE teachers protested, as they'd realised the perfidy, but the result didn't change: rejected for too much football.

The president of Roma was the senator Dino Viola, the man of the *scudetto* of '83, a true legend, and my knees shook a little bit when, at the Christmas party in 1990, he went through all the teams and, once he'd identified me, wouldn't leave me. The senator was a very thin and ill man, and always had two people alongside him ready to support him, and while shaking his hand I used all the delicateness I was capable of because I was afraid of hurting him. He spoke in a soft voice, but he knew perfectly well how to make himself understood.

'You're Francesco, everyone's telling me about you. Good, good. How old are you, kid?'

'Fourteen, *presidente.*'

'Ah, 14. If you keep going like this, I'll tell the coach to give you your debut in Serie A at 16, as soon as the rules allow.' I wanted to take my hand out of his, but he wouldn't let me go yet. 'Francesco... Totti, right? Good, good. Roma will need you.'

He released my hand, but his gaze still lingered on me, even after another of my teammates was in front of him. I was shocked when, less than a month later, Gildo Giannini brought all of us together to tell us that President Viola had died. I think back to his words, and to the effort that he made to tell me them, as if he were entrusting Roma's future to me with them. I volunteered to hold the coffin at the funeral. It was the least I could do.

I jumped from one team to another, always playing underage. Vito Scala, who had arrived at Roma in the meantime and who I was getting increasingly close to, said that the coaches were throwing me in because they all wanted to use me, they were in love with the way I played with my head up, they considered me a prodigy. I went almost directly from the Giovanissimi to the Primavera (Under-19s), skipping the Allievi, aside from one game: the national final against Milan, which we won 2-0 at Città di Castello. The first goal, which I set up, was scored by Daniele Rossi, one of the guys from that generation who deserved more: in his case, it was his knee that ruined everything.

The march towards the first team proceeded briskly, partly because I had quickly taken on certain obligations. If you want to become a professional, live like a professional right away: this commandment ruled out a bunch of things that guys of my age were starting to get a taste for, from alcohol to club nights, from cigarettes to motorbikes. But I never felt as if I was giving up anything by missing out on all that.

3.

Sliding Doors

IT WAS A BEAUTIFUL SATURDAY IN EARLY SPRING AT TRIGORIA, the temperature was already perfect, and some of the first team players were lazily digesting their lunch, sunbathing at the sides of the main pitch. It's here that we in the Primavera were facing Ascoli, a straightforward game that I set the course of in a few minutes with a brace.

I could still hear some applause as we returned to the dressing room for half time, but I couldn't get a glimpse of who the fan was. Vito Scala – my former PE teacher turned Roma coach – who had more contact with the first team, told me that my talent had been noticed, and that more than one person in the group trained by Vujadin Boškov, the club's head coach, had suggested that I join them for an away game in Serie A to let me breathe the air of my debut. They were pleasant thoughts, but still distant ones: it was the 1992/93 season and I was only 16 and a half, but already playing in the Primavera when I ought to have been playing at the Allievi level.

Francesco Trancanelli, one of the directors, stopped me as I left the pitch.

'Francesco, take a shower because you're not coming back on for the second half. One of our forwards got injured in training this morning, so you need to leave with the first team for Brescia.'

Of all the emotions that I could have felt after receiving such news – the step up into real football – the one that immediately struck me was embarrassment. I'd never even trained with the first team, I didn't know any of them and I could hardly breathe at the thought of joining *them*.

I didn't feel any enthusiasm, and it wasn't a case of joy either. I was embarrassed about the inadequateness that I'd inevitably show in front of Serie A players. I took a long shower, as if I had to wash off some encrustations, then put on a clean tracksuit – thankfully that was how we travelled – and went out in time to see the concern on the faces of my parents, who had come down from the stand to the dressing room door.

'Why haven't you gone back on? Are you hurt?'

'I have to go to Brescia with the first team,' I said, and spread my arms out as they looked at me, astonished.

'To play?'

'Who knows... I don't think so.'

I put my bag in the coach's luggage compartment, hunkered down in a seat at the back, and watched everything while trying to make myself invisible. Some of the 'big' players smiled at me, a couple of them made jokes, and after half an hour's journey we were at Ciampino to board a plane from the fleet of Giuseppe Ciarrapico, the president who took over the club from Dino Viola's widow.

I was starving, but even after take-off I didn't dare approach the cart full of chocolate bars and nuts available to the players. They had all eaten at Trigoria while I'd gone without food. Giuseppe Giannini and Antonio Tempestilli, the two 'elders', came over to break the impasse. They must have understood the situation because they turned up loaded with chocolate. 'Come on, eat, you can't wait until dinner.' I took a bar, maybe too cautiously, as the two exclaimed in unison: 'Trust me, we don't bite.'

They told me that I was going through emotions that they'd once gone through before themselves and that everything would be fine. 'You're good, Francesco,' Giannini added, 'Dad always tells me that Roma have a great future with you. You just have to relax now, and don't get scared by these old guys.'

As he said this, he gestured towards the whole squad: most of them sleeping – how can anyone sleep on a plane? – some were playing cards, a couple were leafing through the papers. 'I'll introduce you to them at the hotel,' the captain finished. I mumbled a thank you, and for the first time I hazarded a grimace that looked like a smile.

The Roma of Vujadin Boškov, who was dozing in the front row, were a team who had long been missing a spark: they were tenth in the league, a long way behind the dominant side of that time, Capello's Milan. After the *scudetto* and European Cup final in the early '80s, Roma's level had continually dropped, reaching a mid-table position that the fans found hard to bear. The trip to Brescia came after being knocked out of the UEFA Cup by Borussia Dortmund in the quarter-finals, and although we were still in the Coppa Italia, we'd lose in the final to Torino.

The hotel in Brescia was luxurious, or at least it seemed like it to me. We arrived late in the afternoon and luckily they booked me a single room. Thomas Hässler was the player missing from the squad list, it must have been him who got injured.

Fernando Fabbri, the director accompanying us, set up a board in the hall on which he laid out our schedule. Dinner was set for eight, but I was already downstairs by seven, excited and at this point curious too. But I continued to be embarrassed by everything, constantly finding new reasons. My mobile phone, for example, was the latest model and I didn't want it to make me look like a geek. I quickly called my parents to tell them that we'd arrived and that everything was fine but I still didn't know what would happen tomorrow, and I finished just in time not to get caught – what the problem would have been, thinking about it now, I really don't know – by Boškov, who arrived before the majority of the group. This time the manager spoke to me: 'I often come to watch the Primavera matches, Totti. You're already too good for them, you score twice a game. Listen to me, when you're scoring twice a game, it's time to go to the next level.' A great lesson in a few words, typical of the Slavic coach: after every victory you mustn't rest on your laurels but raise the stakes of the challenge.

Giannini introduced me to his teammates as promised. I struggled to hold their gaze, but at least I didn't drop mine to the ground. Was I growing up? Judging by the fear that stopped me from saying a simple 'Good evening,' I'd say no. At one point, while the others were playing pool, Giannini was signalling to me again, tapping his watch, and it didn't seem real to me that I could go to sleep after a quick 'Hello everyone.'

I went to bed excited by one thing in particular: I'd counted and recounted the players, and, including me, there were 16 of us. And that meant, even though no one had confirmed it to me yet, the next day

I'd be on the bench.

The following morning we had breakfast at 9am, lunch at 11.15, and then met at 1pm to talk about the game plan that obviously didn't involve me. Rattling off the names, Boškov confirmed that I would be on the bench, wearing number 16. The stadium was full because Brescia were sliding towards the relegation zone and needed to secure their safety. The atmosphere was hostile and we could hear all sorts being shouted at us from the stands, but the game was over within half an hour.

It was all thanks to Siniša Mihajlović: first he crossed into the box for Claudio Caniggia to win a header, then he made it 2-0 with one of his powerful free kicks. There was a superstar playing for Brescia, the Romanian Gheorghe Hagi, but he couldn't put his team back on track all by himself. The second half was all about managing the game and the defensive spaces in order to not take any unnecessary risks. After 83 minutes, Boškov brought off Giannini to put Fausto Salsano on. Then, suddenly, he turned to me and told me to get ready.

At first I didn't realise he was talking to me, I thought he was looking at Roberto Muzzi, sat next to me, and I gestured to him. Roberto looked at me amused: 'He's talking to you, move.' To me? My heart leapt into my mouth. I jumped to my feet, started to take off my tracksuit bottoms but, to do it more quickly, I didn't take my boots off, which became an embarrassing obstacle: I had to sit on the ground and struggled to pull them off my feet – a real mess.

'Come on, come on,' Fabbri gestured for me to hurry. Boškov eventually became irritated by my clumsiness and glared at me. 'What's wrong, Totti, don't you want to make your debut?' Just before he told me that my time was up, I was finally ready. I went on for Ruggerio Rizzitelli. It was the 87th minute. I had time to touch the ball, and take it to the corner flag to win a few precious seconds. Then the referee Robert Boggi whistled for full time, and confusedly I realised that I'd just played in Serie A. For the first time since the beginning of the weekend, I felt happy.

On returning to the dressing room, more than one person ruffled my hair: 'Congratulations kid, now bring some *pastarelle* to Trigoria for us, OK?' There was a general joy in the air from the win, and my debut only brought congratulations. The awareness of having taken an important step gave me courage, and on the return flight I ate a couple of chocolate bars and a bag of nuts. I think I'd earned them. A little party was waiting for me at home, half the extended family gathered together – too little time to get everyone together, but that was fine. The next day I took the pastries to Trigoria, God forbid I didn't fulfil the request, and Fabbri gave me some new instructions: 'Francesco, from now on, you'll train with the first team twice a week, in addition to your usual work with the Primavera. I'll notify you about which days each time.' I left the sports complex with my heart ready to burst.

The next Sunday I was selected in the squad for Roma-Fiorentina, but I didn't play. The one after that, I travelled again to Ancona and was given another three minutes, this time when it was 1-1 and the result was still in the balance, in Muzzi's place. From then until the end of the season I only got on the bench once more, at home against Torino, but the main thing was that there were training sessions with the first team, in which I learnt a lot more than a whole season with the youth team. My approach was always extremely respectful, and that remaining bit of embarrassment pushed me to keep changing in the Primavera dressing room, alone, which was also because there weren't any free lockers in the first team's and I didn't want to cause any fuss. Finally – and don't laugh – I felt very timid about the idea of showering with *them*. In fact, I really didn't like it.

This attitude of mine evidently appealed to the senior members of the team, particularly Giannini and Tempestilli, who always had a word to say to me, but also to others, including the 'syndicalists' Giovanni Cervone, Amedeo Carboni and Valter Bonacina. I got proof of this when, at the end of the season, I got a big surprise: before leaving for the holidays, Umberto Spada, the club comptroller, handed me a cheque for 218 million lira (€112,500).

'It's what you're entitled to for getting through three rounds of the UEFA Cup.'

'But I was never even selected for a UEFA Cup squad.'

'You don't have to tell me. It was the syndicalists who decided you should get a share of it too. Take it up with them.'

Take it up with them? I'd have kissed them, if I could. By giving me a share, an objectively disproportionate one, they wanted to send me a message that 'you're one of us'. I didn't go home that day, because we'd all already moved to our holiday apartment in Torvaianica. I walked around with the cheque at the bottom of my pocket, feeling it constantly because I dreaded it would be stolen. When I arrived at the apartment, I flew up a flight of stairs and, in front of my parents' curious gaze, took out the most precious piece of paper that I'd ever seen. 'Look!'

Phase one, absolute amazement: 30 seconds with mouths open. Phase two, overwhelming joy: five minutes of singing and dancing. Phase three, blind panic: 'My God, it's Friday, we can't bank it before Monday, and there have been thefts in the building! How can we keep it safe?' By watching it day and night, which in fact they did for the entire weekend. On Monday morning, we all got in the car to go to the branch where Dad worked. Once the cheque was safe, Mum called Spada to give him an account number: she told him that I'm too absent-minded to be walking around with large amounts in my pocket, and from then on Roma would pay me by bank transfer.

From the next season, 1993/94, I was fully part of the first team and I signed a contract worth 500 million (€250,000). A nice figure for a 17-year-old boy, but which needs some clarification: it didn't represent any social liberation, nor did it redress any sort of difficult childhood. In our house, not only did Dad make sure we never lacked anything, but we also went on holiday every year, something that not everyone can afford. And the money from football, immediately considerable and regular, was auspicious, but my passion was my 'drive' more than ever. In fact, I spoke freely about my salary with relatives and friends, to the point that Mum had to intervene several times to remind me that it's a good idea to keep a lid on certain topics to avoid seeming cocky or, worse, arrogant. Naturally, she was also thinking of keeping me away from the crowd of acquaintances who, upon learning of my sudden wealth, couldn't understand why we hadn't seen each other in so long…

The new season began with the arrival of Carlo Mazzone, and this was one of the best things that ever happened to me. Roman and Romanista like me, he perceived the increasing expectations around me and, since he was well aware of the dangers posed to me by the local environment, he acted as a shield to allow me what I needed: a season in which I could strengthen myself away from the spotlight. When a journalist asked him why he was waiting to start me, he replied angrily, 'The more you insist on seeing Totti, the more I'll keep him from you.' He expected the delirium around me to dissipate. Sometimes I read these responses and felt bad about it, but it wasn't my fault if people were pushing to have me in the team – I'd have liked to play at least a bit too – but I didn't get onto the pitch in Serie A until February 1994. But Mazzone really treated me like a second father, and it was evident that for him it wasn't just a job, it was much more. As grouchy as he could be, his affection was obvious.

There's a famous story about the press conference before the Coppa Italia game against Sampdoria in December 1993. Just as the training session was about to end, Rizzitelli and Caniggia collided, a terrible clash of heads, and there was a mix of blood and fear. The two stayed on the ground, Mazzone didn't leave them, the doctors intervened while they waited for the ambulance, and the day's schedule was up in smoke because of the emergency. I'd already finished and was alone in the dressing room when one of the directors came by. 'Totti, thank God you're here. You're playing tomorrow, right? Come with me.' I followed him, relaxed, realising too late that he was bringing me to the press room, where there were 50 journalists lined up, cameras and microphones scattered about. They'd been waiting for the coach and instead found themselves faced by the player who had been denied to them since the start of the season. I was afraid I'd ended up in a situation that was bigger than me.

Mazzone saved me, of course. Just as the press officer, albeit reluctantly, was about to start the questions, a great slamming of approaching doors could be heard, and finally the coach appeared, out of breath: 'Go and take your shower, kid, while I talk to them,' a phrase that has gone down in history, which I gladly agreed to even though I'd only just got out of the shower. Later on, when we were alone, Mazzone told me that I wasn't yet seasoned enough to talk to journalists and that if they wanted to use me for a good headline, they'd lead me to say whatever they wanted in three seconds.

*   *   *

My first victory of the 1993/94 season was my ability to stay in the 'senior' group without feeling embarrassed anymore. I was still very quiet, and in the days we were on training retreats I spent hours watching them play pool or sat next to them while we watched games on TV and listened to the comments they were making. On the pitch, though, my personality started to emerge, and not a single training session went by that didn't see me progress tactically or enjoy myself technically. I tried tricks, and they often came off. I also nutmegged some of the veterans – Giovanni Piacentini, Bonacina, Carboni – which was normally frowned upon, but I was 'forgiven' for the instinctiveness of the move. They understood that I wasn't making fun of them, otherwise they would have kicked lumps out of me; it was simply that if a nutmeg was the most direct way of getting past them, I'd try it.

Giannini, the captain, was increasingly becoming my reference point. He took me under his protective wing like his father, who recommended Franco Zavaglia to me as an agent capable of helping me through my first steps. For away games, Il Principe and I would share a room, and not infrequently – as he's someone who can fall asleep as soon as his head hits the pillow – I'd look at him admiringly before turning off the light, or I wouldn't pee for fear of making a noise while going to the bathroom and waking him up.

Someone else I liked a lot was Giovanni Cervone, the goalkeeper, because although he's the nicest man in the world, he has two shovels for hands, and when he gets angry you have to call the civil defence to stop him. Once there was a misunderstanding between him and Massimiliano Cappioli at a corner. The two told each other to go to hell and, unlike what usually happens, things weren't smoothed over at the end of the game. The next day, at Trigoria, after having mulled over that 'eff-off' overnight, Cervone thought he'd hang Cappio on the wall, and it took five people to intervene and split the two apart. Much better to be friends with certain characters, and in Rome there are a lot of those.

I noticed this in that very Coppa Italia game against Sampdoria, which I started. Just eight seconds passed when I got hit with a heavy challenge from behind by Pietro Vierchowod. The referee blew his whistle, I got up as if nothing had happened, and soon after, a second heavy tackle came in. Still biding my time, I started again, and after 10 minutes came the third tackle that didn't get anywhere near the ball. This time I stayed on the ground, my ankle really hurting. When I got to my feet again, I met Vierchowod's questioning gaze and told him to cut it out. He brought his finger to his lips, indicating I should be quiet, and that's when it all kicked off because three or four teammates intervened in my defence, and for a couple of minutes there was a big melee. Then everything calmed down and his tackles, still hard, became acceptable. I got the feeling I'd passed a test.

Having been left to watch the entire first half of the season, in the second, I made a couple of starts and got some other minutes here and there. Roma improved on their tenth position from the previous year but finished 1993/94 seventh and, not qualifying for Europe, certainly couldn't be satisfied, because the increase in points – just two – was really poor. For me, on the other hand, it was a year of great progress, because Mazzone's care bore fruit: my reading of the game improved a lot, and the more I understood the tactical developments the better I used my technical ability. Which, yes, was better than the average in the first team.

A test? The way in which I entered the game in my first derby, a very difficult situation: at half time we were 1-0 down after a volley by Beppe Signori, and as I headed towards the dressing room Leonardo Menichini, Mazzone's assistant, held me back on the pitch: 'Francesco, go and do a good warm up because we're putting you on straight away.' I ran hard in those 15 minutes. I wanted to come on like a cannonball. The stadium was packed, the Lazio fans were singing, ours were grumbling: I was a little worried, but I felt I could make a difference. I replaced Piacentini and the formation changed. I played as a second striker because we had to come from behind, and the start was a sprint, so much so that Paolo Negro immediately gave me a kick, initiating what would become a venomous duel. In the final minutes, after a few good moves that didn't pay off, I ran at him down the right-hand side, beat him, got into the box and, as I went to cross it from the byline, I felt a touch from behind. I could have stayed on my feet, I admit it, but it knocked me from my stride and I risked seeing the ball run out of play, so I let myself fall, because there had been contact, and the referee couldn't not have seen it. He whistled for a penalty, and I was immediately embraced by my teammates. I wanted to take it too, but when I realised that it was Giannini who had picked up the ball and was heading towards the penalty spot, I shut my mouth and silently cheered him on. But there was no happy ending to my first derby: Giuseppe aimed for the corner but it wasn't far enough, as Luca Marchegiani had a very good reach. It ended like that, and my good performance didn't console me. There was a lot of anger, and after the game even the president, Franco Sensi, came down to the dressing room – he had only recently arrived but knew how to make himself heard.

If that was the most emotionally intense moment of the 1993/94 season, I didn't have to wait long for the next season's. The day before the first game, Mazzone fielded the team for the opening match with Foggia at Trigoria, and it wasn't Abel Balbo who was alongside the new signing Daniel Fonseca – it was me. There was a rule at the time that said only three foreigners could play, but Roma had four, and this – without European commitments – would become a problem that needed to be managed. But if it was Balbo who was left out for the first game (Aldair, Jonas Thern and Fonseca played), the 'merit' was mine too, because by then Mazzone trusted me both on the pitch and off it. He no longer feared that I might let it go to my head if things went well.

And they did go well, at least for me. After half an hour, Thern chipped the ball into the area, Fonseca was well-positioned but found himself with his back to goal. Seeing me coming at full speed, he laid the ball back to me with his head. My left-footed half volley came off perfectly, an unstoppable strike into the corner, and the roar that followed stirred my soul. My first goal in Serie A. I practically lost my mind.

How should I celebrate? Hell, I'd talked about this with Riccardo a thousand times, and he'd always replied: 'You just think about scoring,' as if the proper way to celebrate would inevitably come to me. The problem was that I'd imagined that first goal a million times, but under the Curva Sud, where I had all my points of reference, where I'd know immediately which area to run towards. Under the Curva Nord I didn't know what to do. I ran towards the corner flag, then I punched the air; it was all a bit of a mess really, but the real joy was inside me, and it was beautiful.

Roma, however, didn't win the match. In the second half, Enrico Catuzzi's side got into the game and equalised through Igor Kolyvanov. In the dressing room, Mazzone wasn't happy at all and said in no uncertain terms that we shouldn't be either, and while he said this he looked at me, as if to check my state of mind. I imagine he was satisfied, because the joy of my first goal in Serie A had been wiped out by Foggia's goal. I was just totally disheartened by missing out on the win. This is a drive that came naturally to me: in time, I'd learn that no champion is ever happy with his performance if the team doesn't win.

This didn't mean that I didn't cash in with my uncle Alberto – who had promised me a mountain bike after my first Serie A goal (a nice gift but don't be moved: he sells them) – or that it kicked off my first season as a regular. My debut goal wasn't enough for me to keep my place, as from the second gameweek onwards the starting pair was Balbo-Fonseca, and as it worked well, Mazzone was essentially restricted in his choice of foreign players to a perennial toss-up between Thern and Aldair. But the coach sent me some very strong signals, such as starting me in the second leg of the last 16 in the Coppa Italia against Genoa. We'd lost badly at Marassi, 2-0, and the return game was a bullfight that ended 3-0 and was opened with the first of my 'great' lobs – they would become a trademark. I scored the first goal of my career against Juve in the Coppa Italia too, a strike across goal that beat Angelo Peruzzi, but it didn't have any real effect: they'd won 3-0 in Turin, so our 3-1 win at the Olimpico wasn't enough to get through to the next round. In the absence of Balbo and Fonseca, however, I played up front in tandem with Giannini, and we left the field to applause for our courageous attempt at an impossible game. I think Lippi, the Juve coach, first noticed me that evening: as well as the goal to make it 2-1, I set up Cappioli to make it 3-1, I was denied a penalty, and I generally gave the Bianconeri defence a real headache.

1994 was also the year of the 3-0 win in the derby and of Mazzone's run to the Curva Sud in the 90th minute. I remained on the bench for the whole game, but in the end it felt as though I was playing in it, because experiencing it next to a coach like that increases everything: enthusiasm, anguish, joy, fear, excitement. In reality, the game was all one-way: Balbo scored after 2 minutes, we were 2-0 up by half time, and Fonseca settled the result at the start of the second half. But Mazzone was still like the Energizer Bunny. I'd have liked to have filmed him to make people understand what the derby means to a Roman. At the final whistle it was wonderful to see him run towards the *curva*, he was soon tired and staggering a bit, but with a clenched fist towards people who had experienced the game exactly like him. I know what you're thinking, and let me tell you that, years later, the day after his famous run at Brescia's ground towards abusive Atalanta fans, I called him to express all my solidarity and sympathy to him. In that run, there was the proud affirmation of a *romanità* vilified beyond all limits and, even more importantly, the defence of the memory of his parents. Seeing him go mad with rage, a very strong feeling of affection came over me, the same that he gave to me every day he was in charge at Trigoria. And I think the ultras themselves respected his action, in a way. Mazzone proved that he had blood in his veins, that he was a real man.

His second season – 1994/95 – went much better. Roma improved from seventh to fifth place, qualifying for European competition again, and, counting points in the old way – it was the first season in which a win was worth three points – finished with eight more than in the previous campaign. I scored another three goals, in addition to the one on my debut, and I brought home the confidence that Balbo and Fonseca, two very strong forwards, showed in me. I know that Abel suggested more than once to Mazzone that he should play me behind them as a *trequartista*: 'Because when Francesco's there, the chances come, boss.' The next season, I entered the attacking rotations straight away but I rarely scored, just two goals in the league. I got my first European goal, true, against the Belgians Aalst on a strange evening, because the fans were whistling even though we won 4-0. Mazzone secured fifth place again and we reached the quarter-finals of the UEFA Cup, but there was a bad atmosphere. Sensi wanted a change, and he wanted to broaden his horizons in the search for a new coach because he was convinced that too little work was being done at Trigoria. When he announced Carlos Bianchi in the summer of 1996, not everyone knew who he was. Or perhaps they pretended not to, to make the separation with Mazzone less painful.

Bianchi is an Argentine who, after a long career in his home country and France, had won everything while in charge of Vélez Sarsfield. He came in to replace a Roman coach considered too lenient with the dressing room, and he immediately made it clear that he had a lot of preconceptions about the Romans in the squad. I think he had asked Sensi and Giorgio Perinetti, the new sporting director after the departure of Emiliano Mascetti, for a number of 'his' players, and that the club had promised them in the medium term. First, they wanted to make sure that Bianchi's qualities would be evident in Europe too. It's well-known that it was the president above all who wanted him, and that the good early results – the squad didn't work much in the summer, so it shone – excited him, convincing him that he'd made a brilliant choice.

Perinetti was less enthusiastic and pretended not to hear the president's orders to extend the Argentine's contract immediately. Neither he nor us players liked certain practices that Bianchi had brought to Trigoria, such as the Romans versus Rest of the World training games, in which we could feel his dislike towards us. He would shamelessly cheer on the others and enjoyed seeing us lose. It's embarrassing to say this because no one believes me. It didn't take me long to realise that he was targeting me in particular because he thought I was a slacker, and there was no way of making him change his mind, not even by working three times as much, which was the usual ration he reserved for me.

At first, it wasn't easy to understand the puzzle that Bianchi was piecing together, because I was still playing in various games and even doing some good things, like the chipped goal from outside the box into Milan's empty net – Sebastiano Rossi had misjudged coming off his line – or the very late goal that secured a 3-3 draw in Roma-Fiorentina, a game that could have seen 20 goals, mostly for them. Every time a journalist asked him for his opinion of me, however, Bianchi replied in exasperated tones: he said that the city gave too much to supporting 'this Totti', that it wasn't easy managing me while not caring about public pressure, and that ultimately I was still a very young player with a huge amount to learn. In essence, he made it clear that, for him, I was not a 'normal' footballer and that the expectations around me were disproportionate.

Bianchi would have preferred Jari Litmanen, Ajax's Finnish attacking midfielder, instead of me. Litmanen was certainly an excellent player but also my double: he did the same things that I did in the same areas of the pitch, perhaps a little better thanks to his greater experience. Certainly, if he had arrived – and he was already being talked about as the first new signing for the following season – I would have had to leave.

In fact, Bianchi, who continued to have a close understanding with Sensi while the other directors were more uncertain, wanted to send me on loan to Sampdoria to get some playing time. It was an idea that was welcomed in Genova: Vincenzo Montella started to call me, praising Ligurian life, and Roberto Mancini let me know that he would be delighted to have me alongside him. Considering our characters, we wouldn't be able to say it to each other's face, but there would have been few precedents for such a refined combination of techniques.

Nobody spoke about it openly, but I understood that a transfer had been sketched out. That offended me, and privately I made an irrevocable decision. No loans, no options to buy. If I was forced to leave Roma, I'd never go back. It was a matter of principle, because I didn't agree with going from being the cornerstone for every future project to a failure to be cleared out to make space for a new star within a few months. I promised myself that if Roma got rid of me, I'd become a 'normal' star: a couple of years at Sampdoria to fully mature, then one of the big northern clubs: Milan, Inter or Juventus. *If* Roma got rid of me.

I revealed my thoughts only to Vito, with whom my relationship had become closer, and I swallowed the bitter pill that was provoked by the very thought. Mazzone, who has long antennae for certain things, called me to implore me not to do anything stupid: 'France', you were born to triumph in Rome,' he told me. I wanted to think so too, but it seemed to me that this wasn't the case.

The hand of destiny, however, moved in the direction that Mazzone was hoping. On 9 February 1997, we were on a break for internationals. I should have been with the Under-21s – I'd just won the European Championships with Cesare Maldini, but I was young enough for another cycle – but for some unknown reason, the new coach, Rossano Giampaglia, didn't call me up. So I stayed in Rome, where the club had arranged a triangular tournament with 45-minute matches at the Olimpico for those who had stayed behind at Trigoria to keep in shape. Borussia Mönchengladbach were invited, and some of the proceeds would go to them as part of the agreement for the 'restitution' of Martin

Dahlin (who didn't really break through with us), and on the explicit request of Carlos Bianchi, the third side invited was Ajax, whose ranks would include Litmanen.

I turned up to the tournament, which was called the Città di Roma, determined to vindicate myself. Yes, my head had got used to the idea of leaving the team I'd suffered for since I was a child. But before I left I wanted to leave a sign, to create some regret over what could and should have been and yet will not be because of the choice of an Argentine who – uniquely in the world – saw me as a normal player. The atmosphere was very tense because the city was split: there were some who saw me as dumb and immature – the famous *Pupone* (big baby) – and others who considered me the victim of a coach who had no connection with Rome. It was a rift that divided fans and the media and sparked discussions, arguments and verbal fights on the radio and on TV. I've never called a journalist to ask them to support a theory that favours me. Never. And so I was doubly pleased in those difficult days to see the number of those who wanted to keep me at all costs genuinely increase. More than one of them realised that if I left it would be forever and asked themselves if Roma were throwing away the winning lottery ticket. I was flattered. And determined to be remembered, thanks to that tournament.

The first game, between Ajax and Borussia, was decided by Litmanen himself. Bianchi was overjoyed, and it was clear that this triangular tournament was crucial to his transfer market strategy. Then it was our turn against the Germans: we played in a new 4-3-3 formation with Marco Delveccchio centre forward and Checco Moriero and I on the wings. After Tommasi put us in front, I flighted a pinpoint pass with the outside of my right foot through to Moriero, whose cross saw Delvecchio make it 2-0. Then I took centre stage: I dribbled past three opponents and, as the keeper came out, crafted a lob that brought the whole stadium to its feet. OK, in reality, there were 12,000 people there, it was a cold evening and they were all wrapped up. But the feat is undeniable, and it was celebrated as such. I imagine there was some activity in the executive box.

Roma-Ajax thus became the final and, as far as I was concerned, a personal duel with Litmanen, who was probably unaware of the reasons behind it. I scored another great goal: a shot from the edge of the box that flew into the top corner and left Edwin Van der Sar stunned (this wouldn't be the only time this happened in the fine Dutch goalkeeper's career...). The sounds of '*Totti non si tocca*' ('Don't touch Totti') started to be heard from the stands, and Bianchi looked like a pillar of salt – or perhaps that was just my spiteful impression.

I confess that I was full of contrasting emotions that somehow had to get out. That evening, I was able to channel them in the best way possible. Vincent Candela scored his first goal for Roma, starting what would become a Giallorossi career to be remembered. It finished 2-0, I was the standout performer by some distance, and late that night I saw the president on TV, besieged by journalists as he left the stadium, proclaiming that 'Totti is much better than Litmanen, and I'm not saying that to save money on the Finn. I rule out the possibility of Francesco leaving Roma: he's our future.'

Sliding Doors is a brilliant film with Gwyneth Paltrow, in which a random event like taking or missing the metro has profound effects on the life of the protagonist. It came out the year after the Città di Roma, in 1998, and its title quickly became synonymous with destiny. If poor Giampaglia – he passed away a few years later – had called me up for the Under-21s, as seemed only natural, I wouldn't have played in the triangular tournament, I wouldn't have scored those goals, and Bianchi would probably have finished convincing Sensi to sell me to Samp. From where, I repeat, I wouldn't have gone back. My life would have turned out completely differently. It makes me shudder, thinking about it again.

That same evening, however, the directors who had the closest ties to the team, from Pruzzo and Conti to Perinetti, increased the pressure on Sensi to put me at the centre of his future project. In the meantime, results were starting to disappear, partly because the team was running out of steam, and the president's enamourment with Bianchi was simultaneously diminishing. However, I don't believe that the coach ever gave him an ultimatum of 'either me or Totti,' as has been rumoured, because such a juxtaposition wouldn't have made sense. But Bianchi was sacked two months later, a defeat against Cagliari proving fatal: before leaving he briefly said his goodbyes to us, and to me he said 'Good luck,' and looking in his eyes I saw a sad man. He would win other trophies in South America, with Boca Juniors, and in an interview many years later, he stated that I was one of the highest quality players that he ever coached, on a par with the great Juan Roman Riquelme. But these are thoughts that must have come to him in hindsight, after following the trajectory of my career: when we worked together, his esteem was extremely limited.

Bianchi left Roma in seventh place. Sensi wanted to take his time in choosing his successor, and as such asked the elderly Nils Liedholm to oversee the work of Ezio Sella – promoted from the Primavera – until the end of the season. From a results perspective it was a difficult time, because half of the squad gave up and we finished quite close to the relegation zone. From a personal perspective I'm glad I came across a character of Liedholm's ilk, the boss for the second *scudetto* and rightly a legend in Rome, even if it was only for two months. He was 75 years old at the time, this was his last job and it didn't go especially well, and yet I've kept the memory of a very kind man, in love with my technique. 'Show me, show me,' he'd urge me, tossing balls at me, and I'd trap them, shoot on the turn, and check we were continuing, often managing to get a smile from him. He liked me because I was an elegant player, he said. I, on the other hand, liked him because he was elegance personified.

4.

Stella

PRESIDENT SENSI'S DREAM WAS A CERTAIN GIOVANNI Trapattoni. Trapattoni had just won the Bundesliga with Bayern and was still contracted to the great Bavarian club for another year. Contact was made several times during spring 1997. We were told at the club that he would gladly come, but Germans are Germans: a coach doesn't leave if he's under contract. So, after the umpteenth attempt that didn't lead anywhere, Giorgio Perinetti played his hand and proposed Zdeněk Zeman.

The president's first reaction was a cry of horror: Il Boemo (The Bohemian) had been fired by Lazio in January, how could he think of bringing him to Roma now? Perinetti retreated, but it was a tactical move: he returned to his task as soon as he could, backed by an unexpected ally.

According to Perinetti, the die was cast on a rainy night on the way back from an awards ceremony in the Castelli. The sporting director was in the car with Franco and Maria Sensi and, while trying to fight the inferno of water outside and keep the vehicle on the road, he approached the subject again: '*Presidente*, we made a clear choice in firing Bianchi: what we need most is a coach who values Totti highly. Roma's future goes from there, and Zeman knows what to do with forwards, you saw this yourself at Foggia and Lazio...'

Sensi repeated yet again that he didn't want a coach discarded by Lazio because the supporters wouldn't understand, but a seed had been planted. Shortly before arriving at Villa Pacelli – their residence on the Via Aurelia – Maria Sensi, who had been listening to the discussion in silence for the entire journey, uttered a sentence that suddenly changed the scenario: 'Franco, you know, in my opinion, Giorgio's right...'

Sensi's wife Maria was the president's conscience, his most trusted adviser and a woman of intuition. Her husband paid great attention to her, and with her patronage, the road to Zeman was all downhill.

Part of it was because the fans' reaction turned out to be anything but negative. The idea that Il Boemo would bring his ultra-offensive and spectacular style that he'd developed elsewhere – including Lazio, of course – to Trigoria excited their imagination. His was a different style of football, in which the quality of the build-up play was taken into consideration much more, and after trying to get results for so many years without any joy, the idea of trying to get them while playing attractively was a welcome one. Zeman is also a serious professional guided by very strict morals, and therefore was respected by everyone. Given all this, no one cared about the fact he'd coached Lazio.

According to Vito, who immediately became part of his coaching staff, Zeman is the coach who gave me the athletic base that kept me going for my entire career. Top-quality work, clearly, given the age at which I retired. Preceded by the reputation of being more suited to the preparation of a platoon of marines than a football team, Il Boemo observed our worried faces on the first day of the 1997/98 pre-season with his usual wry expression. I, for example, jokingly said that I'd cry off sick because otherwise I wouldn't come back from our training camp in Kapfenberg alive. Well, I actually should have done: on the first day, he made me run 3,000 metres, a few minutes rest, then 3,500 metres, a second pause, then I finished with another 3,000 metres. I crawled back to my room. The day after, he selected a small group comprising me, Delvecchio, Cafu, Di Francesco and Tommasi, and moved onto reps: run 1,000 metres 10 times, broken up by brief pauses. The club had let it filter into the dressing room that Zeman had been chosen as a bulldozer capable of breaking up a system of privileges and restoring a working culture. Given that the previous management teams hadn't been that bad – to say otherwise would be disrespectful to Mazzone – the comparison between Zeman and a bulldozer isn't unfounded.

From day one, the boss gave me a nickname that would last forever, even when he came back to Trigoria 15 years later. He called me *Stella*, meaning, I imagine, the star of the team: he doesn't lack an ironic streak, but the tone with which he says it removes any doubt that there's sarcasm there too. Zeman considered me the best Italian player, or at least believed that's what I had the potential to be, and behaved accordingly: he treated me with the same toughness as the others to show that there was no favouritism at the new Roma, but at least he did it with an amused smile on his lips.

Take the weigh-ins, which we did every day and which led – especially at first – to a barrage of fines. He didn't use the scales from the infirmary, convinced that some of us could tamper with it at night, instead bringing his own from home every day. As soon as he saw a pound more than he should, he wanted to know everything you'd eaten the night before ('How many teaspoons of oil? Any sugar in your coffee?'). He also knew every trick to make that extra kilo disappear from the scales: 'Don't lean with your hand, Stella. No, raise them up, both of them.' There was no dietician on his staff: he was more than enough. I've always been very careful with what I eat, but even I struggled with Zeman.

If that was the downside, the upside was bright. After years of changing positions and roles even during the same game, Il Boemo finally assigned me with a precise role, left wing in his classic 4-3-3, with the licence to cut inside to take advantage of my right foot's passing precision and shooting power. In my apprenticeship seasons in Serie A, I grew from a tactical point of view and was able to expand my skills repertoire, but I didn't score many. Zeman pushed me to consider shooting at goal to be my first option because he was convinced I'd be capable of scoring 20 goals a season, despite not being an out-and-out striker.

His teams had always scored a lot, and after the first few months of work it wasn't hard to understand why. The two hours a day spent on attacking work during our training camp was a vast amount of time, and it didn't reduce by much when we went back to Trigoria. Incidentally, for lovers of strength and conditioning training, in weeks when we didn't have a game, Zeman put on double training sessions on Wednesdays and Fridays, the old system in vogue in Eastern European countries (obviously it was Vito, enraptured, who told me this).

With my characteristics, I basically replicated the movements that Beppe Signori made at Foggia or – to take a modern example – those of Lorenzo Insigne at Maurizio Sarri's Napoli. And things worked out, at least until the blow of the derby, the first turning point of the season: we lost 3-1 despite playing almost the entire game with an extra man after Giuseppe Favalli's early sending off. Not all games are the same, even if at that time Zeman was concerned with treating them like that to take pressure off a game that we felt too strongly about. Losing like that against Lazio reset the clock, and all the good things we'd done up until then vanished into thin air. Luckily we started strongly again, winning at Bari with two beautiful goals from me: a low free kick into the corner and a very difficult volley. By early November, Roma were fourth, and it was looking promising.

In reality, if, on the one hand, the squad that in four years' time would win the *scudetto* was being put together – Mazzone's last transfer activity brought in Marco Delvecchio, we welcomed Damiano Tommasi and Vincent Candela during Bianchi's season in charge, and in the summer Cafu and Eusebio Di Francesco unpacked their bags – on the other, numerous new signings (it's pointless naming names) were of too low quality to fill in adequately when the starters were missing. We got up to third place, but another blow was around the corner in early December: we lost 3-0 against Inter, and at the end I was sent off.

Let's acknowledge the defeat in San Siro. Those are years in which we always lost in Milan. We were making the sign of the cross the moment the plane took off from Fiumicino. We lost because we felt somehow out of place in that magnificent stadium. The early stages of my career coincided with a historic period in which both Milan and Inter were very strong – they could often rely on the best players in the world – while Roma couldn't even aspire to a podium finish. Having said that, the excitement of going out onto the pitch in San Siro is second only to the Olimpico – my home, let's not kid ourselves – because the Scala of football isn't just a beautiful picture but a reality. I understood this when I started to shake off that reverential awe and played without that fear of making a mistake that inevitably accompanies you in front of those four walls of fans.

Beyond the defeats, which in time would start to become victories, I understood where I was, and most of all who was watching me, from the murmuring that followed a well-executed display of technique. Those in San Siro are thirsty for quality, and when you show it to them, they recognise it like in no other stadium. They could jeer you and insult you – especially when they fear you – but they want beauty no matter what shirt you're wearing. It might have happened first elsewhere, but I don't remember it: at the San Siro, on the other hand, I clearly remember the applause after a difficult piece of skill, or as I was being substituted after a quality performance.

For all these reasons, losing there hurt, and it took us two months to recover from that blow from Inter: two months in which we slipped from third to eighth place in the league and our number of goals conceded significantly worsened, the statistic that everyone looks at given Zeman's previous form. Some of us, quietly and respectfully, asked him whether it might not be better to replace one of the many hours of attacking work with some training on our defensive line. He, as a very intelligent man, understood our doubts but didn't acquiesce: 'Think about scoring one more goal. That's what comes easily to you.' He said it slowly, taking a drag on his cigarette, aware that he was making us uneasy. 'Did you want to talk to me about this too, Stella?' he added, and frankly it was hard to press the issue.

What ruined the season, though, more than the goals conceded, were the four defeats in the derby – two in the league and two in the Coppa Italia – a collapse that created an understandable tension with the fans. Every defeat has its explanation, but the general picture spoke of a psychological inferiority. A breath of fresh air in the atmosphere came three matchdays from the end when we beat a Milan side in transition 5-0: on the bench, angry at first and then despondent, was Fabio Capello. We said goodbye without imagining – at least, I didn't – what lay in wait in the future, and not the distant future either. Roma finished fourth in Zeman's first season in charge, with the best attack in the league together with the champions Juve, and the seventh best defence. The fact that Lazio finished below us didn't sweeten the pill. Far from it. They won the Coppa Italia, and for them it was the start of a winning cycle.

Thinking about it more objectively, the 1997/98 season ended with what was then my best finish (we'd finished fifth under Mazzone) and a record for goals scored: 13, and that was without taking penalties. It certainly didn't go badly, and in the summer my name was being bandied around in the newspapers, not so much in terms of transfer rumours – my choices were quite clear, at least in that phase of my career – but rather as far as the national team was concerned. Italy had been knocked out of the World Cup on penalties by France, Dino Zoff replaced Cesare Maldini, and mine was the most called-for and publicised face of the Azzurri's new generation. This popularity wasn't sudden – I'd long since forgotten having the freedom for a walk around the centre of Rome – but I noticed the jump in attention at a national level.

In January 1998, another key signing arrived: Antônio Carlos Zago. Zago was an atypical Brazilian, because he signed for Roma aged 29 after having already passed through Japan. He was not a young guy, and he spent most of his time with the clan of his compatriots led by Aldair, reserved and seemingly innocent. He decided when to give you his trust, but on the pitch he proved to be a top-quality defender. He would be invaluable.

In his second summer, Zeman continued to demand staggering workloads from us, and the bad thing for me was that that wretched Vito had bought into Il Boemo's methods, lengthening my runs because he knew that I tended to cut them short. The nerve!

October 1998 was one of the most important months of my life. I'd just turned 22, and Zoff gave me my Italy debut against Switzerland. I'll talk about this fully later, in the chapters dedicated to the Azzurri. The following week, Aldair had to serve a one-match suspension and, for the first time in my career, I wore the Roma captain's armband: emotions were soaring, but the home game against Fiorentina was going badly because Gabriel Batistuta – who else? – gave the Viola the lead, and after an hour we were playing 9 v 10 after Di Biagio, Candela and Falcone had all been sent off.

However, fate decided that my first game as captain wouldn't be dishonoured by a defeat. Since fate's means are often surprising, it turned out that the game's protagonist was Gustavo Bartelt, an Argentine who had arrived that year and wasn't destined to remain long. Poor guy: we smiled at him too, when he arrived for the training camp, because from the way he dressed himself up, the way he moved and the way he expressed himself, it seemed like we'd found Claudio Caniggia's younger brother. But on that day, launched into the fray by Zeman out of desperation with 15 minutes to go, Bartelt found his best performance for Roma and, judging by the rest of his résumé, perhaps of his entire career. He caused havoc on the right wing, tearing Fiorentina's defence apart, and in the 89th and 94th minutes he sent two balls into the box – actually, the second was a shot parried by the keeper – that first Alenichev and then I turned into goals in an incredible comeback. The celebrations for my first game as captain were the peak of joy.

After another unsuccessful trip to San Siro – we lost 3-2 to Milan – we played in Bergamo on the Wednesday in the Coppa Italia Round of 16 first leg against Atalanta. It finished 1-1, and in the dressing room Aldair asked for a bit of quiet. I was sat in the corner, just out of the shower, and I couldn't even remotely imagine what he was about to say.

'Tonight I wore the Roma captain's armband for the last time. From the next game on I will pass this duty, this honour and this responsibility to Francesco. He's a Roman boy, as we all know he'll become a great champion, and his love for the club and the city are the guarantees that he'll represent us for years and years. I want you to wish him well and for you all to be by his side. Thanks.'

Although he may have forewarned Zeman, what Aldair did was a personal initiative that left me speechless, and while my teammates came over to hug me and shake my hand, dazed, I look around for him but didn't see him, because he'd already left the dressing room. Years later, he would say in an interview that he also took that decision because he found himself in a bit of a stand-off with the club over a contract extension, and he feared that it could affect his nerves.

Aldair's move left me wrong-footed, because I was still at a point in my career where my teammates came to defend me after I got kicked. To defend me from myself, I mean. I've never been a chav but impulsive, yes; the desire to throw a punch at a particularly aggressive full back was absolutely there. A captain really has to get certain idiocies out of his head.

My second 'first time', the definitive one, was on 31 October 1998. I was excited about shaking hands with the Udinese captain Alessandro Calori, and with the referee, Domenico Messina. I mentally noted at that point that going forward I'd have to soften my attitude around the referee – and there's no need for you to remind me that I didn't always do that. That day, everything was easy. Roma won 4-0 and their new captain scored two goals, the first of which was a beauty. Chimenti clears a long ball downfield, Delvecchio headed it on and I, with a left-footed volley, launched it perfectly beyond Turci. A special goal for a special occasion.

Two weeks later – in mid-November – came the high point of our season. With a 2-0 win against Juve, who had just lost Del Piero for the entire season, we climbed to within a point of the leaders, Fiorentina. The first goal came from that joker Paulo Sérgio, but the trigger was a move from the street, something that looked brilliant in Serie A but which anyone who has started off by passing and shooting in a courtyard knows well. It's a clever trick, but perfectly legitimate. I was fouled midway inside Juventus' half, I got up and none of the opponents had the intuition to block the ball. While they were arranging themselves to set up the wall, I glanced at Paulo Sérgio, who understood immediately. I struck it right-footed, chipping the ball over the suspended landscape of those who were expecting a direct shot at goal, and it landed on the foot of the Brazilian, who beat Peruzzi first-time. A crafty goal.

Another two weeks passed, and in a dramatic game – because at one point we were 3-1 and a man down – we started to turn the Laziale tide of recent derbies. It finished 3-3 and I scored the equaliser, my first goal in the *stracittadina*. The scene was set for the return game, which we went on to win.

Two taboos dispelled in a few days, then: Juve and the derby. So why did we stop? Partly it was the usual story in San Siro, 4-1 to Inter and a dejected return home. Partly it was the goals conceded, it's pointless avoiding the subject: at Cagliari, for example, we lost 4-3, so while we scored three goals away from home, the problem was that we let in four. After being just one point from the top of the table, at the halfway point we were eight behind with – would you believe it? – the best attack and the tenth best defence.

The second half of the season began with two away defeats – against

Salernitana and Venezia – and a draw at home to Empoli. At the start of February, Roma were seventh, 14 points from the top, practically in a different league, and were already out of the Coppa Italia, hanging onto a UEFA Cup quarter-final tie with Atlético Madrid in March (which we lost too).

President Sensi never revealed this to me, but I believe that the first contact with Fabio Capello dates more or less to that time. He was out of work: after winning the league with Real Madrid and the unhappy return to Milan, he took a year's break, aware that offers would arrive. Among the reasons why he continued the discussion with Roma is his love for the city, that's for certain, because he's a man who loves beauty, and his memories of the three seasons he spent in the capital as a player often appear in his interviews. Before he established himself at Juve, Capello was an important part of the Roma side of the late '60s.

In the meantime, Zeman recovered a little. At the Olimpico we beat both Milan and Lazio, the contenders for the title after Fiorentina's collapse (without Del Piero, Juve are a long way back). But every time the ship seemed to have found an even keel, another incident occurred that wrecked everything once more. Inter were in free fall, yet they came to our home patch and won 5-4 in a festival of leaky defences. It was devastating. We finished fifth with five points fewer than the previous year, crystallising our positions in the goal rankings: we still had the best attack, but just the tenth best defence.

I was sorry that Zeman left, because of the many coaches who have been fond of me he was the one who was truly enamoured, and this is obviously flattering. If I turn to look at where I was before his arrival and where I was when he left, the leap in quality is evident. Il Boemo called me Stella when he arrived, but I didn't deserve it then. I was simply Capitano, and that's the nickname that accompanied me until I retired and even beyond.

I've never quite understood where the boundary between sadness for those who leave and enthusiasm for those who arrive lies, but, as deceptive as it might seem, I swear that they're two compatible feelings. Zeman left and my gratitude towards him was enough to make me grieve.

When the news came out that Capello had been hired – I learnt it from the TV like everyone else, Sensi certainly wasn't asking for my opinions at the time – I was on holiday in Torvaianica, and it didn't take long before I was down in the street doing cartwheels, just like the rest of Rome. Capello was the symbol of victory, its personification. The club that hired him was openly stating what its goal was, and if he accepted then it meant he considered the mission possible, otherwise he'd have gone elsewhere. As fond of Zeman as it is, Rome was a city literally going mad with joy. To those who asked me for my opinion, I responded with a very simple sentence: 'No one hires Capello to come second.' Sensi's move was a declaration of war.

The first day of the 1999/00 pre-season was scheduled for 5 July at Trigoria, after dinner. At 10pm, the space in front of the sports complex was completely packed, the police said that there were 5,000 people there, a real frenzy of excitement because somehow there was the feeling that this could be a historic moment.

Capello was waiting for us at the bar. I imagine he was pleased with the anticipation that he had created but, if so, he didn't show it. The first thing I thought was that he put pressure on you just by looking at you: it was intimidating just how determined he appears. That evening we only introduced ourselves, but he had time to tell me that the next morning I'd be the first with whom he'd speak individually. I was captain, and Capello treated me as such. I slept little and badly, thinking about that face-to-face meeting a lot.

'Francesco, you're the most important man in the squad. I'm not referring to your technical ability, which of course I know very well, but to the captain's armband: you must wear it with responsibility and be an example for your teammates. I'll involve you in everything, because for me the captain represents the squad not just in the 90 minutes of the match but always. If there are any problems with the team then I'll talk to you about them, and then you'll report to the team.'

The tone of the conversation was militaristic, and in effect the iron-clad organisation that Capello wanted to bring seemed to me to be the first sign of discontinuity with the way in which Roma had previously been (little) governed. The actions he took were inclined this way too. For example, he ordered mobile nets to be set up behind the goals so as not to waste time chasing after balls that have missed the target, and to double the thickness of the mesh fencing to stop anyone outside from being able to spy on us. They're simple things, but no one had thought about them before him.

Capello's first transfer dealings brought other future champions of Italy to Rome, from Francesco Antonioli to Cristiano Lupatelli, from Cristiano Zanetti to Vincenzo Montella, but it was still not enough to win, because we were left by quality players like Di Biagio, who went to Inter, and Paulo Sérgio, destined for Bayern.

The season went more or less like the previous ones: an excellent start that at one point saw us rise up to first place in the standings, and we stayed near the top until the end of the first half of the season (we were third, four points behind Juve, still with the best attack and the fifth best defence). Then came the decline and finally the collapse. We finished sixth, worse than with Zeman. As if that weren't enough, Lazio won the *scudetto*. In short, it was the perfect storm.

I didn't have a good season. Only a few goals, just seven, of which four were penalties. My first goal from open play only came on matchday 12. Given that I was personally finishing badly, I dedicated myself to setting up Montella, who scored 18 goals and yet only convinced Capello up to a certain point. The coach was disappointed by the overall quality of the team, arguing that Roma needed some expensive additions to win, and despite the final league position the people were with him, thus increasing the pressure on the president.

In the first season in which I 'had' to win, I didn't even like my disciplinary performance. A few minutes from the end of the game in Florence, which was already won, I clashed with Heinrich and we were both shown red cards, which meant I was suspended for the game with Juve the following week. In Perugia, forgetting how touchy the referee Gennaro Borriello could be, in the middle of an argument I put a hand on his chest: another red, and the squad had to sweat the proverbial blood, sweat and tears to bring a point home. This wasn't the behaviour of a captain. I had to get that into my head.

Of the many stories that have been told about me over the last 25 years, the most ridiculous is that I would have pushed against the signing of other superstars in order to maintain my status as Roma's number one. Rubbish. The exact opposite is true: I've always pressed my presidents to bring great players to Rome, the ones we needed to win. Not only that: unlike what happens today, where everyone sticks out their antennae to find out how much everyone else is earning, I never wanted to know my teammates' wages, and if Batistuta happened to earn more at Roma than I did then all I can say is that I'm happy for him. I haven't chosen Gabriel's name at random: he was top of Capello's shopping list, and when Sensi announced that we'd signed him I celebrated like a child. He was one of the last pieces of the mosaic, the others being Walter Samuel, Jonathan Zebina and Emerson, a strong spine. And if anyone continues to doubt my commitment to the team being strengthened, I call on Gianluigi Buffon and Fabio Cannavaro as my witnesses. Given how much I got on their nerves trying to persuade them to join Roma from Parma, I'm lucky they still talk to me.

5.

The Long March

THE *SCUDETTO* SEASON BEGINS INAUSPICIOUSLY. WE HAVE A saying, *pesci in faccia,* which means 'fish in the face'. It's a way of expressing displeasure. And our season literally began with fish in our faces. The fans threw them at us, furious over our elimination in the Coppa Italia by Atalanta on a hot afternoon in late September 2000.

The need to wait for those who had been playing at the Olympics in Sydney to return caused the start of the season to be postponed by a month – the league started on 1 October – and the endless summer had created some air pockets. So, after holding us to a 1-1 draw at the Olimpico, Atalanta beat us 4-2 in Bergamo the following week, and the first target for the season vanished.

Exasperated by the sixth-place finish from the previous season, and above all by the fact that that coincided with Lazio's title win, our fans took it very badly. The following afternoon, three or four thousand people surrounded Trigoria, and when they heard that we players were in the car park, separated only by the boundary wall, a heavy bombardment of fish – I don't suppose they were very fresh – and eggs began. We had to quickly retreat inside the sports centre and wait for them to run out of ammunition. Cafu, who had already gone out through the gates, hurriedly rushed back inside as kicks dented his car. Outside, the police, alerted by the large gathering, fired a couple of canisters of tear gas. It was an intolerable situation, and it needed to be addressed before anyone got hurt.

We all went out, the players and Capello. And we responded decisively to the first wave of insults: it was total chaos, everyone was yelling, but after a few minutes of tension, the leaders of the *curva* found their way to the front of the group and we were able to talk with them in a more orderly fashion. Not surprisingly, as soon as some sort of dialogue was re-established, it moved on from indiscriminate attacks about our loss in Bergamo to asking why it happened, what we were lacking in order to win. I was very clear: 'We aren't lacking anything, we've made some great signings and the atmosphere in the dressing room is excellent. Let's not ruin that with protests after the first setback. We're playing for you, this year, at the end, we'll be celebrating together.'

It was a convincing speech, given that the fury subsided within minutes. At the end, there was almost tender advice and the promise that the next fish would be totally fresh and delivered in baskets. Provided, of course, that we deserved them.

The truth is that many individual fans have a reasonable football culture, in the sense that they understand it both from a technical and a psychological point of view, but the masses reason exclusively on the basis of the result. Or, rather, they let themselves be guided beyond what they should: you always play to win, but setbacks on the road happen even when you're a very good side, like Roma were that year. For some fans, though, when you lose it's because you've been out late clubbing and you don't care about the team. Without a doubt this introduces some limitations to the life of a footballer, and seeing the looks on the faces of foreign players I've come to think it's a particularly Italian phenomenon.

Historically, as captain, I always tried to explain to new teammates who have come from abroad that it's not appropriate to be seen around too much after a defeat. 'Why?' they would ask in amazement. 'If I've done my best to win, what do I have to blame myself for? Defeats are part of the game.' I had to cut them off after a while, because I don't have any more arguments against their logic. 'Listen, just do as I say. Trust me, it's some friendly advice.'

In an already fiery atmosphere, our first league game quickly became an extremely delicate test. We faced Bologna at the Olimpico, and in the first half our mental state was evident: Roma played badly, and without several top quality saves from Antonioli we'd have gone into half time behind. Instead, we were actually in front, as in injury time I manage to break free from Olive's marking to head Assunção's free kick back into the far corner. A crucial goal, because it liberated us psychologically. In the second half, Batistuta, who wasn't supposed to play but couldn't miss the opening game, scared Castellini so much that he caused him to score an own goal. It was a good game against an in-form opponent, as Bologna would go on to win three games in a row. The surprise of the first day of the season was Inter's defeat in Reggio Calabria, which led to Lippi being sacked.

Serie A proceeded in fits and starts. An international break in October meant we were only back on the pitch on the 15th – these days you'd be up to round 8 by then. Luckily, our early season fixture list wasn't particularly tough, which allowed Capello to improve on the construction of his team without losing points along the way. We won easily at Lecce, a nice 4-0 that saw Batistuta's first two goals: the first arrived at the end of the first half and was a splendid header from the penalty spot, twisting his head so aggressively – from a cross by Cafu – that it gave the ball the power of a strike with his foot. Tommasi doubled the lead at the start of the second half with a right-footed shot into the corner from the edge of the box. Bati made it three with a left-footed strike into the roof of the net from close range, and I converted a penalty in the 91st minute, awarded for a foul on Delvecchio. It was very important that Gabriel got on the scoresheet, immediately cutting off the defeatist debates that always happen when a big signing doesn't hit the ground running. After two games, only we and Juve had maximum points.

The third match was Roma-Vicenza. It was more complicated than expected, considering that they arrived without a point on the board. But they defended well, and we had to wait until the end of the first half to go ahead. Delvecchio ran down the left and crossed in a medium-height ball for me to sidefoot home with my right foot. Aesthetically a nice goal, but we had to wait until the last 10 minutes to get the safety of a 2-0 lead, and it wasn't a trivial goal because it was scored by Montella, brought on by Capello after an hour to improve our presence in the box. Vincenzo scored with his head, just getting there before Batistuta, who was attacking the same ball, and the dynamics of the action brought up the question of the 'number 9,' which was the shirt number Gabriel had asked for when he arrived at Roma and which Vincenzo was defending tooth and nail.

Let's start with a fact. Montella was a brilliant striker. The previous season, his first with us, he had scored 18 goals, so Capello's request – that he wanted Bati because, in his style of football, the centre forward has to be physically dominant – surprised and annoyed him. From his point of view, though, Gabriel had all the credentials to claim the striker's shirt number: after many years at Fiorentina, during which he even beat Kurt Hamrin's goal record, he accepted Roma's offer because he felt that time was starting to run out. It was time to win. The argument he made to me on one of his first days was completely logical: 'Francesco, no one can understand you better than me. I did everything to win with Fiorentina, like you've done with Roma, and it wasn't enough. We have to join forces.' That was the reason he joined. An urgent need for titles.

Capello was a frank man, sincere bordering on brutal. Considering that next to Bati was me, and I had great confidence in front of goal, he didn't need another thoroughbred striker as his third attacking player but a workhorse like Marco Delvecchio, who scored a few goals but above all helped the midfield while we were out of possession. As such, from that summer, Montella became Batistuta's backup. It was a formula that proved to be a winning one, partly because Gabriel, who was physically in much worse condition than expected and often played through pain out of pure pride, couldn't handle the strain of every game. Being able to replace him with a centre forward with different characteristics but equal threat was the privilege of a great side.

Today it's quite normal that top clubs have 20 stars in their squad who they can rotate on the pitch: but at the time, the stars always played and those who were left out didn't 'start from the bench,' as is said with a certain disingenuousness today. They were reserves. And for someone like Vincenzo, swallowing that pill was deeply challenging. When he learned during the *ritiro* – the training retreat – that Batistuta was also after his shirt number, he didn't say anything to him but made it clear to the directors that he wouldn't compromise on that point: 'If you take that away from me then find me another team too because I'll go.'

I found myself in a delicate situation because I was friends with

Vincenzo, our girlfriends spent time with each other as well, but as the captain I had to help put the pieces of the puzzle together. I spoke with both him and Gabriel, and in the end it was the Argentine who took a step back, understanding Montella's reasons. It was a wise choice by someone who didn't want to humiliate their teammate/rival, aware that they'd already won the battle for the starting spot. Instead Bati took the number 18 shirt, which in the days of Ronaldo's Inter, Iván Zamorano had astutely reinterpreted as 1+8, but which can also mean 9+9, in other words, it's worth double. I realise that this could all seem like nonsense from the outside, but in life in the dressing room, these are power relations to all intents and purposes, and no one gives way without a fight. Montella and Batistuta could both get quite envious, which inevitably attracted pranks and jokes, and frequently piqued responses from them. Once the shirts had been assigned, the matter was closed. Bati showed respect by not making a point of it, while Montella surrendered in the face of a phenomenon who, despite training very little due to his ailments, scored 20 goals in the league alone.

On matchday 4 we lost, 2-0 away at Inter, who were trying to pick themselves up again after Lippi's sacking and Marco Tardelli's arrival on the bench. It was a relatively painless defeat (as much as defeats can be) because the team played well and because Juve – who everyone thought were our real rivals for the title – lost at home to Udinese. It was the Friulian side who went top of the table, together with Atalanta, while we were a point behind with Bologna, two ahead of Juve and Lazio.

Our first defeat could have been a lot more costly. The real surprise was how we managed it psychologically. Losing in Rome is always a bit more difficult compared to other cities, because the pressure of the wait transforms defeats into dramas, especially when things look promising. So coming away empty-handed is seen as the beginning of the end, or of dreams being dashed. It's very childish, I know, but that's how it is in Rome.

Despite the grumbles, the team remained united in its positive attitude. The impression was that President Sensi had done everything in his power – and more – for us to win the *scudetto*: we had Capello, and now we had Bati. Consequently, the team felt like it was on a mission. We were convinced of our strength. We really believed we could score three goals against anyone. And this positivity spread and grew at the weekly dinners that we organised at one person's house, then at another's. The ones who always joined me were Di Francesco, Candela, Cafu, Zebina, Cristiano Zanetti... We were a close-knit group, we got on well together even outside of the dressing room, and above all there was a common goal on everyone's horizon. It might seem trivial, but it wasn't always like that.

After the defeat in San Siro, the trip to Brescia became very delicate: everything went well in the end, but losing another game would have had a depressive effect that would have been hard to shake off. I didn't take part as I got injured at the end of the game with Inter, and so I cheered on from my sofa at home and observed the details that are best seen from the outside, when you aren't playing.

Individual personalities had grown a lot. I noticed that when a move started to develop, the player on the ball always had at least three passing options, and each of those options was shouting 'give it to me.' If you didn't pass it, they got annoyed. The ball wasn't a hot potato anymore; on the contrary, everyone wanted it. After Candela put us in front, a clever placed finish into the corner from the edge of the box, Brescia turned it around and went 2-1 up. It was a moment of crisis that Batistuta resolved brilliantly in the second half with three goals, one every 15 minutes. A detail that I appreciated on TV was that two of the three goals arrived after others' shots had come back off the post: the hunger with which Gabriel launched himself on those rebounds, getting to them first, was emblematic of the new season. Only Udinese remained ahead of us.

Reggina arrived at the Olimpico on matchday 6, but the day before, Bati waved the white flag for the first time. He just couldn't do it, his ankles were tormenting him. Having played through the pain – which he'd done for years and years – his cartilage and tendons were perennially inflamed. Every now and then, he needed to stop. Montella played instead and he made the difference. With my active participation, because I won and converted the penalty that made it 1-0, and after Bogdani's equaliser, it was my header – from a pass from Zanetti hit with such power that if my head wasn't firmly planted on my shoulders, as I always assure Mum, it would have taken it clean off – that put it on a plate for Vincenzo to make it 2-1. Of course, we couldn't have known it that Sunday, but it was a victory that was destined to become a milestone in our season, and ultimately in our history: Udinese lost at Parma and Roma rose to top spot alone. No one would take it away from us, not until the *scudetto* was won.

Looking back at Verona's line-up on matchday 7, you see the beauty of three future world champions: Alberto Gilardino, who after four minutes won the penalty to make it 1-0; Massimo Oddo, who converted it; and the Argentine-born Mauro Camoranesi, who had just arrived in Italy and was then unknown to everyone. Verona held onto the lead for more than half an hour, during which time we made a target out of Fabrizio Ferron, their keeper. Then one of our three World Cup winners, Vincent Candela (the others are Cafu – no one in Europe can rival our full backs – and of course Aldair), decided that he'd had enough; the keeper got a touch on his right-footed shot from outside the box but wasn't enough to stop it, and it slowly dropped into the net. A few minutes later and it was my turn: the ball in from the left from Delvecchio was slightly behind me but Batistuta drew two men away and so, alone in the middle, I had the time to stop and finish it left-footed. From the match at the Bentegodi, which finished 4-1 with a brace from Gabriel, the third goal should be remembered: a literal bullet of a free kick that flew straight into the top corner. I was always greedy with free kicks, partly because I was good at them. That year, however, I had two teammates who were spectacularly effective at them too: one was Bati, and the other was Marcos Assunção, a Brazilian who kicked by opening his foot. He scored several free kicks in Serie A too, but in his three years he never found much game time, otherwise he would be remembered today as the number one specialist.

The next game was the most difficult for Batistuta, because it was Fiorentina who were arriving at the Olimpico, and he had to face them having been their superstar for nine years. Honestly, I can't even imagine what it would have meant for me to play against Roma. It would certainly have been torture, and I'd have gone into it lightly. So I had great respect for his feelings, because he didn't do anything to hide his discontent all week, exposing it to make us understand how much it was hurting him. Fiorentina were an interesting side that year, led by an odd Turkish coach, Fatih Terim, pompously known as 'the Emperor' – a character. They were a mid-table side but they played well, and in the eyes of Gabriel's old teammates, we could see friendship but also the desire to prove something that evening. Every departure by a star from a mid-level club carries an implicit condemnation of their teammates: as long as I stay with you, I'll never win anything. And it's not always an easy thing to accept.

The game was difficult, arduous, disjointed, because although we were now used to basing our play around Bati, that evening he had Tomáš Řepka – a fine defender – marking him, and on the rare occasions he managed to get free of him, another two men closed him down. We struggled on until the 83rd minute. Just as a 0-0 draw was looming, there was an act of courage: Guigou, who had just come on, headed Bati the ball 20 metres from goal, in a central position. The bounce was perfect, the impact of Gabriel's right foot devastating, because the trajectory of the ball was high enough to loop over my friend 'Spilungone' (Beanpole) – that's what I called Francesco Toldo at the European Championships. The volley flew over him and made the Olimpico roar. Finally, 1-0.

We all ran to Gabriel, who didn't celebrate out of respect for his old supporters. These are somewhat strange situations when everyone is celebrating – there's no more overwhelming moment in our lives than the 10 seconds after a goal – while the goalscorer cannot. Bati hugged us tightly but didn't say a word. It was a hugely important goal, taking us three points clear of second place, which Atalanta moved into, in the table. As Fiorentina prepared to restart and we returned to the middle of the pitch, I saw Bati wiping away tears with the sleeve of his shirt. It wasn't sweat, they were real tears. He wouldn't celebrate even in the dressing room.

I mentioned Gianni Guigou, a member of the supporting cast who didn't accumulate many minutes, but was invaluable both because he did his job whenever he was called upon and because he integrated himself perfectly in the dressing room. He didn't sulk if he wasn't playing much and helped to keep the atmosphere cheerful. Gianni is a likeable Uruguayan, a full back who's comfortable in the attacking half too, as on the occasion of his assist for Bati against Fiorentina. And he's also a guy who smiles at the affectionate but slightly odd chants of both the fans ('He sold chestnuts / under Cafu's house / Gianni Guigou / Gianni Guigou') and us in the dressing room, sung to the tune of the *Addams Family*. A great companion.

Traditionally, we struggled in Perugia. Two years previously we'd lost 3-2, and there had been a crazy match the previous year when the referee, Borriello, had sent me off. When I read in midweek that he had been selected again, I understood it as a sign of destiny: watch out, Francesco, to win the *scudetto* you need to improve not only your performances but also your behaviour. Capello reminded me about this too. In the end, everything went smoothly in the game except for the score, which stayed at 0-0, and the fault – so to speak – lies with Andrea Mazzantini, their keeper. At least three unbelievable saves, and the first draw of the season arrived. It didn't affect the table; on the contrary, we gained a point on second-placed Atalanta. Juventus drew in San Siro with Inter and remained six points behind. In short, everything was OK.

The fans noticed this as well. Trigoria became the destination for increasingly large pilgrimages, and a nice delivery of fresh fish was the pleasant compensation that we were given after the urban warfare of the end of September. That had been only two months earlier, so don't tell me that it isn't results that drive the collective sentiment. On some afternoons there were two or three thousand people waiting outside the gates, sometimes we had to hide ourselves in the kit men's vans to get out – and leave our car there – and onto the road back home. It's the famous Roman enthusiasm that causes the rest of Italy to make fun of us, especially in the North, but which I consider harmless. Indeed, it's comforting to know that your fans love you even if you don't win every year, as happens elsewhere.

Another day, another dollar: the fearsome Udinese arrive at the Olimpico. It was a very good match, they'd struggled a bit in recent games but were performing well above the expectations they had at the start of the season. A tricky customer, who Batistuta pushed to one side after 20 minutes when he turned home a cross by Tommasi. A quarter of an hour later it was my turn, and this goal is considered to be among the best goals of my career. And I agree. Roma moved up the field quickly. It was a classic break, with the ball intercepted by Tommasi midway inside our own half and a quick burst forward to keep Udinese off balance. Damiano's run took him towards the right, where Cafu – going full throttle – was getting forward on the overlap. Batistuta was waiting level with the line of defenders to avoid straying offside. Nakata joined him and attracted the attention of another man, and I then chose the opposite side, the left, which was completely open, quickening my stride because I was still behind the ball. Cafu received it 25 metres from goal, and his control on the move won him a bit of time because his cross was practically a dead ball. The arcing trajectory landed on my left foot, and it was as if he found the mythical pot of gold there. A perfect, clean strike, the ball flying straight into the opposite top corner. Turci could do nothing to stop it. A wonder goal. It helped us to win, because shortly afterwards, Roberto Muzzi – my old friend who gave me that wake-up call on the day of my debut – made it 2-1, and there was no rest for us until the 90th minute. A fine game, a fine victory.

And a beautiful goal, I said. For the technique and coordination of the shot in itself, but also for the build-up play, which, not surprisingly, excited Capello like few other times. It was a very direct move from us, one which called two men above all to the fore: Tommasi and Cafu. Damiano had the best season of his career that year. He was at the peak of his physical efficiency, and from a technical point of view he could do practically everything. I was so amazed by him that I renamed him Ronaldo, because he really excited me (and Inter's Ronaldo was the forward who I most wanted to play with) and because I couldn't believe my eyes: Damiano plays like two men. That year he even got a vote (which is worth two points) for the Ballon d'Or: we were the two Romanisti in the standings, I was fifth on 57 points, he was further down but present nonetheless. And he's a wonderful guy, a pure soul with the superior mental strength that comes from faith. That season he only received applause, but it hadn't always been like that: the Olimpico public had targeted him a little bit, yet he always came out of the dressing room with a smile on his face: 'I'm going to take a few jeers, in the meantime, you try and win the game.'

The other figure who emerged from the story of the goal against Udinese was Cafu, who at the time was the best right back in the world, no question. What a voice. I can still hear it now, that's how piercing it was: 'Pass it, pass it, I'm here,' even if he was three metres offside. In the end I always gave it to him to shut him up, there was nothing else you could do.

But he produced, boy did he produce. The cross he gave me against Udinese was perfect. I saw Cafu again recently at a charity game in Georgia organised by Kakha Kaladze. He still runs (almost) like the old Pendolino, giving me feelings of fondness and even a little envy.

There were two games to go until the Christmas break, and we'd known since the day the fixture list came out that these were the ones that would determine the season. The first part was easy, and we got through it without any major mistakes: 25 points out of 30 was more or less the target that we'd set ourselves. If anything, it was our rivals who had been taking it easy, given that Juve were six points behind alongside Atalanta, and Lazio and Milan were both seven back. These were big gaps after only ten games. The two games coming up before the break were the derby and Juve at home, and we faced them with the calmness of league leaders. Capello made a big point of this: they were the ones who had to take risks in playing catch-up, not us.

The derby was a very closely balanced, high-level affair – which isn't surprising, since it was the reigning and future champions of Italy facing each other. The match was decided by a moment that's gone down in Roman football history, an own goal by Paolo Negro. In reality, he can hardly be blamed. There was the usual cross from Cafu – what good form he was in! – and this time it was Cristiano Zanetti bursting in from the left, aiming a header towards the far corner. Peruzzi leapt to parry it, but the ball was still there and Nesta, in his attempt to sweep it clear, hit Negro and the ricochet rebounded into the net. There were twenty minutes left. Lazio poured forward, and a few moments from the end Nedvěd rattled the crossbar. But it didn't cross the line. It was good for us, bad for them, and awful for Negro, and I can't say that I was sorry because he was an annoying opponent, one of those who insult and provoke you as well as kick you, I guess to make him look good in the eyes of his own fans. A couple of days after the game, we started to see Roma shirts with his number, 2, and his name on, and for a while all our supporters were wearing one – making fun of someone who deserved it.

Juve won easily at Lecce that Sunday and, together with Atalanta, remained on our tails, but at a distance: six points, while Milan suffered another blow by drawing at Verona and Inter didn't want to pick themselves up again either. Everything was set up for the pre-Christmas top of the table clash, and Capello prepared us for it by making sure that we kept everything under control. After all, he'd been repeating it to us for two weeks: it was up to them to come at us. But not even Juve had a great desire to, so the game was a stalemate. They hit the post, I had a chance on the break but, in the end, Van der Sar got a bit of revenge for my chipped penalty for Italy from a few months before. It finished 0-0.

With a six-point advantage, the Christmas holidays that year were very enjoyable. The most fascinating thing was listening to the buzz around the city, which was certainly excited but, at least in part, still incredulous. There was a sort of fear of giving into hope floating around in the air, because if things didn't go well this time – with a very strong squad, a winning coach, a leader in great form – then it would be an incredibly difficult blow to take. Rome isn't a place of moderation, if you have ten euros in your pocket then you go out as if you had a hundred; yet in football, at least that Christmas, the word of the day seemed to be 'calm'. After pre-emptively announcing a thousand victories, this time actually seemed to be the one: the prospect of not succeeding, as a result, was much more scary than usual. Put simply, the city suddenly felt as though it had something to lose.

We were back on the pitch before New Year's Day, ready to spring into action, because the first game of the new year would be in Bergamo, against third-placed Atalanta. It was a game that Capello prepared very well for from a tactical point of view; the opposition never got a shot on goal, while Delvecchio's goal after just 40 seconds cleared the path for us, and Tommasi sealed it before half time.

Although there was no real competition – we were clearly dominating – when a pitch is waterlogged it encourages slide tackles, which has the effect of rousing the fans: those by your players are all fine, those by the opposition are shameful fouls that all deserve at least yellow cards. It's like this everywhere, myopia is the fan's prerogative. But in Bergamo the whistles towards me were always a little louder, enhanced, I imagine, by anti-Roman prejudices. It happened in other places too, and with the benefit of a few years' experience, by then I knew where they were: the

Rigamonti in Brescia was a stadium that was never able to stomach me; once, in Ascoli, I don't know what they would have done to me if they'd managed to get their hands on me; and there was a lot more ill will towards me in Naples than – say – in San Siro.

We hit the jackpot with victory in Bergamo because Juve could only draw at home to Fiorentina. After 13 games, we were eight points clear of them and ten clear of Atalanta. It was becoming a walk in the park. Too much? Too much. Experience teaches that when you're in such a psychologically superior position you should hope for a strong opponent, one that forces you to have maximum concentration from the very start. Instead, the eight-point advantage coincided with the arrival at the Olimpico of a Bari side who were bottom of the table: an almost lethal combination because of course we underestimated them, even risking losing. They played well, inspired by Antonio Cassano, who was a truly sparkling talent; Cafu and Batistuta were absent, but it was that sense of a collective mission that had spurred us on right from the start that we were missing rather than individuals. We were tense. There was the risk of reacting to even the slightest contact. In short, it was an ugly Roma.

We went behind to a free kick from miles out by Mazzarelli that Lupatelli perhaps underestimated. With twenty minutes left, we poured forward into Gillet's area again, and I won a slightly stupid penalty, because when Markic made contact with me, I wasn't even facing the goal. I converted it. It was a big point, in its way. In the meantime, Juve had won and were six points behind again.

A new crash test awaited us in San Siro, the stadium where we never managed to get a result. Milan's season was an odd one, because it was clear that Zaccheroni was heading towards the exit door and the team had some flaws. But they also had some unrivalled stars. Andriy Shevchenko, for example, celebrated scoring against us twice, while the free kick that Leonardo opened the scoring with was expertly crafted. We still lost, yes: 3-2, with a brace from me, a clean right-footed shot from 25 metres out that deflected in off Maldini and a penalty after a foul on Batistuta when it was already too late to dream of a draw in extremis. We lost, but only after playing well, so much so that at the end of the game, in a furious dressing room, Capello ordered a moment of silence. He needed to talk to us.

'Gentlemen, in five minutes I'll go to the press room and criticise your performance. I'll say that you were naïve, that being top of the table is a responsibility that's weighing on you, that the title race is more open than ever. I'll argue this not because I believe it, far from it, but because I want our opponents to think that we're in crisis and that, like every year, the time has come when Roma's ambitions melt away in the sun. But you mustn't even listen to my statements to the media, because what I think is the exact opposite: you put in a great performance, here in San Siro, and today I'm more certain than ever that at the end of the season, we'll be celebrating the *scudetto* together. Such defeats as this only make you mentally stronger. Even stronger!'

The exclamation mark is apt here because Capello's speech was that of a statesman. In fact, the bitterness over the defeat disappeared quickly, only the anger and the desire to get straight back onto the pitch to turn things around remained. Here, though, we made a mistake. One of the few in a blessed season. It was Sunday evening, there was no flight back to Rome before the next morning, so we went out to have a bit of fun. We went out as a group and we ended up in Hollywood, the most popular nightclub in the world of football and entertainment. We enjoyed ourselves, sure. We drank, we danced for a while, we were out late. Nothing bad, if it hadn't been for the fact that we'd just lost a game. And with many fans – as I've already explained – that doesn't go down well. Some of the papers published photos from our night out in the club. I was single again, so I had nothing to explain to anyone, but those who were married had a hard time convincing their wives that they were completely innocent. And the supporters were resentful. Not to the point that they were throwing fish at us again – we were still top of the table, after all, even if our lead over Juve had shrunk from eight points to three in two Sundays – but nearly.

The warning of a coming storm had sounded, and the next match became as crucial as the first game of the season. One of the most modest Napoli sides that I ever faced in my career arrived at the Olimpico – in fact they'd be relegated that year – but given the situation, there was no risk of underestimating them. Capello took advantage of the moment to make a couple of changes to the team, and they were decisive ones. Antonioli regained his place in goal from Lupatelli, and Aldair was withdrawn from the defence for Zebina. And before talking about the match, which was an easy 3-0 win, it's worth dwelling on the teammates I've just mentioned.

It can't be said that the goalkeepers were the strong point of the *scudetto*-winning squad, but they weren't as bad as the stories about them have made them out to be. Antonioli is a serious and taciturn guy, Lupatelli a likeable and impulsive madman, you only have to remember that he's the only goalkeeper I recall to have claimed – when he moved to Chievo – the number 10 shirt. They weren't too far apart in their ability, Antonioli was probably a little better and after a spell on the bench Capello recalled him, partly because Lupatelli had conceded a few too many free kicks. The other rotation concerned Aldair, who at 35 years old remained an unsurpassed defensive maestro, but he no longer had enough to perform at the highest level every Sunday. Pluto – as the fans had called him for years – gave way to Zebina, one of the strangest and most unconventional characters I ever knew at Trigoria. On the pitch he was a very quick and intelligent defender, because he learned from the expertise of the players in front of him and, thanks to his physical capabilities, quickly overtook them: that was the case with Aldair. But it's off the pitch where it's worth saying something about the phenomenon of Jonathan: far from the cliché of the ignorant footballer – just think of the fact that he opened an art gallery at the end of his career – he was a guy who always dressed with style and elegance, went around wearing a Borsalino hat and... well, I'll say it, he's a big playboy. He got injured against Napoli and missed a few games, but when he recovered, he stayed in the starting line-up.

The game was very easy. We didn't encounter any resistance, and it quickly appeared as though the sky was clearing again. The great news was that in the second half, Emerson finally got back onto the pitch, a very important signing who injured his cruciate ligament in the summer and had been replaced in the side by Cristiano Zanetti. The other long-term absentee, my dear friend Eusebio Di Francesco, was also close to returning, so the midfield emergency that Capello had had to deal with for the entire first half of the season was coming to its end.

The last game before the halfway point was a difficult one, potentially one that might have caught us out, because in spite of their mediocre league position, Parma had a lot of talented players. The problem was with their leadership: after Alberto Malesani was sacked, Arrigo Sacchi returned to his old job, but that week – even though results were starting to come – he had resigned, explaining that he was under too much stress. He never coached anyone again. He was replaced by Renzo Ulivieri, who remained until the end of the season, taking Parma to where they belonged: fourth place.

Many of my Italy teammates were in that squad, so we didn't risk letting the league table distract us. In fact, after about half an hour, the referee Stefano Farina gave us a clear penalty for a foul by Antonio Benarrivo on Tommasi. Since I knew Parma's young goalkeeper well, I told myself to angle my shot as far into the corner as possible, otherwise that lunatic would reach it. That young guy is Gigi Buffon. You'll find out later how far back my friendship with him goes: for now, I'll only say that we were almost two boys at the time. We smiled at each other as I prepared for my run up and he, to intimidate me, widened his arms to show me the immense reach that he has. *I need to angle my shot. Even more. Even more. Another two centimetres.* Too many. Gigi guessed the right way, his right hand reaching towards the post, but my low shot hit it and the ball rebounded away. He sprang to his feet, fists clenched. I remained there with my hands on my hips, perplexed, but after a long moment I shook it off, reanimated by the shouts of encouragement from my teammates.

I've seen many exceptional performances from Gigi, fortunately not only as an opponent. That day, he hit one of his peaks, because he seemed to take on a supernatural aura as he saved everything, particularly from me and Delvecchio. With a goalkeeper in that type of form, and with Thuram and Cannavaro protecting him, it was almost inevitable that just as we were at our most dominant, Marco Di Vaio went and scored on the counter-attack, putting Parma ahead and leaving us with an apparently unsolvable puzzle. How could we score against Buffon?

This was one of the days when Gabriel Batistuta made the difference, justifying the great efforts President Sensi went to in order to bring him to Roma. He scored two goals that were conceptually the same: reading a long pass perfectly, he sprinted into position and arrived at the ball in that no-man's-land behind the defenders. There, where not even Buffon can come out and claim it, and where a well-directed volley into the corner can't be stopped. Bati scored two fantastic goals, turning around what was looking like being a defeat into a victory in the last quarter of an hour. That game against Parma was a critically important stage in the title race: at the end, we all celebrated like kids, Montella hugged Bati tightly, forgetting any rivalry, and even Capello had the face of someone who had suffered a lot and was now enjoying the reward. This was also because Juve lost in Bergamo the day before, and so we were the winter champions with a six-point lead over both the Bianconeri and Lazio.

I had never been the winter champion. Moreover, I'd never even been close to it, and so I'd always dreamed of this halfway goal, including in light of the statistic that says that, three times out of four, the winter champions and the real champions are one and the same. In reality, being in first place also helped to calm my anger over a muscle strain that kept me out for two games, the wins against Bologna – I admired Emerson's goal and his subsequent embrace with Silio Musa, the physio who accompanied him during his rehabilitation, from the sofa at home – and Lecce. As always, this apparently straightforward opponent gave us a game that bordered on the dramatic. Samuel settled it with a header from a free kick, which was perhaps the only way to banish the demons. When Lecce came to the Olimpico, there were always plenty of those.

Walter Samuel was one of the main secrets behind our *scudetto* success. He arrived from Boca Juniors, and he certainly lived up to the reputation of those who have grown up at the Bombonera. Walter was a quick and powerful defender, and with time he improved with his feet, but his main characteristic was his heading. I should add that Walter could be quite wicked, an introverted, quiet and not very talkative guy who transformed on the pitch and (also) became my bodyguard: when someone took me down, he immediately rushed over, ready to put himself in the middle if something broke out or to give the player who committed the foul an unequivocal look: 'Don't do that again.' Sometimes Walter got revenge for me too: going in 'Argentine-style' on the legs of the person who'd fouled me. It's the Boca way: protect your number 10, who can then think about winning games for you.

I made my return on a freezing cold Sunday. Udine at the end of

February can be a real icebox, so I loved how Vicenza – who had a stadium ban – had the idea of playing at the Friuli... It was an ugly and laborious game. Batistuta went off injured after half an hour and it was still 0-0 after 80 minutes when Montella, finally, with a great shot from distance, allowed us to get our noses in front. A few minutes later, Emerson made the result safe, but it was a 'costly' victory because it was immediately clear that Bati's knee injury would keep him out for a while. A month, more or less. And Juve were keeping pace with us. The lead was still six.

What came next – on matchday 21 – was a wonderful game that confirmed the argument that if you want to win the *scudetto*, you need to have a deep bench. Inter arrived at the Olimpico after beating us earlier that season, and in addition to Batistuta we were missing Cafu, Emerson and Zanetti; two players from the same position. With Montella playing instead of Bati, we shifted to a four-man defence because there was no real alternative to Cafu, and Assunção took on the role of midfield playmaker. Remember what I said about his free kicks? The first one he took was wicked: it slowly crossed the entire penalty area in search of a touch that didn't come, and dropped into the far corner of the net, leaving Sébastien Frey first stunned and then furious.

It was definitely a lucky goal but a priceless one, because two minutes earlier, Bobo Vieri – in amazing form – had beaten Antonioli with a great volley.

Yet Assunção's free kicks weren't over: just before the half hour he took another that zigzagged through the air like a crazy missile. Frey followed it with his eyes as it hit the crossbar, but the quickest on the rebound was Montella, who headed it into the net for 2-1. Too bad that a great breakaway on the counter by Vieri – it was impossible to get the ball off him that day once he'd got it – made it 2-2 in first half injury time, sending us into the break in a bad mood.

The script didn't change in the second half, with us on the attack but with a little prudence – today it's called defensive covering – because as soon as they got a metre of space, Inter became very dangerous. For a long time the game seemed undecided about which way it would go: when it went our way in the end – the 86th minute – it was down to Vincenzo's eye for goal, because the laws of physics suggested he shouldn't be the one emerging from a group of players to jump highest. Yet he did, gaining the centimetres he needed with timing so perfect it was as if it had been decided by a computer. *L'Aeroplanino* took off and never landed, pursued by all of his delighted teammates.

The incredible Assunção scored a free kick the following Sunday too, against Brescia, and this time it was a real missile because his strong and precise shot flew into the top corner exactly as it should have. Here, again, Montella, after Andrés Yllana's equaliser, sealed the game with a brace. In the Brescia side was my old friend Fabio Petruzzi, but unfortunately for him, he evidently felt the pressure of the game, given that he got two yellow cards and had to leave the pitch.

With a week to go before the final break, our run of consecutive victories ended at seven in Reggio Calabria: not only did Reggina hold us to a 0-0 draw, but I can still feel the ice in my veins when that chance fell to Mozart at the very end, but he skied his shot from near the penalty spot. We were a bit tired, because the injuries were forcing the rest of us to play all the time. It was no coincidence that no one shed a tear when we exited the UEFA Cup in the Round of 16 against Liverpool. But that Sunday, Lazio came to our rescue: by beating Juventus in the direct clash between our two nearest rivals, they allowed us to increase our lead over the Bianconeri to seven points (while they moved up to nine points behind us). And there was nothing more galvanising for morale than a gain, even a small one, from a potentially unfavourable situation.

When the league resumed after the international break, we faced Verona at the Olimpico, and as often happened before, we went behind. Camoranesi scored after Antonioli made a mistake in coming out. Luckily we were able to play with the same calmness even though we were behind, and this was an invaluable quality. We were still behind at half time against Verona, but only after having missed half a dozen golden chances. The breakthrough against the Veneto side came around 10 minutes into the second half: I crossed the ball from the left to make it 1-1 when Montella and Apolloni put it into the net at the same time. Then it was Cafu's turn to replicate this twice from the right hand side to the delight of Batistuta – who had returned from his sprain – and Montella again.

The Olimpico evidently had faith in us, given that the loudest roar of the afternoon didn't come after one of our goals but rather for the one – now famous for its beauty – that Baggio scored in Turin in the final minutes of Juve-Brescia, making it 1-1. As Lazio lost to Milan, with ten games to go we reclaimed our biggest lead: nine points over Juve (and twelve over the Laziali).

The first victim of such favourable standings is superstition. In the dressing room that week, we were all talking openly about the upcoming *scudetto* and – as soon as Capello turned his back – we worked out how many points we, Juve and Lazio were likely to get between then and the end. The answer, common to all the 'working groups', was that the title could be made mathematically certain on matchday 32, the third-last game of the season: Roma-Milan. If we could finish that match with a seven-point lead, it was party time. At that point our lead was nine, but we still had to face the return derby and then go up to Turin. We couldn't wait: if we could have played two games a week, we would have asked to.

Was it a coincidence that, after all that talk, the third defeat of the season arrived? I'd like to say yes, because when we took to the pitch in Florence we were neither relaxed nor cavalier: the performance was good, we lost for the simple reason that an Enrico Chiesa in extraordinary form appeared in our path. He scored with a typical free kick to make it 1-0 – this time there was nothing to blame Antonioli for, the execution was perfect and unsavable – and, after Emerson's equaliser and Candela's own goal, he ended it for us with a beautiful right-footed volley. An old rival of ours, Roberto Mancini, had just taken his place on Fiorentina's bench for his first experience as a coach. After three draws, this was his first victory. He'd chosen the right rival to make people talk about him immediately. Naturally Juve and Lazio won, reducing the gap to six and nine points.

No one was daring to make calculations anymore, because there was tension around Trigoria again. It exploded the following Saturday, on the eve of Easter, in a highly dramatic game. Arriving in Rome were Perugia, who were having a brilliant season under Serse Cosmi and who had already been able to hold us to a 0-0 draw thanks to a good overall performance and to some great saves from Andrea Mazzantini. But the ones he made on his own turf were nothing compared to those he pulled out at the Olimpico. The story of my life in Giallorosso was full of 'normal' keepers who found their day of grace against us, and in some cases – I'm thinking of Marco Storari in an unreal Roma-Samp several years later – they even derailed us from the path to success. Mazzantini tried that day, and he really came close to succeeding; without our 90th-minute equaliser, which, by the way, was unlawful because Montella handled the ball, we would have added defeat to defeat. In a red-hot atmosphere that had suddenly turned negative again, that would have been the end.

A lot of things happened that afternoon. At the end of the first half, Davide Baiocco found the top corner from 30 metres to put Perugia in front – yes, we went behind again – and shortly after the break, I had a go from outside the area, a right-footed shot into the corner that the slight deflection off Marco Materazzi helped to make unstoppable. Our attacks were relentless. Mazzantini had to fly from one side of his goal to the other to keep us at bay, and it really seemed to be just a matter of time until we made it 2-1. Instead, less than a quarter of an hour from the end, Antonioli stumbled as he came out of his goal, lost the ball, and Luca Saudati was lightning quick to turn it into the net. We were behind again, our keeper was prostrate from the error, and the Curva Sud started to whistle and insult him. A nightmare.

Before resuming the game for the final assault on the Perugia fortress, I had to fulfil a captain's duty. I walked over beneath the Sud and, with as much volume as I could muster, I began to shout that Francesco Antonioli is Roma's goalkeeper, that Roma are still top of the table, and that they were abandoning him with those protests and instead they should be behind him to help him to overcome the incident. I was indignant, and this was evidently plain to see because the volume quickly subsided, and the fans started offering us their support again. We needed it, in order to climb the Everest of Perugia.

The goal that made it 2-2 came in the 90th minute. Technically it was an own goal by Giovanni Tedesco, because he was the last person that the ball hit in the furious free-for-all that broke out almost on the goal line, in which Batistuta and Montella were involved. Vincenzo touched it with his hand, and he did so instinctively. There was a fleeting sensation about this on the pitch, but later, watching it in slow motion, the foul play was clear. We were lucky. And also calculating: by staying off the pitch celebrating for a long time, I forced the yellow card that gave me a one-match ban, since I was one booking away from a suspension. Better to miss the trip to Udine than either of the following two games: the derby and Juve. Who, by beating Inter 3-1, narrowed the gap to four points. It was all to play for again, and it could even have been worse.

Fortunately the team got going again in Udine. Although I couldn't play, I travelled with them anyway. It was a moment that the captain couldn't miss, and I had to endure an excessive amount of jeering in the stands because I had a long-distance dispute with Roberto Sosa during the week, and evidently that didn't go down well with their supporters. No harm done though. Montella, Tommasi and my replacement Nakata handled the test, and Juve failed to break through Buffon's wall in the late game. On the eve of the decisive two games, we were six points ahead again.

The return derby was a very tough game, not at all eased by the fact that that afternoon – the match at the Olimpico was in the evening – Lecce had incredibly drawn away at Juventus, stopping them from snapping at our ankles in the table. Lazio weren't only playing for their last chance to fight for the *scudetto* but also to 'help' Juve stop Roma from winning the title. That was what was essential for their fans.

It was a dirty game, no one was pulling out of anything. Not even I held myself back, and a heavy challenge on Nedvěd cost me a yellow card. Rightly so, and I had no regrets: it was the sort of game where you had to earn respect not just for pieces of skill. The first half ended 0-0. It had been a long staring (and kicking) contest, waiting to see who lowered their gaze first. The second half began with a turning point in our favour: in the space of six minutes, first Batistuta scored with a delicious sidefoot finish from a cross by Delvecchio, then Marco himself, stretching himself to his limit, scored left-footed from Zanetti's long ball. A beautiful and difficult goal that only a perfectly flexible body can aspire to; otherwise, the risk of straining something is just around the corner.

At the start of that year, a lot of people had asked for Marco to be set aside so that – playing in front of me as *trequartista* – Montella could partner Bati. Capello, on the other hand, selected and supported Marco because he was the best at playing that double role, he ran back and forth endlessly, and when it came to the business of goals, he scored them too. He was the first to celebrate by gesturing to his ears, because he felt a little underrated, but there's no doubt that he made the most of his abilities. This, in my opinion, is a great testament to his intelligence and psychological robustness.

When you're 2-0 up, you just have to manage the ball to run the clock down, and maybe try to get a third to kill the game off completely. For a good ten minutes, Lazio seemed like a boxer on the ropes. We should have kept pressing them, but the dynamism of the start of the second half had cost us a lot of energy. So, when Zoff re-energised his team with a couple of changes, we started closing up and the pitch suddenly felt like it was sloping uphill. The minute in which we capitulated for the first time was the 78th: a finish from Nedvěd from the edge of the box, the kind he often did, he was a good ball striker even when he was off-balance. Our defence tightened even more, and as we went into injury time – five minutes, an enormity at the time – Capello introduced some fresh legs with Guigou and Mangone. We got our heads to Mihajlović's last venomous corner, Tommasi sending the ball out of the area. But no one could have expected Lucas Castromán, a young Argentine who had been sent on, to launch a powerful right-footed shot that flew low and straight into the corner.

Fantastic goal, but I'll say it now: of those moments, I remember only an uncontrollable fury, kicking everything as we returned to the dressing room, an anger that, that evening, no consideration of the table could assuage. We had overcome the first of the last two hurdles unscathed, but the derby is the derby: the way it had unfolded, it was as if Lazio had won it.

The mood improved in the following days because we needed to focus on Juventus and because the federal court issued a ruling that allowed an unlimited number of non-EU players to be used. It so happened that the provision would have an immediate effect on the upcoming match, and debates about that by Juventini have never calmed, but at the time at Trigoria we were happy about that more than anything else because that limitation had been the source of a lot of long faces, those of teammates who couldn't play even though they were fit and ready. And at certain times, any barrier to unrest is welcome.

We were no longer at our peak, but it's not like Juve were doing that much better: in the two previous games, they only picked up two draws, and the second in particular was a crying shame for them. Had they been four points behind, the prospect of being able to close the gap to one point with a win would have given them wings. But actually, they got off to a flying start: Del Piero scored a header in the fourth minute, set up by Zidane, and in the sixth minute the Frenchman – magnificent at the start – scored himself, partly thanks to our defence, which melted away in front of him. In the last team meeting, Capello had recommended that we kick into high gear straight away to withstand the predictable battle of the first half hour. After six minutes, we were 2-0 down. Mission accomplished...

I played really badly, I struggled to get in the right place while the Juventini flew around me like pinballs for a good half hour. It wasn't even an issue of the physical battle, they were simply going at three times our speed. We had to hold out, hoping that they'd live to regret it: Edgar Davids came close to making it 3-0, which would have ended the game prematurely, and from then on we started to pick up the pieces of a game that we'd imagined but never begun to see what we could do with.

At half time, Capello reminded us of the derby and of Lazio's feat: 'You have even more time available, last Sunday it was still 0-0 at the break.' I don't know how many believed in him. I felt quite empty, the expectations of the big game were like the result of a bad joke on me. I went back out and tried a couple of things, but they didn't work. After a quarter of an hour I saw two teammates on the touchline about to come on, and unusually I stopped to look at the board to see the numbers of the substitutes. I was right to do so, because the first one was the number 10.

I was surprised. And, immediately afterwards, annoyed. I was playing badly, true, but taking off the captain in a game like that... I'd never cared about the image or the hierarchy, I didn't think I had to stay on the pitch because I had more of a right to. But I was still the one who could find a goal out of nothing: keep me on, you never know what might happen in the next 20 minutes. Fine. I clapped hands with Nakata, who was coming on for me, put on my tracksuit jacket because it was still cold in Turin (in May – I'm just saying...) and sat down without making even a mildly controversial gesture. Even though I was being replaced, it was definitely not the time to add fuel to the fire.

There have been many miraculous substitutions, but Nakata's is the most incredible I can remember. In the 79th minute, Hide hit the top corner with a great shot from distance. Roma had already reclaimed control of the game, but it needed a goal to reopen it, and now there it was. I jumped up from the bench too, encouraging everyone and trying to give some basic instructions, just to feel like I was involved. The stadium was frozen with tension. There was a feeling that we weren't out of it, just as Lazio hadn't been out of the derby.

Another sign of fate arrived when the amount of injury time was announced: five minutes, as many as the previous Sunday, but at least we didn't need to wait for the last one to level the score. Another great shot from outside the box from Nakata was only parried by Van der Sar, and Montella was quick to pounce on the rebound ahead of Montero and Batistuta. He scored acrobatically, and the roar from our support was unforgettable because that was a game that was abundantly lost, while now it felt like the opposite.

I ran to Nakata to hug him and kiss him, everyone was already all over him, while he had his usual quiet smile, almost brushing it all aside. 'You're a legend, Hide!' I yelled into his ears, several times, and eventually he turned to me, exclaimed, 'Thanks!' and then moved away. I think he was a bit ruffled by the physical contact, the carnality of a group of players who had just scored the *scudetto* goal, and who were now embracing each other in a state of ecstasy. Nakata was the first to disappear into the dressing room. An alien, courteous but detached, quiet, who was with us but without ever leaving his inaccessible world. Of the few things that we said to each other, I still remember one because was a man of his word: 'I'll stop playing soon because I want to do other things too.' That's exactly what happened.

Once we'd made it through the two head-to-heads without taking any serious damage, the countdown began with a fresh look: Lazio had overtaken Juve and were now our closest challengers, five points behind to the Bianconeri's six. There were five games to go, the first of which was at home to Atalanta: a game to be handled carefully, and in fact before the winning effort from Montella – Vincenzo was on fire at that point – there was a good hour of play, during which there was a splendid save from Antonioli to stop Nappi's shot. A small bit of revenge for our much-criticised keeper. Just consider that after the game against Perugia, the one when I defended him under the *curva*, he hired a bodyguard because he felt the atmosphere around him was so dark that he was afraid.

Once again Capello substituted me – just before we took the lead – to send on Nakata. First consideration: I played badly that day too, it's true. But for the entire second half of the season, I'd helped the team rather than my own personal satisfaction. I could feel how close the *scudetto* was and since the opposition always put at least two men on me, I gave the ball to a free teammate without giving myself the problem of trying to stand out in any other way. Second consideration: I didn't want being replaced to become a habit. This time as I came off, I muttered something at Capello, and it was heard. But it wasn't anything that could set the atmosphere alight. We shouldn't be arguing as we reach the title.

Matchday 31, and it was finally easy: we got a big win in Bari, 4-1, started by Candela. Also on the scoresheet were Cafu – and the two wing-backs scoring at the same time is a reward for the team's tactics, now indestructible – and Batistuta, twice. Capello sent on Nakata again, but this time for Montella. I played until the 90th minute and enjoyed the unprecedented exodus of our fans. There were nearly 30,000 Roma supporters who had used any means possible to get to Puglia. At the end, I got to the middle of the pitch and turned around, getting a 'panoramic view' of this Olimpico that had moved to Bari. Unforgettable.

The 32nd game was the one we'd pinpointed in our predictions from two months before as the game where we could potentially seal the *scudetto*. We hadn't been that good, though, so it wasn't just up to us. If Milan won in the Olimpico, we'd need Lazio and Juve not to get anything more than a draw in their respective games. In any case, our maths soon went out the window because Milan took the lead at the end of the first half thanks to a header by Francesco Coco, and to get us level again we needed another feat from Montella, who was furious after being benched again despite his extraordinary run of form. No one would think to chip a very tall keeper like Sebastiano Rossi. No one except Vincenzo, who saw him slightly off his line, considered the penalty area to be too crowded, and decided to take the high route with an outrageous lob. A goal worth shouting about, and as soon as I reached him to celebrate with him I had to shut his mouth, because you can imagine who that scream was directed at. Milan were good – it's a mystery why they were so far behind.

A draw was a good result, because Lazio conceded a last-minute equaliser to Inter and were practically out of the picture, five points behind with two games left. Juve remained four points behind, but in those moments we felt we were almost champions.

I left the pitch embraced by Di Francesco. I declared to him that we'd win the game and the league in Naples on Sunday, and he strengthened my enthusiasm with a series of yeses. Other teammates joined us, and we paused under the stand to yell that we were just seven days away, and all the people were with us: 'To Naples! To Naples!'

I started to count down the hours.

6.

'Roma Have Won!'

NAPLES. IT'S 30 DEGREES THE EVENING BEFORE THE GAME,
9 June: the end of a championship that began on 1 October and finishes as
summer starts. Rather than being beneath the volcano, I feel like I've
ended up in it. People are in a frenzy on the waterfront, where our hotel is,
and hundreds of people are in the lobby, not exactly ideal preparation for
a game that could be worth the scudetto. Likewise, we're feeling it too. As
always happens on these occasions, no one knows who took care of it but
travelling with us in some trunks are the celebratory T-shirts and iceboxes
of champagne for the big celebrations. The game will be played in the
afternoon, when it's expected to be 35 degrees, and those who don't like
air conditioning are forced to open their windows overlooking the sea,
and Via Caracciolo remains noisy until dawn. And it's not just because of
Napoli supporters. As the hours go by, the number of Romanisti increases
– after all, it's only two hours on the motorway – and many of them feel
compelled to come by our hotel to let us know that they're there...

A wedding was being celebrated in the hotel where we were staying.
This was a slight organisational lapse because the rule followed by Capello
from the very first away game was to isolate the team completely. It
avoided any deception. In football's old days, in my very first years in Serie
A, it wasn't uncommon for some girl who was looking for a fling with a
footballer, famous or not, to sneak into the team's retreat. Since Mazzone's
era though, coaches had moved on from passive surveillance to a

progressively more active one, partly based on prevention. If you booked a hotel where keeping the squad and 'normal' guests apart was easy, taking liberties becomes impossible.

This situation caused a massive misunderstanding that has been embellished in Rome for years, partly because Capello has long been convinced that he was right and has never hidden that. (Next time I meet him, now that we're on good terms again, I really should ask him if he still believes that.) But let's go back to the wedding. That evening, the coach was very unnerved by the coincidence, and I can understand why, because contact at the hotel bar between us players and the guests at the wedding dinner – among whom were some beautiful women – was inevitable. There were requests for autographs, photos, some exchanges, a couple of remarks. But it was all completely innocent. Believe me. Since the end of the previous season, Capello's method had involved two private guards on the floor where the team slept, and no one had ever dared to try any improbable subterfuge. As for me, I was single at the time: if something had happened, seventeen years later, I wouldn't have a problem saying so; at this point, the embargo is over. But the truth is that nothing happened.

That evening, we went up to our rooms more or less all together – we had taken over the entire eighth floor – and before going to bed, we got some fresh air on the terraces overlooking the Castel dell'Ovo. It was a wonderful place. I was sharing a room with Alessandro Rinaldi, a charming guy, Roman like me, from Cinecittà. At one point I heard a knock on the door. I opened it, and found the embarrassed face of Tempestilli, who was now the team manager. He tried to make me understand something with his eyes. I didn't have time to ask him what was happening before Capello appeared from behind him and entered the room, furious.

'Where are they? Where are the girls?'

'Boss, what are you talking about? There aren't any girls...'

'Yes there are, I'm sure of it.'

The search wasn't a long one because the room was twenty square metres, more or less, but it was very thorough. Capello opened the wardrobe, he checked the shower cubicle, he even looked under the bed. Nothing, of course. I tried to make a joke about it, telling him, 'All I know is they made a jump for it', but he got even angrier. He left, convinced that he'd been deceived, and he was right: only not by me, but by whoever tipped him off (and after so many years now, I'd like to know who it was).

The next day, the coach journey to the San Paolo, which usually took a quarter of an hour with the police escort, took more than fifty minutes. Everything was odd that Sunday, including the desperation of the Napoli fans: if we won, then they were relegated. We were aware that we weren't going out onto the red carpet but were also aware that we were the better team: 39 points separated us in the standings, so we would find that difference somewhere and make it count.

Of course, not right away. It wasn't really a habit of ours: for the twelfth time in thirty-three games – I think it was a record for an Italian title winner – we went behind. The defence was shaky from the start, and in the 37th minute Nicola Amoruso managed to anticipate Samuel and beat Antonioli from the edge of the box.

Luckily we equalised immediately. I took a corner that, as it dropped, bent at the right moment to evade the keeper and land on Batistuta's outstretched foot, an easy finish, and it was 1-1 at half time. Thank God, because there was a lot of tension in the dressing room.

In the previous few games, Montella had started to let his irritation show. Even after his fantastic goal against Milan he was convinced that he had earned his place. And he wasn't the only pressure point. From what I read and heard, at other big clubs, the issue of the starting eleven was treated in a less visceral way by the players; in Rome, on the other hand, those who missed out smoulder, and there's nothing that can calm them down. After all, I'd been the same: substituted for Nakata twice in a row, I was already getting pissed off.

Despite the oppressive heat, I had one of my best games. You could see that there was a long-repressed desire within me. The goal that made it 2-1 started with a cross from Cafu, I controlled it with my chest and fired a right-footed shot into the net more or less from the penalty spot. The Neapolitans protest because I'd jumped with my arms wide, and it's true that as the ball dropped it brushed past one of them, but the control was exclusively with the chest. Let me tell you: it's a talent reserved only for a few. If you don't have technique in your blood then nothing will come to mind. Other than handball.

Could that have been the *scudetto*-winning goal? For 29 minutes, yes, and in any case I celebrated it as if it were, pulling my shirt off and running to one of the areas of the ground filled by our fans. For 29 minutes, we stayed 2-1 up, taking no risks and even wasting three or four good opportunities to seal the game. The San Paolo was silent and depressed, they felt that the sentence was coming, and I found it hard to imagine what relegation could mean for such a city and its supporters.

A shadow of resignation was beginning to appear on the faces of the Napoli players themselves when Francesco Moriero's entrance brought a bit of sparkle to the air again. He was the one who won a free kick on the edge of the box in the 81st minute, which Fabio Pecchia went to take with a precise idea in his head: not to go over the wall but to try to go through it. He struck his shot straight at it, and incredibly he was justified: the wall opened up, Antonioli was surprised by the ball flying through where it shouldn't, and though he got his hands to it late, he couldn't stop it: 2-2. Juve and Lazio had had big leads since the first half, so if it ended like this then the championship would still be alive on the final day. And I didn't like that idea at all.

Capello then called on Montella, and he came on, sure, but not before a brief and bitter discussion with the coach. There was the famous kick of the water bottle: Vincenzo was furious not just because he hadn't started the game but also because, after my goal, the coach had taken off Delvecchio for Zanetti. A logical change, you're winning the title game and so you cover yourself a bit. But at this point the issue had become gangrenous; Montella was one of the top two or three Italian forwards, he couldn't do his job in fits and starts any longer. He considered it an injustice, not least because in the second half of the season he had a very high average of decisive goals.

Who knows what would have happened if Vincenzo had scored the title-winning goal: he had the chance for it, but the Napoli goalkeeper – poor Franco Mancini – denied him with a courageous block. Final whistle. A bitter pill, very bitter, and in the dressing room a lot of my teammates and I had to work to keep Capello and Montella well separated, as they were now close to laying hands on each other. The next day, Vincenzo realised that he had gone too far and publicly apologised to the coach.

The journey back home on the coach that evening was awful: very irritable and full of bad moods, of fights threatening to break out, of scowling faces. Sometimes it happens that a simple slogan manages to make you change your perspective on things, to make you change your point of view. I read in a Roman newspaper that 'It will be much more beautiful to win it at home' and suddenly I thought that this was an obvious truth. Of course it would be a thousand times more beautiful at the Olimpico. In the midst of our people, in our packed stadium, in our crazy city, in our magical places. I immediately said this to Candela, my 'champagne' friend, and he nodded – 'I thought so too, we'll beat Parma easily' – and then I talked about it in the dressing room when we returned to training and negative thoughts were still pouring out. And the idea reinvigorated everyone, prompting jokes like: 'Where can I find the 200 tickets I've been asked for?' – which actually weren't jokes, each of us would have to deal with massive demands – or 'How are we going to leave the Olimpico afterwards?' The answer was obvious: we'll worry about that *afterwards*.

In the final week, Capello regulated our work on the pitch with great care, mostly in the late afternoon, because the mid-June heat was now relentless. In that week, the experience of those who had already won trophies could be clearly perceived, because they maintained a perfect balance between a certain positive tension and taking care to play down the expectations that inevitably cause stress.

But I, at home and with friends, devoted myself to another aspect of the feat we were about to complete: the epic one. In March that year, *Gladiator* won an Academy Award, an exceptional film that really caught my imagination. It even inspired one of my tattoos. For a true-born Roman like me, the enormity of our weight in history is a source of pride and interest: at school, I could lose attention in other subjects, but certainly not when the primary and then secondary school teachers recounted the events of the Roman Empire to us. Being able to go back to them by watching the best film of the year was a privilege. I know *Gladiator* almost by heart. When Russell Crowe takes off his helmet in the arena in front of Commodus and says in a momentous voice, 'My name is Maximus Decimus Meridius, commander of the Armies of the North...', my eyes start to well up. Every time. I can't help it. So, every evening that week, I shut myself away in my basement at home, where we have a big screen, and I put on the *Gladiator* DVD. It was a kind of collective excitement that I experienced with Riccardo, Angelo, Giancarlo, the usual friends from all my trips away, and when the cry went up with 'Roma victa!' we all jumped to our feet and joined in enthusiastically, obviously thinking about winning the *scudetto*. The first few evenings, Mum, worried about the shouting she could hear coming from the basement, would come down to find out what was happening and went away laughing. Dad shook his head, but he seemed amused too. It was a fantastic way of getting psyched up, I should patent it. Let's face it: we footballers were fighting for glory, followed by armies of impassioned fans who wanted to see us prevail against everyone or, on the other side, suffer and succumb. What are we, if not modern gladiators?

It wasn't just my favourite film that I watched that week. TV stations were broadcasting specials on our long march towards the *scudetto*, and I watched them again on tape, savouring the importance of what we'd done. It wouldn't count for anything if we weren't able to beat Parma, of course, but in all honesty I couldn't feel more than a small and distant doubt. We were much stronger, and their season had been over for some time: after the problems of the first half of the season, they'd climbed back to a fourth place that reflected the level of the squad. I read somewhere that in the second half of the season they'd picked up 33 points like us, and this was actually a slightly troubling statistic. But the difference in motivation couldn't fail to be felt.

If I can't take a walk around Rome in normal times, sticking my head out of the house that week was unthinkable. My friends, though, told me about a city that was simmering, sure, but in a certain sense still quiet, savouring the expectation amid a thousand superstitious rituals – the tension was there, it's pointless to deny it – and a very… patient impatience. It's like when you have to kiss a girl for the first time: you're pretty sure that she wants to as well, but you never know, imagine if she rejects you, you must have completely misunderstood. Every time you're about to try, the doubts return. What if Parma had prepared a blitz to go down in history? I put *Gladiator* on again to avoid thinking about it. And since many of the team lived near me in Casal Palocco, there were constant comings and goings in the basement.

Saturday morning. Attilio, our friend from the Al Pescatore restaurant in Ostia, had a seven-seater minibus: he stopped at our homes to pick us up so that we wouldn't have the problem of having to get our cars from Trigoria after the game. There was me, Batistuta, Montella, Delvecchio and Candela. There was no special goodbye at home, we'd speak to each other numerous times before kick off: but mum still looked at me in a curious way, and when she hugged me, her eyes were shining. Fortunately, the minibus has tinted windows, because if the people camped around Trigoria had seen us, it would have been difficult to reach the sports centre. The barrier at the entrance gate rose, and it was at that moment that I felt the weight of an adventure that was coming to its end. The last twenty-four hours. Tomorrow we'd be the champions of Italy – either that, or we'd be fugitives on the first plane out.

Training. Team meeting. Pool. Dinner. Small talk. Dreams. I spent hours imagining what the Olimpico would be like, because the videos I'd seen from 1983 showed a celebration – Roma-Torino on the final day – rather than a victory, which had been secured in the previous game, in Genova, with the draw that gave the Roma of Roberto Pruzzo, Paulo Roberto Falcão, Agostino Di Bartolomei and Bruno Conti mathematical certainty of the title. So this, technically, would be its first time (in 1942, the year of the first title, Roma were playing elsewhere). It would be excited too…

Generally, on the night before a game, people head to their rooms at around 11pm, but this time the adrenaline was too strong, no one could sleep. Capello came past, made a face, but didn't say anything – not 'Go to bed' or 'It's late'. He knew it would be pointless, he knew how we felt: like his Milan players, or those at Real Madrid, the clubs he had won at before. Those who are able to sleep in these types of situations are very few indeed. I remember an interview in which the great Enzo Bearzot spoke about the 'coyotes' among his players – one was Marco Tardelli – those who just couldn't fall asleep, so they wandered through the corridors of the training camp like wolves on the American prairie. We were all coyotes at Trigoria that night. I turned my light off at 3am, after a last round of phone calls with friends. Hardly anyone was sleeping in Rome, I think.

The sun filtered through the shutters early, but I stayed in bed, dozing, until 9am. At breakfast I read the newspapers. I liked the *Corriere dello Sport* a lot because it was dedicated entirely to our journey, a celebration before the title had been mathematically sealed. Zero superstition, but never mind.

Two beeps sounded. My phone had received its first text message from a friend inside the stadium, which had opened the turnstiles early for the occasion. I was speechless. 'It's packed here already!' the message said. *It can't be true...* But I saw that some of my teammates were on their feet, enraptured by the TV. They were holding slices of bread and jam in mid-air, as if time were standing still. There were images on the TV... of a full Olimpico, and it was live. *So it is true.*

I took a quick jog to get the muscles moving, but it was already excessively hot. At 11am I went back to my room to call my mum: 'I've just sat in my seat, Francesco. Yes, we're all set, thanks. It's... it's incredible, it's full to bursting here.' After that, I couldn't wait to leave, but first, lunch and our last team meeting to sort out set plays. I got on the bus and hit the horn three times to make everyone realise that there was no time to waste. They were waiting for us.

That day we set a record for the quickest journey between Trigoria and the Olimpico: twenty minutes, no more, and the ten police cars escorting us were only part of the reason. The other, more relevant reason is that there wasn't a soul around because they were all already inside the stadium.

Generally I don't take part in the pre-game stroll, that ten-minute walk for the players in club uniforms to get a taste of the atmosphere and feel what the pitch is like underfoot, which is much more useful when playing away than at home. But I made an exception and I went out onto the field too, because I wanted to see the fans, and the roar when we went out there added itself to the many unforgettable things connected with the *scudetto*.

We passed by the Parma players on the pitch, and there was a certain modesty in our eyes. For two reasons. The first, widely commented on that week at Trigoria, is that their squad seemed like an offshoot of Lazio's: Diego Fuser, Matias Almeyda, Roberto Sensini, Marco Di Vaio...

All people who had played there and who would do their utmost to stop us winning, if only to maintain good relations with their old fans. Many roads lead back to Rome, so it's best not to leave it with unfinished business. The second cause of embarrassment was down to friendships. Gigi Buffon had been like a brother to me since the Italy Under-15s – everyone knew that – and Fabio Cannavaro was another member of the Azzurri who I'd been very close to, between the Under-21s and the senior side. I made it a point of honour not to call them all week – an odd thing, because we usually talked frequently – to avoid jokes and misunderstandings. But now I couldn't pretend not to see them; it would be too much. Partly because the two of them were looking at me, pointing at me and laughing unrestrainedly. They were really poking fun at me.

'Idiots, what are you laughing at?'

'Sssh! You can't talk to us, otherwise we'll call the Investigations Bureau.'

'No jokes, not today.'

'Shut up, you mustn't talk to us.'

And so it went on, they wouldn't let go of the fact that they hadn't heard from me all week. I went back into the dressing room, still followed by their voices. The previous summer, they had been on the verge of coming to Roma. Now I feared that they wanted to make sure they wouldn't regret it.

Ghosts were hovering over the stadium. *Come on, let's get going, the sooner we play, the sooner we'll banish them.*

In the end, Capello didn't waste time and, playing alongside me and Batistuta, was Montella. He wanted to send a clear signal: this time, it will be an onslaught. At kick-off, I had the feeling that I wasn't at the centre of the pitch but at the centre of the world. It was enough to make my head hurt, but referee Stefano Braschi's whistle finally stopped the whirlwind of thoughts that had lasted a whole week. Running, kicking, fighting, falling, striking: I'd never needed the physicality of a match so much.

We started slightly in neutral: you could hear the engine accelerating but it hadn't been put into gear properly, there were a few transmission problems between the different parts. We needed to play shorter, getting closer to each other so we didn't misplace our passes.

Capello shouted as much as usual, if not more. He wanted to correct our weak points immediately to avoid us using up too much energy in the recovery phase. It was a killer heat, the heat that's often waiting for you as the second half begins, and especially the last twenty minutes, when there's the risk of undoing all the running done in the first half in one fell swoop. Parma played their game without hesitation. They were a strong side and they wanted to show that, especially their former Lazio players. As expected. On the plus side was the fact that, not having any league objectives, they played openly. They didn't raise the barricades; they wanted to take away the satisfaction of winning in the title hopefuls' back yard. So, when we got the ball back, we found large enough spaces to get going again; even I managed my 30-metre bursts forward with the ball at my feet without finding three players trying to foul me along the way.

The first real chance fell to Montella from a ball from Candela, but his angled shot hit the post. At the same time there was a prolonged murmur among the people, a sound that had the same frequency as the Mexican wave, but it was no celebration. I didn't pay any heed to it until Cafu, playing on the wing by the technical area and so the one who had access to the news, told me that David Trezeguet had scored in Turin. Widely expected, no one thought that Juve wouldn't win, but it was still a goal that raised the level of pressure a notch. If it ended like this, there would be a playoff.

We knew we had to win, now the time to do that had got a little bit shorter. After a quarter of an hour, it was still 0-0. At least we hadn't gone behind, as we had too many times this year.

It was in this context of stress that was building, but hadn't yet exploded, that the goal of my life was born. Not the most beautiful – however good it was – but the leap my heart took at that moment is only behind the birth of my children, and not by much. There was a long ball from Tommasi from the centre out towards the left. Candela controlled the ball after an opponent's header. There was a touch back from him towards the centre of the box, an action repeated so many times that we could have repeated it with our eyes closed by then. This time, though, there was something different: Montella. Delvecchio was elsewhere. Vincenzo, who was a centre forward at heart, inevitably got onto the pass's trajectory. I was charging in at full speed and shouted 'Mine' even though Montella had somehow sensed my presence, and a moment before he controlled it he instinctively dodged out the way. It really was a fraction of a second, the impact of my right foot needed to be perfect and I thought I was getting to the ball a bit too quickly, that I should have slowed down a bit. These were thoughts all whirling around that disappeared on contact, a masterful right-footed strike that I caught early, sending the ball into the corner that Buffon had just left in order to cover the rest of the goal. Wrong-footing him, just as in a well-struck penalty. There it was, the goal of my life. The one that will stay with me forever, my message to the Roma fans of the future. This is who I was. I was the goalscorer who made it 1-0 on the most important Sunday in our history.

Of course, I can't remember what the exact moment was like. It's impossible. It's such a blinding flash that you can't help but look at it and enjoy it, for ever and ever.

The first reaction was a roar in harmony with everyone in the Olimpico. Then I was all smiles as I started to take off my shirt, jumping over the advertising hoarding, flying to meet the Curva Sud as promised – not that week, but much earlier: the day on which, still a child, I arrived at Roma.

There were many tears in the *curva*, of love and euphoria: the same ones that I saw many years later, on the Sunday of my retirement, when they were tinged with melancholy. I didn't win much in my career. But the intensity of those few days of triumph, especially that 17 June 2001, more than makes up for any deficit. Happiness can't be counted, it's felt. The Roman and Romanista captain who leads Roma to the title is a concept that transcends pure sporting joy. 'My name is Maximus Decimus Meridius, commander of the Armies of the North...'

Capello made sweeping gestures for us to return to the middle of the pitch, fearing that the effect of being ahead would take something away from us in the minutes that followed – as sometimes happens. He wanted the defensive fortress to be perfectly operational when the game restarted.

The great thing about facing an opponent without any objectives to fulfil on the last day was found in the fact that the scoreline didn't affect their attitude. Parma continued to play as if nothing had happened, looking for a way into our area where Di Vaio was chasing a prize – by that point he'd scored fourteen goals, so he needed one more to get a bonus for fifteen. They knew how to cause us problems, but they were open in defence, as is inevitable when you attack in numbers.

Before the break, Batistuta set off, chased by two defenders, who forced him out towards the right. Once he was in the box, Bati shot anyway, a powerful right-footed shot as Buffon came out and stopped it with his foot, pushing it away. But in the centre, where the ball landed, Montella was the quickest, as always. He struck with a surgeon's precision the moment the ball touched the ground, and immediately he was the *Aeroplanino* again. While I followed him as he ran towards the *curva* I thought, *It's over, no one can take the title away from us now.* When I raised my head from our embrace, I didn't see the fans' faces anymore. Only flags, which were absolutely everywhere.

Half time was a succession of gestures of understanding, of thumbs-up, of smiles, of preparing ourselves for the party. Capello was forced to raise his voice, recommending that we didn't ruin all the good things we'd done, asking us for a last good 45 minutes, but even he struggled to find a foothold to keep us alert, as when he turned around I sensed him smiling with Italo Galbiati, his assistant. The title in Rome would be a medal that described his talent as much as if not more than his trophies in Milan, where winning isn't so rare.

A cold shower was the best way to rejuvenate ahead of the second half. Afterwards, I went out into the corridor where I found Buffon, who told me how well I did to fool him at his near post, 'I expected you to go across me, you played me like a fish.' Coming from him, it was a mighty compliment.

The second half wasn't a contest. We wanted to keep our distance and, if possible, seal the season with a few symbolic things. The first was a goal from Batistuta, his twentieth of the season but most of all the signature on the title from a man who was key to its achievement. Gabriel hit the target with a left-footed effort from the edge of the box, about 10 minutes from the end, and it triggered wild celebrations because many people had already climbed over the fencing, and as we hugged Bati, the first pitch invaders joined in, though they were immediately driven back by the stewards off the pitch.

The other symbolic acts were the substitutions, because before Delvecchio and Nakata, whose importance I've emphasised extensively (and so it was right that they took part in the final celebrations on the pitch), Capello sent on Amedeo Mangone, a defender who was always prepared to come in and was a man capable of 'holding' the dressing room like few others. His nickname, 'the white Thuram', played on the fact that two seasons earlier, Parma's highly talented Frenchman had turned out to be among our targets in the transfer market. Instead it was Amedeo who joined – he was good but not that good – and we made that enough for us, won over by his charm.

If it were possible, some of the other substitutes deserved a few minutes too: Cristiano Zanetti first of all, starter for more than half of the season and then willing to step aside without complaint to allow Emerson back in. The others were Marco Amelia, who was always there when I won (as we'll discover at the 2006 World Cup), Di Francesco, who paid too dearly for his injury at the start of the season, the ageing Balbo, who came back to close his cycle, and Gaetano D'Agostino.

In the Olimpico, hundreds of people were climbing the fencing, making Capello tenser and tenser. Once it was 3-0, which at the end became 3-1 when Di Vaio earned his prize, the coach almost never looked back at the pitch to focus on what was happening all around us. The truth is that after about 70 minutes, someone ordered the gates to be opened, with the result being that half of the city was pressing forward, trying to get into the Olimpico. Five minutes from the end, Braschi whistled for a foul and someone misunderstood, running onto the field: as always happens in these situations, after one person does it, thousands follow.

Capello was raging, his neck swollen with anger, yelling at everyone that we'd lose the game by default. The bench and the kit men helped him, trying to cut short the growing celebrations, while on the pitch we players were stripped of our shirts. But then we were able to push the pitch invaders back and get ourselves dressed again as best we could with what was available on the bench.

Capello had lost his voice by this stage, but Braschi signalled to him to be calm. The match resumed, under the watchful eyes of the now thousands of fans crowded around the edges of the pitch. After a while,

Braschi came up to me and murmured, 'Get the ball near to the exit, as soon as I get there, I'll blow for full time,' and that's what happened about thirty seconds later.

Vito ran up to me, and for a moment, just a moment, we embraced each other with joy. We couldn't help it: we looked into each other's eyes, both of us crying. Immediately afterwards, he acted as my shield to help me get off the pitch. But it was a challenge.

At the Olimpico, the distance between the pitch and the dressing room isn't very short, and in normal situations it takes at least a couple of minutes to cover it. That day it took me fifty minutes, because when I arrived at the entrance to the corridor I found it clogged. Everyone was there, well-known faces and people I've never seen before, actors, journalists, politicians, people literally going crazy singing, dancing, pushing, drinking, pouring their drinks over others. It seemed like a Formula One podium, just much more crowded. Of course, my appearance didn't go unnoticed, but since I was left with only my underwear, fortunately no one thought to grab that last trophy: I'd have defended it tooth and nail. Actually, and no one realised it because I'd rolled it up so much it seemed like a towel, I also saved my shirt: it was a memento that I didn't want to part with.

When I got in sight of the door to the dressing room, I shuffled up against the wall trying to make myself seen, because two kit men were there on the lookout, probably worried by the fact I hadn't come back yet. In fact, as soon as they noticed me, they came towards me, creating a mini-corridor with their considerable size that I could walk through to reach the dressing room. Phew.

'A full fifty minutes,' Vito said. I was the last one back. As I entered, the cork of a champagne bottle popped. It wasn't the first, judging by the atmosphere.

The singing and dancing involved me immediately. I toasted everyone and, like everyone, was amazed and then more than amused by Nakata, who in that immense chaos was sat in a corner, reading a book. A Martian.

There must have been some trays of fruit and chocolate in the dressing room, but when I arrived, there was nothing left. So, on my third gulp of champagne, I felt sick. I don't drink alcohol, so doing it on an empty stomach was a really stupid idea.

The dressing room was flooded by people from the radio and TV, everyone begging for a guest for their broadcast. Montella was the best at lending himself until Franco Sensi arrived, and then we all respectfully gave way to him. I kissed and embraced Rosella, his daughter, who was also a friend of mine. I then led a song for the president, and I had a lot of fun watching what people are capable of doing when euphoria loosens their inhibitions.

At one point, Buffon also peeped into the dressing room, and as soon as I saw him I invited him for a round of drinks and said to Sensi, 'President, stop him, don't let him leave the Olimpico.' But I then stopped straight away, because I realised that certain jokes might not be so funny to Antonioli's ears. (I repeated to Sensi, separately, that signing him could be doable. The problem was that that same summer, Juventus sold Zidane to Real Madrid, and the first person they spent their new-found mountain of money on was Gigi.)

We didn't all celebrate together that night. In fact, if I can admit to a little bitterness, there was never a reunion with the whole squad, not even at Antonello Venditti's concert at the Circus Maximus a few days later. Many had already left for their holidays, so there were only five or six of us on the stage for that concert and huge party. The Brazilians spent the night of the title victory by themselves, Batistuta organised something with Delvecchio, other people gathered at Montella's house. I know this because Capello rang his doorbell at midnight. 'Vincenzo, it's the boss, happy birthday. Can I come in?' 18 June is both of their birthdays. What better occasion to smooth over all their falling outs? The coach did well to show up at midnight with a good bottle, Vincenzo did well to embrace him and make him the guest of honour at his *scudetto* party. Winning is a wonderful thing because it helps to put everything into perspective.

Because I'm a Roman, that night I couldn't do anything other than go around the city on a moped, obviously with a full-face helmet on, to snoop on my people's happiness. It was an incredibly foolish thing to do because I'd drunk too much champagne in the dressing room and was seeing double as I drove. But I went slowly, surrounded by friends and relatives on mopeds, to enjoy those endless processions of flags, those colours –

the yellow and red – that all of Rome was painted in, that boundless and carefree joy, the most beautiful night of my life and of the lives of many who I travelled past and who couldn't imagine who was under that helmet.

Mum, Dad and all our friends were waiting for us at Claudio's La Villetta – where I like to celebrate – but I needed a trick to get in because there were so many people who knew my preference for that place. There were almost two hundred people outside waiting for me, an appetiser for what would happen in the months to come. We stayed at Claudio's to sing and dance until 3am, and of what happens afterwards I remember very little. I know that we ended up in a club near the Pantheon which I'd never been to before, and that in the end I was brought home at around 8am to lie down as the happiest and most relaxed person in the world. Finally.

When Juventus win the *scudetto*, which happens practically every year, the fans always taunt each other with the same argument: the contrast between the habit of success, which leads you to short celebrations, and the rarity of victory, which extends its celebration beyond all limits. And the great thing is that each of them, instead of worrying about themselves, questions the other's style of joy: Romanisti – and not just them – accuse Juventini of celebrating for just one day, and Juventini in return laugh at us for celebrating for an entire summer, and there are certain spots of colour that are still visible on the walls of houses that date back to those days. I'm not crazy enough to think that I did better than Buffon or Del Piero: I would have liked to have won more, at least a couple of league titles, and also the Champions League. But the intensity of that single *scudetto* is something I'd never experienced before and never would again, not even for the World Cup, and that's the highest goal any footballer can possibly achieve.

It's right to say that the celebrations lasted practically the entire summer. The truth is that they finished on 11 September, when the city was preparing for a great night in the Champions League against Real Madrid, but what happened in New York changed the world we live in forever (and of course, no, we shouldn't have played, but UEFA didn't know how to rule on it in time). Each of us players has his own memories of that summer, because its all-encompassing feelings of strength and love aren't repeatable or, above all, forgettable.

I have a funny story to tell: it happened a week after the *scudetto*, dinner with all the family. We booked in at Consolini under the Aventine, a nice restaurant with a large terrace. Once he'd understood who was arriving, the owner put up a sign saying 'Closed' in an attempt to limit access. In those days, word got around wherever I went, and soon the premises were under siege. There were 150 of us and I managed to enter without being spotted, and we had dinner in peace, all happy, until I did something foolish. I went over to the railing on the terrace and leant out to look down, towards Testaccio. The first cry was almost instantaneous: 'There's Totti!' The second and third followed soon after: 'Totti's at Consolini' and 'Call everyone'. At that point it was pointless to step back, even though Riccardo and Angelo almost grabbed hold of me to move me back from the most exposed position. I returned to the table, but within about twenty minutes, the buzz that rose up from the street was more and more noticeable, and somehow intimidating. Vito had turned on the radio, and all the private radio stations were broadcasting from the Aventine 'because Totti has been spotted in a restaurant in the area'. Spotted? What was I, a wanted man? The answer was yes. People start pushing on the restaurant's heavy wooden doors, which the owner had shut. Very cautiously, I leant out from another – more discreet – spot to get a glance at the situation, and despite my knowledge of Rome and her impulses, I was still stunned. There was a tremendous crowd of people, there must have been 5,000 down there, almost all of them in Roma shirts. Via Marmorata was completely blocked. I really didn't know how I would get out.

The restaurant owner saved us. He took me, Angelo, Vito and Riccardo to the back of the terrace, at the point furthest from the street. There was a very steep uphill embankment and, at the top of it, a two-metre-high wall with spikes.

'It's the only escape route,' he said. 'Beyond it is the Pontifical Athenaeum of Saint Anselm, no one will be in the garden at this time of night. You'll have to climb up the embankment, climb over there, and then cross to the other side of the property to get out: I'll give the address to the others now so that they can wait outside with the cars.'

A crazy idea, but certainly less crazy than going out onto the street and facing 5,000 fans. We rolled up our sleeves. There was something dramatic but also irresistibly comical about the situation. I climbed the embankment first, sliding a couple of times but without going all the way back to the bottom, and after a couple of minutes I was holding onto the wall, helping the others who were still climbing up. When we were all below the wall, Riccardo interlocked his fingers and gave me a boost up: for a long moment, at the top, I observed the new view. Even in the dark you could easily see the park's beauty. There were a couple of sharp iron spikes to avoid on the top of the wall, but fortunately no shards of glass. I pulled Riccardo up; Vito and Angelo were already in position.

'Ready?'

'Ready.'

'Shall we jump?'

'Let's jump. It's not like a priest is about to come out with a rifle...'

We landed on soft, freshly cut grass. No matter how hard we tried not to make a noise, muffled laughter was inevitable. We crossed the large garden under a full, bright moon, bent double like in the movies. As if we were less visible that way. We passed in front of the entrance to the building, which is old and magnificent. I was almost sorry to be leaving so soon, but Vito was already next to the front gates that overlooked the Piazza dei Cavalieri di Malta, where there's the famous keyhole through which you can see the dome of the Vatican.

'Who are you? What do you want?'

The tone was peremptory. I turned around. A friar had come out of a small door that opened out of the heavy front door. He was wearing a habit, and I wondered if he was a Capuchin monk. I instinctively raised my hands, although I quickly saw that, fortunately, he wasn't armed.

'We're not doing anything. We're just trying to get out, we were at Consolini's...'

I realised that no explanation would be believable. Unless...

'Hang on, you're Totti!'

'Yes, father, brother, I'm not sure what to call you. I'm Totti, and there are 5,000 fans outside Consolini's waiting to throw themselves on me. We escaped through your garden. I'm sorry, but we didn't know what else to do.'

The friar chuckled, coming over and looking at me in the face. As happy as a fan.

'Come, come, I'll open the gate for you.'

On the other side, my father was already in the car, waiting with the engine running.

'*Ciao*, Totti, *ciao.*' The friar hugged me, and I reciprocated affectionately.

Before getting into the car, I asked for a moment. I too wanted to see the Cupolone through the keyhole.

7.

Batman and Robin

ANTONIO CASSANO IS THE MOST TALENTED PLAYER I EVER played with. Between Roma and Italy, I went onto the pitch with many top players, but I have no doubts about the fact that the most sparkling talent was his.

Such a binding premise is necessary to explain our relationship, or rather the depth of a bond that has stood the test of time, beyond the vertiginous ups and downs that it's seen. Antonio means a lot to me, and I know he feels the same about me. He's the younger brother I never had, whose career I tried to 'save' unsuccessfully, or at least not as successfully as I'd have liked. Today, when we happen to meet each other again, he always ends up telling me that he should have stayed at Roma, and that together we would have won a lot more. I change the subject, because bitterness lies at the bottom of such debates. Better to think that what's done is done; it hurts less. But Antonio is right: if he had stayed with us we would have won a lot more. And he would have showed the world more than the thirty percent of his potential that he limited himself to showing us.

Cassano was bought by Roma in 2001, the icing on the cake of the *scudetto*. In two years at Bari, he had shown himself to be the most gifted young player in the country. Juventus had been following him for a long time, but in the end, Sensi won the race. It was a deal with a strong symbolic value and confirmed that we were now the strongest, and not just on the pitch. Antonio was the last expensive purchase in lire, as six months later the euro came into force: Roma paid 50 billion lire for him plus Gaetano D'Agostino, one of the most promising youngsters at Trigoria at the time. Newspapers spoke of an overall valuation of 60 billion lire, or €30 million, a considerable sum even today, seventeen years on.

In reality, the negotiations with Bari had been finalised since the spring, and in May everyone knew that Cassano would join Roma. Four games before the end of the season, though, we were due to travel to the San Nicola. Bari were already relegated. Our advantage was clear, but when it turned out that Cassano wasn't playing against us, controversy broke out. He had got injured in the previous game, and in fact he wouldn't take to the pitch again before the end of the season, yet many protested, proof that he was a highly regarded player.

That was the day I 'officially' got to know him. 20 May 2001. We'd already had a couple of photos together, in the middle of the pitch, before other games between Roma and Bari, but those are the sort that you forget about the second after they're taken. For him, though, it had been different. I understood this before the game, when Vito escorted him into the dressing room and he, candidly, asked me for my shirt at the end of the game.

'But next season you'll have as many as you want, we all know you're coming to Roma,' I told him light-heartedly.

Antonio replied very seriously: 'I want yours, because you've always been my idol.' There was a glint in his eye. I promised it to him, flattered by the firmness with which he expressed his esteem. He was not the loudmouth that I would have met in the seasons to come, he seemed rather overawed. At the end of the game, in addition to handing him my shirt, I introduced him to my father, who had come down from the stands. Antonio greeted him almost deferentially.

Less than two months later he was at Trigoria. But while he remained kind and respectful with me, he quickly became a thorn in the side of others because there's no filter between what he thinks and what he says: he's honest and frank beyond any sense of appropriateness. During training sessions he spoke his mind, tormenting his less technically gifted teammates with ferocious teasing. Tommasi and Delvecchio were his favourite victims, telling them 'you suck' every time they miscontrolled a ball, and if they didn't retaliate it was only thanks to their good nature.

He didn't just play the big man with those who didn't react. Not at all. He also got on the nerves of Batistuta, someone who would run after you when he lost his patience. Moreover, he did it in a difficult period for Gabriel, because after being decisive in the title-winning season, he began to pay for the pains in his ankles that would affect him so much even after his retirement. His strength had always been in his power, and if that declined then he became just a normal player. Cassano didn't fail to point that out to him without worrying about being tactless.

I've read that more than one star athlete – the late Kobe Bryant, for example – stimulates his teammates by treating them very badly and openly challenging them to prove that they're better than he thinks they are. That was never my style. On the contrary, I always tried to encourage the less able. But if Cassano was different, as we've seen, the reason wasn't malice. Antonio isn't spiteful. Quite the opposite: he's a golden boy, kind and generous with those who lead him in the right direction, and above all different from anyone else. It's easy to imagine that it was a difficult childhood that made him into who he is: a ticking time-bomb, ready to go off at any moment. I remember that he managed to adjust his attitude on his first day at Trigoria, and that was natural too: he found himself amongst the champions of Italy, listening to Fabio Capello, the most successful coach in Serie A. It was natural for him to be nervous. But from the second day, his nature took over.

When his adventure at Roma began, I was prepared for the fact that Antonio was crazy, but honestly I didn't think he was *that* crazy. On the other hand, I also knew that he was talented, but seriously, I didn't think he was *that* talented.

Cassano was a carbon copy of me. And not just that: I could push myself to call him my clone because he didn't just play like me. He thought like me, too. In every game there were situations in which it came naturally to me to look for an unpredictable solution. Because of my body's position, because of where the opposing players were, because of how difficult the pass was, no one expected me to put the ball there. No one except Antonio, who was invariably in the place where it went. They were link-ups that wouldn't have succeeded with others even if I were to explain to them where to position themselves with diagrams. Instead, between him and me, a glance was enough, and sometimes not even that. It was football telepathy, never tested to that level again.

Antonio observed my movements and automatically rebalanced the attack with his. In any case, he did what it took to win the game. He didn't play much in his first year, since Batistuta and Montella were still around, but at Trigoria, after certain link-ups, I heard Capello muttering, 'At this rate we won't need a centre forward,' and his tone was that of someone licking his lips. I developed an opportunity, Cassano not only understood it but refined it by transforming intuition into a masterpiece, then whoever was better placed scored the goal, no selfishness. We were basically Batman and Robin.

Antonio landed in Rome with his 'cousin' Nicola, and the quote marks are intended to make it clear that he isn't a relative, even if he was presented as such. Nicola is a friend who ran his errands and kept him company; such people are fairly widespread among footballers, especially among those who move cities and don't yet have a girlfriend.

The two went to live in a place in Casal Palocco, not far from my house, and the search for a villa to rent immediately encountered difficulties. My father also lent a hand to help them out, but all of the solutions proposed had some flaw. One was too small, another didn't get enough sun, a third didn't have a swimming pool, the fourth 'sucks'.

Cassano earned hundreds of thousands of euros a month, and thanks to that salary he went around as if he were in Beverly Hills. He felt like he was at the movies, so he wanted a villa from the movies too. Since he couldn't find one, and the rapport between us was excellent, at the end of the summer training camp it felt natural to me to suggest that he came to stay at our house. We have a nice guest room. Before I'd even finished the sentence, he threw his arms happily around my neck. We had a new tenant, and thankfully I'd mentioned it to my mother earlier. Seeing him suddenly come into the house, with his two suitcases, would have given her a stroke.

His 'cousin' remained at the residence, charged with continuing the search for his Hollywood villa. I was happy with myself, because Rome can be a very difficult place for a nineteen-year-old millionaire who isn't ready to withstand its impact, and the role of captain implies this sort of help too. I didn't do it out of duty, though. Antonio has something that can't help but touch you. In a world where many are very phoney, he's pure.

In the summer of 2001, my first serious love affair, with the actress Maria Mazza, had just ended. Ilary was yet to appear on the horizon – that would happen next spring. In other words, I was young, famous and single: I went out with Cassano almost every night. He joined my usual circle of friends and cousins – mine were real, though – and he hit it off with them immediately because he's a really funny guy. And incomprehensibly generous. Sometimes I'd go out for dinner with other people, perhaps on work-related business, in one of my favourite restaurants, like Claudio's; if Antonio happened to be there too, the first thing he did was come over to me to say hello, entirely naturally, giving a minute to my dining companions before heading over to his table. When, at the end of the evening, I'd get up to see Claudio to settle the bill, he would raise his hands: 'I don't want anything, Antonio's paid for you all.' The first time, I thanked him, and the second time as well, though that time telling him it was the last time, and after the third time I told him to leave it because there's no way he was paying for ten people every time, not to mention the fact he only knew one of them. But there was no choice, and I couldn't even assert myself with the host because Antonio, when he gets started, is much more exhausting than me.

When you're a young footballer, especially if you're a successful one, you don't waste time wondering about the behaviour of others, especially if they're kind to you. It all seems like you're owed it. It's only later, after getting to know people better, that you stop to think – perhaps on a night when you can't sleep – what's behind the habits, the choices, the oddities of those who are part of your life. I've already mentioned that Cassano came from a difficult childhood, with a father who vanished when he was very young and a mother who had to take on the burden of raising him in an environment as difficult as Bari Vecchia must have been. His football talent brought him out of there, but mentally he never completely got out of his childhood. An enlightening example: in the evenings, we often went out in groups on mopeds, because thanks to the helmet it was more difficult for people to recognise us. I can drive a moped, of course, or at least I thought I could, until Antonio bought one and joined us on our trips. The way in which he drove his was something else completely, and I'm not just talking about the speed, the angles he took the corners at, the acrobatics he entertained us with as if we were at the circus. Most of all, what's different is the way he sits. What I mean is that I look ahead of me, and if I need to say something to someone travelling alongside me, I turn my head around just for a moment. Antonio, on the other hand, sits directly facing the person he's talking to, as if he were in an armchair, and occasionally turns his gaze to the road, which he's obviously checking at all times with the corner of his eye, but without looking like he is. We poked a lot of fun at him for this posture, which none of us could copy without risking crashing; we told him that he must have learned it when he was mugging people in Bari, and he laughed loudly without revealing whether we'd guessed right or not.

A compulsive desire to pay for everyone is a sign of generosity – as I've already said, he's a noble soul – but also a way to be accepted. If one is accustomed from childhood to considering money as the key to inclusion, it's logical that once you've made a fortune, you'll use it. Antonio wanted to feel like a recognised and appreciated part of my life, because the impression I got was the same one expressed in the dressing room in Bari's stadium: I was his idol. There were times when such esteem was almost embarrassing. Around girls, for example. Some evenings we went out with two girls – as I've said, we were both single – and if I noticed that he liked the prettier one a lot, I didn't stand in his way. He quickly realised – you don't need to explain the same thing twice to him – and whispered in my ear: 'Look at how much she wants you, you can see it a mile off, why would she care about someone like me?' He didn't say it because he lacked self-esteem, quite the contrary. He said it because, having idolised me since childhood, he didn't believe it was possible to surpass me.

He must have told me a million times that he wanted to be my friend without the slightest ambition of being my successor, because in Rome, whatever happened, no one would ever be able to be like me. Is that a thought that flattered me? Yes, greatly, because with Cassano, I knew that he was being sincere. And then, when we happened to share a room for trips with the team – it was rare because I preferred to sleep alone, but in certain hotels that couldn't happen because there weren't enough rooms – a couple of times I woke up to see him watching me, and I remembered when I did the same thing while sleeping in the bed next to Giannini's. My own idol at the time.

Sharing the family home in Casal Palocco lasted a few months and it was a happy time, because while Dad had become fond of him ever since that afternoon in Bari, it didn't take long for Mum to start loving him as if she'd adopted him. He let this happen, though: he treated her as if she was a queen, showering her with attention and exorbitant gifts. He really was a model guest. So perfect that, when Mum read about one of his stunts, she asked me if it was true because she couldn't believe it. 'Anto', poor thing, did he really call the referee a cuckold?' Um, yes Mum, that was more or less it.

Often we ended up not going out and inviting friends and girlfriends to our place instead so my parents could sleep peacefully. Even if we partied until the small hours, there was no problem with getting home: we were already there. I guess that some, at this point, might think that our behaviour at that time wasn't very professional. I accept the objection, but let me respond: we're talking about the start of the week, we certainly weren't up late on Fridays or Saturdays. Furthermore, at that age, you can recover much more quickly; impeccable habits are needed to extend a career, but it's a need that increases once you're over 30. Finally, let me add that neither I nor Antonio drink alcohol and neither of us smokes, let alone does drugs. If ours are sins, I'd call them venial ones. By the morning, as we have breakfast together before rushing to Trigoria, we'd already forgotten them.

Cassano's first year coincided with the first of the *scudetti* that we could and should have won, but which instead vanished into second-place finishes. For Antonio, it was a high-quality apprenticeship season, because he was somewhat sidelined by the other forwards. But at the end, when the overall energy levels were declining and I missed a few games through injury, it was his freshness that kept us afloat. For example, in Venice, in a game that weighed heavily in the race for the title against a team that had already been relegated, we went 2-0 down without even understanding how. I had stayed at home for my recovery and watched the TV, amazed at a debacle that was only partially fixed in the last five minutes.

Pierluigi Collina gave us two penalties: they were both clear, but it took a referee with his personality to give two so close together. And it took someone with Antonio's character to set off on a mazy run with time already up, looking for an opportunity to shoot or, more shrewdly, the naivety of a defender. That Sunday – the fifth last game of the season – Inter, the leaders, lost at home to Atalanta, and if we'd won then we would have joined them. It was a championship that will go down in history for the way it finished on the final day, 5 May 2002, and for being overtaken by Juventus in extremis. As I see it, though, it's a title that we threw away ourselves. We were the strongest team, but we don't win it.

By the end of the season, Cassano had left the house, following the first crisis in our relationship. It was entirely his misunderstanding, and it concerned the monthly salary payment: big stuff, obviously, we were on around €300,000. One morning Antonio went to my mother and told her that his cheque had disappeared, he'd looked for it everywhere, and so his conclusion was that it had been stolen. According to him, it could only have been the maid. She had been working in our house for years, though, and in those years nothing had ever gone missing, not even a cent. First Mum and then I tried to reason with him: beyond the fact that we'd swear blind for her, did he think that a maid could steal such a large cheque? What would she do with it? What bank would cash it for her? These were entirely logical questions that Antonio didn't even listen to; he needed a scapegoat. He repeated that he'd looked everywhere and, since we wouldn't give him the satisfaction of blaming the maid, he left. He packed his suitcase in an atmosphere full of tension, called Nicola to come and get him, and left the house with a quick goodbye to Mum. And that was it, end of story.

We didn't speak to each other for a month. We still had an understanding on the pitch, and it was interesting to observe that our technical skills continued to speak to each other as if they had a life of their own. That was until Vito, who has always been an open channel of communication in difficult times – both with Cassano and others – told me one day that Antonio found his cheque in the car. It had ended up in a fold between the seats. We looked at each other like two adults struggling with a child: I was relieved by the innocent explanation, but now I was expecting an apology. And in fact the next day I was having coffee at the bar in Trigoria when suddenly I was hugged tightly from behind. It was Antonio. 'Sorry. Sorry. Sorry. I found it a few days ago, but I was too ashamed to come and tell you. I've been a child, tell your mum I'm sorry too, and the maid as well, of course.' There was no need for that, because no one had said anything to her.

Another time the iciness lasted a lot longer, and not even the peace was able to dispel all the shadows. I've been friends with the TV stars Maurizio Costanzo and Maria De Filippi for years. They're people who have always been close to me, and every season I give up an evening for *C'è Posta per Te*, Maria's show that brings together relatives, friends or acquaintances that for one reason or another have lost touch. Roberto, the head of production, once proposed that I organise a meeting between Cassano and his natural father: it was known that the relationship between the two of them was non-existent, because Antonio had understandably accused him of disappearing after he was born.

When a long interview came out with Cassano's father in the *Gazzetta*, in which he tried to patch things up, I realised from Antonio's furious reaction in the dressing room that it was really not something to press. Thus we arrived at a second proposal, a much lighter one: to bring Cassano to the studio and have him meet the traffic policeman from Bari Vecchia who, over his years of reckless fun, had sequestered his moped many times. A man with whom he had often argued, but who he loved deep down, as Antonio himself recognised.

C'è Posta per Te is a very successful show that pays very good fees. I don't know how much they gave to Cassano for that episode, it was his business and it didn't seem right to me to ask. The evening went smoothly, the 'reunion' was moving, Antonio was happy, and I thought nothing more of it.

After a couple of days, however, I noticed that he tended to steer clear of me when we passed each other in the corridors of Trigoria. What happened? Had I missed a pass to him on Sunday? I didn't think much of it: Antonio has these spells, you'd go crazy if you went after him every time. But when the period of frostiness extended to a week, and especially when it extended to Vito for the first time, I asked Montella – he and Emerson were closest to Antonio – if he knew anything. Vincenzo said: 'He's offended because he was told that you'd asked for a €15,000 commission for him to take part in De Filippi's show.' I was stunned. It was a massive lie, and I didn't understand who could have told him this rubbish. 'I asked him about it, because that story stinks to me too,' Montella continued. 'He didn't want to tell me. He only said that he found out in the dressing room.'

Was someone in the squad working against me? I was very doubtful, because it would have been the first time. Cassano's great flaw was in believing anything that anyone told him, but on such a delicate subject there must have been something in it. Otherwise he would at least have come up to me, nose-to-nose, to question me. I started looking into it and aimed to talk about it with Antonio at the same time. The tension had grown and we looked like a divorced couple on the pitch and Capello, who had noticed it, bombarded us with 'Pass it to him, what's wrong with you?' Once, during a training game, Antonio challenged me: 'Will you tell him or will I?'

At the end of the session I confronted him. I told him that he was a moron if he thought I could have stolen €15,000 from him. I earned a lot more than that for each of my appearances, so I really didn't need it. It was a braggart's reaction. I didn't like it and it didn't reflect who I am, and I immediately regretted it. But I was really angry, both with him and with the phantom talking about me behind my back. I never found out who it was.

The rift with Antonio lasted longer this time, a few months, and it was a period when Roma didn't play well either, I think partly because of us. He was very close to the group of Brazilians, especially Emerson and Lima, and in an environment that, for all its weaknesses, had always been united, the fracture was noticeable. After the business with his lost and found cheque, Antonio had returned home to hug my mum again, who was overwhelmed by her bouquets of a hundred roses every birthday, and their relationship was repaired in a second. Not this time. The iciness remained for a long time even with my family, and when something finally convinced him that he had believed some utter nonsense – and he came to apologise to me again – he made his peace. But it wasn't the same as in those early months. A few splinters remained.

In 2003/04, Capello's last season on the Roma bench, we finished second again. Milan won the *scudetto*: they were more consistent, while we paid the price for dropping off the pace in March.

It was a season in which Cassano showed his enormous talent with good regularity, and there were many Sundays when we celebrated together after both scoring. I remember Bologna, for instance: I made it 1-0 with a great left-footed volley, he set up Montella's second goal and scored the fourth after gliding past the defender. You can understand how special Antonio was by the fact that the more difficult the game was and the more competitive the opponent, the better he played. This is the surest sign of star quality that exists, because there are many Thursday training game stars in football, while those who can raise the level of their game to match that of their opponents are much rarer. They're called superstars, and it was a joy to partner Antonio when we were facing Milan, Juventus or Inter.

That year he scored against all three of the big clubs, even a brace in that famous 4-0 against Juve, when I gestured at Tudor, who hadn't been gentle in his treatment of me, by holding up four fingers. Antonio was devastating that evening, and the penalty he won for me to make it 2-0 was one of the many examples of two-player games that succeed because class communicates with class.

As always, though, you had to accept the complete package with him: heavenly goals and skills, but also the water he squirted over the goalkeeping coach Francesco Tancredi after my penalty or the nonsense of breaking the corner flag when he kicked it after the goal that made it 4-0. While we were celebrating, Collina arrived, furious, pointing to the shattered corner flag, and shouted at him, 'Why do you do these things?

Now I have to book you!' He seemed like a teacher who had to punish an impudent though not a bad child. Antonio accepted the card and hugged Collina.

I said before that our technical abilities somehow spoke to each other even during the times when there was frostiness between us, as if they had a life of their own. In fact, there's a better way to explain this rapport: sometimes, love stories lose the emotional power of the early days, but the couple stay together just the same because the sex is still great. Antonio and I sometimes fought and told each other where to go, but all it took was for a ball to come between us for the magic to come back and for the problems to be shelved again, at least for the duration of the game. Of course, our 'total' coexistence of the early months vanished in the spring of 2002. The reasons for this go beyond the fact that the incident with the cheque took him out of the house. I simply came to know Ilary, and so I started spending the time that I previously dedicated to my friends with her.

The situations related to Antonio continued to entertain me though. Like that time when we were lurking outside Consolini's with the usual group because we knew that he had invited the TV hostess Pamela Prati to dinner there. But the presence of a fake paparazzo hired by us set the evening alight: the actress was waiting for him on the steps, Antonio – who has a phobia of gossip papers – arrived but noticed the guy with the cameras and slipped away, though not before sending an insulting message to poor Pamela. He was convinced that it had been her who had called the paparazzo to get a bit of publicity.

If I'm telling you about a prank that was played on him, it's because we suffered from dozens of them from him. For Antonio, joking around is simply the meaning of life, the occupation to which he dedicates most of his time. Some people got annoyed, but most people in Trigoria tolerated him because after a successful prank, the roar of his laughter somehow reconciled you with the world.

Franco Sensi, for example, found him adorable and willingly let himself be made fun of. The president, who had had serious health problems, came to Trigoria every morning during his convalescence to do his exercises in the pool. At the end of training, before going for a shower,

Cassano passed by him and started jokingly insulting him: 'Old paralytic, where are you going?' You've no idea how much Sensi laughed, amused by the boy's impudence. The problem is that Antonio struggled to understand that confidence is a privilege not to be abused, and which in any case has its limits. So, after a couple of defeats because we have 'mediocre' players – I'm using his words – he got in the pool with wild eyes and started shouting: 'Ugly miser, spend your damn money and buy us some superstars.' That time Sensi wasn't amused at all, and Vito and I had to intervene to pin Cassano up against the wall and explain to him how to behave.

The 2004/05 season, the season of four coaches, was the most difficult of my career, and Antonio was its protagonist, first for ill and then for good. I say for ill because he was really unbearable with the coaches at that time. The year before, he'd already lost all his inhibitions with Capello, who he began to follow around the pitch during training sessions, taunting him about his limp – 'Ugly cripple, you only won a *scudetto* here because you had Totti and Batistuta' – and the situation exploded immediately with Cesare Prandelli. In Perugia, for a friendly at the end of August, a few days before the start of the season, the FA happened to make it known that Marcello Lippi, the new Italy coach, would be in the stands. Cassano, who was the only one to redeem himself at the European Championship, cares about the national team much more than his attitude might suggest. So, when Prandelli took him off at half time, he launched into a series of loud insults that left everyone shocked. The situation didn't degenerate because there were a lot of us there to intervene, but it was clear that a rupture had opened up in the dressing room that was at the heart of Prandelli's resignation a few days later. Of course, the coach also found himself facing a difficult personal situation with his seriously ill wife, but it was that furious argument with Antonio that pushed him towards resigning.

The problem was that that year, the carousel never stopped. Rudi Völler, a legend in Giallorossi history, was hurriedly appointed, but after four matches he too resigned in deference to his past. He couldn't control the team, and he didn't want to ruin the memory that people had of him. In the first game, against Fiorentina, Antonio got himself sent off for hitting Giorgio Chiellini. In the fourth, at Bologna, we went 3-0 down, but at the start of the second half, we found ourselves playing with 11 against 9 because two of our opponents were sent off for second yellow cards. But despite the two-man advantage, we only scored one goal – a shot from me from outside the box – and Völler realised that our heads weren't right. In training, Antonio said openly, as is his habit, that Rudi wasn't suited to being a coach, which didn't help to calm the atmosphere.

After the German came Luigi Delneri. The team initially struggled to recover, but we put a string of results together and climbed up to the European places. But it wasn't our season: a couple of bad defeats, in the derby and against Juve, and we fell back down the table again. The coach's way of speaking, very quickly, meant that sometimes he was a bit unclear, and Cassano was merciless: 'You can't understand shit,' he repeated several times, loudly and to his face. Someone laughed, and inevitably Delneri's grip on the dressing room weakened.

Of course, these stunts from Antonio were the subject of constant confrontations between me – the captain – and him. I intervened both in public and in private, but in reality the discussions were always very short because he agreed with me, admitting that his way of doing things made every coach's job harder. Yet the next day it was the same thing all over again. 'I can't help it,' he said, spreading his arms out, and I reiterate that this was true. It wasn't malice that drove him but an obviously irrepressible need to cause trouble.

The problem was that we risked going into freefall. Ten games from the end of the 2004/05 season, we lost badly at Cagliari, a 3-0 defeat inspired by Gianfranco Zola, still very talented at 39. In the dressing room, Delneri told Rosella Sensi that he'd had enough. He left. The scenario of having three coaches resign in a single year – Prandelli, Völler and Delneri – in a world where no one ever resigns perfectly illustrates how sensitive the situation was.

That afternoon, Rosella asked Cagliari's president Massimo Cellino, with whom she is friends, to use a private place for a brief discussion and to make a decision: other than the sporting director Daniele Pradè, she only summoned me and Montella. By now we were the wise old men of the dressing room. So wise that, when Cellino accompanied us to the stadium caretaker's house, we were distracted by the smell of the breaded escalopes of meat that his wife was preparing in the kitchen. Even Rosella, despite the drama of the moment, made the face of someone who would love to attack the pile of meat: the lady sensed the situation and kindly offered them to us. They were impossible to resist. It was a surreal atmosphere: an urgent summit between directors and senior players to decide the new coach took place while nibbling on (delicious) cutlets and looking for a paper towel to clean our greasy fingers. In any case, we all came to the same name, and since the man in question was outside the room chatting with his son, we left, though not before saying goodbye to the exquisite chef of the Sant'Elia.

As soon as he saw us and noticed that our eyes had focused on him, Bruno Conti raised his hands as if to protect himself, saying, 'No, no.' It's clear that if he'd wanted to become a coach in life, he would have made different choices a long time ago. He had been talking with his son Daniele, unaware of the meeting, and when he realised that we wanted him, he tried to avoid us. But he couldn't. Roma were empty, in the legs and in the head, for a final sprint in which safety from relegation wasn't yet certain. Hiring a fourth coach wouldn't make sense, there was no time to implement another tactical system: this was the moment for a Romanista – in this case, a Romanista legend – who knew how to bring together a worried dressing room and angry fans in his name. I don't remember if I was so clear at the time, or if I kept my most extreme fears to myself. But today I can say that Roma were in serious danger of relegation that year: with ten games to go, we still had a good cushion – 12 points above third bottom – but without even a litre of petrol in the tank. 'Don't put me in the middle of it,' was Bruno's final defence, which in the end he gave into, as the generous person he is.

I certainly didn't give him a hand. In the game we lost at home to Milan, I got myself sent off in the last minute for kicking out at Massimo Ambrosini. A one-match ban. Three games later, on matchday 32, we lost in absurd fashion again, at home to Siena, and when we were already a goal down, I lost my nerve and struck Francesco Colonnese with a punch.

We had actually once been friends when he played for Roma in Mazzone's day. We went to bars together, he sent me to his hairdresser, he was one of those I visited most often, and happily so. But then we kind of lost touch, he played for Napoli and Inter, and once he moved to Lazio there was a violent, spiteful derby. He was finishing his career at Siena, and it remains a mystery to me why he started insulting me from the first minute. What I mean is that provoking and kicking Totti in a Lazio shirt can guarantee you the applause of your fans, but doing it in a Siena shirt makes no sense, other than to make me lose my cool.

The judgement against me was merciless: a five-game ban. Essentially I was only able to play again on the final Sunday. Panic. The team was sliding further and further down the table, and I wouldn't be able to help them. Bruno, who had the courage to resist the temptation to resign, had to find another saviour.

Antonio. In the toughest weeks of our recent history, Antonio decided that it was time to make fewer jokes and more of a difference. Perhaps it was the memory of his relegation with Bari that troubled him, perhaps it was my sudden absence, but he certainly took on his responsibilities. Alongside him were Montella, Panucci, De Rossi; in short, the remaining leaders in the dressing room. We lost twice more but we manage to hold onto an important 0-0 in the derby. In the 37th game of the season, a wonderful right-footed shot from Cassano gave us a crucial 1-0 win at Atalanta and we secured safety, while they were relegated. It's like I've already told you: when the opponent is strong or when the moment is serious, Antonio raises his game. He did it the year before, too, for Italy at the European Championships, scoring the winning goal against Bulgaria which, without the *biscotto* between Sweden and Denmark, would have seen us progress in the tournament.

Unfortunately, though, it was the swansong for his journey at Roma. We came out of such an ill-fated season by changing everything and starting again from scratch, and Cassano had run out of patience. He wanted to win. Rosella Sensi appointed Luciano Spalletti, the man who took Udinese to the Champions League, as the new coach, and it was a decision I approved of.

Antonio, however, didn't really take to him. There's a well-known story from the first days of the pre-season training camp at Castelrotto, when we were working in the gym: Antonio put music on as usual and, after a while, Spalletti, without saying anything, went to turn the volume down. Then Antonio, likewise silent, went to turn it back up. In an atmosphere that was caught between amusement and tension, because everyone wanted to see who would win that tug of war, Spalletti turned it down for a second time, making it clear – as it should be – that the last word would always be his.

But Antonio exploded: 'Look, you're not at Udinese anymore where everyone's silent, this is my turf.' It was an outburst that didn't have any effect: the volume remained low, Cassano lost his status as vice-captain, and the squad realised that certain behaviour wouldn't be tolerated any longer. Antonio definitively decided that it was time to leave, which the supporters contributed to by whistling him at the first opportunity, immediately making it clear whose side they'd chosen.

Another cool period in our relationship followed, and he didn't ask me for advice about what to do, nor did I take the initiative to talk to him. Autumn 2005 was tormented by barbs and tensions, but in the meantime the squad was taking shape and it was clear to everyone that the path we had taken was finally the right one. Antonio remained on the sidelines until, in January, the recurring rumours about Real Madrid gathered pace, and one awful day we found him in the dressing room emptying his locker.

It was an awful day, yes. It was seen by many as a liberation, because an angry Cassano was also an enormous problem for the group's calmness, but it caused me profound regret. I felt the weight of failure on me. I know that most of the culpability wasn't mine, but it pained me anyway because for several years I'd had the teammate I'd always dreamed of by my side, and the pure appeal of my talent – which had led him to choose Roma from among many suitors – wasn't enough to keep hold of him. Technically Cassano was irreplaceable, nothing would ever be the same again, but from this perspective I trusted that Spalletti knew how to find a solution (and in fact he did). Personally, I reflected bitterly on the wasted capital of a relationship that even involved sharing a house together and, in some ways, two parents. At Franco Sensi's funeral in August 2008, Antonio would go up to my mother to embrace her and she – still offended by certain circumstances around our 'separation' – would push him away, and confided in me immediately afterwards that it hurt her deeply, not being able to hold him to her chest as she would have wished. Once the peace was restored, she would be a happy woman.

We all laughed at lot, at Trigoria, as we watched Antonio's presentation at Real Madrid live, because the unthinkable fur coat that he wore in the presence of the impeccably tailored suit of the vice-president, the great Emilio Butragueño, was emblematic of what Real, without knowing it, were signing themselves up for. Antonio was perfectly capable of playing alongside Ronaldo, Zidane, Raúl or Robinho on the pitch. It was his impact in the most traditional atmosphere in the world that left us slightly puzzled...

After a few months of silence, his first statements in the press room came out. Antonio is always very generous when he talks about me, just as I am when someone asks me for my opinion about him. Our professional esteem for each other is indelible for both of us, and as a result, the old friendship began to strengthen a little again. I followed Real Madrid's results for a year and a half with a certain interest, and when Antonio returned to Italy to Sampdoria, a club that has always been good to me, I was happy to see him happy. In reality, he continued to get us into trouble even from a distance: in the books that he wrote in those years with Pierluigi Pardo, there were stories of women brought into Trigoria at night that none of the rest of us ever saw. Equally, explaining that to our wives wasn't easy for anyone. Luckily, the right partner was about to arrive for him too: Carolina is an intelligent woman, and she's tough enough to make him think even when he doesn't want to. It's no coincidence that since they got married in 2010, the number of interviews in which Antonio expresses his regret over what he lost by leaving Roma has multiplied. Over what *we* lost, I should add.

We saw each other many times again on the field, but there's one that matters: the cursed game par excellence of my career, Roma 1-2 Samp on 25 April 2010. It was matchday 35, we had overtaken Inter two games previously at the top of the table, and our path seemed to be downhill all the way to the *scudetto*. The last obstacle with an element of difficulty was Samp at the Olimpico, and that week – as always happened on these occasions – the invitations and jokes of my teammates were wasted, 'Call

Cassano', 'Remind him of your old friendship', and so on. Obviously I kept well away from it, but that Sunday, while I was getting a massage before the match, Antonio was knocking on the door. He knew where to find me. It was just the two of us and the masseur. We both started laughing.

'Hey, don't bust my balls,' I told him, and they were generic words that could refer to anything, starting from his presence there just before the game was about to start.

'I can't, come on,' he replied with a cheerful grin. 'We're playing for the Champions League and we have to win.'

I replied that I was well aware of that, and that I'd be sorry to disappoint them. We parted by telling each other to go to hell with a big smile, and I thought about how nice that short interlude was in which we pledged our allegiances, as it should be, but with a deep and profound respect. Antonio felt obliged to come and tell me that he'd do everything to beat us: I didn't doubt that, but I interpreted his visit as paying homage to our history.

And he did, damn it. Actually, the real star of the game was Marco Storari, because his was one of the greatest performances from a goalkeeper I've ever seen. After, of course, my goal that gave us the lead in the first half; at the start of the second, Cassano produced a simply wonderful cross for Giampaolo Pazzini, who made no mistake with his head. It wasn't revenge, as many commented, it was only destiny that was being fulfilled: when facing a very strong side, Antonio raises his game as much as is necessary to overcome them. I was surprised and floored by Storari's saves, not Cassano's skill. If I didn't applaud him, it was only because the title was beginning to slip out of our hands – Pazzini completed the job in the final minutes – and the gnawing anger was now full-on. But he deserved it.

A quarter of an hour after the end of the match, while I was still lying on the bench in the locker room asking myself how it had been possible to throw away the title like that, Antonio appeared in front of me. He chuckled. 'I told you.' The others looked at him as if he were an alien, except for De Rossi and Perrotta, who shook their heads – they were all people who arrived after he left. Perhaps they were expecting that, faced with that inappropriate comment, I'd get my hands on him, and I admitted that for a long moment the temptation was there.

Then, slowly, it became clear to me that it was the same old Antonio in front of me, the one who I loved like a brother. A pure man, instinctive to the point of self-harm. Capable of coming to rejoice over a fine victory in a dressing room, funereal because of the decisive defeat, but without any malice or disrespect. He just didn't understand the situation. Since I didn't touch him, no one else dared to. '*Ciao* Antonio, see you.'

'*Ciao, ciao.*' He sounded almost surprised by the abruptness of my goodbye.

He'd dip his finger into my coffee to stir the sugar, which he found incredibly funny. But on the other hand, he'd get angry when someone's control ended up two metres away: 'You play in Serie A, you can't be that bad.' Every morning you had to make the sign of the cross, because he'd do something to upset the peace in training. He'd make the sign of the horns to referees, and it was rare that they took it well. Now he's retired too, and when we see each other at charity matches, Antonio tells me that he plays tennis in the mornings, and in the afternoons – when Carolina goes to water polo training – he spends his time playing with his children, where he's happy.

Soon, he'll tell them about the time we were Batman and Robin.

8.

6 unica

THE BALL MOVES QUICKLY DOWN THE LEFT SIDE OF THE PITCH, carried by Candela, and when it comes to Montella, we're midway inside Lazio's half. Vincenzo sees me out of the corner of his eye and uses me, then takes off towards the area, instructing me where to play the return pass. But he's already scored four goals. It's an evening he'll never forget, he can do without that last pass. It's mine.

It's 10 March 2002. There are 20 minutes left in the most one-sided derby in my career. We're winning 4-1, with four goals from the frenzied Montella, and once the victory is sealed, I have a personal mission to fulfil. I can afford it: the first goal came from a backheel that set Candela free to put in the crucial cross, the second from the keeper parrying away my shot, the third from a free kick that I put on Vincenzo's head. In short, I've earned the right to think about my own affairs for a moment. Affairs of the heart. I see that Angelo Peruzzi – my poor unfortunate friend – has moved a few metres off his line, and I decide in a flash to try a lob. If it has to be one of the most important goals of my life, let's try to make it a beautiful one. I dig under the ball with my right foot to get the maximum possible arc on the trajectory, and what comes out is a lob from twenty metres out that flies over Angelo without giving him a chance of getting to it before dropping down into the goal just below the crossbar.

Yes, I created a masterpiece. I needed one.

Now I have to 'find' her in the Monte Mario stand. I know more or less where she is, that's the direction in which I need to hold up the shirt.

And to think that Sunday had started really badly. Silvia, Ilary's older sister, had warned me that an invitation to the derby was most likely to fall on deaf ears. Ilary had remained in Milan with her boyfriend, so the personalised T-shirt I'd made with Angelo and Giancarlo wouldn't have come out of the drawer, and my mood was terrible because I didn't know how to behave. Should I send her a text? What if I got the wrong response? It was pointless. I had the feeling that whatever I did, it would be wrong. I'd have liked everyone who says 'Oh it's easy for footballers, women are falling at their feet' to have been there, just then, in front of me. *Go ahead, give me some advice, seeing as you think it's so simple.*

Of course, in certain circumstances, being the captain of Roma helped. But when I met that special girl, the one who made my legs shake just when talking to her, I was just like any other guy, anxiously in love. And when things don't go the way you were ready for, you consider yourself facing disaster. And so it was that day. It was the morning on the Sunday of a nighttime derby, and all I could think about is Ilary. What could I do?

Love at first sight. That's right, 'sight': in the sense that the first time I happened to see her she was on TV, on the gameshow *Passaparola*. I was speechless. '*Mamma mia*, how beautiful she is,' I told Angelo and Giancarlo, and they agreed without hesitation, telling me that she was called Ilary Blasi and that she's a Roman.

Falling for Ilary came some time after the end of the most significant relationship I'd previously had, with Maria. That was a fairly calm break-up, without much heartache on either side, but the fact that I'd put in some mediocre performances had contributed to an absurd argument, with some fans blaming Maria, and her potential new partners, for my loss of form.

At that time, a Roman actor, Massimo Giuliani, was doing an impression of me that didn't reflect well on me – I'd be a liar if I said I liked it – but which I certainly didn't lose any sleep over. Even he, though, ended up in the crosshairs of some fans who were a little too worried about my composure. And that's the most unpleasant aspect of popularity: the fact that someone you don't know can harass other people in your name without having exchanged a word with you. These two experiences got me thinking, and since then I've paid more attention to what I say, especially in controversial situations. Too much love can have dangerous consequences too.

When I saw Ilary on *Passaparola*, I was immediately besotted. Her situation was more complicated: she lived in Milan and had a boyfriend. She grew up in the Portuense district in a family of Laziale on her father's side and Romanisti on her mother's side, and at the age of 20 she decided to take the big leap into the world of commercial television. Unaware of everything, as soon as I saw her on the screen I said 'I want to marry her,' and I must have been very convincing as Angelo and Giancarlo started to work out how straight away.

Of course, Ilary was known among the Roman youth who gravitate around sport and entertainment. The connection I found was called Alessandro Neccetelli, who does PR for events and clubs, and when I asked him about Ilary, he immediately introduced me to Silvia. I owe her a lot, because I started tormenting her in order to get to know Ilary and she, instead of telling me where to go, indulged me. She told her sister that she'd met a famous footballer who was very taken with her and, faced with her indifference, insisted – 'At least let him introduce himself' – until she agreed. Ilary spent a weekend in Rome every fortnight, and a good opportunity came at the start of January, in a bar on the Nomentana where the band Ragazzi Italiani were playing.

I went there full of hope, but our first meeting was quite negative, as her group had just come from a party and she was furious because she had lost her phone. The volume of the music was very loud. Ilary borrowed her friends' mobiles to make calls here and there in search of hers, and when Silvia managed to isolate us for a moment, we just shook hands, and I realised that it wasn't the right evening for us to get to know each other a little better.

A couple of days later, Alessandro gave me Ilary's number, making it clear that she had authorised him to give it to me. This was the second bit of good news. The first was that she, completely indifferent to football, had a very vague idea of who I was and above all what I represented, and this was a relief because whatever direction our relationship took, I felt like she'd be sincere. I sent her a very relaxed text – 'Hi, it's Francesco', something like that – and she replied in a manner that was equally polite.

And detached. I didn't keep going. I didn't want to come across as pushy, but after a while I got back to her, asking if she'd be back in Rome the following weekend (which wasn't exactly when I was most free, but I'd explain that to her later). We agreed on the end of January, then for the end of February: on both occasions, we went out as a group, and at the end of the evening I took Ilary home with Silvia, who was partly my accomplice and partly her bodyguard.

Not that there was any need for that. If I was already shy, imagine what I was like around the girl I was falling in love with. Ilary was not only beautiful: she was intelligent, kind, very down-to-earth despite only being 20 years old, I'd even say serious. Different to everyone else. So different that it makes me remember my casual encounters with other women on nights out with deep embarrassment. Let's face it: often it's those who didn't see the person in me but the personality – captain of Roma, face all over the TV and the newspapers – who expressed their appreciation in a very explicit way. So when it happened in Ilary's presence, my first reaction was anger. 'Now she'll think that she'll always have to be on the lookout if we get engaged.' In fact, some time later, she confessed to me that this was her biggest doubt ('When I'm in Milan, is this what happens?').

Thus we arrive at 10 March. The feelings were good: I was getting to know Ilary better, and she too seemed happy when we spent time together. She never talked about her Milanese boyfriend, so I went out on a limb and, in midweek, asked her if he would allow me to invite her to the stadium to watch the derby. Obviously I'd prepare the entire trip for her; for those who have never been to the Olimpico, the first game can be an organisational shock – let alone if it's a derby. She said she was doubtful but didn't say no, and I interpreted that as a postponed yes. In short, a high school story with advances and retreats, hopes and cold showers, complicated plans and sharp braking. Or did you really think that love stories between footballers and showgirls are really as glossy as they appear on the pages of gossip magazines?

Angelo and Giancarlo arrived at the training retreat on Saturday, and together we made the T-shirts that I'd wear under my Giallorossi shirt during the game. We prepared two, one for the first half and one for the second. I had to send Ilary a clear message, and '6 unica' ('You're unique') seemed unequivocal to me. And to her. Since journalists, in the event that I managed to show it, would demand an explanation, I could always bring up Roma, the team or the fans. In short, I needed to camouflage it: we weren't even engaged and I had to be careful not to throw half the city on her.

Everything seemed to be going well until the first stop sign came, which was a message in which Ilary reiterated that most likely she wouldn't be able to come. By then it was Saturday evening and the message was repeated the next morning with a warning from Silvia. My spirits went through the floor.

We were resting in our rooms after eating. Trigoria was immersed in silence, but there was no chance of falling asleep. Lying on the bed, toying with my phone as if I needed to deceive myself too, eventually I couldn't hold out any longer and typed the most neutral message that came to mind.

'How are you?'

'Going to the station soon.' The reply was immediate, and for a moment I didn't make the connection. She was leaving?

'Where are you going?'

A short silence. I imagine the next message being delivered in an impatient tone.

'Where am I going? I'm coming to you in Rome, didn't you invite me to the stadium?'

How can I describe my state of mind at the news? Let's just say that I leapt up from the bed, almost hitting my head on the ceiling. *She's coming to Rome! Ilary's coming to Rome!*

'What time do you get into Termini?'

'At six.'

'I'll send my friend Massimo to collect you on his Vespa, if you need to go home he'll wait for you outside and then take you to the Olimpico. He knows where to pick up the tickets.'

The text exchange was interrupted. I called her because I wanted to hear her voice so badly. She was in a taxi heading to the central station in Milan. I'd have liked to have told her that I'd dedicate a nice goal to her, but I never make promises that I'm not sure I can keep. In reality, once I was reassured Ilary would be there, and after speaking with Massimo to organise the transport, I could finally concentrate on the game. We were 14 points ahead of Lazio in the table, but the derby is always the derby.

Well, not that evening.

As I ran towards the Monte Mario Stand in search of Ilary's face – Angelo and Giancarlo got up to make themselves seen, but honestly I couldn't see more than an indistinct group – I thought that the stars couldn't have aligned better: a wonderful goal in a historic victory, all on her first time in the stadium. The message '6 unica' obviously came into the spotlight after the game, and the journalists who had known me for longer must have guessed something was up because it was very clear I urgently wanted to leave. 'The Curva Sud is unique,' I said.

'But you were heading towards Monte Mario...'

See you later, until next time.

That night we all partied together, but before taking Ilary home, I made sure that the next evening it would just be the two of us, and she agreed. Classic plans: first to Cineland di Ostia to watch a truly terrible horror film, and I'm not joking (we both love the genre, but you just couldn't follow that one; in fact, I don't even remember its name), then luckily we raised the bar by going for dinner at Il Fungo, in EUR. It was the evening of our first kiss, 11 March 2002: Ilary told me that she'd been thinking about it for a while, and that the day before, deciding to come to Rome, she had practically dumped her boyfriend. I had wanted that since the day I saw her for the first time, on TV. We were both very happy, but the stereotype of the couple that we embodied seemed strange to her: 'Have you realised? We're the footballer and the showgirl, the most banal thing in Italy today.'

'So let's be the ones to make it special,' I said to convince her.

I didn't have to try too hard – she wanted to as well. We both saw the great love in each other's eyes, and it was a sensation that has been with us ever since. I was so happy that if someone had asked me where Roma were in the table I wouldn't have known what to answer, and I'd have continued to stare dreamily into Ilary's eyes. And yes, after the derby, we were back on top of the table...

The story is immediately overwhelming, which was inevitable because being my girlfriend in Rome isn't easy, and withstanding the impact takes great passion more than just simple feelings. At that time, I already lived in quite a withdrawn way, always going to the same select places, those where I was able to seclude myself without attracting too much attention. With Ilary, life 'reopened', partly because she was part of the entertainment world and therefore had her own circles in which to mingle. But if we ended up in places where we were unprotected, it became difficult: she was shocked, for example, by people who saw me and tried to touch my right foot as if it were a holy relic, who burst into floods of tears while I tried to cheer them up, who wanted to take a photo but it took all night because their hand was shaking, who threw themselves dead weight onto the bonnet of my car to greet me through the windscreen. All 'normal' situations for me, as I'd been dealing with them for years, but absurd for those around me. And it was precisely that.

Sometimes there were incidents caused by resentment, and these happened on more than one occasion. Once, Ilary and I were lying on the sofa, watching a film in the apartment I'd bought on Via Amsterdam, in Torrino, when her phone rang. It was one of her friends – or rather, an acquaintance, since there's certain crap that friends don't do.

'I have to tell you something unpleasant, but I can't keep quiet: I've just been told that ten minutes ago, Francesco was at the Gilda fooling around with a girl.'

Ilary was icy. 'You're mistaken: Francesco has been here at home with me for at least two hours,' and she put the phone down while the other person began to stammer excuses to regain some face. Yes, the envy that a couple like us can generate is frightening, even sad.

Our first trip away together was quite an important one: to Japan, for the 2002 World Cup. Not that she was bursting with desire to go. But when I told her that I couldn't stay away from her for more than a month, she agreed. The trip she was burdened with was hardly tough, given that the journey from Rome to Tokyo is broken up by a stopover in the Seychelles, where she was due for a photoshoot for suntan oil. That World Cup wasn't just a nightmare on the pitch but also logistically: apart from the leave we were given after games – though we certainly weren't in touristy places – we could only see each other for about 20 minutes a day in the hotel lobbies, and after a little while, Ilary told me that she'd had enough. She had nothing to do, apart from avoid journalists who want to extort who knows what scoop from her. She went back home after the national side, having finished the group games in Japan, moved to South Korea for what would be a very short time. A week later and we were together again, this time on holiday.

The perception that this relationship is very serious was immediate, and in fact we soon started talking about marriage. We initially thought of a date in 2004, but this is where the debate started because I'm an old-fashioned guy, and I added the fateful question to the prospect of marriage: when we're married, will you leave TV?

I admit I'm a bit ashamed of it now, because it's an outdated request and time has shown that Ilary, while working in a very tough and competitive sector, is raising three children in a masterful way. Among other things, she is much firmer and stricter than me, and by toying with her so much I sometimes seem like an older brother… However, when the old-fashioned guy argues with the modern girl, he always ends up coming second. Not by being worn down, but because, day by day, life teaches you how much the person matters regardless of their profession.

In this sense, the long journey that we undertook from Milan to Rome in a Smart car was symbolic, and at the same time precious. After two years away from home, Ilary had decided to return to Rome: for our future, and because she was sufficiently established to be able to decide on her own work. She sent the luggage for the move ahead, but there was no room on the train for the car that she bought to get around Milan.

'What's the problem? I'll drive,' I told her, and it was an endless, tender, romantic and fun journey, with people watching us in amazement – seeing a Smart on the motorway isn't common – and when they recognised us, they began hitting their horns wildly.

We decided we'd get married on 19 June 2005. The preparations began. We wanted to do something big that brought together the many friends that we had with the people who would definitely want to be there, whether out of affection or even simple curiosity. We both love the Basilica of Santa Maria in Aracoeli, so the choice of the church was easy. Sky proposed broadcasting the event live, and an agreement was soon found on the basis that our fee would be entirely donated to charity.

As the ceremony approached, we encountered only two problems. The first is a wonderful one: in March, Ilary discovered that she was pregnant, but in the midst of so much happiness, the unforeseen complication of having to redo the two dresses of that momentous day, one for the wedding and another for the party, needed to be sorted out. The tailors at Armani took care of it, and although Ilary had to get completely measured up again, we were as excited as two teenagers.

The idea of becoming a father was simply thrilling, as was the way I got the news. In March, we both had a couple of days off, and we decided to spend them in the mountains, in Roccaraso. Getting into the car, I saw that Ilary put a white packet with the logo of her pharmacy on the dashboard. I didn't say anything, as I wasn't suspicious, even though we'd said it would be nice to expand the family right away. We drove for a few kilometres, chatting about various things, then she asked me to stop at a service area because she needed to use the bathroom. I waited for her in the car. She took a few minutes, so to pass the time I picked up the packet from the pharmacy and opened it to see what it was.

A pregnancy test. Positive. Chills. I started trembling. Fireworks were going off inside my head. The most intense, searing hit of my life. I sat there for a while, dazed by an emotion that was rapidly turning into pure joy. I closed the packet and put it back on the dashboard, trying to remember the exact position. I didn't know what to say. Ilary returned, we set off again, and for a few kilometres neither of us opened our mouths but, out of the corner of our eyes, each of us could guess at the other's smile.

'What's in the packet?'

'See for yourself.'

'I'm driving. You tell me.'

'It's a surprise. You have to open it.'

I looked at her. She looked at me. We burst out laughing together, and we didn't stop. There were no words: only long, tender, sweet laughs. Then she leant over to give me a kiss, and I said, 'Easy, be careful, there are three of us in the car.' Unforgettable.

I mentioned two problems. Unlike the first, which was a dream, the second was a nightmare. It materialised in the famous interview with *Gente* in which the actress Flavia Vento claimed to have spent a night of passion with me at her house. It was all false, but as always happens in such situations, first a rumour went around that a spanner was about to be thrown in the works and then, once the news came out and been denied, the talk began that the story contained too many details to have been invented and had to be true. According to this argument, every novel, every film should be about something that really happened: in fiction, details abound...

The truth is that I got to know Miss Vento one evening when Ilary wasn't there, at an event on the Via Tuscolana: footballers and showgirls, the usual mix at Roman soirées, were invited to a party for the launch of a new model of air conditioners. She was introduced to me, she was a nice girl and we talked for a few minutes, and then, as happens in such situations that are full of people, we went our separate ways because both she and I had seen new people to greet, and we didn't see each other again that evening. The following week, I was with friends at Prado, a restaurant in Trastevere, when Giancarlo and Angelo told me that there was a girl at another table who was trying to attract my attention. It was Miss Vento. Greetings and smiles were sent from one side of the room to the other, by which I mean that no one got up to say hello, then each of us turned our attention back to our own tables. As we left, there was a series of goodbyes from afar, and that was it. I went home to bed. That's what happened that night.

The interview was very troubling for Ilary, which was only natural: she'd recently discovered that she was pregnant and there were only a few weeks until the wedding, so it wasn't a good moment to deal with the infidelities of her husband-to-be. Especially if they had existed. I, on the other hand, went back and forth over my two encounters with Miss Vento, which are the ones I've just described, and I implored her to believe me because it was my word against hers, and mine should be worth more to her.

Ilary believed me, and that would have been the end of it had the paparazzo Fabrizio Corona not called Vito a few days later to tell him that there was a second part to the interview, more detailed, together with some compromising photos. He was ready to sell them to the gossip magazine *Gente* for €50,000, but if we wanted to take everything off the market then he'd be happy to give them to us for the same amount. Vito got the call while he was at the Campidoglio, preparing the security plan for the wedding. He consulted with my brother Riccardo, because the two of them were managing the bank account opened just for the nuptials, and together they decided to pay it regardless of my lack of involvement in the story: they judged that, at that time, precedence must go to keeping Ilary calm, anything that could upset her must be got rid of. They also sought advice from Maurizio Costanzo, who knows everything about the world of media and had been close to me for years.

I was notified of the agreement only after the payment had been made, and I didn't like it at all because I'd got nothing to hide. Not surprisingly, when it came down to it, Corona gave Vito a typewritten document in Miss Vento's name in which there was very little that was new compared to the first part of the interview, and no photographs. It had all been a big bluff.

Two years later, my case was looked into as part of the 'Vallettopoli' investigation – a public probe into wiretapping by parts of the Italian media – but it was shelved because Corona hadn't made any threats, so it wasn't considered extortion. The difference to me is subtle, but what interests me is a particular check that was carried out by the police during their inquiries: that infamous, incriminating night, my phone was never triangulated to the specific area where Flavia Vento lived. I really hope that this previously unknown detail will remove any remaining doubts.

It was at this time that I dedicated a new celebration to Ilary, my thumb in my mouth, destined to become permanent. It was thought for a long time that it was a way to signal a child was on the way or, after their birth, the tenderness of their first steps. It wasn't that. When Ilary's concentrating, whether she's reading a programme schedule or studying the menu for my birthday party, she puts her thumb in her mouth just like when she was a child. She doesn't even notice it, it's the most 'her' gesture of all because it evidently comes unbidden. Copying it after every goal – my professionally important moments – was a tribute to the woman who changed my life.

It was a way to tell her that I continued to love her just as I did when I saw her on TV for the first time and was left speechless, or when I decided not to give the ball back to Montella because I had to build our future.

9.

No, gracias

ONE OF THE FINEST ROMA GAMES IN THESE 25 YEARS WAS THE Supercoppa of 19 August 2001. As the new Italian champions, it was the first time that we played with the *scudetto* on our chests. The detail matters because it worked like an injection of that enormous dose of passion produced (and consumed) in June.

What our detractors argued with needless sarcasm was quite true, the title was celebrated every day of that long, hot summer. But the first official outing with our champions shirts soon became the most highly anticipated event for a city that had not just learned to live with victory fever, but was thoroughly enjoying it. Our opponent was the one we'd been hoping for, Fiorentina (who we'd supported in the Coppa Italia final against Parma), because they were one of the sides that had beaten us in the league so we wanted to get our revenge. The Olimpico was as full as the day we won the title. I saw faces in the stands of those who would normally still have been on the beach, but who instead had all poured into the city, despite the heatwave, because missing a match involving that Roma side was simply unthinkable.

I had been training at Trigoria for days to make sure we lifted the trophy, which everyone told me would be tough. Pradè and Bruno acted like know-it-alls and recommended me a fitness supplement to help me out, which goes to show how cheerful the environment was. In fact, the game wasn't tough at all, in the sense that we were so good – we found each other with our eyes closed – that it was like playing cat and mouse with Fiorentina. The outstanding performance came from Candela, who made it 1-0 with a great right-footed shot from 25 metres and set me up to make it 3-0 with another strike from distance: Pino Taglialatela didn't hold onto it and I clipped the ball over his body as he was lying prone with a very deft touch. But the real refinement of a game that could have finished 6-1 was the goal that made it 2-0, a chipped pass that Montella, from the edge of the area, struck left-footed with supreme pureness. It was one of those goals that makes you say, 'This year, no one's got a chance.'

Too bad it didn't quite go like that. We started with two draws and a defeat – in Piacenza, for whom Di Francesco scored after just being sold to them – and immediately we were on the back foot. It was a stop-start campaign throughout, in the sense that we never found the continuity we had the previous season. It was such a strange championship that for a few Sundays it was led by Chievo, for whom Lupatelli had ended up playing in goal. It was us, just before Christmas, who ended their hopes of finishing at the top of the table with a 3-0 win at the Bentegodi. So we reached the top at the end of the first half of the season – we were winter champions again – and we held that position, alternating it with Inter, almost until the end, only to throw everything away when we played each other, but also and above all in that absurd draw at Venezia, the one where we had two penalties given to us. It was the first of two titles we missed out on in those years – on 5 May, Juve won it – despite probably being the best team.

The truth is that the energy of Batistuta, an extraordinary protagonist in the *scudetto* win but at the cost of untold suffering, was being consumed by his exertions. Gabriel made it through the first half of the season, but it was an ordeal for him: from Monday to Thursday he had injections on his knee, on Friday he did a couple of short runs, on Saturday he took part in the final training session, and on Sunday, when he felt he could, he went out onto the pitch. He was a fighter and a goalscoring animal, but an exhausted one: he scored his final goals in January, then that was it. From then on, Montella performed really well and Cassano improved, but we didn't find our old ferocity at key moments and we finished in second place.

For me personally, though, there was a novelty that year, or rather, the trailer for a film that would become a blockbuster a few years later.

But let's go chronologically, because the story began on a terrible day, 11 September 2001. While the hijacked planes were heading for the World Trade Center, the delegations of Roma and Real Madrid were at an official lunch at the Hotel Cicerone: it was the first Tuesday of the Champions League, and the draw immediately set us against the biggest team in the world in a group that also included Anderlecht and Lokomotiv Moscow.

According to what Rosella Sensi and Daniele Pradè told me, things went like this. The first to speak was Florentino Pérez, who turned to President Sensi: 'My dear Franco, you know that I'm trying to bring all the best players in the world to Real Madrid. So, I'd like your permission to ask Totti to join us next year.'

Sensi's reaction was a loud laugh that left Pérez speechless. 'What is this? A joke?'

The Spaniard got a little nervous then.

'No joke, no trick. Give me a price for Totti and I'll pay it.'

'We aren't even going to discuss it. Totti is like a son to me, I'll never get into a discussion that involves selling him. And, please, don't talk to me about this again.'

A chill fell over the fancy table, but a few minutes later, there was breaking news from New York, and inevitably no one was thinking about football anymore.

We were in a training retreat and followed the live coverage on TV, and after the towers collapsed, contact with UEFA became frenetic, but the decision that arrived was – absurdly – to play. Only games taking place the following day would be suspended. Forced to go out onto the pitch, we were like so many ghosts, both us and them. We lost, but no one's mind was on the game.

President Sensi's response to Florentino Pérez was very clear: not only did he say no, but he also asked him not to press the matter. Under the radar, though, Real Madrid didn't let it drop completely, partly because I got involved by scoring the opening goal in the return game: the usual combination of Candela cutting the ball back from the byline and me arriving in the right place to score left-footed (Figo scored a penalty to equalise near the end). It was ideal to further entice Florentino.

The job was entrusted to Ernesto Bronzetti, a famous agent who's very close to the Madrid club, who periodically asked Roma for information about players' availability. But Sensi was in his heyday: he had finally won the *scudetto*, he had signed one of the best youngsters in Europe in Cassano, and he could see an increasingly strong and competitive Roma side, including in the Champions League, on the horizon. So he not only refused to meet Pérez's emissary, he even refused to answer his phone calls.

The first part of the story (that could have been) between me and Real Madrid ends here, but this was only the prologue. Out of curiosity, I went to look back over the list of Galacticos signed by Pérez during his first spell at the Bernabéu: at the rate of one per season, he signed Figo in 2000, Zidane in 2001, and in 2002, the year in which I was to have gone, he eventually signed Ronaldo. Not a bad alternative. I found myself up against him at the start of the following season, when a draw that seemed to have been made on purpose put Roma and Real in the same group again (Ronie only played at the Bernabéu). They smacked us 3-0 at the Olimpico in the first game. Unfortunately, by this time, President Sensi had begun to understand that he had gone too far, taking more financial risks than he should have, and he slowed down. The effects on the squad were felt, because to remain at the highest level you have to invest something every transfer window. But there were no longer the funds to invest. In fact, that season, halfway through which came the farewell of a now burnt-out Batistuta, finished really badly: eighth place, 23 points behind Juve.

He was doing what he could in Serie A, but Capello continued to be a magician at the Bernabéu, a stadium that had already been his once before and which would welcome him back in the future. In the return game, we even managed to win there: it finished 1-0 with a goal from me in an amazing collective performance, with two miraculous saves from Antonioli to stop Ronaldo. In front of us, defeated, was a more than galactic Real side, given that, as well as Zidane, Ronaldo and Figo, their team contained Raúl, Hierro, Roberto Carlos, Makélélé, Cambiasso... It was one of the most priceless victories of my career, with its crowning moment of the spontaneous applause after the goal, a first-time right-footed shot into the corner, after Montella's shot had been blocked. It was enormously pleasing, and I imagine that someone in the VIP seats was updating their transfer plans...

The following year, the 2003/04 season, we were competitive again: the investment on Cassano was bearing fruit, Christian Panucci had become a leader, Cristian Chivu and the Brazilian Mancini were perfect additions, and a certain Daniele De Rossi was beginning to find his feet. And I, with 20 goals, in addition to my usual role as an attacking playmaker, didn't miss a thing in front of goal.

For the third time under Capello's management we were winter champions, albeit jointly with Milan, but immediately after the halfway point came the misstep – a draw at home to Udinese, who equalised in the 88th minute, and a subsequent defeat at Brescia – that cost us the *scudetto*. That's exactly how it went, because in those two games, Milan built up a points advantage that they never let slip. Then we recovered, beating Juve 4-0 in that famous game with the banter with Tudor, and we put together a good run ourselves. But Milan didn't let up and, three games from the end, in the clash at San Siro that could have brought us to within three points, Shevchenko scored after two minutes and ensured victory. It so happened that in the last three games, the ones where we should have sprinted to the finish line, we picked up just one point. We came second again. And Capello was furious.

Five years with the same coach is tough if you're competing for the title and if this coach is a specialist of Capello's calibre. He was a professional who not only demanded a lot, but he knew that once you'd won, you had to work even more to do it again, not less, as would be only natural. No one else had Capello's ability to assemble a squad and make it competitive. He was accused of being good at having the best players bought for him – and this was certainly a talent he possessed – but the way in which we came so close to the *scudetto* that last year, after a transfer campaign that certainly wasn't lavish, only increased his worth. To win, however, you have to be very demanding with your players, from the training sessions to their private lives. And on this subject, in that last period, there were moments of tension.

I had always helped him, faithful to that first conversation we had had when he arrived, the one in which he invested me with special responsibilities as captain. I helped and respected him even during quarrels, and there were some of those. Capello was touchy, you couldn't directly answer back to something he said, even if it seemed wrong to you; to try to assert your point of view you had to tread towards it lightly, otherwise it was pointless. Capello is an all-round expert, he knows a lot of things and is cultured and educated, but he has the flaw of always wanting to have the last word. Flying over Europe, he'll tell you that that's Vienna and there's Budapest in a tone that doesn't let you respond, and sometimes it happened that the stewardess – careful not to let him see – denied his assertion by shaking her finger. These are minor flaws of a very strong personality, nothing serious, and everyone has their own. However, football continuously throws delicate moments at you, during which my flaws and yours collide and temperatures rise, sometimes risking getting out of control.

After the bitter end to that season, as I said, Capello was furious. A couple of days later, at Trigoria, there was a big fight: on the one side, me, Samuel and Emerson (yes, Emerson, who always behaved as an example of a virtuous professional), on the other, the coach, who attributed our last three results to our training having been too inadequate. 'You were slacking,' he shouted, and it was an accusation I wanted to cast off because it wasn't true: we played badly – there was little to argue with there – but with the title at stake, our commitment was absolutely there. We were as broken as him, if not more, and it was because of this that our reaction was as harsh as his criticism. We were unpleasant, certainly. We told him he had a big mouth and that he was a fraud, we told him that he only sang *Grazie Roma* when he saw the TV cameras were on him. Assorted spitefulness which was the result of a season that ended badly, but nothing insurmountable or permanent. Nothing that couldn't be cleared up when the pre-season activity started.

The problem was that Capello left long before pre-season. On 27 May, ten days after the end of the season, Juventus announced they had hired him. It was sensational news: no one had been aware of the negotiations, which were probably finalised within a few days, if not hours. The coach with whom I'd quarrelled was a man tired of Roma, so I was less surprised than others. Unfortunately we couldn't talk about it at the time we said our goodbyes, because there were no goodbyes at all: on 27 May, those who passed through Trigoria found his locker empty. Capello was gone, and of my many coaches, he's the only one with whom there was no farewell.

Intense debates have arisen on the subject of his 'night-time escape'. He has always denied it, claiming to have collected his things in the morning because he was due to be presented in Turin in the late afternoon. Be that as it may, it's obvious that there was no great desire to say goodbye at that point, either on his part or on ours: yet another argument would have broken out. Mindful of that quarrel straight after the end of the season, though, I had worked out a series of things to tell him, or rather to clarify, and it weighed on me that I had to keep them to myself.

In the following twelve years, we never spoke again. There were times when we met each other on the pitch or at some event, but in both cases, it was possible to turn aside, because evidently the time wasn't ripe, the break-up had been too traumatic. We even taunted each other from a distance with peppery interviews, so to speak. It was certainly a road that needed a special occasion to find its end.

This was provided to us by Pope Francis, in October 2016, with the Match for Peace: Fabio Capello was coach of the team in which Maradona and I were playing. A handshake, a smile, and we simply started talking again as if we had said goodbye only yesterday, and certainly not with an argument. It was a thaw warmed up further not long afterwards with another meeting: in Dubai for an award, just before the New Year, me, him and Lippi, each with our respective wives, found ourselves at the same table. Two peaceful hours of football and laughter, two nice hours because they ended up rebuilding a relationship that couldn't not be strengthened. Capello and I had won a title in Rome together, a very rare feat that inevitably ties its protagonists together for life. Of course, there were also disagreements, differences, arguments, as I think are natural in any workplace. But the greatness of what we achieved, that must remain above all.

Let's rewind the tape now. We'd reached the abrupt separation from Capello that initiated the worst season of my career, 2004/05, the one with four coaches. By the time we went to Madrid at the end of September – the draw was getting a little tedious – Prandelli and Völler had already gone, and Ezio Sella was on the bench for that game while the club were negotiating with Delneri. In short, chaos.

In these ideal circumstances, I was told that Ernesto Bronzetti was in the hotel and wanted to meet me. Before I even had time to go downstairs, I was informed of quite an animated discussion at the hotel bar between Franco Baldini, who had stayed at Roma as sporting director after Capello's departure, and Bronzetti himself. Simply, his initiative of arriving at the hotel without anyone's knowledge had pissed Franco off.

I didn't meet Bronzetti or his assistant Giampiero Pocetta, but I learnt that, in the end, they spoke with someone from the club. Pérez wanted to return to the issue of my transfer to Madrid, partly because he hadn't won anything for two seasons, and the name that he had chosen to continue his collection of Galacticos – enriched in the meantime by David Beckham and Michael Owen – was mine once again. This time, however, he knew that Roma were no longer in their position of strength of 2001, and so he was motivated to act with added determination. That evening at the Bernabéu, we went 2-0 up with goals from De Rossi and Cassano, but Real were a storm that was impossible to escape when it started to rage: they came back to win 4-2 – I remember the splendid goal from Roberto Carlos to seal it – and at the end, their stars, from Beckham to Zidane, came to hug me, saying things that sounded more or less like 'We know we'll be teammates soon.' I had a very odd feeling. The best players in the world were ready to welcome me, and yet I knew nothing about it.

While the season went from bad to worse, and Bruno Conti was tasked with saving us after Delneri, Bronzetti periodically passed through Rome, announcing the arrival of an official offer the moment that the team pulled away from the relegation zone. A touch of class, very Madridista. At that point, even I was directly informed of what was about to happen, and the day after the victory over Atalanta that guaranteed our safety – on 22 May – the offer really arrived.

In 2005, I was yet to turn 29, and it was the period in my career in which Roma were paying me the most: €5.8 million a year and image rights that were entirely mine. It was thanks to the latter that, in certain moments of great difficulty for the club, I could allow myself to wait, inviting them to pay the other players first and, above all, the people who worked in the club on 'normal' salaries; all I needed was a commercial. A crucial detail: my contract had another year to run, until 2006, which meant that while Roma could ask Real for a fair amount for the transfer, as it should be, it would be hard for them to say that I wasn't for sale. In theory, they risked seeing me leave for nothing the following year. Rosella Sensi told everyone that she would never agree to sell me, and I believed her. Not only does she like me, she also knew that the city would revolt. But alongside her were directors, from Daniele Pradè to Bruno Conti (Baldini had since left), who could make her think about the risks of intransigence. In short, the weight of the decision was essentially on my shoulders.

Real Madrid offered me €12 million a year and hybrid management of image rights, both personal and the club's: in other words, I would have a percentage on 'my' items – personalised shirts, for example, or little figurines with my face on – and another, obviously less, on all Real-branded merchandising. The percentages dropped as the numbers rose, but a first estimate indicated possible earnings of €15 million, even more than my salary. Absolute madness. I'd definitely have become the highest-paid player in the world. The offer was accompanied by the €60 million initially offered to Roma for my transfer. Initially, I'm told, meant Real could have gone up to €70 million without a problem. If we'd been in a film – and if I wasn't teetotal – then this would have been the moment when I said, 'I need a strong drink.'

Ilary and I were preparing for our marriage at the time, and we'd already spoken about the subject of Madrid. She was free to put her television commitments on hold for a couple of years, and she commented that it would be an interesting experience, even if she was sceptical about my real desire to move. 'You're one of those Romans who are convinced that there's nothing to eat outside Rome,' she always says to me, and there's part of her that's right. But I'd thought all about Real's prestige, about the probability of winning the Champions League and the dream of the Balon d'Or, and I was willing to fast for those trophies... That was before the official offer arrived.

I wasn't comfortable at all. My head was spinning. I broached the subject with my family with great caution, especially with Dad and Riccardo. Dad's response was clear-cut: 'Where would you be going? When you're in such a good place here...' Riccardo was more detached: 'Think about it Checco, that's really a lot of money.' I also asked Pradè for advice, we went to eat at Scapicollo, and I realised that I'd put him in a difficult position. I couldn't ask him 'What would you do in my shoes?' because it was only from my perspective that the whole picture could be seen. And therefore, only I could decide.

What do you want to do with your life, Francesco? You've got the chance to become a 'normal' star player: a big transfer, victory after victory in a team of superstars, world fame and fabulous riches. Moreover, Real are also selling Figo, which will also free the number 10 shirt that Florentino Pérez has promised you. The child who played Ducks becomes the star of Real Madrid, their number 10, their projected captain. You never even dreamed of a career ending like this. Too big even to conceive.

But have you done enough to repay Rome before leaving it? Of course, you guided them to the *scudetto*, and that's a rare feat. But the river of love that you've been swimming in since the day of your debut, the affection with which it supports you and protects you, the faith that it has in you – not trust, faith! – can these know their end? The season that's just finished has been the most absurd of all, and there are no new projects on the horizon. Can you leave it with a light heart? What will you do on a Sunday evening, before taking to the pitch at the Bernabéu, when someone tells you Roma have lost the derby? Or that they've slipped into the bottom half of the table? You'll hit the locker, making a dent in it, you'll massage your sore fist, and you'll murmur something in your hesitant Spanish to your shocked teammates... You'll want to be 2,000 kilometres away from there to organise the Giallorossi's rescue. You'll want to, but you won't be able to.

I didn't talk to my mother about it. She knew, I knew that she knew, but the idea of telling her that I was going to Madrid was unbearable for me. I thought of when she accompanied me to my first training sessions, of the history lessons that she studied for me while waiting for me in the car, and which she'd then repeat on the journey back. I thought of the air vents in the Fiat 126 with which I dried my hair in winter. I thought of her face when I showed her the cheque for 218 million signed by Ciarrapico, of her fear that someone would steal it from us, of the rush to the bank to pay it in on the Monday morning. I thought, and I was moved.

And I decided.

I wouldn't go to Real Madrid, because it wasn't my story. My story was Rome, Roma, and a series of reference points that allowed me to express the best of me as a man and therefore as a footballer. Forever my family. Both the one that was being born, because Ilary was expecting Cristian, and the one at Trigoria, which wasn't an ordinary sports complex but an entity made up of individuals, of people who had loved me from day one, from before I became a champion. I'm talking about the masseurs, the kit men, about those who woke up early in the morning so that I could find towels folded neatly in front of my locker and the pitch in perfect condition for training. They did it because they receive a salary, of course. But believe me: they felt a particular pleasure in doing it for Totti. I could tell from the way they looked at me. I couldn't tell them that I was leaving, they'd feel like I'd betrayed them. I couldn't do that to them.

I wouldn't know how to tell the people either. A press conference? 'It was a life choice, I couldn't refuse Real!' Eh? I couldn't imagine myself saying that sort of shit. I'd have felt utter shame. The truth was that all the love that there had already been, and there had been a lot, was based on a tacit pact: the Roman and Romanista captain would never leave his club. The people were invested in me, and they'd used up those reserves of love that you generally keep aside for safety and don't touch, because in the event of disloyalty, you would lose absolutely everything. Seriously, I couldn't betray them.

And then there was my mother. I'd have had to tell her, 'Mum, we're going to Madrid – me, Ilary, your future grandson, and the others who will follow us. But don't worry, as soon as you want to see us, call me, and I'll send a private plane to Ciampino to bring you to us.' Could I say that to Fiorella Totti, who brought me up in Via Vetulonia, who got kicked in the shins by my brother Riccardo when he was afraid that she'd choose Lazio, who took me to Testaccio or Trastevere to my relatives every Sunday, who kept a gang of thirty kids at bay in the summer in Torvaianica?

A private plane? No, I couldn't do it.

It was the middle of May. I went to dinner with some childhood friends to breathe the air of the old Rome of when I was a young boy. Of my teammates, only Candela was there. My anguish was over, and after dessert, I picked up the phone and called Pradè: 'Daniele, we need to have a meeting to extend my contract. No Real, my place is here.'

I've never regretted it. In the long years of second places, scrolling through the Balon d'Or rankings and finding everything except my name, not for a moment did I think, 'If I'd said yes...' It's worth saying again: it wasn't my place, it wasn't my story. It was wonderful to go back to the Bernabéu in a Roma shirt and win there again, in 2008, amidst the rueful looks of their fans, or at least that's how I saw it. It was thrilling, truly thrilling, to go on with a quarter of an hour left on 8 March 2016, in what I knew would be my last time in that magnificent stadium, and receive a standing ovation. They all rose to their feet at the stadium announcer's voice and applauded me for a long time while, running towards midfield, I passed Marcelo, who gave me a high five and immediately afterwards joined in the applause. This is the most important and most noble legacy of the path I travelled, the thing that has truly stayed with me: respect. The testimony of having been part of a world of millions of people, of having been a reference point even as an opponent. In the case of Real Madrid, in particular, of being appreciated despite the rejection.

I brought thirty shirts with me for my goodbye at the Bernabéu. The first one was for Florentino Pérez, who embraced me and, while pointing at me to the directors around him, said, 'Look at him carefully, this is the only player who said no to me.' He even asked me for a dedication as a reminder. Then, with great pride, I handed over the others to the stars of that fantastic team: a pride multiplied by their joy in receiving them, from Ronaldo to Marcelo – who was so enthusiastic that he bowed to me – and from Modrić to Bale.

All players collect opponents' shirts: to know that the red and yellow 'Totti 10' shirt would have a special place in their galleries flattered me as much as the standing ovation. At the end of the game, I exchanged the one I'd worn with Sergio Ramos, the captain, someone who has won everything that there is to win, someone who scores decisive goals in injury time because the champion is always the last to surrender. Ramos had played at Real since 2005, the year I was about to move there. In some parallel universe, I must have been his captain.

10.

The Silver Spoon

IT'S AN APPROPRIATE MOMENT TO TAKE A BIG STEP BACK NOW, because the story of what happened to me in an Azzurri shirt – the only one other than the Giallorossi one I wore in the many years I played football – requires some dedicated space and time. It wouldn't make sense to dilute all the various experiences I had with Italy in the chronological narrative that I've kept to so far. That's reserved for Roma, the 'woman' in my life. I won't go so far as to say that the national team was a clandestine relationship, but objectively speaking there was something of a mistress about it: burning passion at particular moments, a long series of disappointments, finally released in an unforgettable night. Then, it was over. I didn't have the energy to manage two relationships any longer, and the question of which love took precedence never came up. But I still had a great story in the Italy shirt, from my first day at Coverciano – I was little more than a child – to the celebrations in the Circus Maximus when we were world champions. And it's for this reason that I prefer to tell it all in one go.

My first call-up came in 1991 for the Italy Under-15s for the Reggello tournament. The coach was Sergio Vatta, and we came together at Coverciano, the Italian FA's technical headquarters. We were all rookies. I went with Marco Caterini, my teammate at Roma, and we found ourselves in the midst of dozens of other kids who were bubbling with ambition. I remembered two in particular from that big group: a Tuscan goalkeeper named Buffon – yes, the early days of our friendship date back to that time

– and a midfielder from Cremona with excellent feet, Alessio Pirri. He deserved a different career.

I faced those first training sessions with a quiet but urgent curiosity. Despite the shyness that leads me to slip away from discussions about rankings, which are so frequent among my peers, by then I'd realised that I was the most gifted 14-year-old footballer in Rome. This, though, might not have meant much: if I discovered in Coverciano that there were many from the rest of Italy who were better, I'd have had to scale down my expectations. The Under-15 training camps also serve this purpose, for you to compete with others from the same age group who are following the same path in other regions of Italy: will the Milanese, Roman, Friulian or Sicilian be further ahead?

It was me who was furthest ahead. It took a couple of days before I really admitted it to myself, because I needed to get a good look at them all for the test to be reliable. But from the very first training games, from what I could do and from the way that others started looking at me, I realised I'd found my place. I wasn't just the best in Rome, I was probably the best 14-year-old in Italy, and what I felt was pure euphoria.

Two years later I was selected for the first big tournament of my life: the Under-17 World Cup in Japan. At the time, I didn't want to go: it was the middle of August in Torvaianica, I was on holiday with friends and cousins, and having already made my debut for Roma I was enjoying the advantages of my early popularity… Should I throw it all away in order to go to Japan? The answer was yes, but very reluctantly.

It was the first time I'd left Italy, and when I left, Mum burst into tears with emotion, or maybe it was the pain of seeing me sweating inside the team uniform, in a suit and tie, when an hour earlier I'd been in swimwear. I had a lump in my throat too, and I cried my eyes out on the way to Fiumicino. Thinking back about it now tugs at my heart. The tournament was a disaster. We finished bottom of the group with one point from three games. In the first game, the one we lost 2-1 to Mexico in Kobe, I scored the goal that temporarily brought us level, and it was a great goal: a right-footed shot from 25 metres that can still be seen today on YouTube with enraptured Spanish commentary – 'Golazo!' I guess it's Mexican television. (Fun detail: I celebrate by running towards the bench, where the coaches

Sergio Vatta and Giancarlo Corradini can be seen, but before I reach them I'm cut off by the embraces of my happy teammates, and standing out among the many blue shirts is the grey one of the big lad who's in goal for us, arriving in a whirlwind of joy. Guess who it is? Buffon, of course.)

Three years later, in 1996, the same story repeated itself. At the end of May, I was already enjoying my holidays – I spent some great evenings in Ostia with my Giallorossi teammate Massimiliano Cappioli, someone who has always known how to have fun – when the message calling me up for the Under-21 European Championship finally arrived, a four-team tournament in Barcelona. I pretended not to have seen it because I didn't want to go: regardless of the holidays, Cesare Maldini only selected me because Christian Vieri and Filippo Inzaghi got injured, and since I'd felt a bit of regret at missing out on a call-up, in my head I didn't want to give him the satisfaction. So I didn't even answer the calls of my parents, who were very worried that a refusal could result in me getting a ban. In order to convince me to go, my father literally had to come and pull me off the beach by the ear, and thank God he did: even though I hadn't trained for about ten days I was flying, so much so that Maldini, at half time in the semi-final, sent me onto the pitch in place of Marco Delvecchio.

It was a difficult game because we were facing France. I didn't know it yet, but they would be my eternal rivals, and some of the guys on the pitch at Montjuïc that day will return later on in the story: Patrick Vieira, Sylvain Wiltord, my future friend Candela, that damned Claude Makélélé (you'll understand why later)...

I soon scored the decisive goal, a determined strike through a crowded penalty area, wiping the smile from the face of their peevish coach, a certain Raymond Domenech, in doing so. It was only the beginning of the story with him too.

It ended 1-0, enthusiasm was high, and awaiting us in three days' time was the final against a Spain side with highly talked about youngsters of their own: Raúl, Ivan de la Peña, Gaizka Mendieta. We drew 1-1, I went off near the end – at that point I was feeling my lack of preparation – with another sparkling talent coming on to take my place, Domenico Morfeo of Atalanta, and it was he who converted the penalty that gave us the title in the shoot-out. It was my first victory in blue: I was a European Under-21 champion, and I hadn't even wanted to come. Back in Ostia, seeing the people who had witnessed my attempts to escape it, I felt a touch of shame.

A few months earlier, in February, Arrigo Sacchi had called me up for a try-out with the senior national side. The message arrived on a Sunday evening, after a derby lost amidst a thousand controversies, and at first I didn't enjoy it, thinking I was being taken for a ride. Then, having established it was true, I was shocked because I wasn't yet 20 years old, and yet... The national side was a big deal. Sacchi immediately clarified that it was merely about making first contact, Morfeo and Enrico Chiesa were there as well as me, and the experimental aim was also evident because there weren't any games to prepare for: Monday and Tuesday at La Borghesiana, firstly, to learn the – rather serious – code of conduct required by the coach, and secondly, to get more at ease around star players. It was the first time that I happened to play with Paolo Maldini, with Antonio Conte, with Pierluigi Casiraghi... Actually, I established a really good rapport with Casiraghi, so much so that in the practice match at the end of the training camp, when we scored about ten goals against Lodigiani's Juniores, I scored twice, with two pretty good lobs. Sacchi was very generous in his comments, he said that he liked me and that I would definitely have a future with the Azzurri. That was exciting – he was and is a legend. However, he took Chiesa to the European Championships that June, while I was left out. It was better that way, otherwise I wouldn't have won the title with the Under-21s.

In reality, my debut with the senior Italy team came a long time later, because the terrible season under Carlos Bianchi meant I dropped off the radar of Cesare Maldini – who took over from Sacchi in the autumn of '96 – and the first season under Zeman wasn't enough for me to get a late call-up to World Cup '98. I confess I was a little upset, to begin with. It should have been Del Piero's tournament, and in fact he took the number 10 shirt, but a thigh strain in the Champions League final cost him his place in the starting line-up; Roberto Baggio, who was still very strong and is still the Italian player most loved by journalists, took his place. In that situation, better not to be there. The World Cup went as it went – Italy went out in the quarter-finals, on penalties as usual, against France – and Dino Zoff was appointed as the new national team coach. Despite having only recently left the role of Lazio president-coach (he had replaced 'my' Zeman, what are the chances?), he immediately showed his full confidence in me. I got my senior international debut in his second game, 10 October 1998, in the last twenty minutes against Switzerland in Udine, replacing Del Piero, who scored the two penalties that won us the game, and the next month, in a friendly in Salerno against Spain, I was starting.

Describing the first match that you play for the national team isn't easy, because it's one of those events that you hear about many times – every year someone else makes their debut – and the emotions it arouses are more or less the same for everyone. If you fear banality, as I often do, it's a subject to steer clear of. The senior national side – the youth sides are another thing, certainly important but not comparable – is a dream you cultivate from childhood. I was born with the desire to play for Roma, all my childhood fantasies took place in red and yellow. But in the summers of World Cups or European Championships, when Dad sliced up enormous watermelons for us kids waiting for the games in Torvaianica, I realised that there was a different form of excitement in the air, one which involved absolutely everyone, even the fruiterer's wife who really didn't like listening to talk about football. When her husband dawdled to talk about Roma's transfer dealings, she scolded him harshly, making it clear who was in charge. Here, though, on matchdays, she was more indulgent, if not somewhat interested. And I remember that this detail, more than a thousand words, made me realise the importance of playing for Italy. So, in Udine, when Zoff called me back from my warm-up because the time had come to go on, I considered that debut as a kind of graduation. I wouldn't just be a good player, able to play in Serie A for his city's team; if, while wearing the Azzurri shirt, I was able to win over fans of other clubs, those who didn't share my faith and so didn't love me no matter what, then I would become a true champion.

When Zoff put me on for Del Piero in that first match, as Ale – with whom there was a budding harmony – came off, he winked at me. He had scored twice, so he could certainly rest easy with me replacing him, but I also read it as an OK for me to make the final step to the top. I'd just turned 22 years old. In Rome, I was already Francesco Totti, and though I didn't

At the age of 6, in my mother's arms, I receive a caress from Pope John Paul II in the Sala Nervi.

On the snow at Roccaraso as a kid and cycling down Via Vetulonia, not far from my front door.

On holiday with my parents and my brother Riccardo in Porto Santo Stefano.

Starting out in football. From the top: wearing the number 4 shirt in a summer tournament in Torvaianica; posing with my SMIT team-mates in Testaccio; launching the ball with my right foot during my Lodigiani days.

From the top: one of my first individual trophies, best player at the Cetorelli tournament in Fiumicino.

1989. My first derby on the Campo Ruggeri in Montesacro. Behind me is Lazio's captain: Alessandro Nesta. Friends and rivals from the very start.

In a secondary school class (with my jacket on because the radiators were broken); and as a cadet at Cecchignola during my military service in June 1998.

Christmas 1990. 'Francesco… Totti, right? Good, good. Roma will need you.'
Dino Viola, my first president.

Cards have always been a passion of mine: here I am with Francesco Moriero
in Lavarone on the first summer training retreat of my career in 1994.

My two mentors: Carlo Mazzone and Zdeněk Zeman, under whom I became the captain and star (his nickname for me was Stella) of Roma.

The scudetto celebrations: in the dressing room after Roma-Parma, with my team-mates and Fabio Capello; and at the Circus Maximus with President Franco Sensi and Vincenzo Montella, in front of a million people.

Four of a kind: the 2001 Supercoppa, celebrated with Zebina, Bati and Assunção, and the Coppa Italia, won in San Siro against Inter in May 2007.

A few months later, we returned to San Siro to claim the Supercoppa there too, and in 2008 we won our second consecutive Coppa Italia, which I lifted together with Rosella Sensi.

The road to the World Cup: the injury in Roma-Empoli that nearly forced me to stay at home, a discussion with the national team coach Marcello Lippi, the penalty against Australia, that night in Berlin.

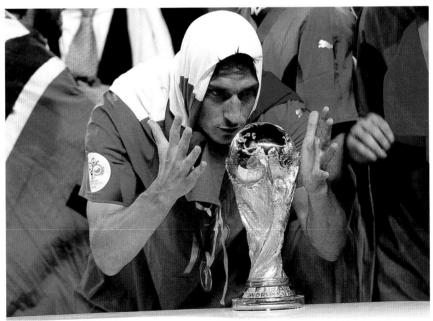

10 March 2002. I've just scored the goal that made it 5-1 against Lazio and am running towards the Monte Mario stand, revealing the celebratory t-shirt dedicated to Ilary, who was watching her first derby in that stand. It was the start of a story that changed my life forever.

Scenes from a wedding: on the Aracoeli staircase, on the Campidoglio, and at the reception with Angelo and Giancarlo, lifelong friends.

Vito Scala, my irreplaceable squire from the very beginning. Here, he's looking after my muscles during a pause in our strength and conditioning training.

Daniele. The brother to whom I left the captain's armband.

In the middle of the pitch alongside Gigi. Eternal rivals in the league, team-mates for Italy from the Under-17s to Berlin in 2006.

Antonio Cassano, the most talented player I ever played with.

We all loved each other so much. With Luciano Spalletti in the days of his first spell at Roma and several years later during my final season.

On the previous page: with Claudio Ranieri, Luis Enrique, Rudi Garcia.

The goal against Manchester City with which I became the oldest goalscorer in the history of the Champions League. A few weeks later, against CSKA Moscow, I extended the record to 38 years and 59 days.

June 2007. With my son Cristian and President Sensi at the ceremony for the award of the Golden Boot for the best goalscorer of the European season.

Derby emotions: my last goal, which set the record for the most league goals in the stracittadina at 11, and the selfie that capped off my celebration under the Curva Sud.

28 May 2017, my last Sunday as a footballer. In the morning, Ilary and I review the farewell letter that I'd read in the Olimpico a few hours later, and Isabel brings me my boots before I leave home and join the squad at Trigoria. The Curva Sud's farewell. Vito, in the dressing room, hands me my final Giallorossi shirt.

My stadium, the embrace with my wife and my children, my fans, saying goodbye to football.

My first appearance in the Olimpico as a director. I even wore a tie for the occasion, and I got to my feet to acknowledge the fans who had applauded me after seeing me on the big screen.

What does it mean to be a captain? It's about shouldering your responsibilities, being at the centre of the group, helping your team-mates, giving everything for your shirt and your people, rejoicing in victory and accepting defeat. But it's also about finding time for a joke with the youngsters during a training session, about leaving them a legacy. That's how it should work in football. That's how it works at Roma.

know it yet, exactly one week later I'd wear the captain's armband for the first time. Outside of that connection, though, I was someone who had only won an Under-21 European Championship and a *scudetto* with the youth team, while Del Piero already had three 'real' *scudetti* in his trophy cabinet, as well as a Champions League and an Intercontinental Cup, and had taken part at a World Cup and a European Championship. In short, he had all the silverware to decide if I was part of his own circle, and that wink signalled his yes. I've gone back to look back over the team that evening, and aside from Ale and me, there was Buffon, Cannavaro and Inzaghi: not bad, a core of future world champions. Furthermore, on the left side of midfield, was a name that would cross the path of my Romanista story many times: Eusebio Di Francesco.

The first goal for the national team took a while to arrive. It happened in April 2000 in Reggio Calabria, in the final minutes of a friendly before the European Championships against Portugal. A worthy opponent – featuring Figo, Rui Costa, Paulo Sousa, Flavio Conceição and Fernando Couto, to name the most famous ones – who we beat 2-0. After Mark Iuliano's opener, I took advantage of Quim, their goalkeeper, senselessly coming out of his goal to score from Stefano Fiore's precise assist. I celebrated a lot despite the fact that the goal was clearly unimportant, because I've always loved doing things for the first time, and this one was certainly worth framing. We left for the Euros determined to demonstrate our young potential, even if the absence of Buffon, who got injured in Norway in the final warm-up, put us in a bad mood. Francesco Toldo became the starting goalkeeper, and his would definitely not be a story like many others.

We had a great tournament. The team had the courage and desire to impose itself, the after-effects of the league season – Juve let themselves be overtaken by Lazio on the final day, it's the year of the perfect storm in Perugia – had disappeared in a few days of training. Zoff clearly set his sights on me, lining me up alongside Inzaghi in a two-man front line, with Del Piero ready to come off the bench.

The Euros are a quicker and more merciless tournament than the World Cup. There's no time to wait for a player who is slow to find his form. I was in excellent form and, after a good opening game against

Turkey, I scored the first goal in two splendid 2-0 wins, against co-hosts Belgium and against Romania in the quarter-finals. I felt fantastic, and in the four matches that separated us from the semi-final against the other co-hosts, the favourites Holland, I regularly trained with the starters. Without even thinking about the distant fact that I'd have to sit on the bench at the Amsterdam ArenA.

I didn't read the newspapers at that time, so I missed the scoop of *La Gazzetta*, which on the morning of the semi-final put Del Piero in the team in my place. I sensed something strange in the air at lunchtime. Someone told me, but I couldn't believe it; then, when Zoff gathered us after coffee to tell us the starting eleven, the confirmation floored me, as if I'd been hit in the head by a flowerpot while walking down the street. Alessandro would start, I was on the bench. I let my mobile, which was in my hand, slip into my fingers, and I wrote a couple of texts to my closest friends in which I insulted the coach. My teammates didn't know where to look out of embarrassment, they were amazed by the incomprehensible choice, and if it were not Del Piero – a champion who we all respected regardless of the somewhat troubled period he was going through – who replaced me, it was likely someone wouldn't have managed to keep quiet. The session finished. I was numb with anger and Zoff – I don't know if it's because he'd seen I'd changed or maybe he had already decided to before – ordered me to stay behind for a moment, alone with him.

'I imagine that you're upset, Francesco. I've put you on the bench because I've seen you've been tired in the last ten days, the game could be a long one and I want you to be sharp at the end. So take this positively.'

I have a hard time swallowing this without responding badly. Me, tired in the previous ten days? Rubbish. Five days before I'd been the best against Romania, and going back another five I'd been rested, given that in the third group game, a dead rubber, Del Piero was rightly given playing time to get some minutes into his legs. But I kept quiet. I didn't let it go because I didn't say 'OK, I understand,' but nor did I express what I suspected, namely that some sponsors had put pressure on the federation and the coach to impose their poster boy on them. Let me be clear: completely without Ale's knowledge, who exactly like me would disgustedly refuse certain sources of help. I've never liked thinking the worst, but at that moment I couldn't think of any other explanation.

At the stadium, I hadn't yet dispelled the anger about what appeared to me to be anything but a logical choice. We were playing at the home of the favourites, and you leave out the man in the best form? I have to admit that I behaved like a prick in the pre-game, because when I saw the TV cameras at the exit of the tunnel from the dressing rooms, I slowed my step until I stopped, adjusted my headband with ostentatious calm, and in short 'communicated' to everyone that I wouldn't be starting, because otherwise I'd have been running out onto the pitch to warm up like the others. Of course, the rumour was already going around, and the fans who saw the scene on the stadium's big screen started railing against Zoff for a choice that evidently seemed absurd to them as well. Thinking about it in retrospect, the scene I put on to annoy the coach was challenging for Del Piero, who instead deserved the most united support. For that, I regret it.

Holland-Italy was less a football match than a treatise on human endurance that we followed with resignation from the bench, in the sense that games like this, attackers versus defenders without ever changing roles, always end in the same way – in the end the goal comes, and all your suffering is in vain. On that day, however, something happened that until then I'd never seen before and that I'd never see again: the goal didn't come. Bergkamp hit the post, Zambrotta was sent off, and after half an hour we found ourselves down to ten. Toldo saved a penalty from De Boer and Kluivert, later in the game, hit the post with a second. Everything happened, yet we managed to survive. Even with ten men, even with two penalties given against us.

In the last part of that afternoon on the bench, in the minutes preceding the moment when Zoff finally sent me on, I thought many times about what is said about us Italians and about the incredible mental strength that we know how to bring out in certain situations. Football is made up of clichés, and I'd always considered this one an exaggeration, if not nonsense. Instead I, and particularly the Dutch, discovered that it was true, and the Dutch gradually got more and more desperate despite their evident, enormous, overflowing superiority. Running alongside them, you could distinctly feel their growing dejection, because they knew that if they couldn't score a goal in those circumstances, it meant that the game was predestined.

I have to say that Del Piero's performance was excellent, because after Zambrotta's sending off, Zoff didn't use up a substitution but simply asked Ale to cover two roles: 4-4-1 with him dropping back onto the wing. Had it been me, given I didn't run as much as him, I would probably have come off after a while. Instead, Zoff first used Inzaghi up completely, replacing him halfway through the second half with a tireless runner in Marco Delvecchio, then he put Pessotto on for Albertini to strengthen the defence and finally, after 83 minutes, sent me onto the pitch, looking to make a decisive impact. It was a tactic that was so close to succeeding: I picked up the ball on the edge of our own area and, with an immediate, very long pass, I set Marco through against the goalkeeper, one-on-one. If he'd scored, it would have been the robbery of the century: instead, he was forced wide and it was easy for Van der Sar.

It went to extra time, but the atmosphere had lightened. The Dutch energy reserves were now in the red, and we felt as if we were impassable, like the three hundred at Thermopylae. (It's an example I love because a few years later I went to see *300*, and once I understood the differences in the forces on the field, I commented, 'It seems like Holland-Italy from 2000,' causing loud laughter in the cinema. As well as the usual autograph hunt in the middle of the film, but that's another story.)

Penalties. The first thought was positive: there were some good penalty takers among us, our practice in training proved it. The second was much less so: in the previous three World Cups, we'd always gone out on penalties, so a certain complex existed. Zoff gathered us briefly in front of the bench to agree on the first five penalty takers and the order in which we would go up to the spot.

I looked at my friend Luigi Di Biagio, visibly agitated by the memory of the decisive mistake he made two years before in Paris. Zoff called on him, he nodded sombrely, then interrupted the coach, who was about to tell him when he'd take it: 'Coach, I'll take it but let me take the first one, let me get it over with.' When he walked towards what must have seemed to him to be the executioner's platform – he had a haunted expression on his face – I cheered him up with a killer quip: 'Man, how big is Van der Sar, he looks like an octopus.' He looked around, told me where to go, but made a grimace that could have been a half-smile. And in fact, he scored. Thanks to me! (Come on, at least a little!)

It was Toldo's day, by then everyone had realised that. He saved another penalty from Frank De Boer as if it were the most natural thing in the world, and it was clear now that the Dutch, going up to the penalty spot, were in total panic. Pessotto sent his perfectly into the corner. Jaap Stam was choking on the absolute necessity of scoring, and since you always end up missing whenever you don't know where to aim your penalty, his went high into the stands. We were 2-0 ahead, and it was my turn next.

For several days now, we'd been finishing our training sessions by practising from the spot. As long as Zoff and Francesco Rocca, his assistant, were watching, I took my classic penalties, hard and angled. But when they left, after telling us to keep going for another five minutes, I liked trying a few in the Panenka style, where the ball goes down the middle and taunts the keeper, who has already dived to one side. In short, a chip shot. As far as I know, it was done for the first time by Antonín Panenka, a Czechoslovakian player, in the final of Euro 1976, the year I was born. It's a risky move, because any keeper who doesn't move only has to catch the 'pass' from the penalty taker, but if you're good enough to hide your intentions until the last moment, you're almost certain to score, because ninety percent of goalkeepers will pick a corner sooner or later and dive towards it. In those days, I tried it in training against Toldo and especially against Abbiati. And every time I succeeded, I'd add proudly that if I got a penalty in a game I would take it like that, letting my claque of teammates loose: 'You're a talker,' 'No one believes you,' and so on. Nesta smiled, Maldini laughed, Inzaghi smirked scornfully, Di Biagio roared with laughter, and I warned them: 'If it happens, you'll see...'

So there we were, and I had no choice: I had to chip it, otherwise I'd forever be the Talker. Yes, with a capital T. It will seem strange, and maybe it will sound tone-deaf, that at such an important moment in the sporting destiny of my country, my concern was about avoiding getting that gnawing feeling inside afterwards, but it was the absolute truth. It had always been like that.

As you're going to take a crucial penalty, if you're thinking about the millions of people who are being anxious for you in front of the TV, you'll be crushed by the pressure and end up hitting the corner flag. If, on the other hand, you live the moment with the lightness of a bet at a sports bar, everything becomes easier. So, after whispering 'I'm going to do a Panenka' to Di Biagio as I passed him, I walked towards Van der Sar followed by his 'no, no' in a low voice, because if he shouted out then some of the Dutch might have suspected something and signalled to the keeper to expect something out of the ordinary.

Man. I'd joked before with Gigi to ease the tension but now, seen close up, Van der Sar really did resemble a massive octopus. The orange wall behind him was imposing, and suddenly the goal looked small. I was very afraid of making a mistake, but there was a rock-solid idea in my head. No posing. Be clinical. The chip came out perfectly. The goalkeeper, who had tried to screw with me by feinting left and diving to his right, saw a mocking ball fly over him: it must have seemed so close to him, yet it was unreachable because the weight of his falling body denied him that glancing blow off his torso that might have been enough. 3-0 to us, and no one would be calling me the Talker now.

I looked at the bench and saw stunned faces. Inzaghi had his hand on his forehead as if to say 'He's crazy.' When I passed Toldo as he went to retake his place in goal, I saw him laughing as if he already knew everything and couldn't wait to enjoy the finale. In fact, shortly after, the spotlight fell back on him: Kluivert scored, Maldini missed, and Francesco saved another, from Bosvelt, sending us through to the final. I was one of the first to run to him, to jump on him and grab him about the neck: 'Spilungone,' (Beanpole) I shouted many times, because that's what I called him. Big guy, I love you.

The final, however, isn't a story with a happy ending. We'd cheered for Portugal, and therefore against France, while watching the other semi-final. Zidane and his teammates were world champions, objectively a very strong side. In the first half they dominated the game, but our defensive tactics were organised and led us unscathed to the second half, when our quality came through. I had a great game, one of my best with the national team: the backheel with which I released Pessotto to set up Delvecchio's goal, for example, was a brilliant move, considering that I was faced with two Frenchmen and theoretically there shouldn't have been space for a pass. I also created the chance to make it 2-0, which at that point we deserved, but unfortunately Del Piero missed it, as had happened to me and to everyone else a thousand times.

I say this because the case that was then mounted against him made no sense, but it floored him, to say the least. A player who has made a mistake pays the price for it immediately, in the dressing room at the end of the game, when he just wants to be alone with his bitterness and instead has to put up with his teammates consoling him, who obviously have sympathetic intentions but end up increasing the weight he's feeling on his shoulders. In certain situations, after triumphs that become disasters by a matter of seconds, there's something cruel about the search for a scapegoat. I went through it too, albeit to a lesser extent, when I was accused of not having held onto the ball in the final third for long enough in that last accursed minute of injury time.

The truth is that I'd already wasted a bit of time and couldn't keep going: either I sent the ball straight out for a throw in or I try to find a pass for Montella, but he looked offside to me. I took the second option, and it turned into a total disaster. Fabian Barthez got things moving again, and with Cannavaro, Nesta and Iuliano on the pitch – three beasts, especially with the head – the ball should always have been ours. Misfortune wanted it to end up with Wiltord instead, and his shot from a very narrow angle passed below Toldo's hand. We're really talking about nothing, a few seconds, a few centimetres, zero luck; if the ball had been controlled by one of us, the referee would definitely have blown for full time. I don't remember another feeling like it, of the world collapsing on you: we had won, and to do it we'd gone beyond the 90th minute totally on our knees.

We looked around at each other, faces crushed by disappointment and exertion. Maldini clapped his hands to try to revive us, but there really was nothing left. We started extra time and some of us were so broken that we didn't even remember that it was golden goal, that whoever scored would win...

We felt like we no longer had a chance, and unfortunately we were right: the sentence came from Trezeguet. I watched him celebrate, chased by his teammates. It would be nice to say that at that moment I thought: 'One day you'll repay us this joy with interest, David,' but it would be fiction or, rather, a lie. All I was thinking about then was how to get out of there, because I didn't want to remain in Rotterdam for a minute longer than I had to.

Instead, I was forced to stay there for another couple of hours, under medical observation, because after going back into the dressing room I went out like a light. Passed out. I hadn't replenished the lost fluids as I should have, and for a while – I was told – I even struggled to recognise the doctors.

I lost a lot in those few seconds. The European title and, I believe, the Balon d'Or too. That year it was awarded to Luís Figo, who had had an excellent European Championship, going out in the semi-final, as he had done in the Champions League with Barcelona, before his famous transfer to Real Madrid. Without false modesty, at that time I was definitely one of the top five players in the world. If Italy had won the Euros, the biggest tournament of the season, the judges would probably have rewarded their star player. And between goals, assists and pieces of skill that remained in the collective memory, like the chipped penalty, in 2000, that man was me.

Zoff and I parted on good terms, as was only right. The anger at being left out of the semi-final had gone by the time the news of his resignation arrived, which I have honestly never understood. His successor was another icon of Italian football, Giovanni Trapattoni, but it only took a few games to realise that his call to the national side has come too late: he no longer had the energy and the positivity necessary for the job, nothing like the lively coach that all the journalists talked about, evidently recalling a younger Trap. In reality, he was well-liked in the dressing room because he let us do what we wanted, but there was zero motivation, it was more us motivating him than vice versa.

The 2002 World Cup was born from these uncertain premises, and we probably also paid for the fact that our camp ended up being in the north of Japan, in Sendai. In terms of how we integrated with the place and the people – I remember a room on the fringes of what was known as 'Casa Azzurri' and our faces of 'What are we doing here?' – we might as well have been on Mars.

Nonetheless, it started well, because the understanding between me and Vieri resulted in an easy opener against Ecuador; Bobo and I got on both on the pitch and off it, because he's a guy who's always having fun, a joker, the sort who fills up those hours on training retreats. And he had an impact on the pitch, and how.

Despite these good feelings, though, things quickly became complicated. We didn't win the group, and we were sent to South Korea for the Round of 16 to face the co-hosts. Not only that: we weren't hosted in a classic hotel – which can be more or less luxurious, but which still guarantees certain facilities – but a huge university sports complex, totally deserted. Freed up for us, I guess. A series of buildings connected to one another by endless corridors; to reach the dining room from the bedroom area, you had to walk for more than a kilometre. Anyone who has seen *The Shining* won't forget the Overlook Hotel, the remote – and frightening – hotel in which Jack Nicholson goes mad. At certain times, when I happened to walk alone through those corridors, I expected that at any moment, just like in the film, the child with the tricycle or the murdered twins would appear from behind a corner. Horrifying, in short. Add to that the beds were made to measure Koreans, and were therefore too short, the Turkish toilets and the stench of garlic that was everywhere… you might suspect that we lost on purpose in order to go home.

But no, it wasn't like that. It was the infamous referee Byron Moreno who wanted South Korea to win. The reason has never been discovered. Had he really been bought? Did he think that FIFA would appreciate the favour to the co-hosts? Did he dislike us? I don't know. From memory, the treatment that he subjected us to, which reached its peak with my red card, was certainly unprecedented.

We heard a lot of rumours before the game, but we never gave much credence to the allegations among ourselves. We went out onto the pitch in a calm state of mind, not preoccupied by what might be done to favour South Korea. But after the first four or five decisions, which all went one way, we started glancing at each other: *Don't give them any excuses; if he can, this guy will help them.* My first yellow card, for example, was ridiculous: while jumping I extended my arm a bit, but I didn't touch the opponent. The whistle went and that was fine, but the booking was completely over the top: with the tone set, from then on I planned to be twice as cautious when going in.

In any case, we took the lead through Vieri – who headed in one of my corners – and almost doubled it on many occasions. It needed a great effort, since Moreno always gave the impression he was there, lurking, but we nearly saw it home. Nearly. Unfortunately, South Korea equalised two minutes from the end, and it went to extra time.

I'll come straight to my sending off because I remember little else – the anger was so great – other than that we continued to miss easy chances to close the game. The penalty on me was clear, because in the duel with the Korean defender, I'd got into the right position at the moment contact was made, and when someone touches your leg while you're running at speed, it's always a foul. Always. I never simulated anything at all. Of course, I didn't make any effort to stay on my feet, but having arrived at that point in such an important game, you can only win it in one of two ways: with a special piece of magic or a mistake from the opposition. And the Korean defender made a mistake. I heard the whistle from the ground, and I thought, *It's over. I'll take the penalty, and since it's the golden goal rule, I'll take Italy into the quarter-finals.*

No. Moreno wasn't pointing to the spot, but was coming towards me. *No, please.* He rummaged in his pocket. *No. Fuck. No.* Yellow card, and a few moments later, a red one. Anger. Protests. For the first time, I had the feeling that it was useless to fight. I entered the tunnel that led to the dressing rooms with my vision clouded with fury, and since the door didn't open immediately, I kicked it until it broke, and our kit men had to intervene to stop me, because none of the Korean officials had the guts to say a word to me. I remained there, lying on a bench, without hope. A quarter of an hour later, I heard the roar in the stadium and I realised that it was over. It was there, at that precise moment, that I promised myself two more attempts – one European Championship and one World Cup – and then that would be it. You can't suffer like this over and over again.

The anger began to subside in the showers. More than one person half-heartedly said that we'd allowed the referee to steal it from us by missing too many chances, and despite everything, I had to admit that it was the truth. Trapattoni was mad with the FIFA investigator. Franco Carraro, the ex-FIGC president, ordered a press blackout. He said that we were too irritable and it would be pointless to add to the damage caused with the insult of a ban for overly controversial statements.

I didn't care anymore, or at least I thought I didn't, but the next day we encountered Moreno at Seoul airport and I discovered that was not the case. He hadn't travelled with us for reasons of security – his – but in the capital's large airport, we saw him through the window that separated the international zone – where we were, about to return to Italy – and the one for domestic flights, where he was, on his journey to some other Korean destination. There was no chance of contact, of course, but he mustn't have been so sure because, faced with our shouting, our insults and – I admit it, but you have to understand – our threats, he dashed off away from the glass so quickly it was comical. We ended up ridiculing him, but it goes without saying that had we come into contact with each other, no one would have hurt a hair on his head. But don't tell him that.

The following season wasn't a happy one for me, neither for Roma nor for the national team, given that between injuries and drops in form I played just two international games. The season building up to the European Championships in Portugal went smoothly, however, and the team wasn't bad at all given that Cassano, in great form in the days before his debut, was added to those already there. In fact, Trapattoni sent him out onto the pitch in the second half of the opening game against Denmark, because we were struggling to break down their defensive barrier. He couldn't do it either, and it finished 0-0.

Of that game, played in Guimarães, I remember the excruciating heat, my feet being almost on fire, and little else. It was already disappearing from my memory when, the next day, Vito Scala – who had added the national team to his work at Roma – came into my room and asked me, bluntly, if I'd spat at Christian Poulsen on the pitch.

'What, are you nuts?' I answered.

Since there was still doubt etched on his face, I told him to go to hell, but not without adding that no, I hadn't spat at anyone, the very thought of it made me sick and that he should know me better. There are certain things I don't do.

'There seems to be a video...' he murmured, and I was thrilled, because I was absolutely certain that I hadn't spat at anyone.

'Let me see it,' I say, and in the meantime, the head of the Azzurri delegation, Innocenzo Mazzini, the director of communications Antonello Valentini, and other directors had arrived too, all with puzzled expressions that gave me a very bad feeling. The video was on a Danish television channel's website. It was them, who had had a camera following me for the entire game, who had discovered what had happened. I clicked play. And I saw it.

Spitting at Poulsen is the episode in my life that I'm most ashamed of. Not in my sporting life, my entire life, the whole thing. I was so ashamed of it that I had immediately removed it from my mind: if it hadn't been for the video, I would have denied having spat at him until the end of my days, and I would have done it in absolute good faith, convinced I was telling the truth. Watching and rewatching the clip, there was no doubt, and I felt like I'd been hit by a train. They told me that UEFA had opened an investigation, that I'd have to go to Lisbon for a hearing in front of their panel of judges, that the federation was studying everything to get me the minimum penalty, blah blah blah. I wasn't listening to them anymore. I felt bad because I still didn't understand how I had been capable of something so vulgar and disgusting. Let's be clear: I must have suffered millions of fouls in my career, and as long as they didn't put my health in danger, I always put up with it. No one ever spat at me, however: if they had, I would have bitten their head off, because the very idea of it makes me sick to my stomach. Which explains why I didn't want to believe it until I saw the video and why I've since considered it the greatest shame of my life.

Christian Poulsen was an awful character. A provocateur who, while the ball is nowhere near you, didn't stop pinching you, hitting you in the sides with little punches, getting on your toes to make his studs felt, in short, someone who used the entire weaponry of the mediocre marker. What's more, he told you to keep quiet when you told him, 'Do it when we're fighting for the ball, if you've got the courage,' and the more you told him where to go, the more he laughed and toyed with you. Luckily I never saw him on the pitch again, not even in the two years he played for Juventus, because I wouldn't have resisted the urge to give him a kick, and I would have got myself sent off. But in our players' code, a kick is acceptable foul play, spitting is not. Spitting is total cowardice. And it's this that continues to burn me up, even many years on.

The incident was really unpleasant, and the federation told me that an enormous wave of negative press reports was coming. It came, and it actually exceeded my worst expectations. It was a massacre. A tsunami. I accepted everything. I was aware that I had made a mistake, but at the same time I noticed once more the anti-Roman prejudice and the considerable antipathy that inspires many comments. These were reactions that by now I'd learnt to endure and, above all, to ignore, but not to forget, and it was clear that in the long run, they'd weigh on my decision to leave the national team.

There had already been difficult situations with the Azzurri, though not like that, and I always had the impression that the media in the North were waiting for the right incident to take the moral high ground not just with me, but with all of Rome. Perhaps it was a counterweight to the indulgences that could be read, and not just between the lines, in the comments of the press and television in Rome.

To defend me, the federation hired an acclaimed lawyer in Giulia Bongiorno, the same one who defended the former prime minister Giulio Andreotti. Walter Veltroni, the mayor of Rome with whom I'd established an excellent personal relationship, sent a letter to UEFA in which – while condemning my act – he assured them that he didn't recognise me in that bully and testified to the many charitable occasions at which I spared no effort by his side. This is what I call 'affectionate severity': recognising the error by accepting the resulting punishment, but after pointing out that it was a one-off, not habitual behaviour. With this letter and Bongiorno's closing statement, everyone assured me – Carraro first of all – that the disciplinary commission wouldn't overplay their hand. So, when the three-game suspension was announced, frankly, I was disappointed, because I'd hoped to get away with two. They swore to me that a reduction had been made, from four games to three, but even so, it would be very difficult for me to play in that European Championship again; we'd have to reach the semi-finals. However, that problem didn't arise: that was the tournament of the famous *biscotto* – the term we use when two teams engineer a particular result – between Sweden and Denmark, and a week after my suspension we were back home. And I, outcast, was more or less public enemy number one.

This second flop in a big tournament cost Trapattoni his job. To replace him, the federation chose the most important coach around, Marcello Lippi, fresh from his second spell at Juventus. Fantastic, I thought. The last time we had faced each other, in February, Roma had won 4-0 and I couldn't resist the temptation of the famous 'it's four, go home' gesture aimed at Tudor, who had talked too much. Someone wrote that I'd also dedicated it to Lippi: an absolute lie, but because we hadn't encountered each other since, there hadn't been an opportunity to clear things up. And now, after what I'd done at the Euros, I wondered about what the new national team coach might think of me with no little anxiety.

I missed the first game, a friendly in Iceland shortly after the Ferragosto holiday in August, because I was full of aches and pains. Roma communicated this to the Azzurri doctors, no problem. At the start of September, two World Cup qualifiers were scheduled, in Palermo against Norway and then in Moldova: since I couldn't play the first one because I had to serve the last game of my ban, I was authorised to continue training with Roma and to join up with the Azzurri on the evening of the game against Norway. That same morning, however, in a warm-up against Lodigiani at the Flaminio, I took a whack on the ankle and ended up in the dressing room with an ice pack. Dr Brozzi called Castellacci, his counterpart with the Azzurri, to tell him that there was nothing to be done, that I wasn't in a position to play against Moldova, and that it would be better if I stayed in Rome to follow the appropriate treatment. Normal procedure, followed previously on several occasions, certainly not a way to cry off sick. So imagine my bewilderment when, an hour later, a fax from the federation arrived, asking for me to go to Palermo anyway for a medical examination. There wasn't explicit hostility, but the message was clear: there was a lack of trust.

I departed for Sicily the next morning with the feeling that the next few hours would be decisive for my future with the national team. Lippi needed to talk to me, he had said as much to Vito, who, knowing both of our characters, feared that it could lead to a heated confrontation. When I arrived at the Mondello Palace, the hotel the squad were staying at, they were out doing cooldown exercises. The atmosphere seemed cheerful. It was maybe slightly forced, because Luca Toni's goal to make it 2-1 had only come ten minutes from the end, but we'd beaten Norway.

The coach arrived, and the first teammate I embraced was De Rossi. He had made his debut the night before, and had even scored the first goal. When Lippi saw me, he came up to me smiling, asked me how I was and told me that after we'd eaten, while the others were resting, he'd like to talk to me alone. He didn't seem ill-disposed, and none of the doctors scheduled me in for a check-up. I didn't understand. I hurriedly ate a plate of pasta; at that point, I couldn't wait to talk to the coach.

'Francesco, we need to get to know each other better,' Lippi began, 'because we'll spend a lot of time together in the next two years, and I'll be asking a lot of you. You'll have read some of my interviews in the papers, the passages in which I say that I accepted the national team job because I'm convinced that we can win the next World Cup. So, you need to know that if I've gone that far, it's because I'm certain I have the men to do the job, and you're one of my key men. As the coach of the opposition, I've spent many nights studying how to limit you, because stopping you completely was impossible. Now I'm eager to enjoy the other side of the coin, to organise a game that can bring out the best in you. But for this to happen we need to get to know each other, to be in tune with one another. So let's stop talking about football, that's the least important thing, and start telling each other what sort of people we are.'

I was open-mouthed. I'd never seen such an approach. Wonderful. I started to tell him what my family was like. I told him that things had quickly become serious with Ilary, he told me the latest news about his son Davide – we're friends, we did military service together – and we had a few laughs while remembering the foolishness of those times. We sat there for two hours talking about everything: music, politics, women, Federer and Kobe Bryant, the pursuit of style and the pursuit of victory. By the end, I had the feeling that he liked me, and I certainly liked him.

'Now go back to Rome and take good care of yourself, Francesco, because I'll have serious need of you from October,' he told me, sending me away without any medical exams. I imagined the disappointment of those who had expected strong tensions between me and the new Azzurri coach. Once the personal rapport had been established, the technical one naturally followed. Lippi wasn't exaggerating, he really wanted me at the centre of his national team, and to do that he rightly took full advantage of me in the qualifiers in order to let me rest during the friendlies. It was the perfect man-management of someone nearing 30, someone still determined to pursue the greatest of results in an Azzurri shirt but weighed down by the overly long training retreats.

And it was in this privileged condition that the year of my last World Cup began. Did it all go smoothly? No. I'd have to pass one more difficult test before heading for Berlin.

11.

The Great Fear

CRACK.

The uphill path to the world title began like that, with a broken fibula on Sunday 19 February 2006, a few minutes after Roma-Empoli had kicked off.

At the time, I didn't feel any pain after falling to the ground after a tackle from Richard Vanigli. I grabbed my foot with both hands to check what had happened to it, and for a moment everything seemed OK. But only for a moment. As soon as I took my hands away, it hung to the left in an unnatural way, dead weight, and I felt myself dying too. *The World Cup. I've lost the World Cup, damn it.* I'd been waiting for four years for revenge for South Korea, but now I'd never get it. I'd already decided, and even announced, that I would retire from the national team after this World Cup. This was my last chance. *It's not fair, damn it, it's not fair, it's not fair...*

Just a week before, in agreement with Dr Brozzi – Roma's team doctor – I had raised concerns about the excessive number of fouls from behind that I was suffering. Let's be clear: taking kicks is part of the job of a number 10; those who accused me of being a 'cry baby' didn't understand anything because I'd always tolerated it up to a point. Even if you're the best, or maybe it's because of this, you can't expect your opponents to stand there applauding, admiring your talent show.

Foul play is partly a question of quantity, and at that time I was suffering in excess; Brozzi had thought that showing off my bruises, as well as how red and swollen my ankles were, even days after the previous game, could convince the referees to protect me a little better. I'd struggled to train for weeks because of the pain: from Monday to Friday, I mainly did physiotherapy, on Saturday I joined up with the team for the final training session, and on Sunday I went out onto the pitch, hoping not to find a killer waiting to mark me. I've already told you about the welcome I got from Vierchowod when I started for the first time under Mazzone. Two other really tough guys were Couto and Montero, real nightmares before the derby and Juve-Roma, while those of Milan – from Maldini to Costacurta – made you understand who you were up against immediately, but without hurting you too much. They were masters of the role, as were Nesta and Cannavaro. Someone who gave a worse impression of himself than what he was actually like was Materazzi, because the most glaring fouls didn't come from malice but from the lateness that he sometimes went in with. Of course, there were those who went too far at Roma too: I've already talked about the way in which Samuel took charge of my protection, but I also remember Leandro Cufré when he was preparing to go in all guns blazing against Juve because he had an ongoing feud with Del Piero, and every time it ended in blows. No, there were no saints-only teams.

Roma-Empoli, then. It was Spalletti's first season. After a slightly faltering start, we'd picked up the pace, we were on the back of nine consecutive victories and no one seriously thought that they could stop us. The following week it was the derby, and we wanted to be in good form going into it. Marking me was Richard Vanigli, who didn't usually start but wasn't a young kid either. He played with the desire of someone who needed to win his place in the team. Three fouls in five minutes. I asked the referee Messina for a yellow card – not because they were violent tackles, but if you don't put a stop to it, it isn't a game anymore and every challenge is a foul. Nothing. He turned the other way. I guessed the yellow card had just been postponed. You'll have to take another kick, be patient Francesco…

That's exactly how it went. One minute later: six minutes into the first half and a fourth foul. Yellow card. But it was too late. Vanigli went into me from behind in the middle of the pitch. Yes: the middle of the pitch, and I wasn't even facing his goal. It would have been 'just' another bruise if my left foot hadn't stuck in the ground, staying there while my body slid forward, passing over it. Later, I was told why I didn't initially feel any pain: the nerve had broken, removing all feeling. I realised the disaster when my foot 'fell', and then, for the first time in my life, I understood what panic is. An unspeakable terror. The precise, chilling feeling that it was all over.

I cried and screamed all sorts of things about Vanigli. But I was only told about this later because for a good minute I lost track of what was happening around me. I ranted there for ten seconds and then held my face to the ground for another ten, then the cycle began again until Brozzi and Vito and Silio Musa, the physio, were on top of me, and I screamed at the three of them: 'I broke everything.'

I saw Vito get to his feet and wave his hands in frenzied gestures. I thought he was calling for a substitution but Spalletti had already told Montella to get changed, he was already getting ready. Vito was simply calling for the ambulance on the touchline. Someone put my tracksuit jacket on me, it was still February after all, and a few moments later I was set down not particularly gently on the stretcher in the vehicle. 'Quick, quick, to Villa Stuart,' Vito shouted at the driver, while the doctor, who learned from the clinic that Professor Mariani was in his country house in Anguillara like every Saturday and Sunday, was trying to track him down on his mobile. Luckily he succeeded straight away, while the ambulance travelled around the bends of Monte Mario with sirens wailing.

It's amazing how, of those convulsive moments, you remember everything with merciless lucidity. The wheelchair waiting for me at the entrance to the clinic, the digital clock that read 15.26 – just twenty minutes after the incident on the pitch – when I went in, the two lines of nurses and attendants who escorted me discretely to have my scan, even the guy who, in a generous attempt to give me a little relief, whispered that Perrotta had scored and that we were winning 1-0. My foot ended up inside the machine for a quarter of an hour. I was in the room alone. I closed my eyes, trying not to think about anything while the hum of the scanner signalled that the verdict was being prepared. I still had my match shorts on. My thighs were coated in grass and sweat. The tears had dried but my nose was running. I really wanted to have a shower.

Fifteen minutes later, the machine stopped with a last metallic sigh. The doors of the room opened and Ilary was there, upset yet calm. We'd spoken on the phone before the warm-up. She had been in the car with Cristian heading to Fiumicino because she had to get to Sanremo for the rehearsals for the festival, which would be held there in a week's time. They had called the flight at three o'clock, but someone had alerted her about the incident before she got on the bus to reach the plane, and there had been no way of stopping her. Now that she was with me, she hugged me, kissed me and told me that Mariani has already arrived and was assessing the results. We stayed there for five minutes, hand in hand, with Cristian in the nanny's arms. I tried to hold it back, but I burst into tears, and cried uncontrollably, consoled by my wife. I managed to compose myself again just in time before Professor Mariani entered the room and, without even saying hello, he shook the X-rays and delivered the verdict: 'Ten minutes and the room will be ready. Santucci and I will operate on you immediately, Francesco.'

I read somewhere that, no matter how bad things may be, man can still manage to find a composure he finds hard to lose. Here, discovering this characteristic of the human soul, I uttered an absurd phrase, impromptu, that went against the very professional urgency of the doctor.

'Immediately? Couldn't it be done tomorrow?'

Mariani was astonished. He's a luminary. He wasn't used to having his decisions challenged. He spoke to me by punctuating his words, as if I were a child. 'Francesco. You've been seriously hurt. At a rough estimate, it's going to keep you out for seven months, and the World Cup is in less than four. If you want to have a chance, you need to win back every minute possible.'

I wanted to say something else, because panic is a jolt that comes and goes in a few seconds, while fear – even of surgery – is a less brutal but more lasting emotion, difficult to dispel. But Ilary was looking daggers at me, and I realised that I had no back up, especially among the people who cared for me. I begged for general anaesthesia, because if I heard the professor ask his assistant for a drill I would die of fright right away, and at

16.30 I entered the operating theatre. The game was still going on. Before the anaesthetic took effect, I tried to overhear what the various doctors were saying, but I didn't understand anything, and maybe it was better that way.

I woke up again at 20.30 with an acidic taste in my mouth. I sensed that there was someone else in the room, so I left my eyes half-closed before opening them, to investigate. Everyone was there. They were speaking in low voices so as not to disturb me, but they were all there: Mum, Dad, Ilary, Riccardo, Angelo, other relatives, a dozen people, those closest to me. Outside the room I noticed a larger crowd, the frosted glass let me perceive only the colours. There was the dominant red of tracksuits. *It must be the team.*

I coughed, and everyone rushed to the bedside straight away. Fortunately the quickest was a nurse, who knew exactly what she needed to do: lifting my head up a little, she allowed me to drink through a straw. It was then I understood how much I needed water to rehydrate myself and get rid of that bad taste from my mouth.

The small commotion was obviously noticed outside, and the army of doctors and other nurses that I hadn't noticed were scrambling to stop an invasion of my teammates and dozens of other curious onlookers who had mysteriously arrived there. 'Captain, we won,' someone shouted, and that was all I wanted to hear. From them. For the rest, I waited for Mariani, who entered the room after seeing to the crowd's withdrawal.

'Let me tell you right away, you can do it. You broke your fibula and the ligament in your instep. The surgery lasted two-and-a-quarter hours. I inserted a plate with thirteen screws that will remain there permanently, plus a screw in the instep that will block the ligament for a month and will then be removed. The rehabilitation will be long, laborious and even painful, but I know your body well, I know that calcifications are faster than normal with you, so I feel I can promise you that you'll be able to play games in June. Don't ask me how, though, because the timescale is really tight and a World Cup is no joke, it requires total physical efficiency. What I mean is that you'll get there, but I don't know how much preparation you'll have had. A lot will depend on you.' As always, I thought. That was the penultimate thing I remember before a long dreamless sleep. The last thing was learning that Vito, well aware of my phobias, had stopped Mariani or Santucci, the surgeon, from warning me that my fibula was broken before the operation. I would have been too scared.

When I opened my eyes again, at nine in the morning, only my mother was in the room. She had a magazine in her hands, but wasn't leafing through it because her eyes were fixed on me. Being a child again is quite inevitable, in certain situations, and my thoughts went back to the past when a touch of fever convinced her not to send me to school, which I wasn't exactly saddened by. I couldn't do much else, though, because she kept an eye on me by touching my forehead every five minutes to check that my temperature hadn't risen. And so, we'd gone back twenty-five years and she, with the faintest of smiles, put her hand on my forehead to feel my temperature and – I imagine – then explain what I needed to the nurse. I'd like to tell her that I'd broken my leg, I didn't have the flu, but I keep this short moment of newly discovered intimacy just for the two of us. Very short, actually. An outline appeared behind the glass, knocked on the door, and entered the room without waiting for a response. It was a few minutes past nine, I hadn't noticed how my foot felt yet, and Marcello Lippi was already in my room. The coach of the national team. Our coach.

'Boss, how are you?' Only the most trivial words came out, because I was bewildered. My thoughts focused on the time that Lippi must have got into the car in his home in Viareggio in order to be there in Rome at nine.

'How am I?! How are you, that's the issue. Who cares how I am. So, Francesco, tell me…'

In the end, considering the World Cup and the breaks for friendlies and qualifiers, I must have spent no more than three months of my life with Lippi. But they are worth more than thirty years, because I've never met another man who is capable of understanding me so deeply and therefore of guiding me in the right direction, even when he had to give me some bad news. At least in football. That day at Villa Stuart, I had two paths in front of me: to believe with all my heart in my recovery, accepting its difficulties. Or to give into depression, letting myself be held back by doubts. Smiling like the film star he has always been compared with, it was as if Lippi took me by the hand to lead me down the right path.

'Francesco, I've come to tell you that you'll go to the World Cup, no ifs, no buts. Last night I spoke to Vito, who gave me an overview, and later I'll go to see Mariani to find out more details about the situation, but whatever he tells me, you'll be coming to the World Cup because to win it, I need you, even at thirty percent. I need you. We need you. Don't think negatively even for a moment, and trust in your ability to recover. It will be hard work, sure, but I'll be there alongside you.'

We're used to thinking that everyone is useful but no one is indispensable, a fine maxim that keeps us humble. But it's not humility that I needed that day, lying on a hospital bed with my leg in a traction splint. On the contrary, I needed to feel indispensable and Lippi – who has a magical touch in identifying the needs of his men – perceived that immediately, just by looking me in the eye. I felt an almost physical push in his words. And to reinforce it gradually came the phone calls and messages from my Italy teammates, all saying the same things. I've never asked him, but I wouldn't be surprised if Lippi had ordered them to hammer me with messages incessantly to keep me in good spirits. When situations are in the balance, as objectively mine was, the head decides almost everything.

That morning, Vanigli called as well. He was not in good shape. After his challenge on me, the Olimpico gave him a difficult afternoon, because as the news reached the stadium, the anger of the fans mounted. I know that he cried in the dressing room as he asked for news about me. I told him that I didn't doubt the fact that he didn't want to injure me, and I really didn't, but that maybe a few less fouls might also help his image. He reiterated that he isn't a thug, and I replied: 'OK, don't worry, it was just bad luck.' Inside I think that it was *mostly* bad luck, not *just*, because four fouls in six minutes is still too many. But it was right to draw a line under it there.

My hospitalisation at Villa Stuart lasted for four days, and the staff of the clinic struggled to channel the continuous procession of people – relatives and friends on the one hand, simple fans who just wanted to show me their affection on the other – who climbed the hill of Monte Mario every day. It was a human touch that made me feel proud but also created a certain embarrassment, because I could see the annoyance at the unplanned overtime on the faces of the nurses. In short, I realised that I was a nuisance, and my availability for an autograph, for a photo, for a couple of words on the phone 'to my brother who's such a big Roma fan' wasn't always enough.

I thought about it a little in the evening, when the lights went out and even Mum and Dad, the last ones, had left. Who knows how I'm seen by people who, despite not having an interest in football, somehow come into contact with me – as is inevitable, sooner or later, in this city – and suffer the side effects of this incredible relationship of love. To what point are they tolerant and from what point do I become a big pain in the arse, as, for instance, could have been the case at Villa Stuart? These were thoughts that were already coming to me at the end of the first day of my convalescence, the ones that stop you from sleeping, which was also because I'd been in bed since the morning and I had quite a need for a nice walk.

I turned over onto my other side in an attempt to fall asleep. The customary digital clock ticked past eleven, and in the silence of the elegant clinic that overlooked Rome, I first noticed the shuffling of feet in the corridor and then a knock on the door, which was evidently intended only to be heard by me. There was a shadow beyond the frosted glass. Saying 'Come in' was a reflex.

It was Luciano Spalletti. It was eleven in the evening, and the coach was sneaking into my room. He had a fairly bulky package with him. He signalled to me to be silent by putting his index finger to his lips and unwrapped it, taking out a collapsible stand and a block of large white sheets of paper. As if suddenly struck by a distant doubt, while he was assembling it, he turned towards me to ask: 'Were you sleeping?'

'No, boss, I just can't get to sleep.'

'Ah! Good, good...' and he went back to work, as if reassured. Thirty seconds later, the setup was ready. He took a black marker out of his pocket, and began. 'Now, dear Francesco, we'll design next year's Roma. I'll show you the various options, then we'll study the pros and cons of every player together.' I was totally stupefied. He realised that, he must have expected it, and then continued with assuredness, accelerating his preparation of this strange game of Monopoly. He wrote down the names of three goalkeepers, six defenders, six midfielders, and five forwards. 'Let's begin: choose one for each role as if we didn't have budget problems, we'll consider those later.'

For four nights, I stayed at Villa Stuart. For four nights, Spalletti arrived at eleven and left at three in the morning. What we did, in essence, was chat about football: the analysis of the players that Roma could buy was obviously a pretext, because actually we talked about everything, from the style of play of the top European sides to the total distinctness of the Roman context, the biggest he'd come across so far, having come from Udinese. And of course by me too, having never encountered any others.

They were four long and at the same time untroubled nights, in which the boss gave me great confidence and, with his transfer market game, kept my head well inside Roma at a moment when a certain distance could have built up, if for no other reason than because there wasn't any talk about me playing for the club until August. I have the memory of great harmony between us in those moments, even of affection, and this accentuated my inability to understand his behaviour years later. But there was a time when Spalletti was brilliant with me, and it's only right to acknowledge that.

A week after the operation, I was in the stands at the Olimpico, on crutches, to watch our victory in the derby. It finished 2-0, and Rodrigo Taddei and Alberto Aquilani didn't forget me as they were celebrating their goals, coming across jubilantly towards the area in which I was seated.

If that evening was an interlude of joy, the rest was just effort, effort and more effort. According to Mariani's predictions, the fact that my bones calcified faster than the average would win me a month. I had to come up with something to steal some more time, and the right idea came to Silio, who, by cutting up some rubbish bags – the black ones, you have them at home too – and sealing them with some elastic bands, managed to create some waterproof leg protectors for me that allowed me to work in the pool when the wound was still scarring and, out of the water, the screw that was blocking the ligament forced me onto crutches. I won back another twenty days like this, because when they removed the screw, I'd already recovered some elasticity and, above all, muscle tone.

In fact, on the first day without crutches at Trigoria, less than a month after the operation, I ran around the edge of the main pitch very slowly, but I was already feeling steady on my legs. I felt so steady that when I got to the last corner flag and found a ball next to it, as if it was waiting for me, I couldn't resist and, with my right foot, kicked it back towards the goal. I hadn't lost my touch because the accurate trajectory took it into the net, but I didn't have time to compliment myself because everyone was on me, shouting 'What are you doing?' or 'Are you stupid?'

Actually, in order to hit it right-footed, I put my body weight onto my left, as is normal, but I'd forgotten that the ligament had just been freed from the screw and that the fibula had shattered less than a month earlier. I put on the face of a child who had just been caught with his hands in the jam jar, but at the same time, I 'listened' to my left foot, and that was saying absolutely nothing. 'Look, everything's fine,' I said, in a low voice, as if afraid of offending them. Vito, Silio, the boss… I think that, if they could have, in that precise moment, they would have broken my other leg.

The need to speed up time as much as possible meant I was working for eight hours a day, testing my left foot more and more each time to strengthen it. Jumps, little steps, big steps; I started by stopping after each jump to check that everything was alright, then I moved on to stopping every two movements, then every three, every five, gradually increasing it. I was already running smoothly by around 30 March.

Lippi came to Trigoria once a week and watched my progress with an increasingly optimistic expression. Spalletti had been running with me since the beginning, imperceptibly increasing the pace and slowing down only when he saw that I was limping. It happened regularly, but a little later every day.

These were weeks of great emotional intensity, because around me was a world of people who were pushing me to do it, and I distinctly felt that they were behaving like that because they loved me, not just because the World Cup was at stake for everyone. And so this time, the famous questions that I always asked myself about what the hell I'd done to deserve so much affection, so much respect, so much popularity had a simple, immediate, clear answer: *I have to be able to recover in time for June.* The growing confidence and the feeling of being able to do it, which became clearer and clearer day by day, gave me wonderful sensations. *Yes, I'll make it. Yes, your extraordinary work won't be for nothing. Yes, I'll play in the World Cup.* How much and how well remained to be seen, but I felt like I'd be there.

The last sign-off came from Professor Mariani, who visited me at the start of April to authorise me to go back to training with the squad. I told him that the ankle had never swelled up, not even after the heaviest workouts, and that I felt great: he studied the X-rays and approved them with a broad smile. 'Francesco, I wasn't exaggerating that afternoon when I told you that such a calamity would normally have required seven months of convalescence and rehabilitation. But I knew that your body is special, and I've seen confirmation of this. It's not even been two months, but let me tell you that the World Cup is close now.'

Another month of work, obviously while being prudent in avoiding tackles, and the phone calls with Lippi became daily. The encouragements from my teammates, both at Roma and Italy, were increasingly convincing. Then, at the start of May, the national team coach called me and, in a candid but slightly excited voice – or at least that's how it seemed to me – asked me the question he had to: 'Francesco, it's time to send our initial squad list to FIFA. Can I count on you?'

Do you remember that, as a child, I used to ring the intercoms in Via Vetulonia saying that I was Gerry Scotti? There, at that moment, I thought of his famous 'Shall we turn it on?' from his quiz because, despite its courtesy, Lippi's question had a meaning of equal finality. But I had no doubts. We'd turn it on alright.

'Yes, boss, I'm there.'

He was obviously expecting it, but I sensed a certain difficulty in disguising his enthusiasm. Or maybe Lippi didn't have any intention of disguising it.

'You couldn't have given me better news, Francesco. See you at Coverciano.'

12.

The Eye of the Needle

THE REAL SITUATION DAWNED ON ME AFTER THE FIRST training session at Coverciano. After an hour filled with athletic drills, Lippi blew the whistle for the end and, quite worn out, we all headed over to the sidelines where there was a table with water bottles. A couple of gulps and the coach's voice sounded from behind us. 'Shower for everyone except Francesco, he's staying on the pitch with me.' I turned around. Lippi had two balls in his hands and smiled: 'Show me that you can still hit the target.'

The provocation was good-natured, but in fact, after the injury, I'd played less than ninety 'official' minutes, all in San Siro, between the second leg of the Coppa Italia final against Inter and the last game of the league season against Milan. I completed my physical recovery at Trigoria: running, ladder drills, changes of direction, lots of rondos, and a few training games with teammates who were very careful not to make contact with me.

But competitive football is a different animal. Before throwing me back into the mix, Lippi wanted to regain confidence in 'my' fundamentals, so he went in goal, challenging me to beat him from outside the area, and I had to strike the shots as quickly as possible. He also went to collect the balls that went off target, and after the tenth one I saw that he was panting a bit. Many years later, he would admit to me that those extra training sessions – which were repeated throughout that first week for half an hour a day – took a lot out of him physically ('After a while I couldn't

182

think straight anymore'), but that didn't make him stop. This was the last piece in reconstructing the mosaic before the definitive test, the one on the pitch.

The moment of truth was in Geneva, on 31 May, a friendly against Switzerland. One hundred and one days had passed since the injury, and there were twelve days to go until the World Cup opener against Ghana. Lippi slotted me into the starting line-up without setting any limits: I had to play for as long as I had the energy. Like when you get a new car and, in order to find out the tank's capacity with absolute precision, you drive it until it stops because it's out of petrol.

I was a bit sluggish in the first half. I played behind Gilardino, who put us ahead by turning home a low cross from Fabio Grosso from the left. It was a 4-2-3-1 with Camoranesi and Del Piero occupying the wings, the alternative system to the *trequartista* behind two forwards that Lippi used most frequently. The Swiss equalised with a fine shot from range. I moved cautiously because after a calm start, some of them were becoming aggressive. They'd reacted badly to something, but I didn't know what that was all about.

At half time, Lippi made a questioning gesture at me, checking if everything's alright, and I reassured him: technically I'd not contributed much, but the leg was fine, and as the minutes went by it felt better and better to me. In the second half, I raised my game, partly because we'd gone back to the usual formation, two centre forwards and me behind them, with three midfielders behind to support me. No other goals came, but the full ninety minutes – I didn't need to be replaced even towards the end – were the most eagerly anticipated confirmation. I was fine.

We stayed in Switzerland because two days later, this time in Lausanne, the second and final pre-World Cup friendly was scheduled against Ukraine. Naturally, it was mostly those who had had to watch in Geneva who played, but after an hour, Lippi, who wanted to know what point my recovery was at, put me on for Del Piero. Little happened in that half an hour, just a blow from Andriy Gusin that served as a crash test for the convalescent leg: if it held up to that tackle, it meant that the bone was stronger than before. Which didn't prevent me from giving the blond guy a heartfelt f-bomb…

But I was running, and that hadn't been a given. Around me, I saw the relieved and smiling faces of my teammates. During the World Cup, and in later years as well, Lippi would tell me many times: 'You have no idea of the affectionate attention with which they followed your recovery. They called me and sent me messages, all with the same tone. "Boss, we're taking Francesco even if he's at fifty percent, he scares the opposition no matter what and opens spaces up for us." Going against the famous maxim, they begged me to choose the dead lion instead of the live donkey.' Which is just an expression, there were no donkeys in that context.

We left for Duisburg, the location assigned for our base camp, with the certainty that we were a good squad. We were well-equipped in every area. Buffon was unanimously recognised as the best goalkeeper in the world. In central defence were two stars of the position in Cannavaro and Nesta. The midfield axis ran from Pirlo in front of the defence to me behind the strikers. Up front, there was an embarrassment of riches: Del Piero, Toni, Gilardino, Inzaghi, each one dangerous in his own way. And in addition to these champions, there were quality players ready to play their part in times of need.

It shouldn't be said, because it's not right to take hope away from young people, but I don't believe we'll ever have such a strong national team again. Or at least, we won't have one until a way is found for clubs to play an adequate number of Italians, because the sea of players to choose from has become a pond: you can always find one world-class player, but not seven or eight superstars all together, the odds are against you.

Let me be clearer: English is spoken in Roma's dressing room today, and this still doesn't seem normal to me. Of course, we all dabble in a bit of English, and for years, the newly arrived foreigners were helped by their teammates until they learned Italian. Now, many of them don't even study it anymore, knowing that they'll stay in Rome for a year or two, so there's no point in making the effort. The result is that a dressing room like ours, which over time has been able to rally around Roman captains, from Di Bartolomei to Bruno Conti, from Giannini to me and Daniele, speaks as though we were Arsenal or Chelsea. Is that normal? Come on... The 2006 Italy side was the result of years of rich options and of common paths in the youth teams. Do you remember my goal against Mexico at the

Under-17 World Cup in Japan, when Buffon ran the length of the pitch to come and embrace me? Even in 1993, we were already teammates in blue.

The other aspect of modernity that I find harmful to team spirit is the smartphone, with its power – in other ways fantastic – to take you to distant worlds and isolate you at any time. Including those in which you should be experiencing a group dynamic. The 2006 national side – like all teams at that time – arrived at the stadium by bus listening to the same music, with the incredibly loud speakers brought by Materazzi. It wasn't only the famous Seven Nation Army, there was an entire playlist to get us psyched up for the simple fact that we listened to it together. In the following years at Roma, there were several occasions that I decided to propose a return to the past: mobiles off, no headphones, shared music. Well, that was no longer possible, everyone had a reason to keep their phones on: someone needed to tell their wife exactly where they'd left their tickets, someone was waiting to hear from their friends on WhatsApp to find out which restaurant they were meeting at after the game, someone wanted to wait until the last minute before kick off to find out how high his kid's fever had got... All legitimate things, but which fatally distance you from everyone else.

When there's an hour to go before the game, and you know that before long you'll have to make sacrifices for someone else or that someone else will have to make sacrifices for you, your teammates are your family, your refuge, your motivation. You can't treat them like strangers, they're not office colleagues. They're brothers, and the result will be the same for everyone: there's no situation in which you win and they lose. Individual emotions have to be synchronised, and however strange it might seem, listening to a song together on the coach creates chemistry that can be felt on the pitch. I'll finish my digression by thinking back to my last season as a footballer, when it was expected that I would feel old in my legs while instead – because of the frequency of these thoughts, this nostalgia – I, if anything, felt old in my head. Old, but not wrong. I'll come back to this in my new role ...

Let's pick up the story with the departure for Germany and the air of trust that we all breathed, in contrast to the heavy atmosphere that we felt around us because of Calciopoli.

There was an internal meeting on that subject at the start of the training camp in which we unanimously took two decisions. The first was to reject any question on the subject from journalists, and the second was not to speak of it among ourselves either, even banning jokes and jibes, because we were all deeply convinced of the honesty of our teammates. Not of the directors though, and in fact we devoured the articles on the investigation every morning. But there was no doubt about the fact that Buffon, Cannavaro, Del Piero and the other Juve players had nothing to do with Calciopoli directly. And understanding the difficulty of their situation, it was better to avoid jokes too.

I'll confess something to you: when rumours about their transfers in the event of Juve's conviction began to go around, I strained my ears so as not to miss a single syllable from Buffon. I didn't ask him openly out of respect – except for the night of the party at the Circus Maximus, when the atmosphere was special and a little alcoholic – but if he'd even hinted a word about the possibility, I would have tormented him to the point of 'forcing' him to come to Roma. But Gigi never gave me the chance.

As the first game approached, however, all other subjects faded and disappeared. We were up against Ghana, a tough African side who were full of high-quality 'European' players. If it would be going too far to say that we were fearful, it would be difficult to get away with just 'respectful', because that's a bland word, which doesn't convey the idea enough. There was a lot of restlessness.

The game was scheduled for 12 June, the fourth day of the tournament, and on its eve, before flying to Hanover, we noticed that Holland had joined Germany, England and Argentina on the list of favourites to have passed their first test without excitement, but with three points. I envied them. They'd already made it through the test of their opening game, but growing within each of us was a ferocious desire to play, to measure ourselves, to fight, and it was a desire that took hold and became infectious. We were very tense. I struggled to sleep in the afternoon break as well, so I watched a little of the other game in our group, where the Czech Republic beat the United States quite easily, and then – since it would use up half an hour – I asked the hairdresser to cut my hair. It was a sudden decision, completely spontaneous, my mood and state of mind took me. It was as if I wanted to go into the World Cup differently to how I'd been leading up to it, and I needed an aesthetic change to rubber-stamp it. At the technical meeting at 18.45, more than one teammate looked at me questioningly, but if I think back to it now, the bemused faces belonged to the reserves. We starters, rattled off one by one by Lippi, were as focused as if we were frozen in time.

Bang. The whistle from the referee, a Brazilian, sounded like a starter's shot. I played behind Toni and Gilardino in a very attacking formation. The intent of the coach was clear: start with a bang to increase the self-confidence within the group and, outside it, to increase the perception that we were dangerous. Ghana's best player was Michael Essien, a tireless midfielder for whom Chelsea paid a lot of money to Lyon to please José Mourinho. I ran into him a few times, but the one who was keeping a close eye on me was Eric Addo, a defender who played in Holland for PSV. And when I tried to escape his man-marking, I ended up close to John Paintsil, who at one point aimed a hard kick at me, at the ankle I'd had the operation on, and thankfully he wasn't able to catch me fully.

But Ghana were a high-level opponent, physically very strong, technically decent and far from ignorant from a tactical perspective. We started better, I found a good amount of space between the lines as long as I played with one touch, two at a push, and it's just a shame that a surprise pass – not for us, of course – by Pirlo from a free kick set me up for a horrible shot from sixteen metres. I took it with my body too far back and what came out was something like a rugby conversion.

Never mind, because when it was my turn to give it to Pirlo, from the corner flag, he came up with a great goal from the edge of the area: it put into practice a routine we'd planned beforehand, but I certainly didn't feel like calling it an assist. The merit was entirely his, and we were in front.

The best thing about my game, which was a good one, was the laser-like pass that I played to Gilardino at the start of the second half for him to take a shot, but unfortunately their keeper was alert. Soon after, another blow from Paintsil arrived, and even though it didn't cause any damage, Lippi preferred to take me off for Camoranesi. Rightly so. There was a lead to protect, 4-4-2 was the appropriate protection, and in the last minute,

Sammy Kuffour – my teammate at Roma that year – even made a mistake passing the ball back to the keeper, letting Iaquinta make it 2-0. Victory. Rising from the bench at the final whistle, I poured a bottle of water over the curls of Ciro Ferrara, who was there as Lippi's assistant, while the Tannoy in the stadium in Hanover blasted Adriano Celentano's version of *Azzurro* out at full volume.

It was inevitable that such a brilliant opener, after the many questions that those outside the squad were asking about our real worth, led to relaxation. Lippi gave us a day off but I, not having anyone there yet, stayed in the hotel to play cards with Gattuso, unaware that I'd make way in the next game to make space for him.

At a World Cup, time passes quickly. Two days of training and it was already the eve of the second game. This time we took a plane to the south – Kaiserslautern isn't far from the French border – with a much more relaxed spirit. Too much, evidently, because after the further good news of Ghana's victory against the Czech Republic in the afternoon game, the feeling that the group had been taken care of was widespread. A huge mistake: the Americans physically battered us for the entire game because they ran faster and were tougher too. We somehow managed to take the lead with Gilardino turning in a nice header, but a slice from Zaccardo, with the resulting own goal, soon levelled the game again. And a minute later, De Rossi capped off the disaster.

I love Daniele dearly. His absolute, exorbitant, almost schizophrenic love for Roma was obviously the ground on which we understood each other right from his arrival at Trigoria, but over time our relationship has grown in every sense. We see each other off the pitch as well, and now it's a relief to see him calm and happy after the years in which he went through his vicissitudes. Daniele also stayed at Roma for his whole career, but to do so he had to say no many more times than me, because evidently the big international clubs didn't believe in his desire to stay there for life, so big offers came in every year. I think he silently put up with the progressive ageing of his nickname, Capitan Futuro, but if you go back and watch the video of my farewell, you'll find him devastated by emotion, a sign of sincere affection. I couldn't have left the armband on a more worthy arm.

That evening in Kaiserslautern, shortly after halfway through the first half and with the score at 1-1, in an aerial duel, Daniele elbowed an American, Brian McBride, under the nose of the referee. Inevitably, it was a red card. He tried to explain himself with broad gestures of his arms, meaning that he had only used them to give himself leverage. We were immediately by his side, as we should have been, but actually no one had had a good view of the incident, so we took him on faith while he yelled uselessly at the referee, 'I didn't do anything, I didn't even touch him,' with the urgent and desperate tone of someone who's leaving his teammates with ten men in a World Cup match.

Daniele went off distraught, his head in his hands, and we frenetically regrouped. I dropped back to the halfway line and, immediately, I was able to slide a pass between three Americans to Pirlo, who in turn set up Toni for a shot. It's a pity that he was off balance because the chance wasn't a bad one. But I was aware that the formation, even readjusted like that, wouldn't last. In fact, in the 35th minute, seven minutes after the incident, Lippi called me back to the bench to send on Gattuso. I had no objections.

It was a game that looked kindly on us only because the Americans were very naïve: in the 45th minute, Pablo Mastroeni provided the Uruguayan referee with the opportunity to restore numerical parity after a frightening challenge. And at the start of the second half, a senseless tackle by Eddie Pope, who had already been booked, reduced them to nine men. That was lucky, because we really weren't in good shape mentally, we risked losing even then. If we'd been facing a more experienced national team, we wouldn't have brought the points home safely.

In the dressing room, Lippi was very angry with De Rossi. I realised this from the fact that he never mentioned him. Daniele was seated, already changed, keeping his head down. In the friendly against Switzerland, he had booted an opponent on the ground, and the boss had given us a ten-minute lecture on the need to avoid certain nonsense (this explained the aggressiveness of the Swiss that I hadn't understood at the time). According to Lippi, the referee had seen everything on that occasion, but had refrained from taking action so as not to ruin the World Cup for Daniele, so it must have seemed incredible to him that he'd fallen for it again. In any case, he didn't say anything to him, and he also signaled to us to let him work off his rush of adrenaline by himself. There were a couple of quick observations on the game and on the fact that we still had two useful results to be able to qualify against the Czech Republic, and then the session was over. We were about to leave when Daniele got to his feet and, still keeping his eyes lowered, pronounced aloud the words that he needed to: 'I'm sorry. Honestly, I'm sorry to all of you. I fucked up, it nearly cost us badly. I'm unforgivable, sorry again.' He was then the first to leave.

Aside from the gesture, which was serious, the aspect that struck everyone most was the discrepancy between the conviction with which Daniele swore on the pitch that he hadn't done anything and the bleak truth of the video. There had been an elbow, definitely, and in the following days, when the wound started to heal, a couple of courageous people tried to joke with De Rossi ('His cheek opened up, imagine if you'd caught him...'), who smiled reluctantly. He didn't smile at all, however, when the sentence arrived: a four-game ban, his World Cup effectively over; we'd have to reach the final before he'd be available again, and at that point, no one was thinking that far ahead.

The despair was such that Daniele wanted to go home immediately, the same day, and that was the moment when it was my turn to intervene, because at Roma I was his captain and his oldest friend. I heartened him. I told him that the keyhole through which we could see the final would get bigger as each day went by. I delved a little deeper into the frenzy that had seized him, without imagining how many times I'd have to go back to the subject over the years. It would happen with Mauri in a derby, with Lapadula in Genova at the end of 2017, and every time Daniele would repeat robotically, 'I don't remember anything, sometimes my vision clouds and I'm not aware of what I'm doing.' And an increasingly desolate sorrow spreads across his face: towards the opponent he struck, towards his teammates, who he left with ten men, and towards himself, feeling it's like a curse. Nowadays, a thousand cameras are trained on the pitch, it's impossible to escape them all. When you make a mistake, it's inevitable that you'll pay. Rationally, you know there are certain things you mustn't do, but there was nothing rational in those frenzies.

The third game, against the Czechs, was the last for Sandro Nesta, who stretched his groin in the first half, went off, and had already learned the diagnosis by half time: he'd be out for a month, and there were less than three weeks until the end of the World Cup. I grieved for him, my Laziale 'twin' since we were teenagers. I felt for his fate of being an injured player at a big international tournament, because there's always one every time. Yet, despite his certainty of no longer being able to play, Sandro never thought for a moment about going home: his involvement in the adventure remained total, and his choice had a positive influence on Daniele, who definitively shelved the idea of returning – he still had a chance of playing, albeit a remote one – and kept Sandro company during the games. We ended up calling them Chip 'n' Dale...

Just as De Rossi's suspension brought Gattuso back into the side, so Nesta's injury opened the door for Materazzi. Thinking about it, the part chance plays in the creation of a World Cup-winning side is impressive. To say that Marco was ready isn't going nearly far enough: a few minutes after he came on, I went to take a corner and I saw him arrive running full speed from the back, with his finger pointing to the sky, implying I should aim deeper towards the far post. The expression on his face was so convincing that I was compelled to comply, and it was an inspired choice because I saw him leap above all others, turning the ball into the corner, beyond the reach of Petr Čech. 1-0.

I clenched my fists and ran to embrace him. It was an important goal because the Czech Republic – who needed to win to stay in the tournament – had been attacking us with great intensity in the opening minutes. Nedvěd was in irresistible form that day, and it pains me to say it because I'd never been able to bear him on the pitch: a unbelievable whiner, you brushed against him and he flew ten metres, forcing the referee to show a card, it made you want to beat him with your hands, and I said all sorts of things to him. But he was good, boy was he good, and even more so in that game, so much so that Buffon had to come up with three or four top-quality saves to keep him at bay. (Having reiterated how much he got on my nerves as a footballer, and I admit that I've never hidden it from him, I must also acknowledge that he was very kind to me the first time that we met off it, at the draw for the Champions League group stage in Monte Carlo. He came up to me – and it was me who was the rookie – and asked me how I was feeling soon after I'd retired from playing, jokingly suggested that I pick well and, when I drew Barcelona's name, he shrugged, smiling, as if to relieve me of the weight of the worst possible draw I could have given him. Although my friend Buffon, sat next to him, was ready to shout 'damn you' at me from the front row...)

If the corner for Materazzi's opener is my first personal contribution to the win against the Czechs, the second and definitive one is due to my ankles, hit a dozen times from behind by Jan Polák who, in first half injury time, after his umpteenth foul, had a second yellow card waved in his face by the Mexican referee.

The second half was purely about game management, even if Nedvěd didn't stop attacking Gigi's goal. Lippi kept me on the pitch until the end: he'd withdrawn a striker from his starting formation to include Perrotta, a move dedicated to me given that Simone, for both Italy and for Roma, was the best at running into spaces, instructing me to play long balls. Gilardino played as the lone striker for an hour, then he went off for Pippo Inzaghi, who after missing two chances made it 2-0 in the 87th minute in a way that triggered general hilarity. Or rather, we all started laughing at Simone Barone, who had also come on after half time, who ran after Pippo on a counter-attack into a wide open pitch as if there was actually a chance that he'd get the ball. In the end, Inzaghi dribbled around Čech to score his only goal of the tournament.

Hamburg smiled on us: we finished top of the group, entering the knockout phase on the opposite side of the draw to the favourites Brazil. In the evening, we found out that our opponents in the Round of 16 would be Australia, not Croatia, as we all thought: it ended 2-2 between them, and I can't say that the result was welcomed with disappointment.

But it was the evening after that the famous corridor opened up in front of us, because even France, second in their group, ended up in the other half of the draw, and a graphic from German television removed any doubt: after Australia, we'd face the winner of Ukraine-Switzerland. With all due respect, a World Cup quarter-final could be a lot worse.

Lippi called us together the next morning, in the breakfast room, and with his dialectical skill gave us a double message. On the one hand, we had to focus exclusively on Australia, because in a World Cup the only possible way of thinking is one game at a time, especially when the knockout phase begins. On the other hand, we had to realise that the opportunity of getting at least to the semi-finals was a one-off, and that everyone in Italy now considered it to be the minimum objective: and rightly so – he added – considering our ability. It was useless to hide that then.

In the dressing room, we did nothing other than talk about the 'corridor' and the potential traps hidden on a path that seemed to be downhill all the way. We clearly felt that we were stronger than Australia, and Switzerland and Ukraine were two sides that we'd faced recently, in the last two friendlies before we flew to Germany. We'd drawn against both of them, but in both cases we had the distinct feeling that with more energy, and not held back by our preparation for the tournament, we'd have won easily. All talk, therefore, moved after a while to the chance of a lifetime, because when fate seems so favourable it's as if it's sending you a message: Use this chance well because you won't have others. Which is scary at first glance, but then it gives you extra determination.

There was only a very short space of time between the last group game and the Round of 16, just four days, the minimum in a World Cup, which meant a warm-down, a training session, and then it was already the eve of the flight to Kaiserslautern.

So far, I'd played almost an hour against Ghana, 35 minutes against the Americans, and the whole game against the Czechs. Speaking of a planned recovery in a World Cup could seem presumptuous, but it went like this: I presented myself at fifty percent, and by then I felt that I'd progressed to at least seventy thanks to my condition improving and there no longer being any toxins in my body, which were natural for someone who hadn't played a competitive game since February. In short, everything was going well.

And this is why when Lippi came to find me in my room after we'd eaten, just before leaving for the stadium, to tell me that this time I'd be on the bench, I took it badly. 'You've played in all three of the first games, now it's right that you rest because if things go how we want them to, this game will be the exact halfway point of our tournament. We've had one day less to recover, and for someone coming off of your injury, this could make itself felt. And the Australians are also very physical, let's let them wear themselves out a bit...'

The reasoning honestly made sense, but it was still a huge pain in the arse. Ilary had come for the first time, accompanied by her sister Silvia, and the gnawing feeling of having to tell her that I wasn't playing added anger to anger. But I didn't complain. In fact, I supported Lippi by telling him that it was OK, that it wasn't a problem, and that I'd be absolutely ready to come on if needed, without expressing my disappointment in the least. I owed it to him, for how he waited for me and encouraged me in that long spring. Even today, if you ask him how I accepted his decision, he'd answer that I didn't react critically in the slightest and made myself totally available to him. I'm proud that the façade held up, because after having received so much from him, it was only right to give something back with that level of calmness.

I vented with Ilary, but, after listening to my reasons, she cut me off by embracing Lippi's perspective. I was surrounded. She doesn't follow football, but she instinctively understood the coach's words and thought they were right, because in the context of 23 elite players it's normal to have a rest in an easy game. As players we couldn't even let that idea cross our minds, but she was obviously free from clichés and superstitions and could say what the whole of Italy was thinking.

Before leaving for the stadium, Lippi called a technical meeting to tell us the line-up, and I thought about two things: the first was that he had the tact to forewarn me about my exclusion privately, and this was a great sign of respect; the second was that Del Piero had taken my place, and when you're replaced by such a champion, the only thing you can do is swallow any bitterness and support him unrestrainedly.

From Euro 2000 to the 2006 World Cup, I shared four major tournaments for the national team with Alessandro, and there was never a build up to them without some newspaper coming up with a confrontational headline along the lines of 'Arm wrestle for the number 10 shirt' – obviously between me and him. Among the huge amount of rubbish that was said in those years, we were almost fond of this idea of an 'arm wrestle' because it made us laugh so much.

The story of the Azzurri's number 10 shirt can be told quickly: Del Piero rightly had it at Euro 2000, since he was coming off the World Cup two years previously while I – a debutant – asked for and, with great satisfaction, was given the number 20. But the final in 2000 didn't go well for Ale, who, two years later, before leaving for Japan, suggested that I take the number 10: '7 is a number that has always brought me more luck, and I know that the 10 is on excellent shoulders with you.'

He made the same reasoning for Euro 2004, so on the eve of the 2006 World Cup in Germany – given that neither of the previous outings had been a success, blowing any superstition out of the water – I told him that we could easily do odd and even for the number 10. Lippi had also let us know that we'd have to resolve the issue between ourselves, and so it was our duty to show that we were accommodating. It was Ale who went furthest: 'Francesco, it's not just that I don't care, I also know that you do. So there's no odd and even to do, the number 10 is yours and we can both be happy with that.'

This issue of the shirt number, which was never actually an issue, is obviously a pretext to describe one of the best friendships that I've had – and continue to have – in the world of football. Alessandro is a special person, generous, intelligent, a loyal man. As well as an incredible champion, of course. The roles that we had in our careers led us to an inevitable rivalry, and given how the contests between Roma and Juventus were experienced by the respective sides, it wouldn't have taken much for us to hate each other. But at the very first match, the very first meeting in the tunnel at the Olimpico, when our eyes met while waiting for the referee to give the order to go out onto the pitch, a wave of human understanding started between us that our time together in the national team cemented into friendship. And with this esteem for the man who was taking my place, by the time kick-off against Australia came around, I had already set aside all sadness.

Knockout matches are deadly simple: if you lose, you go home. Put like that, you might imagine that before leaving the hotel, though you don't pack your bags – just doing that will bring you defeat – at least five minutes are spent gathering things together, looking under the bed to see if that slipper you haven't found for two days ended up there, squeezing the last gram of toothpaste out of the tube instead of grabbing another one. Not at all. You spend every day of the training retreat as if it was eternal, that the run will never come to an end, and certainly not before the final.

You think of stupid things like that while waiting for a game, and on the bench they linger with you for longer because you can't let off steam by running around.

We didn't play well in the first half against Australia, or rather, we created numerous chances but missed them all, suddenly making the mistake of not being clinical. At half time Lippi raised his voice like I'd never heard him before because he said that we were messing around too much. It seemed like we were in a ballet and not a 'win or die' match.

He was very angry with someone, who he didn't name, accusing him of talking with journalists too much, thus revealing our tactical plans to the opposition. He looked at those who started but also at us on the bench; no one felt excluded from his outburst. He said that the Australians knew our passing lines too well not to have sat down and studied them, and since the team and the system were new, he could see that someone had blurted out the changes and that that damned Hiddink – who was then coaching Australia – had prepared for the game with the right line-up at hand. In retrospect, thinking about it, I believe Lippi was shooting blind, or rather he used a pretext to communicate his anger to us: if I'd only found out a few hours before the game that I would be on the bench, it wouldn't have been possible for someone to have revealed it to reporters in time for Hiddink to find out. In any case, the wake-up call at half time seemed to be acknowledged. But the problems were yet to start.

Five minutes after the break, Mark Bresciano set off, chased by Zambrotta, and Materazzi also went over to put in a tackle. The foul was obvious, and fairly pointless. But given that Marco mostly took out Zambrotta, the decision of the referee – the Spaniard Medina Cantalejo – was chilling for us: the challenge was worth a yellow card, but he brought out the red.

All of us on the bench jumped to our feet, as always happens in those situations, with expressions that were halfway between dismayed and scandalous, but it didn't make the slightest difference. For the second time in four games, we found ourselves playing with ten against eleven, but this time it was a knockout match. We were on the brink.

There were 40 minutes to go until the 90th minute and 70 until the penalty shoot-out, which was an outcome that we'd have all taken at that point. A long time to spend with ten men. A few moments to regroup, and then Australia started to come forward. Nothing dangerous, but Lippi, who had already taken off Gilardino at half time for Iaquinta, more inclined to help with covering, took off Toni to restore the traditional back four with Andrea Barzagli.

The second change made, he sent me to warm up, signalling to me that the third (and final) change would probably be me. From the corner flag, running along the narrow strip of turf between the sideline and the advertising hoardings, I noted Buffon's confidence in saving a couple of shots from outside the area and a header from Tim Cahill that went over. But we were taking risks. The team was dropping back, there was probably a little bit of tiredness creeping in now it was the fourth game: that wasn't the right time to go down to ten men, if such a time ever existed.

'Francesco! Francesco!' Lippi called me, very agitated, as if I'd strayed too far. I was beside him in a flash. 'You're going on now. You have to play Iaquinta into deep spaces, as he's still quite fresh. Let him hold onto the ball so that our defence can take a breather, and after giving it to him, get close to him. If he gives it back to you, maybe you'll have the room to try a shot from distance. Go, go...' His last words were lost in the roar of the stadium, which had seen the substitute board. Ale came off, we briefly embraced. The faces of my teammates were marked with exertion, but they were also determined not to give up. There were 75 minutes on the clock.

I realised immediately that there was room for a counter-attack. The Australians were excellent athletes, but not even Hiddink had been able to give them a decent tactical order: they were running almost on empty, not succeeding in taking advantage of the extra man, and despite their numerical superiority they hadn't yet made a change, a sign that there was very little on the bench. I gave the ball to Iaquinta twice, but didn't get the return ball. There were 90 minutes on the clock now, we were in injury time, nearly extra time, and who knows if we'd have been able to keep going until a penalty shoot-out.

Then, Fabio Grosso, who was truly inexhaustible, started up the left touchline with his stride of a 400-metre runner. I had the ball in the centre circle, saw him out of the corner of my eye and decided to trust in myself: a long ball with my left foot. Fabio was smart to let it drop because then he got an advantage against Bresciano, decisive in taking it past him and getting into the penalty area from the touchline. Iaquinta was waiting in the middle. I hadn't moved from the spot where I'd played the pass.

I'm not sure how to explain it, but in my mind it's like I was seeing everything in High Definition. Fabio pushed the ball past Neill and then fell from the contact with him. The referee took half a moment to think, then pointed to the spot. Iaquinta rejoiced and then ran to hug Grosso on the ground. The ball was mysteriously given straight back to me. Honestly, I've never known who kicked it towards me, or whether he did it on purpose or not. What's for certain is that when I picked it up and looked around me, I didn't see a single blue shirt. Like Moses and the waters of the Red Sea, the way towards the penalty spot had parted for me.

That Italy team didn't have a designated penalty taker. Lippi never wanted one because, in certain games, substitutions change everything – think, for example, of Del Piero, who had just gone off and been replaced by me – and then there's the emotions of particular moments that can't be controlled. Looking back at the team on the pitch, the most reliable takers were me and Pirlo, and if the ball had been in Andrea's hands, I wouldn't have allowed myself to say anything to leave him alone, though perhaps I'd have said something to Gattuso, if, in a fit of generosity, it had been him who was taking it...

I looked around again. Buffon had already turned towards the fans behind him; as usual, he didn't want to watch. Pirlo was next to the bench. He was having a drink. He must have had a terrifying thirst, given how long he was taking... In short, the way to the spot was completely clear. The Australians' protests – I understood them, they'd been forced into conceding the penalty – were dwindling, and since they have an Anglo-Saxon sporting culture, none of them thought to put me off in any way, to block me off, to say something unpleasant to me. I kept walking, looking at Mark Schwarzer, who had started the goalkeeper's pre-penalty ritual: the movements, the short steps towards the referee, a couple of words to take the edge off things. I walked and thought, even spoke, whispering to myself: 'Do I try a chip?'

Later that evening, Lippi would tell me that he went through a terrifying minute because he was seriously afraid that I would try the Amsterdam trick again. Actually, I was close to it, because I was still undecided as I was ten metres away from the spot. Then I thought, *Schwarzer is a smart keeper and he'll definitely have studied our penalty takers.* So he'd know everything about me, starting with the most famous of my penalties: better not to give him the chance to make him look clever, leaving me looking like an idiot. I put the ball on the spot and decided: top left, just under the crossbar, inside the angle, let's go.

There and then, I didn't think about anything other than the mechanics of the shot, but since the referee – I only looked at him, carefully avoiding Schwarzer – was taking a while to blow his whistle, something shifted inside me, to ease the tension that had mounted to crazy levels. Suddenly I was six years old again. I was in front of my old school and was playing Ducks. I had to take down the last one to win the game. The thought flashed for a moment, a flash of lightning to illuminate: *Our whole mission rests in this shot.* I didn't know if we'd survive extra time. Ten against eleven for a long time is agony. Medina Cantalejo whistled while I was still looking at him. I was as focused as I'd ever been in my life. *Go, Francesco. Go and finish it.*

The bomb in my head went off when I saw the net bulge, because that was the moment of certainty. I was so crushed by the pressure that I didn't even trust my eyes. Maybe the ball crossing the goal line was an optical illusion and Schwarzer's hand could still reach it. But the net bulging was the final seal. The ball had gone in, and nothing could take it out again. I'd done it. Duck downed.

I stuck my thumb in my mouth as I was already starting to laugh. Not to smile, to really laugh, because that was the moment when everything came back: the injury, the fear, the anxiety of not making it, the crutches, the race against time. Everything came back and solidified in that moment of absolute joy. One of the three most beautiful and important moments of my sporting life, I'd say.

I looked for Ilary with my eyes. I knew more or less where she was, but before I could pick her out, one, three, ten, all my teammates were on me, and we collapsed into each other's arms.

'We're winning this World Cup!' someone shouted, and immediately the call was echoed: 'Yeah, we're going to win!' and 'No one's stopping us!' and 'We're the best!' A crazy elation. We were past the 95th minute, and the referee didn't even let the game restart. After some unprecedented suffering, we were in the quarter-finals.

Lippi smiled at me like a father. Even his journey at dawn from Viareggio to arrive at Villa Stuart early one morning in February had suddenly found its deeper meaning. I told him that I was back scoring again after the injury, he applauded slowly and theatrically: 'Well done, you really chose the right moment.'

When I was an altar boy as a child and listened a little distractedly to the sermons of the priest, there was a passage from the Gospel that really didn't sit well with me, the one with the camel passing through the eye of a needle. I simply couldn't understand how this was possible until the concept of a metaphor was explained to me and everything fell into place, including the story of the camel. Safe to re-emerge from some forgotten corner of the mind on the night of the Australia game, with the adrenaline still coursing round me, stopping me from falling asleep, and my thoughts returning to the penalty. A shot that for me was generally simple, but not in such conditions: to withstand the pressure, I'd had to call on all my reserves of mental strength. So, with a great deal of effort and my pulse racing, squeezing and contorting myself, I passed through the eye of the needle.

Finally I fell asleep, exhausted. Happy. The last thought was the same as that of my teammates: now let's go and win this.

13.

'Go. Score. Win.'

THE PSYCHOLOGICAL CHANGING OF THE SEASON – FROM THE hope of advancing in the tournament to the awareness of being able to win it – transformed our day-to-day life. Until the Round of 16, the continual build-up to matches was experienced with agitation: from then on, the team seemed to be suffering from a fever, and games coming quickly after one another – there were only four days between Australia and Ukraine as well – contributed to increasing the squad's heart rate. We were no longer waiting for our opponents, we were going out to meet them with a limitless desire to beat them. Not just to beat them, which is a truism in a knockout game, I mean *really* beat them, with a slightly cheeky addition of enjoying testing our strength, convinced as we were of asserting it. Lippi increased his cautionary warnings, because the risk of not taking Ukraine seriously was very high, but I believe that, deep down, he had the same feelings as we did.

And if we needed more motivation, it came at lunchtime the day after the game with Australia, when we were still all over the place after not getting back until late the previous night. Cannavaro and Zambrotta brought it to us, having just had a call from Turin: if they hadn't said it in that voice, grave and quivering at the same time, a stupid joke would have come to mind. 'This morning, Gianluca Pessotto jumped from the second floor of the Juve headquarters. He's in hospital in a coma.'

Among the many shows of solidarity that can arise on a football field, there's a very special one that concerns the penalty takers in a shoot-out.

You're waiting there, inside the centre circle, for it to be your turn. At that point in the contest – I can't call it a game, technically that's over – the pressure is very strong, and it's inevitable that your gaze will run down the line of your teammates to end up looking towards the opposition, and then return to your own side. It's a duel. There are searches for signs of courage among friends and signs of fear among the opponents. It's essential that whoever is wearing your shirt is a solid, mentally strong person. Someone who doesn't tremble, who doesn't succumb to the emotions of the moment. My thoughts were on exactly this as I processed the terrible news, while the others shouted their no's and were rushing around Gigi, Fabio, Ciro and the other Juventini asking the classic question of such situations: why, why, why?

I thought of the terrible, roaring minutes of Amsterdam, six years before, when we were in a penalty shoot-out for a place in the final of the European Championships, against co-hosts Holland. I thought of Pessottino walking towards the spot before me – he was the second penalty taker, I was the third – and I remembered his relaxed walk while he was going through hell inside, as we all were in that situation. I remembered the strength that he conveyed to me with his calm wait for the whistle, with Van der Sar trying to put him off by moving those incredibly long arms, and the effortlessness with which he hit it flat, wrong-footing him. Then he turned and clenched his fist for a long moment, the only visible manifestation of that inner storm that he let out. Coming back to midfield, smiling, he passed Stam, who, bewildered by so much confidence, by so much psychological solidity, would miss his shot, making my chip much easier.

What must have happened for a man with this strength of character to lose his way so completely? So tragically? Someone was talking about depression following his retirement, others about problems at home, but for once the shock and pain far outweighed curiosity, and in short, our only thoughts turned towards knowing how he was. No one dared to say it in those hours, but inwardly we were asking ourselves if he'd be able to pull through.

Gianluca had just ended his career, leaving a lasting memory among teammates and opponents alike of talent and sportsmanship. A strong opponent, first with Torino and then with Juve, but one who you embraced with joy and emotion both before and after the game. He could foul you as well, he was a defender, but if you went down, he would invariably stay there with his hand extended to help you get back up.

I heard that the federation were hurriedly preparing a private flight because Cannavaro was desperate to go and visit him in hospital, and another couple of teammates intended to join him. It was a good thing to do and the right thing to do. Before leaving the camp, Fabio called us together: 'Look, I'm going to promise him that we'll beat Ukraine so we can dedicate the victory to him.' Deep down I thought I'd have gladly done that regardless, but with such an extreme motivation, the Ukrainians lost any remaining chance they had.

After the second game in Kaiserslautern, we returned to Hamburg, where we'd been before. During the flight, I again found myself thinking that Lippi was right once again: despite the fact that I had still found a way to make myself useful (ahem ahem), playing only twenty minutes against Australia allowed me to recover all the energy I'd lost during the group stage. If we really were to get to the final, we'd be facing three games in ten days. Envy had gnawed at me over being benched, but by then I was almost grateful for it. I'd had the classic narrow horizon of a footballer, who struggled to look beyond the ninety minutes. Coaches, who must have a much wider view, pay for it with much more stress. Look at them, sometimes it's frightening: in just a few months they lose their hair, get fat, talk in isolation, feel like they're in everyone's sights. Most of the time they're right, like Lippi was that time, but what an effort it is to make us realise that…

Ukraine were clearly weaker than us, and the widespread opinion in the dressing room was that we'd beat them even if we played at seventy percent. Of course we didn't tell the coach that, he'd have flipped out at us if he knew, but at no time did our self-awareness seem presumptuous to me. The team was now mature enough to approach games without the need for false modesty. I'll add something else: before going out onto the pitch for the warm up, many of us took advantage of the screens in the dressing room area to follow the penalty shoot-out in Germany-Argentina with bated breath to find out our semi-final opponents. I should add 'potential', I know, but honestly the idea of going out didn't even suggest itself to us at that moment. Far from it. Most of us were openly cheering for the Germans, and I won't say we hugged each other when Cambiasso missed the last penalty, but the atmosphere was more than satisfied and there were even a few high-fives.

Argentina were a more technical team, we feared them, because there were youngsters not in the starting line up who everyone was talking about: from Carlos Tévez, who was already quite well known, to the young prodigy at Barcelona, Leo Messi. Those who had seen him live promised that he really was the new Maradona. It wasn't like the other times that some Argentine kid had been likened to the great Diego, only to collapse under the absurd comparison. This time it was a different story, and Messi really was the prodigy that was talked about, but in 2006, at least in my eyes, he was still a prospect, because – after getting injured at the end of winter – he hadn't been able to play in the decisive games in the Champions League, won by Barça.

In any case, Germany were better for us, partly because our tradition of beating them weighed heavily on them at the World Cup. But first we had to beat Ukraine, and at the moment we went out onto the pitch, I saw the same determination in the eyes of Andriy Shevchenko that had grown in me: *It's now or never, at thirty years old, the World Cup to win is this one.* The difference was that he – a brilliant forward – didn't have the teammates to aim for the title. I did.

We scored after just six minutes, and the credit was partly mine because, with a well-directed backheel, I avoided the usual kick from Andriy Gusin and returned the one-two with Zambrotta, setting him up for a left-footed shot. The move was rapid and effective: Gianluca's shot was sharp and precise, and the goalkeeper Oleksandr Shovkovskiy dived a moment too late and couldn't reach it. 1-0 to us, and the semi-final was so close it felt as if I could almost touch it.

Actually, our sense of superiority caused us a few headaches. At this level, the World Cup quarter-finals, the slightest relaxation is noticed and attacked. The defence always managed to keep Shevchenko at a safe distance, but in order to mark him with more men we were forced to leave spaces open elsewhere, and Maksym Kalynychenko almost took advantage of that at the start of the second half, when Buffon did really well to turn a low shot from him onto the post.

I interpreted this chance as a signal: we needed to get a move on and make it 2-0. At a corner from the left, I called Grosso for a one-two, based on a move that we'd practised in training: he passed it back to me perfectly, and with my right foot I found the perfect cross that dropped the ball onto Luca Toni's head. To tell the truth, Cannavaro tried to steal it off him by leaping for the same ball, but his jump was slightly mistimed. Toni did well to get his head to it, and again it was the movement of the net that confirmed to me that it was mission accomplished. Yes, it's over now. An exchange between Pirlo and Zambrotta freed Toni again for 3-0, we were well ahead, and I enjoyed the scenario that had arisen. I'd set up two goals and, aside from the penalty against Australia, this had been the match in which I contributed the most. At the end of the game I smiled as I too, together with my teammates, raised a tricolour flag on which we'd written 'Pessottino, we're with you.' I owed it to him for the calmness that he'd guaranteed me in Amsterdam. I owed it to him because I was very fond of him.

We left Hamburg that night, and by the time we arrived in our hotel in Duisberg it was almost dawn on Saturday 1 July. The countdown of the days was nearly over: the semi-final against Germany was scheduled for Tuesday evening in Dortmund, and there the road forked: either you went to Stuttgart on Saturday for third place, or you went to Berlin on Sunday for the title.

In any case, the victory over Ukraine gave us the certainty that we were going all the way, and this in itself was very satisfying. Vito told me that after so many negative words – it was even written that I'd play in a wheelchair – journalists were starting to realise that I was doing significant things. Thank God. I let him do the press review for me. I didn't want to get distracted or create any bad blood about certain preconceived criticisms. I was fully aware of what had been written after Daniele's sending off: *Two years before, it was Totti spitting, now it's De Rossi's elbow, these Romans are unreliable, they can't keep their nerves under control.* To be clear, there's nothing to argue about with those incidents, but it's an entirely separate thing to go from there and consider them a genetic defect of those who are born in Rome.

The transition from sympathetic outsider to opponent – indeed, enemy – of Germany was sudden and immediately perceptible. After the final whistle against Ukraine, everyone looked at us differently: the organisational volunteers, the police who escorted us, the airport staff. And then there were the personnel at the training camp in Duisburg, all Italian, who loaded us with pressure from the opposite direction: if we beat Germany, it would be the best day of their lives, but if we got knocked out, it would be a mortal blow. On Saturday we even tried to leave the retreat, which was open to families that day, but I hadn't gone two hundred metres before I decided to go back, because a walk was impossible: the area had been invaded by our fans, and if on the one hand you can understand how much hope and how much enthusiasm we'd managed to stimulate in Italy, on the other hand, you couldn't pay attention to everyone. Better to stay in the hotel.

Lippi sensed that the tension was rising, and to soften it he concocted a joke at the expense of Angelo Peruzzi. Before telling it, I have to briefly describe Angelo, a dear friend with whom I played in countless games, though almost always on opposing sides given that, after having grown up together at Roma, he played for Juve and then for Lazio, our two main rivals, for many years. Angelo is what they call – in a good way, mind you – a beast. He has an explosive physique, biceps as big as thighs, and if he pins you to a wall you can't move a muscle. Luckily he's a good-natured person because otherwise he could do a lot of damage. Since he's a very proud guy, it's easy to drag him into things: one evening, for example, in a pizzeria, we challenged him to fold a pizza eight times and cram it down. He obviously agreed – he always agrees – and I won't tell you how he ruined his shirt in the – successful – attempt to win the bet.

There are some crazy rumours about Angelo, who grew up in the Viterbese countryside, like the one that he can kill a wild boar with his bare hands, just with a punch. One feat which he often boasts about is knowing how to catch fish using just his hands, thanks to his lightning reflexes and iron grip. It's an art that he practised in his local streams. In short, he's a beast.

In the garden of the Duisburg hotel was a large pond, which we would sit around during our free time. The water was genuinely disgusting: very dirty, silty, practically sludge. This didn't stop a fairly large colony of fish from swimming in it: when there was fish on the menu, there were inevitable quips that the cook had caught what ended up on our plates from that pond. Jokingly, because not even he was desperate to go in, Peruzzi was tormented from day one: 'Show me you can catch them without a harpoon!'

So, let's go back to that Saturday and to Lippi, who had decided to ease the tension a little. Basically, without being seen by anyone, he went into the kitchen and, with the help of a waiter, impaled a lovely sea bream, fresh from the market, on a carving fork. Then, on the sly, while we were still having our massages, he placed the fish in a strategic point in the pond, memorising its position. After eating (and having warned us), he went up to Peruzzi, telling him that he'd gone too far with his tales of catching fish with his hands, that it wasn't so difficult, and that he too was perfectly capable of doing it. 'Like anyone from Viareggio,' he explained, and the challenge was officially laid down. Angelo laughed heartily. 'Look, boss, you don't know what you're letting yourself in for. It's not easy at all, you'll see…'

Of course, the whole party set off for the pond. Peruzzi stood at the edges with his arms folded while Lippi, after taking off his shoes and rolling up his tracksuit trousers, stepped in cautiously and started to zigzag towards the point where he'd immersed his prey. When he saw a fish go by, he plunged his hands into the water, and as soon as he brought them out empty with a disappointed grimace, Peruzzi's laughter boomed loudly. 'I told you, boss. Look at this, we'll be here all night.' Then came the money shot: the coach sank his hands into the pond again, started to shake them around to make a little foam, and finally squeezed them tightly around the fish, pretending to make a huge effort not to let it slip from between his hands. This was all falsely dramatic, as it allowed Lippi to remove the carving fork, but Angelo's apprehension was growing: 'Wait, what, he's got it?' I heard him muttering to himself, looking much less amused than before. And when the coach triumphantly pulled the fish out of the sludge, triggering a roar from the now sizeable crowd, Peruzzi didn't know whether to laugh or cry. We laughed like crazy, and the good mood returned immediately.

That same Saturday, more news arrived to jolt the atmosphere: the elimination of Brazil, who had lost their quarter-final in Frankfurt to France, 1-0 to a goal from Thierry Henry. We were all in front of the TV, and at a certain point we start trying to bring them bad luck. The result was surprising, because after a slow start, the reigning champions seemed to have picked up speed, and since the previous year – when they won the Confederations Cup in style – everyone had considered them clear favourites: Ronaldo, Ronaldinho, Kaká and Adriano up front, plus old acquaintances like Dida, Cafu and Roberto Carlos. A great squad who we were very happy not to have had on our side of the draw, and who we all imagined would be our likely opponents if we reached the final. The fact that we'd seen them go out like this, while we were still well in the tournament, was a relief: satisfied with the outcome of the jinxing, many commented by saying 'One less,' and I was among them. But we did so without thinking that although Brazil were disappearing, there was still a France side that was coming on strongly, and our previous meetings with them – I'm talking about recent ones – still hurt.

The Italian journalists told me about the controversies instigated by the Germans over Thorsten Frings' suspension – they said that we solicited it – the usual teasing about pizza eaters (as if they didn't like pizza: that month I saw more pizzerias than bars), in short, some psychological warfare that didn't affect me in the slightest, given that I don't understand German and had no interest in going into the subject further. Gattuso took it more personally, and seasoned our endless games of *scopa* with some comments on our opponents' media strategy, which evidently someone was showing him. On Sunday he snapped and asked to go to the press conference, where he gave the Germans a piece of his mind for having disrespected the Italians. We applauded him when he returned, but more because we were entertained than argumentative. In the meantime, mayhem had broken out as our hotel had become a harbour for journalists, FIFA staff, relatives and above all hundreds of loafers who were wandering around in search of a ticket, an autograph, fifteen minutes of fame. When the crowds got out of control, arrangements were made for a security guard to police the area reserved for us players, with access allowed only to those waiters who we knew, and only at our request. You never knew, we were still playing against the hosts.

The Germans' strategy to make us nervous also extended to the hotel in Dortmund. Normally, nights before a game are spent in large international hotels that reserve a wing for the squad and visiting delegation. This time, however,we were sent to an awful three-star one, small and cramped, so covered with carpets that if one of us were allergic to something he'd be screwed. But it was a slight that only psyched us up more. We said it to ourselves openly: 'They're so afraid of us they want to stop us from resting,' and it was all a joke for us to give us courage, to increase the state of fervour. The tension was very high, and yet, incredibly, that night we slept. So much for the three stars and the carpets...

Tuesday 4 July 2006. One of the questions I'm often asked is what I'd give to relive the emotions of that day. Would I pay a million euros? The question is obviously an idle one, but the answer I give is absolutely serious. If the happy ending wasn't guaranteed, no: the very idea of being able to end that day by losing the semi-final would be far too much to bear. But if someone could guarantee that I'd feel the same emotions again and get the same ending, I'd give up even two million euros because there hasn't been another day in which I've felt more alive, dynamic, vibrant, illuminated. It's like walking on the Moon: ask one of the astronauts who have been there what he'd do to do it again... Anything, as long as he can be sure of getting back to Earth again.

Borussia Dortmund's stadium is wonderful because at first, when you enter it, it doesn't seem that huge, but you gradually realise how big it is as you get closer to the middle of the pitch. I'd played there before in a friendly with Roma, but it wasn't full at the time. The impression it gave me that day, bursting with support and hopes and fears even two hours before kick off, was simply sensational. I thought to myself that the Germans had set up a wonderful theatre to celebrate their arrival in the final, and that the disappointment if we went through instead would be brutal. During our walk around the pitch to familiarise ourselves with the environment, I looked for the segment of the stands reserved for our fans.

Naturally, it was small, but it was easily visible (and during the game I'd notice flags almost everywhere): I gestured a greeting and a roar went up. They were fired up too.

When you mentally prepare for a very difficult away game – and that match was the peak of my career in that respect: I never played in such a hostile atmosphere again – there's nothing that heartens you like the sight of your own fans. It's something to do with risk, even if your safety is guaranteed, and with the discomfort of finding yourself alone against everyone. Your people have followed you because they don't want to let you walk alone, as Liverpool's anthem goes. Wonderful. The more the opponents jeer yours to drown out their enthusiasm, the more the desire to win for them grows inside you, to repay them for the sacrifice that they've made to be there at your side. When you play at home, there's never such perfect harmony. In the toughest away games, however, the distances between those who play and those who support are reduced a lot, to the point that you really think of yourselves as being under the same banner. You play for your fans because you want to see them leave the stadium with their heads held high, happy, followed by the disappointed and envious gazes of the other side's supporters.

In that segment of the stand were my parents, Silvia – Ilary hadn't been able to come – uncles and other relatives, a few friends. I couldn't make them out, you could only get so close. But I knew they were there, and that was enough for me. Meanwhile, the usually tolerant German police had chased our ticketless kit men from the field, even though they were wearing their named accreditation, complete with photo, around their necks. In the other games, they'd been allowed to sit on their containers, behind the bench, but this time there was no flexibility. There were looks of intimidation, a brawl was dangerously close, but the nerves held.

We're off! We got into the game immediately, and we attacked continuously and with personality. I found excellent spaces between the lines, and after a well taken free kick, but which didn't cause Jens Lehmann any trouble, came the chance I'd been waiting for. I received the ball just beyond the halfway line and instantly saw that the German defensive line was 'unbalanced' because a full back was out of position. Perrotta also saw the gap between the centre backs and raced for it determinedly. Neither

Michael Ballack nor Arne Friedrich were close enough to block my pass, which landed perfectly in front of my teammate. It was a regular move at Roma. I held my breath hopefully. Every time he renewed his contract, Simone hugged me, telling me, 'All thanks to the perfect balls you give me.' But this time his second touch was a bit heavy, and it allowed Lehmann to come out with great timing and close down the angles. Too bad, it would have been a really great assist.

A few minutes later, Pirlo took a free kick from the right after giving me the predetermined signal: against Ukraine I had hit my shot way over, but this time I considered my body's position more carefully to keep the ball low, freed myself by pushing off... Materazzi and hit it well. But the area was too crowded, it ended up hitting Cannavaro. The fact that it was our two centre backs who were blocking me off in the German penalty area is a good indication of the drive pushing us on in that hostile atmosphere: Germany were strong and their fans believed in them, but the pressure wasn't just crushing us. On the contrary. The feeling was that they had a few more fears, and that our rampant start had worried them further: Klinsmann was gesticulating a lot – I often passed in front of his bench – but rather than tactical instructions, it seemed to me that he was trying to instil courage in those who were lacking it. Lippi, on the other hand, was very calm. We reached half time with the clear sensation that we were ahead on points. A shame it wasn't boxing.

'You have to win it in ninety minutes,' the coach said, moving between one bench and the other. 'You have the chance, you're playing better. Keep it up, you've got the legs to do it, you've been working for more than a month to win this game, nothing can take it away from you.'

The second half was more balanced, and there were a couple of times when Buffon had to remind the Germans how good he is. On a couple of occasions, Grosso and Perrotta got close to their keeper, but Lehmann really was a marvel at coming out, and in both cases he blocked our attackers' best efforts.

End of normal time. Halfway through the second half, Gilardino had replaced Toni. Lippi joined us at the bench while we were taking on water. 'Now Iaquinta's coming on for Camoranesi. We aren't changing our set-up, Vincenzo is fresh and when they have the ball he can cover the wing.

But I want to send the signal that we'll keep attacking because this match must be won before penalties, we're so much more dangerous than them.'

He was correct in his evaluation, and in that first extra period, first Gilardino hit the post after a good counter-attack and then Zambrotta hit the crossbar with a shot from distance. The balance was tipping more and more in our favour. Del Piero also came on in place of Perrotta. In the final break, very short yet invaluable, I realised that we'd got a goalkeeper, four defenders, four attackers, a *regista* and poor Gattuso on the pitch. A vein was throbbing in Lippi's neck. 'Finish them. Now. They've got nothing left in the tank now, they're only dreaming of penalties. But you mustn't give them that because you've been the better team, and they mustn't get another chance. The two midfields don't exist anymore, it's attack against defence, and our defence is unbeatable. Go. Score. Win!'

Returning to the middle of the pitch, I suddenly felt that the noise in the stadium was less intense, and it was mainly our fans who could be heard. The Germans' fear was palpable, almost tangible. Gattuso gestured to me to 'listen' to that silence, he'd noticed it too. I clenched my fists. Now we had to act fast.

The last fifteen minutes passed as Lippi had predicted, end to end: they attacked and collided with Buffon, who saved the most venomous shot of the evening from Podolski; we attacked and gave the impression of having the greater danger. But it wasn't enough. Time was running out. Pirlo tried a great shot from outside the area after a quick move forward, but Lehmann was ready and turned it behind for a corner. He never seemed anywhere near that good when he was playing for Milan...

The dynamics of the move had brought me to the middle of the penalty area, where I'd called for a pass from Andrea. Del Piero was freshest, so he ran over to the corner flag to take it, even though it wasn't his job. Pirlo had stayed in the middle of the D, Zambrotta – another corner taker – had joined him, stopping to the right of centre, while Gilardino had placed himself in front of me, forcing me to take a few steps back, beyond the penalty spot. Grosso headed over towards Ale to offer him the short option. Materazzi and Cannavaro arrived too, they were always there for corners, while Iaquinta set himself in the six-yard box, the closest player to the goal line. From the bench, the signal came that there were two minutes to go. Two minutes until penalties. The siren was about to go off.

Let's pause the scene and look at it like a still life. The number of blue shirts that were part of it speaks for itself: there were nine of us. Missing was Buffon, who was waiting midway inside our half, and Gattuso, who was inside the centre circle. If the Germans counter-attacked at speed, he would have had to face two or three of them by himself. It wouldn't have been long before some of us could have got back – I don't know with what strength – to help him, but initially, Rino would have been alone. Tactical madness, in the 118th minute of a World Cup semi-final against the hosts, but there are few moments like this in life, unconditional moments in which you feel like you're capable of facing any test.

Beyond being a story of footballers, this is a story of men. Take Gattuso. Aside from the fact that he was technically better than is commonly thought, I've never known a player who was more willing to make sacrifices than him. This meant toiling on the pitch, which everyone saw, but also – so as not to be missed, and this was perceived by few – playing through pain that would have kept others not on the bench but at home on the sofa. Rino is a man who gets excited when he feels like someone he cares about needs him. He's the first one you'd always want by your side because you'd know you'd have nothing to fear, he'd be there to protect you. And on that day he was there, waiting for any three Germans racing towards Buffon, and he'd come up with something to stop them. Now, it was up to all of us to get into the box, because it was time to finish it.

Del Piero sent his cross into the middle, Friedrich got there ahead of Gilardino with his head but the clearance had no power. The ball landed in the D, where Pirlo was unmarked, and he only needed one touch to control it. It was there, seeing as he's a genius, that his journey began.

I must have rewatched that goal thousands of times, and I'm regularly ecstatic. Andrea caressed the ball four times, moving it from left to right, parallel to a line of German defenders who were thinking about closing off the gap instead of tackling him. I've always thought of it like a train station at rush hour, with trains passing through all the time, and for a brief moment you can see from one platform to another before it disappears again. The 'window' for the pass to Grosso opened up at the fifth touch, which is a no-look assist like you see in basketball, not football. By that point I'd retreated from the middle of the area to its edge, to provide Andrea with an alternative option if he were to turn around at the end of his run. Even I, standing behind him with no Germans in front of me, didn't immediately notice his pass, because he doesn't move a single muscle in his body in Grosso's direction, except for his right foot. I was just able to react in time to focus on Fabio's perfect left-footed shot, the arced trajectory that gives Lehmann no chance, the glory of the moment when the net barely moves, it's so tense.

Honestly, I don't remember anything of the moments after Grosso's goal. Fabio immediately ran towards the middle of the pitch, and in the videos you can see Buffon coming at him like a rocket. I must have chased after Pirlo, bewitched by his pass, but in that sea of joy and excitement I could have done anything: there were clusters of blue shirts everywhere on the pitch, not just those who were playing but all twenty-three plus the staff, the masseurs, the kit men. Poor Lippi, after allowing himself a brief but irrepressible celebration, had a lot to do to 'reconnect' us to the game with all haste, because there was at least another minute to go, maybe two with injury time. Gattuso helped him with a couple of loud yells that finally woke us up. We were back in shape. Smiling, but in shape.

When the result that you were chasing materialises at the end of a game (and it's impossible to get closer to the end than this), you usually experience the moments that separate you from the final whistle with a mixture of exaltation and terror. The reason for the first is obvious. The reason for the second is also obvious; if you concede an equaliser after having done so much hard work to get your head in front, all that's left is to bash it against a wall. This time, though, I wasn't afraid. It was strange, or perhaps it was the fruit of the spectacular confidence that had grown inside us in that month. We couldn't lose.

In the dying seconds of time remaining, Germany launched a ball into the box as they had to, but Cannavaro first cleared it with his head – and his was a powerful clearance – then went in with his head again to take it off Podolski who, disheartened, had miscontrolled it. And he was in such a trance of omnipotence, Fabio, that he wanted to take it from there all the way to Lehmann.

Luckily his run brought him practically straight to me, and in my position I decided what the best thing to do was. In fact, I'd already got an idea, seeing as Gilardino had attacked the space and Del Piero was arriving at full speed from deep. But I was forced to give Cannavaro a big shove to get hold of the ball, a sort of necessarily decisive 'Let me do it!' Fabio didn't even have time to realise it before my ball – ah yes, it's mine now – was flying quickly and precisely towards Gilardino. Who, like me, had realised that Del Piero was three times as fast as anyone else. He waited for him to pull alongside him to release him in his turn, and Ale's magnificent sidefoot shot with his right curled around Lehmann into the top corner. It was a great way to get revenge after the mistakes of Rotterdam, a beautiful and well-deserved goal. I was delighted for him, because the truth is that we've always spurred each other on.

Dortmund's stadium was overwhelmed by a bigger, supreme pain, a negative emotion that was so intense it short-circuited it. I was one of the first to reach Ale to hug him. The game was over, our fans were going wild, and yet what has stayed with me after so many years is that striking silence. Losing a World Cup at home is an unspeakable torment.

14.

Final Insomnia

THE RETURN TO THE DRESSING ROOM WAS LESS CHAOTIC than you might think, because while we were obviously in party mode, everything around us was shrouded in a deathly silence. We'd really done it, but I'd be a liar if I said that we restrained ourselves in those moments out of sensitivity towards the Germans...

Instead, I feared that I'd twisted the knife in the wound, but without ill will. Simply put, we were all drunk on happiness and tiredness, a dangerous mix because it takes away all your inhibitions. I'll tell you this: after a bit of singing and dancing had finished and all the fruit in the dressing room had been eaten, I plunged into the cold water pool to reinvigorate myself. I resurfaced, and above me was the menacing shadow of Peruzzi, naked and armed with a massage table, raised above his head. What the hell was he doing with it? Before I'd had time to ask myself the question, Angelo threw it into the water. Fortunately his aim was precise and the table sank between me and the edge of the pool with a huge splash; if he'd hit me, it would have smashed me in half. I looked at Angelo in amazement, but he'd already walked away, laughing joyously. I got out of the pool quickly, before his enthusiasm made him think of throwing a locker in there too.

Get changed. Mixed zone. Interviews. The routine of international matches is different when you reach these levels, because on the other side of the mic, the Italian journalists – the ones you've known forever – were in a clear minority compared to the dozens and dozens from other countries. Of course, each of them thrust their recording device or phone at your face to get a few words. You have to stop somewhere, and it was in those moments that the pain of Germany appeared to me in all its considerable size, because the World Cup volunteers were also there and, as always, were escorting and directing us, and these were people who had dreamed of a different outcome that evening.

I remember one girl in particular who, while she was leading me from one picket line of journalists to another – telling me which countries they were from as much as she could – was barely holding back her tears, and when I looked at her, she furtively turned her head away so as not to let me see her bloodshot eyes. It was a game – I'd like to have told her – and tonight we were the better side. Nonsense, because obviously there was nothing to explain and still less to apologise for. But walking next to her, accompanied by her sadness until the coach, it felt natural to me to have a more composed attitude. Measured smiles instead of raucous laughter. Thumbs-up instead of noisy high fives. I patted her on the head as I left. Who knows if she realised my embarrassment.

I didn't see any of my relatives. They came to Dortmund on a whistle-stop charter flight, one of those airport-stadium-airport ones, and by then they'd already be flying back to Italy, busy planning the big expedition for the final. It's strange to say it, because it almost seems like an ugly sentiment, but I didn't miss them much because at those times, you feel as though your family is your squad, your teammates, the group with whom you've just fought until the very end. And with whom you've won. The almost physical need for real family starts a minute after a defeat, after an elimination, when the competitive charm is broken and you realise that you haven't spent an hour with your wife and children for more than a month, and the very thought seems absurd to you. But as long as you're still in the tournament, and maybe you've reached the final by going through an extreme experience like beating the hosts, you live in a bubble of warlike celebration, where there's only room for you and your teammates.

On the return flight to Düsseldorf – and from there to Duisburg – Lippi decided that we deserved a reward and gave us the green light to all the junk food that had been banned since the first day of the training camp: mini pizzas, crisps, chocolate, fizzy drinks – there was an assault on the baskets. They had probably been packed to alleviate the disappointment of a possible elimination, but the boss – thrilled by our feat – decided to give them to us anyway.

Be that as it may, it was a real party, which continued up to the hotel, until two in the morning, when we finally managed to cross its threshold. Waiting for us were Azzurri fans as far as the eye could see, the newspapers said there were ten thousand: at the airport, in the streets of Duisburg, outside the hotel. They were Italians on holiday, but also and above all Italians from Germany, emerging from the shadows to celebrate their national team, happy twice over because we'd knocked out Germany. You sense many things, looking at that joy outside the window, those flags being waved frenetically as we passed by, and it moves you a little. In short, you feel good, you understand that you've done something wonderful for a lot of people. You balance the thought of the German girl who was almost in tears with another about your jubilant compatriots. You've probably given them some revenge. Yes, that's how it has to be.

The hotel staff finished illustrating this by welcoming us with a stadium chant. There must have been four hundred people in the lobby, our 'extended family' with our loved ones, friends of Gattuso, relatives of Gilardino, people who you're used to greeting with affection and enthusiasm. Lippi was visibly exhausted and went up to his room shouting at us not to stay up too late, but no one slept that night: in the area reserved for us – the restaurant, bar and games room – the lights stayed on until dawn. The next day's training session, reserved for those who didn't play, was wisely arranged for the afternoon.

Wednesday. The day after the night before. It was a free day, but hardly anyone went out. It would have been impossible: half of Italy was pouring into Duisburg before continuing on to Berlin. Once again, I don't know what I'd have done without Vito: we took half an hour to work out how many tickets I needed – obviously after hearing from Ilary and Mum – and the final tally was scary. After drawing a line through all the 'non-essentials', which is an ugly way to say it but I can't think of another, I still had a hundred names. A hundred tickets, not one less. I asked the FIGC's general manager Antonello Valentini for help. He first rolled his eyes and then promised me that he'd do his best. Having started the most complicated job together, Vito took control of the situation: 'From now on I'll take care of it. You must only think about the final.' I could never be grateful enough to him for that.

There were two long parts to that day. The first, after breakfast, consisted of reading websites and online newspapers that told the story of how Italy poured out onto the streets to celebrate the win. A beautiful feeling. With the calm of the day off, I savoured the scale of the feat and its effects to the full. Many of us were sat behind our laptops, and from one room to another – all the doors were open – we called out recommendations to a website, a photo gallery, some coverage of the night in Italy that we'd just discovered. We were warriors who were resting briefly, but we'd already be back in combat mode that evening: France-Portugal, the other semi-final, was on the television, and we all gathered for dinner in front of the big screen. Needless to say, we were supporting the Portuguese: they had excellent players like Deco and Figo, as well as the highly promising Cristiano Ronaldo, but pound for pound there was no comparison with France. Who won, in fact, by the bare minimum: a penalty from Zidane to secure a 1-0 win. Them again, then. I wasn't afraid. I think fate had decided to give us some revenge.

Thursday. Vito assured me that the tickets would turn up in the end, and he was speaking to Italy to organise the transport. If I had had to do that, I wouldn't have had time to train. That day on the bus, going to the pitch, I chatted a little with Buffon, as I often did: if I have to think of my best friend in the national team, I think of him, a dependable and sincere man, very frank and quietly crazy, which doesn't hurt. We're almost the same age, teammates in all the Azzurri youth teams, and as youngsters we even shared a room. And now, still together, we were marching towards a World Cup final. The sense of the talk that day was 'Look at how far we've come,' but it wasn't expressed directly. It would have been banal. Instead, we enjoyed remembering incidents that happened off the pitch, such as a tournament in Spain with the Under-18s, when one night we jumped from the balcony on the first floor to go dancing: said like that it doesn't sound difficult, but you try carrying Coco on crutches with you. He'd got injured during a game, but the mere mention of a nightclub was enough to find him in tow. Gigi practically had to 'parry' him to allow him to land without doing more damage to himself. We had a good laugh thinking back about it, a great antidote to the growing tension.

Friday. The hundred tickets had arrived: the federation gave me twenty while I paid for eighty, and that was absolutely fine because the most important thing was that the whole gang were going to be there on Sunday.

I celebrated by playing *scopa* with Gattuso, sitting cross-legged on the bed, and we repeated the same gestures almost robotically. I believe that, after the World Cup started, Rino and I exchanged more points tallies than words. Even better was that we both suspected the other of cheating and so threw down insults together with each hand. Great times.

Going onto the pitch, even a month after our arrival in Germany, the person who continued to lead the group was Cannavaro, as funny and playful off the pitch as he was determined in training. With him there were no light training games, he went in on everyone as if it were a real match and if you weren't quick enough to pull your leg back, you risked taking a whack. There was also another, among us, who was working doubly hard. Daniele. His suspension reduced with each round until it was fully served. As we'd told him to encourage and convince him not to go back to Italy, we'd reached the final to have him available again. To give him another chance. He felt the debt of honour very strongly, and after days of silence had started talking again, getting involved in discussions, living with the group. I didn't know if Lippi had anything in store for him, but if he did, he'd find him ready for sure.

Saturday. The training session the day before the game was early in the morning. There was a plane to Berlin to catch. The excitement around us was at its peak. The staff who had served us all month saw us off as if we were going to war. It was moving. Vito had managed the flow of arrivals from Italy as well as possible, only the edges of it reached me. On the flight, I spent a bit of time with Nesta, who had remained with us despite the injury in the third game that ruled him out. If Buffon was a brother to me, Sandro was my twin. We'd always got on well because we're similar: calm, very reserved. Not infrequently, at difficult points for one or other of us, we'd call each other secretly to confide in each other and exchange advice without it getting around. There had always been a good air between us, a healthy atmosphere, and this was why I was doubly sorry about his absence: he also deserved to experience this fully, but Sandro was always unfortunate with the national team and got injured before other important occasions. This was destiny, too.

The hotel in Berlin was very luxurious, real compensation after the dump in Dortmund. There was only time for us to settle ourselves in before the bus to the stadium was ready: initial reconnaissance and a quick run out, a press conference from Lippi and Cannavaro, and a quick and silent walk through the mixed zone. Our desire to speak was close to zero. It wasn't the time.

As the hours passed, the thought of the final penetrated deeper and deeper. Some became more taciturn than usual, others sought company because they didn't want to be alone. At dinner we joked as always, but really a little less than always. You could feel the tension. Lippi postponed all tactical discussions until the following day, since there was little to find out. We knew France by heart even if, compared to that damned European Championship final of six years previously, only Cannavaro, Del Piero, Zambrotta, Inzaghi, Nesta and I had remained in the squad.

The boss lingered in the hall for a few minutes longer than usual. His family were probably already there while I and many of my teammates had to wait for our loved ones until the next day. Then, before going up to bed, he passed by to say goodnight in his usual way which was... how to put it... a little masculine. Basically, he recommended that we not be up too late, whatever fun we might be able to find that evening. It was clear to everyone though that this was a figure of speech rather than a real possibility, as World Cup hotels are incredibly heavily watched and each of us was just waiting to see our wives and girlfriends. What Lippi really wanted to do was send us a message of trust; unlike other coaches, he avoided surprise inspections and checks because he was sure of us and our professionalism.

That night, however, was different, and even though we shut ourselves away in our rooms with the lights turned off by eleven, it was only a few minutes later when the first sound of footsteps came from the corridor.

I could hear a distant door being opened with little delicacy, then mine was ajar again, and in the chink of light I could see the shape of Gattuso.

'What are you doing, are you asleep?'

'No, I can't sleep at all.'

'Do you want to play? A little *scopa*?'

I jumped out of bed without waiting for him to repeat it, turning on the light. Rino already had the deck ready in his hand. 'Raise,' and yet another round of cards began. *It will help you sleep*, I told myself. *Half an hour and then bed*. It only took two hands, though, before Perrotta appeared as well. 'What are you doing? Can I watch?' From then on, the floor reserved for us started to really come alive. I went out to explore – by then it was past midnight. Let me remind you, we had to play in the World Cup final the following evening.

The door to Materazzi's room was closed, but the noises coming from inside were unmistakable. I threw it open as if I wanted to catch those present red-handed, but the group inside didn't even notice. I remember Marco, De Rossi, Oddo, Pirlo, Barone and Iaquinta were there, but there were others too: they were playing on a PlayStation, a two-on-two FIFA tournament, yelling at every goal as if they were in a stadium. It made me laugh, but I told them to keep it down. Materazzi looked at me as if I were stupid. 'Look, no one's sleeping,' he said, and Pirlo nodded as if he were his lawyer who needed to confirm the statement.

So, I went back into the corridor, and by then all the doors to the bedrooms were open. Buffon was watching a recorded match from Wimbledon – the tournament was being played at the same time – and since he didn't know the result, he was cheering unrestrainedly for one of the two tennis players.

Marco Amelia was the best, because he was reading a book. 'What's it about?' I asked him. 'Philosophy. I'm partly reading it because I'm studying it, and partly because maybe it'll send me to sleep.' In the corridor with me, as the second inspector, was Inzaghi: he too was going from room to room, chuckling. Having finished my reconnaissance, I went back to my game of *scopa*.

The hours passed, and the only one who got a bit of sleep – though only after two – was Del Piero. He passed by to greet us all with an ironic smile.

'You know, I'm used to finals, so the night before doesn't have this big effect on me...' He was sent away after a series of insults and a few slippers were thrown at him. Brilliant Ale.

On average, we turned in at around six. The adrenaline of the most important game of our lives was coursing around us in torrents. A little sleep came only when we were exhausted. I imagine that the same thing happened in the French hotel, and in any case, it was clear that the energy for a game like this, the seventh and the most dramatic in a month, must be found in the head much more than in the muscles.

I slept for around three hours. Breakfast was set for 8.30. I woke up no more than two minutes before: at the buffet we appeared like so many ghosts, and practically no one opened their mouths. There were only tired and tense looks.

Five days before, on the morning of the semi-final with Germany, we were much more cheerful and noisy, but that night we'd slept. There was silence on the bus too. Twenty minutes on the road to reach the pitch set aside to wake up the muscles and there, thanks to a young bull having fun, someone started making jokes again. In short, we laughed at the white night that had just passed, 'How are we all feeling,' and so on, but that only lasted five minutes because, preceded by a big commotion from the federation's staff, Youth and Sports Minister Giovanna Melandri and President Giorgio Napolitano himself stepped onto the grass. Lippi went to welcome them and quickly escorted them to the middle of the pitch, where we lined up in a semicircle, waiting.

The President's speech was more or less what you'd expect under such circumstances. It was clear that he wasn't too concerned about football, but the fact that our victories had brought the country together, prompting him to share this enthusiasm in a fraternal atmosphere, gave him great joy. His words sounded very sincere, and I found myself thinking that there can't be a deeper sense of disappointment for a President of the Republic than governing a divided and rancorous Italy. Napolitano concluded by saying that everyone was hoping for us to win, but that whatever happened, the country would be grateful to us for this month of passion and for the result achieved... and here – to general surprise, initially embarrassed and then gradually more amused – Lippi interjected.

It would be going too far to say that he interrupted him abruptly, but he certainly used Napolitano's first pause to intrude: 'Excuse me, *presidente*, but it's not yet time for thanks. These guys haven't done anything, or at least I'm drilling into them to think that's the case, because tonight I want nothing less than victory. Nothing less than the world title. Gratitude is a pillow to rest on later, while we're still involved it's better not to talk about it to avoid it having any effects. We've reached the final, but if we were to lose, we'd ruin all the work we've done up until now. Excuse me once again, the guys know these things, but it was important to repeat them.' And he went quiet, while eyes fell back onto the President, who briefly collected his thoughts, with the hint of a smile on his lips, and then addressed us directly: 'Did you hear your coach? Go and win, we all have faith in you. Tonight I'm sure you'll let me touch the World Cup.' He shook everyone's hand, Lippi's for a little longer. He must have liked his clarification.

The coach surprised me too, that morning, because before returning to the hotel, he stopped me to say that I mustn't lose sight of Makélélé. It was odd: normally Lippi left me ample freedom while we were out of possession, at most he asked me to unsettle the start of the opposition's build-up play when the centre backs had the ball. Marking a central midfielder, particularly a dynamic one like Makélélé, had never been mentioned before. But I didn't bat an eyelid. As I've already said, the boss had done too much for me to ever debate his choices.

Back at the hotel, we found everything set for lunch and then, at 13.30, the doors to the sector reserved for us were opened and we could meet the members of our families. After an hour, the FIGC staff were tapping on their watches at us. It was the last time we'd see them before the game: next time, it would be either as world champions or as losers.

It was a very special hour that infused us all with new energy because, ultimately, when you say 'I'm playing for Italy,' it's your loved ones that you're thinking of, your family and friends. They're the Italy who you want to win for above all. Not all the recipients of my hundred tickets were at the reunion, that wouldn't have been possible, but there were a lot of people there anyway, and everyone was wearing a blue shirt, including Cristian, who was eight months old and, in Ilary's arms, looked at me as though he wanted to capture these moments forever. My wife was the sweetest, Mum was a bit emotional, Dad was... Dad. No hugs and kisses, it wasn't our style, but we looked each other in the eye for a long time, and there I could see all his pleasure, his affection, his closeness. A moment of absolute intensity, which I needed to feel complete. It was difficult for me to say goodbye to everyone, but then I went up to my room and finally, like most of my teammates, I slept: two hours of deep sleep, without dreams, with my phone in silent mode because there was still a world out there that was sending its good luck to me. *Shhh! I need to rest.*

Alarm. Snack. Shower – long and cold, invigorating – which I always took before leaving for the stadium, whether Roma or the national team were playing. The ritual of the suit: that night, among other things, we also needed to be stylish. We left our rooms and, to the noise of suitcase wheels banging on the stairs, headed towards the conference room.

Lippi had already spoken at length in the days before. The final tactical meeting was only used to finalise the last details. Attention focused on Zidane, which is why I had to take care of Makélélé: to free up another midfielder to mark Zizou. France were a team full of champions, but there was no doubt that everything revolved around Real Madrid's superstar. He was definitely a superstar, the best player I've ever seen in my role, even if in reality Zidane was like a cross between me and Pirlo: he never had my ability in front of goal, even though he scored a lot, but he read the game like a true *regista*. On the pitch, he clearly felt the confidence he instilled in his teammates. That said, Zizou had always fascinated me because of the schizophrenic traits of his character, the cards, the reactions – I certainly didn't imagine there would be another of those that evening, indeed, the most serious of his career – in short because he got pumped up. I happened to talk to him a couple of times, at the end of games between Roma and Juve, and I sensed a similarity between us: we were both anchored in the same, somewhat old-fashioned values. Candela, a mutual friend, confirmed this to me.

We didn't cross paths with the French before the game. The entrances for the team buses were different, the dressing rooms far apart, the warm ups separate. They went out to inspect the pitch first, and when it was our turn the stadium was already full. The trophy was there, on a plinth.

I looked at it spellbound until Gattuso and Vito passed me, who both said, 'Don't look at it, if you look at it it'll bring bad luck,' and then I ran towards the area where our families were seated. Only after the game did I find out that Cristian didn't have a ticket – at eight months! – and that, as a result, the Germans hadn't wanted to let him in.

On returning to the dressing room, to get changed, the tension was evident: exorcised until now in order not to get overly agitated before the game, it gradually possessed each of us.

Naturally, the World Cup final is a one-off, incomparable event. Over the years, Lippi has explained our victory as being down to the group's compactness, and I agree with him one hundred percent: in certain moments, the encouragement that gives you the most is the one you get from a teammate who isn't playing. The ability of a substitute to cheer for a starter without a second thought is one of the main indicators of the health of a team, and in fact it often happens that someone on the bench wishes for bad luck, or hopes that the team wins but that the person who's playing in his position flops. In our dressing room, however, the eleven starters were hugged and encouraged by their possible replacements: I remember the sincerity in the eyes of Del Piero when he said to me, 'Go out and tear it up, Francesco.'

A siren sounded. Time had run out. We went out, walked along the corridor, entered the big hall that opened onto the pitch, took a few more steep steps, and then there we were. The French arrived from the opposite corridor, we greeted each other casually and politely – everyone knew everyone – and someone even managed to take the edge off things with a joke.

The Argentine referee Horacio Elizondo and his linesmen were last. We all shook hands with the mascots who were looking at us dreamily. Then we were moving. In front of me some, passing next to it, couldn't resist the temptation to brush their fingers over the trophy: Materazzi, Camoranesi, Cannavaro himself, some of the French too. I avoided it. I thought, *If I touch it now I won't be able to at the end.* It was pure superstition but – since I think this way – it was an antidote to any negativity. The two columns of players passed between two lines of photographers. The teams lined up, and wherever I turned my gaze I saw people who were clenching their fists, winking, blowing a kiss. Total involvement. We listened to the anthem with our arms on the shoulders of our teammates on either side. They did the same on the bench. Cannavaro signalled for me and Toni to go to the centre circle, because we would kick off. Elizondo waited for a long time for every little detail to be in place, then whistled. Luca, who had already had his foot on the ball for about thirty seconds, touched it to roll it towards my right foot: I stopped it, turned around, saw Pirlo waiting outside the centre circle and passed it to him. We'd started with the usual pattern again. Even though it was the World Cup final.

It can never be a match like any other, and in fact I remember only a sequence of incidents: not a logical progression – there was too much tension to organise my thoughts – but a series of situations that followed one another very quickly. Before even sixty seconds had passed, Henry bumped into Cannavaro and stayed on the ground for a couple of minutes. There was no foul but the French put on expressions like 'typical Italians,' and the referee slipped imperceptibly towards their side. He booked Zambrotta very early on for a studs-up tackle on Vieira, even though it was on the edge of their area, and as soon as Malouda got into ours, he saw a contact with Materazzi that initially seemed clear, but which was much less so in slow-motion replays on TV. Penalty, and practically no football had been played.

I don't think I'd ever tried to jinx an opponent's attempt as I did then, and I celebrated inwardly for a moment when Zidane's chip – slightly high – touched the bottom of the crossbar and bounced near the line. In or out? After a brief moment of indecision, the linesman pointed to the centre circle, Zizou celebrated after waiting for the signal, and the replay on the big screen removed any doubt: the ball was over the line, and it wasn't even close. I thought back to a statistic I'd read the day before: not since 1974, the final between West Germany and Holland, had the title been won by the team who went behind first. Good idea: as if France weren't enough, let's take on history as well. I went back to the midfield, mulling over these thoughts.

The game restarted without radical changes – it was too early to change the tune. After all, if you ignore me following Makélélé, the tactical plan was still the same: the important thing was to stay calm, and that wasn't easy because the balls were flying over me rather than arriving at my feet.

France's advantage put us off balance, some of our players at the back were getting rushed, and they launched the ball forward as soon as they had a bit of space without looking to start up a sequence of short passes, which was our style. Luckily we quickly found the equaliser, a great header from Materazzi from Pirlo's corner. I had taken up my usual position for corners, which was on the edge of the area, ready to hit a short clearance from the defence on the volley. From there I was the first to meet Marco's incredulous eyes, I yelled at him but he didn't even see me, before being overwhelmed by hugs from his teammates. He wanted to dedicate the goal to his mother. He raised his arms and looked to the sky, and it was clear – just like for Grosso against Germany – that he hadn't even remotely thought about scoring in a World Cup final. Then it was just a mass of arms one on top of another, shouts, encouragements and relief for the immediate equaliser. I tugged on his hair with happiness. Marco didn't notice this either. We were starting again from scratch for a seventy-minute match, or at least that's what we were thinking as we headed back to our half of the pitch.

The game was trench warfare with two generals on display: Zidane for them, and his France tried to dig in permanently midway inside our own half; Pirlo for us, and we restarted from deep, trusting in his guidance. My problem was that the passing lines were clogged up, and as I looked for space I knew I couldn't stray too far from Makélélé, who was the man who regularly restarted their moves, getting the ball from the defence and immediately looking for Zidane.

France were playing more. Henry was continually calling for vertical passes, and if he received them at the right time he was very dangerous. If he ended up offside he bent his run and was onside again in a moment: an awful customer for our defence, the worst of the tournament, though this was the final after all; there were no mediocre people out there.

If we were covering more it was also because a second set piece could be enough for us to take the lead: after Materazzi's equaliser, another perfectly taken corner from Pirlo found the forehead of Toni, who hit the crossbar. After around half an hour Perrotta got injured, staying on the ground for a couple of minutes. I went over towards the bench to get a drink, and Lippi hurriedly turned to me. Though not to compliment me.

'Francesco, what's the matter with you? You're not doing enough, this must be your match.' I tried to respond that the ball was flying over me, but he mimed a more continuous movement. 'You need to show yourself, you're always behind a Frenchman.' I gave him the OK gesture – a thumbs-up – threw my bottle at a masseur and went back towards the midfield.

I also knew that I wasn't doing anything special. This business with Makélélé had upset a still delicate balance. I'd only been playing again for a month. I called for a one-two with Pirlo. I tried to replicate the exchange with Zambrotta that set him up for a goal against the Ukrainians. I tried to stay less distant from Toni, who I'd abandoned a little to his fate. But when Elizondo whistled for half time, I didn't feel right about the personal expectations that I'd had. And Lippi agreed. Once we were inside the dressing room, he called me aside and took me into a bathroom, closed the door and exploded again: 'You have to give more, Francesco, these games are decided by champions and you are ours. Think about what you've done to be here, think about how much you've worked in these months and throw everything you've got left onto the pitch, because the final is a game with no tomorrow. I want the title, Francesco, all your teammates want it, you must want it too, with all your strength. Otherwise, I won't wait long before replacing you.'

A short speech, not even a minute, but very intense. Thinking back about it now, the scene, a fully equipped bathroom because obviously there wasn't time to look for a meeting room, makes me smile. I find his choice to do it in private very proper, and I honestly did call on all my energy, but there really was very little left – this was the moment in which I paid for going three months without matches – and to put what I had to use I needed a different tactical context. Impossible in that situation.

When we went back onto the pitch, France started to get on top and I although I continued to run around, I was always a long way from the ball. Lippi's decision to substitute me was right, as was that to reinforce the midfield: I'd noticed a few minutes earlier that Daniele was warming up. I wasn't surprised by the fact that it was him who was coming on for me. Iaquinta also came on in place of Perrotta, and so the entire game plan was changing: I must have touched the ball ten times in total and none of those turned into a long pass to Simone. I just hadn't had the space to do it, and I suspect that Domenech – their coach – had sought to limit a tactic that had caused trouble for other coaches in the past.

Substituted after an hour in the World Cup final, and aware that I wouldn't be playing in any others, I should have been at least a little bit angry, embittered, mortified. Anger should have gnawed at me. I've already told you that my character would be inclined that way. Instead I left the pitch without negative feelings, convinced that, given the way things had turned out, Daniele could make himself more useful.

Know that, of everything that I've said up until now, this is the thing that most resembles a miracle: I played in a World Cup as a starter, praising the spirit of the reserves, and at the moment that I became a reserve, all I was interested in was the people on the pitch winning the game. I'm not emphasising this so that I can be congratulated but to make you understand what a winning group is: the congratulations go to all twenty-three, and consequently also to the coach, because it's knowing how to distance oneself from one's own personal interests, even in the most delicate moments, that describes the goodness of collective work.

I fell onto the bench exhausted, took a long gulp of water, and immediately focused my attention on Daniele, who went onto the pitch burdened by unimaginable pressure: coming on in a World Cup final after missing out on four games through suspension, so you don't have match sharpness, but everyone, if necessary, will blame you for it rather than give it to you as an excuse. In practice it was like playing with ten gorillas on your back, and I held my breath when De Rossi received his first ball: he controlled it well, raised his head and moved it on, completing a pass that wasn't straightforward. From that point on, everything would be less difficult.

The suffering on the bench was unspeakable. We all jumped to our feet when Toni put it in the net, but out of the corner of my eye I'd seen the flag was up, so the disappointment was contained. We sat back down again. I was between Perrotta and Peruzzi. We cheered unrestrainedly, and if any of our team passed in front of us, running down the wing, we urged them on by raising the volume.

When there were a few minutes left, Lippi called Del Piero back from his warm up, and I waited for our eyes to meet to encourage him by clenching my fists. I was happy that he'd play a bit of the final too. Not a small bit either: after 90 minutes the score was still 1-1. We were going to extra time.

At Elizondo's whistle, I jumped to my feet, grabbed a few water bottles and took them to my teammates, who were coming over towards the bench. I smiled, I encouraged, I heartened, as did all the others who weren't playing, or rather, who were 'playing' in a different way.

Lippi had already made all three changes. There was no need for the substitutes to keep warming up, there would be no further changes to the eleven out there. The others had the task of supporting them now. The abrupt drop in adrenaline following my substitution was a distant memory. I was freshly excited and 'switched on' again, as if I were playing. Actually, it made me think that if changes in football were like those in basketball, I could have come back on. And I'd have loved to.

Extra time 'belonged' to Zidane. The first half for the splendid header that no goalkeeper in the world except for Gigi would have saved, and when I think back to it today, my knees still tremble; the second half for the incredible headbutt on Materazzi and his consequent sending off. The last act of his career.

On the bench, no one noticed anything because the ball had been sent upfield and we were all looking towards the forwards. Del Piero was heading for goal, but he gave away a free kick. The French restarted. Wiltord received the ball in the middle of the pitch, and it was at that moment that everyone noticed Materazzi on the ground. The game stopped, Elizondo ran over to where the incident had occurred – where blue and white shirts were mixing together, the atmosphere becoming increasingly edgy – and I understood it must be something serious from the face of Buffon, who had evidently seen everything and was moving non-stop between the referee and the linesman, making furious gestures at the latter, touching his eye, as if to say that he couldn't not have seen it. Gattuso was also very determinedly suggesting to Elizondo that he get help from someone who had a monitor in front of them, and that's what happened. The red card was shown to Zidane, but the anger of the French fell silent when the stadium's big screen showed the replay of the headbutt. There was a unanimous 'Oh' of astonishment, because everyone had imagined a push or at most an elbow, certainly not that act of madness.

Zidane left the field, passing in front of us, but no one dared to say anything to him. Let's be clear: at that precise moment I was happy that France were losing unquestionably their best man, the star who had continued to scare us until ten minutes before the end of extra time. But it's one thing to feel relief at an incredibly important game becoming less difficult, it's another to forget who that man going off is, how bitter that last walk to the dressing room must be, almost touching the trophy that won't be his, how unjust it is for such a champion to end a fantastic career with such a humiliating dismissal. There were ten minutes left but practically nothing happened, the incident with Zidane left such an impression on everyone that the rest of the match simply became a wait for the penalty shoot-out.

This time Lippi hadn't told the team to finish the game, as happened in the semi-final. The reason is obvious: Germany were inferior to us, penalties would have given them a chance that they didn't deserve. With France, however, it was even: forcing the situation would have exposed us to the risk of conceding a goal. The truth is that, in such a dramatic context, we felt relatively calm: there were a lot of penalty takers for their respective clubs in the squad, and although the emotional situation wasn't comparable, the habit of taking them would still mean something.

Buffon couldn't sit still, because he, the best goalkeeper in the world, knew that penalties weren't his strong point. I charged myself with keeping his spirits up, reminding him that his name was Buffon and that any penalty taker would be terrified at the idea of finding him in front of them. I clearly went over the top because Gigi, laughing, said, 'Exaggerate a bit more, come on,' but in the meantime I'd brought back his smile, and that had been my aim.

Lippi had a precise strategy, using a 'safe' penalty taker straight away to start the shoot-out in the best possible way. We would be going first, which is best, like being on serve for the first game in the fifth set in tennis.

Pirlo headed towards the penalty spot with apparent coolness. I went over to the centre circle, I couldn't stay on the bench any longer. I stood in the second row, behind the penalty takers. I couldn't say anything. It was too intense, no one had the strength to utter a single word. The shot was central, but Barthez dived early. Goal. Andrea kissed his ring finger and returned to the midfield with the same neutral expression on his face. That never changed. He had an amazing World Cup. He was the fulcrum of the team, the conductor of the blue orchestra; on the pitch he and I always found each other instinctively, and I was pleased that I gave him the ball for his goal against Ghana – all thanks to him, I was merely making a delivery; he told me that I'd been like a FedEx courier. He didn't lose his composure even after scoring a penalty in the World Cup final, re-entering the centre circle and nodding briefly at everyone's praise. By the time we'd turned around, Wiltord, that man again, had equalised.

Materazzi set off quickly as if he wanted to shorten the agony. Fifteen minutes before, the French sections of the stadium and the bench – starting with Domenech – had overwhelmed him with insults, thinking that he had dived or, at least, provoked Zidane's red card. The big screen did him justice, but the feelings of antipathy remained. It needed a very strong character to stand up to it, and Marco didn't lack that. While the stadium seemed to physically shake from the intensity of the whistling, he struck his penalty hard into the corner, beyond Barthez's outstretched arm. Fantastic. He returned to the centre of the field touching his ear with one hand, a message to the French who were continuing to shout all sorts of things at him. Since that World Cup I've been very fond of him, and yes he continued to clash with me in the league as if nothing had happened, but he's much kinder as a person than as a footballer, and after getting to know him deep down, you can't help but think well of him.

Next it was the turn of Trezeguet, Buffon's teammate at Juve for many years. The fact that the goalkeeper and penalty taker knew each other very well could have a decisive impact on the psychological balance of the duel. In fact, the Frenchman tried a shot that was too difficult, high and into the corner, and hit the crossbar. The surge of adrenaline that came from an opponent's mistake has three times the power of a teammate's successful conversion, because it's there that you feel victory getting closer.

Now a great deal depended on our third penalty taker and I, who didn't remember the sequence set out by Lippi, looked apprehensively down the line of candidates, a few metres in front of me. My heart skipped a beat when I saw Daniele breaking away from it.

The choice was logical, he was the second choice taker at Roma after me, and his right foot was both powerful and precise. But equally, partly due to a sense of protection, the risk that De Rossi had agreed to run troubled me. When I saw the ball fly into the top corner, a kind of fine copy of Trezeguet's shot, I celebrated more profoundly than for any other penalty. I had been a model and a reference point for Daniele for a long time, and it's natural for me to feel like his older brother. It was one of many moments – probably the most famous one – in which I was proud of him. When he returned, I brought him into a hug as Eric Abidal headed towards the penalty spot, and he made no mistake. The French were still coming after us. They were slightly behind, but they were still there. Del Piero clapped his hands and set off. It was his turn.

He couldn't miss. Firstly, because Ale never misses – how many times did I uselessly try to jinx him at Juve... – and secondly because it was time for him to help us out. In 2000, Zoff left him until last and Holland's mistakes allowed us to celebrate early. And this was why Lippi put him fourth, so as not to run the risk of wasting our main penalty taker. And Ale didn't let us down, wrongfooting Barthez and clenching his fists tightly towards us in the centre circle.

Pirlo now watched the penalties embraced by Cannavaro, while the most enthusiastic about Del Piero's conversion was Grosso, and the reason for that would soon become clear: from that point on, every penalty was a match point. If Buffon saved the next one it would be over and Fabio would save himself the last, daunting spot kick. He, in fact, was the fifth on the list.

Willy Sagnol, a full back, set off, and I think it was probably him who replaced Zidane in the quintet of penalty takers. *You'd love to see... No, nothing doing*: Sagnol converted it with confidence, and all eyes inevitably fell on Fabio Grosso.

His wife, in the stands, was eight months pregnant. Ilary told me that three or four people had gathered around to support her – she was very nervous – and she had turned around out of fear. She hadn't wanted to watch him take it. Fabio, though, hadn't batted an eyelid when Lippi had asked him if he felt up to taking the fifth penalty. He was a soldier. And now that it had become the decisive one, look at how direct his walk was, not deviating from the shortest path by a centimetre, look at how he picked up the ball and placed it attentively on the spot, look at how he walked back for his run up, stopped and observed the referee out of the corner of his eye, waiting for the whistle, carefully avoiding making eye contact with Barthez, who wanted to make sure that Fabio knew he was facing a world champion.

Grosso had already won the penalty against Australia and scored the first goal against Germany. Could his shoulders bear the weight of the decisive penalty for the title too? At the beginning of the tournament, honestly, I would have said no. However, as the responsibilities gradually ended up with him and as he managed them better and better, the feeling grew amongst us, his teammates, that he was the man of destiny. Indeed. Run up. Left foot. Goal.

My head exploded. I don't remember who I hugged first, I only remember Pirlo passing in front of me, chased by the FIFA cameraman who had been next to us to film us, discreetly and silently, as the penalties were taken. In the images, which I must have watched again a million times, I'm there, clinging to Daniele and Vito, and that all-Romanista party – Perrotta joined it a moment later – will remain sculpted in my mind forever. Unforgettable. Winning a World Cup is too big an occasion to define, you can try but something is always left out: you're part of the history of football, yes, that's the thought that was dancing around my head while I was waiting for Cannavaro to lift the trophy. But it was all very confused, and every time I rewatch the videos I notice a new detail: Lippi with a cigar at the trophy presentation, for example, was a recent discovery. No one notices the famous absence of the FIFA president Sepp Blatter, about which a lot has been said; imagine if what you're thinking about in those moments is where Blatter is...

The dressing room was absolutely heaving. A mass of people. And no one slipped off when buckets of icy water began to fly: I imagine that being there in that moment was like showing off an exceptionally important status symbol. Even the President got splashed a bit when he came in, while Minister Melandri – who happens to be a beautiful woman

– was calculatedly drenched by her admirers… Fortunately they both took it in the right spirit, and I think it was satisfying for them too to be in those photos. Vito, who always kept his eyes open, sprang on a member of the presidential escort who was stashing away a couple of shirts.

Then we rushed to the airport, because before returning to Italy we needed to pass through Duisburg: we owed it to the guys in the hotel, who welcomed us with their faces still swollen from crying. Outside the hotel there were Italians as far as the eye could see, madness. We saw in the dawn in small groups. I spent that sweet night with Ilary, Cristian, who was dozing, Vito and his wife Cristina. We talked, we laughed, we all had the feeling that nothing would be the same again after this victory. Nobody asked me, but at sunrise – when the sky began to colour – a thought came to me: *I've played my last game for the national team.* Yes, I had. If I'd still had any doubts, the opportunity of finishing at the top would have tempted me, because it's always better to leave when there's still someone who will long for you.

The afternoon plane from Düsseldorf was headed for Pratica di Mare, the military airport south of Rome. I was clean and clean-shaven. We were expected at Palazzo Chigi and then the Circus Maximus for the big public celebration. I travelled next to Ilary and with Cristian in my arms. The World Cup was over, and I didn't want to be separated from them for even a minute.

During the flight, we Romans explained to the others what it means to celebrate in our city, aware that the impact would be particularly impressive for the Juventini, who – as the old and immortal joke goes, a light-hearted and somewhat meagre consolation for the number of their successes – are used to celebrating the *scudetto* for about twenty minutes. At most. Buffon laughed heartily every time we touched on the subject. Twenty minutes before landing, the Frecce Tricolori – the Italian air force's aerobatic display team – flanked the plane to escort us to the ground. The captain explained that this was an honour reserved for very few. Our joy increased.

The soldiers who were waiting for us on the runway immediately gave us a taste of what was awaiting us. They seemed crazy. I mean: it should have been a ceremony; instead, as soon as we touched the ground, the hunt for photos and autographs began.

Our first appointment was in the centre of Rome, where Prime Minister Romano Prodi was waiting for us in the government building in Piazza Colonna. I hadn't been to Via del Corso for ten years, and this excited me a little: I had the chance to see some glimpses of my beloved Rome again, which had been denied to me for obvious reasons. Another small addition to the elation that was exploding in my chest. The journey on the Pontina and then the Cristoforo Colombo was of disarming beauty, because there were thousands and thousands of people celebrating along the way, each one of them with a flag, some unfurling banners as we passed by, all visibly exhausted – that night no one in all of Italy had slept at all – and it gave us unconfined happiness.

Soon the bus was forced to slow down because there were hundreds of scooters in front of us, and the journey to Palazzo Chigi had become a procession. We proceeded at a walking pace along the Via dei Fori Imperiali. I had only seen that many people on the streets for the *scudetto*. We arrived in Piazza Colonna at nine, behind schedule. Prodi came out into the street to welcome us. Behind him was a line of ministers, and I already knew that Gigi Riva, who was part of our technical staff, was coming out in a rash. He doesn't like politicians, especially those who, before the start of the World Cup, had given interviews in which they asked whether it wouldn't have been better to stay at home after Calciopoli. The reception at Palazzo Chigi was still pleasant. Piazza Colonna was swarming with celebrating fans. At one point I took the trophy and looked out of a window to show it to the people: the resulting roar was worthy of a goal in the derby.

Despite the total party atmosphere, I sensed that something was wrong. I asked Vito if he had overheard anything, and he told me that there were some problems with Riva. When he heard that it wouldn't be just the squad and the staff who had been involved at the World Cup who would be getting on the big open-top bus heading for the Circus Maximus but also some federation employees and, above all, some politicians, he had caused a scene. I saw him at the back of the room, his face clouded: people were trying to restrain him, but his mind was made up. He quickly descended the internal staircase, emerged in the square next to the parked bus, made the stunned driver open the luggage compartment, pulled out his suitcase and left, I imagine to look for a taxi. If I already admired him before, for his past as a champion and for his unique willingness to always put himself on the side of the players – even when it's difficult, as it had been for me after spitting at Poulsen – now I felt I truly loved him. I think it's invaluable how he has the ability not to forgive, not to let things slip by him like the rest of us, who, so as not to upset that party atmosphere, pretended not to remember what some individuals had said or proposed or who they had insulted. Gigi, on the other hand, had made it clear that he was willing to go and shake a few hands, but not to let everyone climb aboard the winners' bus. And he kept his word: once he learned that even those who had opposed us would be in the photos too, he left.

The journey from Piazza Colonna to the Circus Maximus was another slow procession down packed roads, so much so that some of the team, those who still needed to catch another flight to get back home, would have liked to have finished it there and then. I managed to convince them, promising them a party like they'd never seen before, and handily the provisions loaded onto the bus arrived just then, among which was plenty of spumante. Before we reached our destination, we were all half-cut, and the usual trio – me, Daniele and Vito – made another attempt to try to persuade Buffon to join Roma. 'Look at how many people there are, how much joy there is,' we nagged him. 'Imagine a *scudetto* here, you'd be celebrating for a month straight.'

Gigi hadn't held back on the drinking, to put it mildly, and actually laughed like an idiot all night, nodding vigorously at our smart observations. 'Yes, yes, I really have to come to Roma, I can't miss an atmosphere like this...' Cue more laughter. The three of us looked at each other speechless: had we finally managed to convince him, or was he stringing us along? It was the latter, of course: after the party at the Circus Maximus and the final buffet at the Parco dei Principi, Gigi hugged us and wished us happy holidays. And that was it, unfortunately. I didn't sleep for a second night in a row, and it was a good thing because the next day, flying to Bora Bora, I had daydreams, holding Cristian to my chest. *Never again let me be without him.*

When I came off after an hour of the World Cup final, substituted by De Rossi, I didn't just leave a great game. I ended – fortunately in glory –

my story with the national team. I wasn't even thirty years old, but I felt the need to spend more time with my family: with Ilary, with Cristian, with his little sisters who would come, and who at the time we already wanted with all our hearts. From now on, I would divide myself between Roma and my family, stripping the retreats, the friendlies, the qualifiers and the major tournaments with the Azzurri away from my life: it's all a lot of time that builds up at an age when it no longer seems to you to be infinite. I had already informed the directors of my decision on the flight back from Germany, though I'd made it before the World Cup, and when Roberto Donadoni, the new national team coach, came to see me in September in a hotel in Milan before a league game, I said no to him again. I was sorry, because it's not easy to deny yourself to a coach who makes you understand how much he would like to be able to work with you. Donadoni is a good person, and it's a shame that we didn't share a leg of the journey together. But at that moment, it had reached its end.

There was talk about a possible return to the national team on other occasions as well. Everyone thought it two years later, when Lippi reprised his role as Italy coach: given our relationship, the idea made sense. But it was precisely for this reason that I never gave him the chance to go beyond a couple of informal chats: if I'd allowed him to ask me outright, it would have been difficult to refuse again.

Finally, a few months before the 2014 World Cup, Cesare Prandelli called Vito to ask him if anything had changed. I actually liked the idea of playing in Brazil – and that was widely known – and if the coach had come to talk to me about it in person, perhaps we would have teamed up. But it didn't happen. Prandelli didn't call a second time, and it was better that way. I would have felt uncomfortable entering a group that had withstood the hardships of qualifying at the last minute, including because I would have taken away a place in the squad from someone who had worked his arse off to be there.

I left as a world champion, the highest peak. It was a heavily criticised choice, because by deciding to favour Roma, I'd demonstrated my attachment to the city in a way that left no room for doubts: even today, many are surprised when I say that, for me, the *scudetto* has a slightly greater value than the world title. They call me crazy and can't accept it, because obviously the World Cup is the pinnacle of any career, but this is more the case for those who win every year, like Juventini, than for those who almost never win. For us, the best thing is the *scudetto*, and my biggest gripe is not having won at least a second.

The national team, well... Whenever there's a major tournament, instinctively I want to be there: the anthems are sung, the camera runs along the line of Italy players, I call Cristian and we sit down on the sofa to watch the game. I'm a little choked up inside, but nobody notices.

15.

Core de 'sta città

THE DECISION TO LEAVE THE NATIONAL TEAM AT THE AGE OF thirty to devote myself entirely to Roma is a good illustration of my relationship with the club and with the city. Visceral, that might be the right word. Symbiotic, that suggests to me a friend who knows a thing or two. Yes, the idea of symbiosis between me and my natural habitat captures the reality. Rome is universally recognised as the most beautiful city in the world, but my longing for it comes largely from a renunciation. I can't walk through it as I'd like to. Since I was forced to move from Via Vetulonia to Casal Palocco because some fetishistic fans stole doormats from my condominium, my freedom of movement has been heavily conditioned. I'm not complaining, it's the price to be paid for all the love that I've received and continue to receive, and there's been a lot. But the symbiosis between Rome and I works at two speeds: the city feeds on me until it's full – the games, the interviews, the public encounters – while I'm only allowed a bite from the apple, then I have to disappear. Maybe by escaping at night through a monastery, as happened after the *scudetto*.

There's one Christmas – in 2011 – when I realised at the last minute that I hadn't bought anything for Ilary. Panic, the gifts under the tree are important to her... I called Hermès, in Via Condotti, where she often shops, and I ordered a scarf. But it was the afternoon of 24 December, too late for them to deliver it to me at home. I either had to send someone or go myself. So I did something crazy. I took Cristian with me, covered up well with a cap and hood, got into the Smart and headed off. I took one precaution: I called a friend who has a shop in Via del Corso, more or less where it meets Via Condotti, and asked him if I could leave the Smart car in front of it, with the hazards on, for five minutes. Enough time to get to Hermès, collect the gift, pay for it, and return. A blitz worthy of a SWAT team.

At 17.30 on Christmas Eve, I was on Via del Corso. I parked the car in front of my friend's shop, who stayed there to watch over it, and set off at a brisk pace along Via Condotti. I was very well camouflaged and by then it was dark, but I hadn't thought of Cristian, whose head was uncovered. *Whatever, let's hurry.* I went into Hermès, and the package was already ready. I handed over my credit card and waited for the machine to connect to the bank. I peeked out of the window, and I noticed that a small crowd was forming. *Come on, how long is this payment going to take...* The machine printed the two receipts. I signed the first and gave all the salespeople a collective smile as I left. *We have to get a move on.*

I went out into the street and there was a roar. There were a hundred people gathered there. I guess it had happened in the usual way: one person will have said that they'd seen me, two will have stopped out of curiosity, a fourth because he had nothing better to do, and gradually the group swelled as others stopped after asking, 'What are you doing here?' I knew about these dynamics, but I'd deluded myself into thinking I could still evade them on Christmas Eve. It must have been Cristian that did for me, as he's widely recognised by the fans too.

I held tightly onto his little hand – he was only six years old – and threw myself headlong down Via Condotti, determinedly ploughing through the crowd. Who let me pass, but then they got in line and followed me. It was like the scene in *Forrest Gump* when he runs in the desert with a growing throng of people behind him. I covered the first fifty metres by walking quickly, but from then on I started running, taking care to hold even more tightly onto the hand of Cristian, who luckily was already a little athlete and kept pace with me effortlessly.

When we got to Via del Corso, there was a surprise: the Smart was completely swamped by people. Again, someone must have seen us get out of the car and had waited there instead of following us, knowing that we would have to return. Some of the people around us wanted a selfie, but taking even one would have finished me, because then I'd have to stop and I'd be overwhelmed. And what I was afraid of, in that moment, was losing Cristian's hand. Everyone else limited themselves to filming the scene on their smartphone because that's all they wanted: video evidence of coming across Totti in the centre of Rome on 24 December.

Next to the car, in addition to my friend, were two policemen. As soon as they saw us, they started to make sweeping gestures. I needed to open the door, get Cristian in first, then I'd follow and we could go. They helped me. I was moving in that direction and the three courageously tried to create a safety cordon around me, but it wasn't an easy task. There was no space to open the door, there were too many people crowded up against the car. I pushed it open centimetre by centimetre. In the end I was able to get Cristian in, and, with the help of the police, I was able to slide inside too, but only after a good five minutes.

I started the engine and set off, though very carefully because there was a big risk of crushing someone. When we were finally off Via del Corso and I could take refuge on the Lungotevere, I told Cristian, 'Never again.'

He, though, looked at me as though he was enjoying it.

As a boy, when we went to visit relatives in Testaccio or Trastevere on Sundays, I always asked to go past the Bocca della Verità because I loved the thrill of putting my hand inside it in the hope that it wouldn't bite it off. I visited St. Peter's as a child, the time when the Pope kissed me, but I hardly remember anything of it. A month before getting married, so that I could admire the Aracoeli basilica, where the ceremony would take place, from above, I climbed to the top of the Altare della Patria, enjoying a little privilege, following a private route that kept me away from the siege of tourists. Ah, I've said the magic word. For a day, I'd actually like to be an invisible tourist, to travel far and wide in Rome without crowds and without selfies. Or to be the star of *La Grande Bellezza*, when he's coming home very late at night after his conquests, crossing the most fascinating places in the city when they're completely deserted. One day maybe I'll do that, at dawn, like him. I'll go running along the banks of the Tiber.

After the *scudetto*, I understood a beautiful (as it's flattering) and yet dangerous reality: what I say and do can influence the opinion of many people, because they tend to put their trust in me. I said I would stay forever and I stayed: this is the thing that cemented the relationship of love between me and the supporters more than anything else. Love and indeed trust. So I've always been careful to keep myself away from politics – a field in which I believe I shouldn't be guiding anyone – and closer to administrators, if anyone. When a mayor of Rome, whichever party they belonged to, asked me for a hand with publicising a fundraiser or other charity initiative, I never hesitated to help. Even in that circle, though, there are personal relationships: I've never hidden, for example, my friendship with Walter Veltroni. During his tenure as mayor we did a lot of things together, but nobody ever knew about them. Such initiatives were a long way from the TV cameras. Walter would call in the morning and suggest them to me: offer a smile to a wing of sick children before they had their operations, or inaugurate a new elementary school or a public football pitch in a troubled neighbourhood. So, with Veltroni, I saw a bit of peripheral Rome, and it was very instructive.

I also got to know uptown Rome, of course. The real privilege of being the champion of such a beloved team is having access to a lot of interesting people. Among those slightly special Roma fans who are famously solemn professionals in their fields but lose their minds as soon as they enter the Olimpico, the first to mention is another dear friend, the comedy actor Carlo Verdone. He is exactly as he appears in the cinema: likeable, sociable, and a hypochondriac. Never tell him that he looks a little pale to you: he'll spend the whole day taking every possible test. Several years ago, Carlo gave me a very exclusive experience: he took me to visit the villa of the late, great actor Alberto Sordi at the Baths of Caracalla. It's now about to become a museum, and rightly so, and incidentally he should be one of its curators. At the time of our visit, however, only Sordi's sister had the keys, and she happily lent them to Carlo because she knew that her brother had liked him. The villa was wonderful, and the anecdotes that Carlo recounted about Albertone even more so.

There's always a lot of cinema in the stands at the Olimpico. Claudio Amendola and Pierfrancesco Favino are true fans, those who don't go to the stadium to be photographed but because they can't miss it, even though they suffer like a dog. I've spent many great evenings at the Vanzina brothers' house, and now that Carlo has passed away I'd like to remember how wonderful he was as a person, his class and his ability to put his guests at ease. I'm very close to Enrico too, more fiery at the stadium compared to his brother, but always because he wants the best for Roma. Maria De Filippi and Maurizio Costanzo have been friends for years, from the first time I was invited onto *C'è Posta per Te*. Maurizio was the one who had the brilliant idea of the joke books with which I overcame the talk of Il Pupone, a nickname born with affectionate intentions (it was given to me by Mimmo Ferretti, a journalist from *Il Messaggero* who is fond of me), but which outside Rome became synonymous with immaturity.

The first holiday with Ilary, between the end of the 2001/02 season and the departure for the World Cup in Asia, was a week in Sharm el-Sheikh. Imagine the surprise when we discovered that in the bungalow next to ours were the pop star Claudio Baglioni and his partner. I have wonderful memories of those days, spent together snorkelling and exploring the depths of the Red Sea. But the real privilege was that Claudio agreed to sing some songs just for us, using only his voice, but his is worth an entire orchestra. Ilary was so excited that she even asked him for a song that wasn't one of his, *L'emozione non ha voce* by Adriano Celentano. And Claudio graciously performed it without even having to Google the words. What a phenomenon. We see each other again for dinner every so often, and they're always enjoyable evenings.

Another well-known and quality person I enjoy spending time with, especially in the summer, is the National Olympic Committee president, Giovanni Malagò. We take a boat together from Sabaudia, where we both have a house, to go as far as Ponza, Ventotene, and maybe even Ischia. I play *calcetto* with Giovanni at Aniene, and every time I manage to set him up with a pass that's so perfect it only needs a slight touch on the ball to score, I announce my farewell from football again. After getting him to score, there's nothing more to ask from my career.

But I only understood how formidable the power of football and Roma was in this city at my wedding reception at Villa Miani. I mean the first reception, the one reserved for VIPs and held a couple of days before the ceremony; the second, for friends and relatives, was the real wedding dinner. Let me tell you about the first one. Despite not knowing him, it was suggested that I invite the former prime minister Giulio Andreotti, an international symbol of Rome like Alberto Sordi and... er... me. Well, I invited him and he came, thanking me for the thoughtfulness and wishing Ilary many children and me many *scudetti*, adding that he was wishing for those for himself too because he was a big Roma fan. Then he went to sit in the area of the reception that had been set aside for politicians – I remember he found himself between the former mayor Walter Veltroni and the former prime minister Massimo D'Alema – and he remained there, all happy, until late. He was eighty-six at the time.

Having finished the pages dedicated to my friends, it's right to remember that a great enemy also lives in Rome: Lazio. I've faced them my whole life, from my first derby at thirteen – I'd just arrived at Roma from Lodigiani – at the Giovanissimi Regionali level, until the last in my career, the defeat in April 2017, when I played without affecting the final twenty minutes. As a child, feelings aren't shielded, what you feel burns your skin, and I hated Lazio to the extent that I'd stick their players in upside down in my Panini albums. The wrong way up. I didn't even want to see their faces. So much passion was taken onto the pitch, we were all going crazy trying to win, both us and them, at every level. But this has never prevented me from rightly recognising the merits and skill of the opposition: my Romanista generation had Nesta, Di Vaio and Franceschini as our Laziale counterparts, and after every battle, in addition to shaking hands with thinly concealed fondness, I thought to myself about how good they were.

Sandro Nesta, in particular, was the finest defender I've ever seen. I remember one of the first derbies in which we faced each other. An impossible pitch and dressing rooms that were three times as bad, flooded under an asbestos roof, and in the driving rain, at the end of the game, I had the feeling of being the muddiest guy on the planet. Here, in that landscape of mud and filth, I remember Sandro being like a prince; clean, elegant, never a bad foul – he didn't need to make them. It was natural to nod and smile at each other, even in the context of such a keenly felt rivalry, because he knew that I was the prodigy in the Romanista ranks and I knew that he was the prodigy in the Laziale ranks. It wasn't long after that the first call-ups for the various national teams arrived and our parallel careers took off. From the Under-15s, in fact, around Coverciano, we were known as 'the two Romans' to everyone. And despite our respective origins, there was an immediate friendship.

I've been really hated by Lazio fans, as is natural, but the situation particularly soured when Sandro went to Milan. With that, I really felt a wave of great frustration because, to be sentimental for a moment, Nesta and I should have been shaking hands in the middle of the pitch before every derby until the end of our careers. Until two such noble symbols were physically spent. But while Sensi, at the cost of undoubted sacrifices, always managed to hold onto me, the Lazio president Sergio Cragnotti eventually gave in. Sandro left very reluctantly, and the fact that he had some wonderful seasons at Milan, being a key part in winning everything there was to win, is only confirmation of his enormous talent. But it crippled Lazio, and I'd widen the sense of regret to the whole city: enjoying a derby with two Roman captains, both very talented and loyal, for years and years would have been a privilege. And so a certain Laziale hatred towards me was accentuated by the frustration of the loss of their icon.

The visceral force of the emotions born when you're a boy remains forever: winning a derby makes you feel great, and when you lose it you get more angry than on any other occasion. As a professional, however, certain things change: the rivalry on the pitch, even fierce ones, ends after 90 minutes. You wash it off with a shower. On several occasions, I'd meet people in a club who had got very physical with me on the Sunday: I'm talking about Couto, Radu, defenders faithful to the motto of the derby, 'If you lose, at least hurt them' (there were some of them in my team as well, let's be honest). Well, it's not like you kick people in a club as well. We'd say hello to each other, we'd have a drink together, we'd even joke about the kickings received and given. This also happened with Materazzi, with Montero... There was respect between us, that's it. That's the key word. And there's no more ridiculous question from a journalist than the one they ask you when you might be fighting for the *scudetto* with Juve or Inter, and your rival is facing your cousins. 'Are you able to support Lazio?' Am I able to? I'd do it with all my strength if the title is at stake...

This doesn't take away from the fact that a defeat in the derby hurts a lot. I won't forget that of Paolo Di Canio's goal – beautiful, by the way – as long as I live, given how annoyed I got. And he celebrated under the Curva Sud, *mamma mia...* Even more painful was the defeat in the Coppa Italia final, with the goal from Senad Lulić, because I wanted to lift the trophy at the Olimpico after a derby, and also at stake was the future of Aurelio Andreazzoli, a good person who I would gladly have given a hand.

Fortunately, there were also happier derbies. Many of them are mentioned in the chapters of my story because they're central to the narrative: the one with Negro's own goal, fundamental in the *scudetto* race; the 5-1 win, with the first dedication to the woman who would become my wife; the one – you'll see – in which Ranieri took me and De Rossi off for being too Roman, and in the end he was right. But there are others to remember too, with their connected stories. Such as the one we won in '99, halting Lazio's race towards the title: 3-1 with my goal in the 90th minute and my display of the T-shirt saying 'I've purged you again' that the fans had given me. The Lazio supporters got very angry, and I can understand that, but that was a time of teasing and stinging jibes, sometimes directed at me and sometimes at them, and ultimately it was just a bit of fun.

Many argue that the huge rivalry that divides the fans makes Roma-Lazio the worst match in the Italian league, and having listened to the stories of people who have experienced its other derbies, my feeling is that this is really the case. There was, however, an occasion in which the extreme wings of both sets of fans seemed to join forces, with decidedly unsettling effects. I'm talking about the interrupted derby, that of 21 March 2004, when, at the start of the second half, news spread among the fans that in the chaos of the clashes before the game, a police van had run over and killed a child. The news was completely false – classic fake news, it would be called today – but no one on the pitch had the facts to be sure of that. So, when some of the fans came down from the stands to talk with the two captains, we listened to them.

Among other things, I knew one of them, or rather I knew his brother; he was from Porta Metronia like me, we'd gone to school together. 'You have to stop the game, the police have killed a Roma fan, a kid.' This is what he told me, in an angry voice, as Mihajlović, the Lazio captain, and the referee Rosetti arrived (and listened). We looked at each other. The police obviously don't kill children, but there was a feeling that something had happened. 'You mustn't play,' reiterated the fans who had come down onto the pitch, and the Digos men themselves favoured suspending the game, because the atmosphere inside the stadium was worsening minute by minute.

Making the decision – communicated by telephone to Rosetti – was Adriano Galliani, the president of the Lega, who ordered it to be stopped. We footballers were grateful to him for this, because we were no longer in a psychological condition to play. In the meantime, the evidence was growing, so the police said, that this was a colossal lie, and while people were streaming out of the Olimpico, numerous appeals were made – including from me – for there to be no violence outside the stadium.

But they were just words in the wind, because instead guerrilla warfare broke out against the police, and that night, although by then it was clear to everyone that there was no dead child (fortunately), even a couple of police barracks were attacked. The trial later ruled out that it was a coordinated plan by the two sets of fans against the forces of law enforcement. A simple case of collective psychosis? Dunno. To me, what happened that evening still seems very strange.

Going back to things that occurred on the pitch, I want to mention two more derbies. The first dates back to 2011. We won 2-0 with two goals from me, and an English-speaking commentator proclaimed: 'The king of Rome is not dead'. The fans loved this phrase, as did I: a few weeks later, when a brace in Bari allowed me to overtake Roberto Baggio in the all-time Serie A goalscorer rankings, I displayed a T-shirt with that phrase written on it. (Incidentally, because I imagine some are curious: there were no 'unseen' T-shirts. That is, I never prepared a T-shirt with a message but was unable to show it because the game's result went the wrong way. Maybe it was luck, maybe it was added motivation, but those unique T-shirts were definitely all seen.)

I'll finish with the final gratification, the intense twilight joy of the selfie in front of the Curva Sud after the brace that rectified the derby of 11 January 2015. Rudi Garcia was in charge. I played very badly in the first half, like all my teammates, and the result was that Lazio were leading 2-0. If the coach replaced me, I wouldn't have said a word. Instead, Garcia put his head together with Frédéric Bompard, his assistant, at half time, and they showed me a whiteboard on which the number 10 was the only one without arrows next to it. 'Don't move from the penalty area anymore, Francesco,' the coach said, 'You don't have the energy to play all over the pitch, but in the box the one who doesn't get nervous is you. Let the team bring the ball to you, don't go looking for it. You'll wear yourself out.' It was a request for help and, at the same time, the shouldering of a responsibility. I left the dressing room signalling to Guido Nanni, the goalkeeper coach, that our plan was on.

In the second half, I scored immediately to make it 2-1, a cross from Kevin Strootman that the Lazio defence let go without realising that I was coming in from the right, on Radu's tail. It was a real surprise to them, one which I basically repeated a quarter of an hour later: this time the cross, a little long, was from José Holebas, and to get between Radu and Cana I was forced to be acrobatic, throwing myself forward while striking the ball in mid-air with my right foot. It wasn't an easy goal. In fact, let's be honest, it was a very difficult goal. You need coordination that football schools can eventually perfect but not create: that is, you've either got it or you don't. If the first goal took me to the top of the list of league derby goalscorers, with the second, I left a high-class farewell on the collective retina. Yes, it was my last goal in a derby. I looked around for Guido, who was coming towards me with the smartphone in hand. It was already in photo mode. The Curva Sud was so mad with joy that it seemed to be spilling out onto the athletics track. I got them in the frame and posed for the selfie. Asking for a smile wasn't necessary. Click.

16.

The First Magic Spalletti

DURING MY CAREER, I HAD TO DEAL WITH TWO VERSIONS OF Luciano Spalletti, and despite the enormous problems with the second – which I will recount in the final chapters – it wouldn't be fair to minimise how much I appreciated the first, even beyond the nocturnal visits to Villa Stuart.

Spalletti is a great coach, perhaps the best I ever had, and this goes for both of his spells at Roma. But in the first there was something more, especially towards me, because he was a coach with whom you could go to dinner and speak freely, without having to worry about keeping an opinion quiet, fearing it would be inappropriate. A crazy and funny guy. Crazy because every morning he'd hammer a Swiss army knife into the desk in his office, and the skill with which he handled it was impressive. Funny because every so often he'd do something absurd, like running naked down the corridor to the dressing room, and this isn't exactly usual for a coach. In short, he was a very different character to the conventional image of a coach. And this was why everyone liked him straight away.

Spalletti was Rosella Sensi's choice for the 2005/06 campaign, the one after the dramatic season with four coaches. She had taken over at the helm because running a club like Roma requires energy that her father no longer had. Conti and Pradè obviously supported her, and Rosella let me know everything in advance, but – let's be clear – in the sense that she was 'communicating' the solution to me, rather than 'proposing' it. What I mean is that I, often considered a controlling figure in the club, never asked for anything, still less imposed anything: I always answered those who solicited my opinion, yes, but I knew my place when the directors wanted to do their own thing.

Rosella and I grew up together. In Mazzone's days, in the summer, she went with her father to the pre-season retreats to Kapfenberg, in Austria, to watch our training sessions, and for obvious reasons of age she bonded above all with me and Daniele Berretta, two of the youngest members of the squad. Rosella and I have similar characters, determined but introverted, and in fact I remember her being excitable when it came to talking to the coach or with a more 'adult' player. With us it was different, you could chat about new songs, the ones that us youngsters liked, maybe secretly making fun of the 'elderly'.

This is how we became friends, and this is how we came to the saddest moment we shared, but which will connect us forever: her father's funeral in 2008. Franco always treated me like the son he never had, and so Rosella was practically my sister. She'd recently learned that she was pregnant, and the mix of emotions – burying your father while carrying your son in your womb – had unsettled her. At the moment when the coffin was shut in the hearse and everyone present went to offer their condolences, Rosella felt faint and was on the point of collapsing in the parvis of San Lorenzo al Verano. Her husband was on the other side of the car, also focused on greeting relatives and friends, and didn't notice what was happening behind him.

Rosella slipped, throwing me a pleading look, and, before falling to the ground, found my arms to support her. I was next to her, in the front row as people gave their condolences, and noticed what was happening before anyone else. I've always had excellent reflexes. Once I was holding her firmly, Rosella came to life again, and in her gaze there was the thanks of the young girl who I went to have ice cream with in Kapfenberg. I thought Franco Sensi would have liked the scene as it moved Maria, his wife: 'brother' and 'sister' united in his name.

Let's rewind the tape to the summer of 2005. I congratulated Rosella when she told me that our new coach would be Spalletti, because he was the man who had had the most support among the leaders in the dressing room. There were three of us – me, De Rossi and Panucci – and in the most difficult moments of the season that had just ended, we said to each other that Udinese played really well, and it would be nice to see a big side try that sort of football. Rosella gave us that opportunity.

If I have to be completely honest, until I saw Spalletti in Trigoria, I didn't entirely believe in the fact that we could pull him away from Udinese. OK, it's obvious that Roma's allure is something else compared to the excellent Friulian club. But the club was in its darkest period then, because the Sensi family had spent a fortune to win the *scudetto* and then to try to defend it, and as the months went by, the economies of the early days became real budget cuts. Batistuta, Samuel and Cassano cost a lot, and the only one of them who we recouped a decent amount for was Walter. Bati actually left for nothing, for Inter, because Roma had to get rid of his expensive wages in any way at all, even at the cost of giving him away.

In this scenario, which coincided with the president's illness, the club's major commitment was to pay its salaries regularly rather than buy new players. When it came to professionals who joined from other leagues, it also wasn't right to expect particular understanding: Sammy Kuffour, to give an example, only played if he had been paid, and coming from Bayern, you knew what he was used to. In any case, no one lost out on a single euro. The Sensi family fully honoured their commitments, even during the period in which the search for a buyer for the club was dragging on.

It's logical, however, that with these premises, the transfer market became a task bordering on the impossible, hence my incredulity about the fact that an extremely ambitious coach like Spalletti had agreed to part with a club as ambitious as Udinese at the time, who had deservedly qualified for the preliminary round of the Champions League (and would progress through it too, reaching the group stage). In effect, Pradè could only sign players on free transfers, but he did it well, seeing as, that summer, he signed Rodrigo Taddei, someone who would be very reliable in the years to come.

But Spalletti didn't come to assemble a low-cost squad. His dream, the one he had pursued for years, was to work with me, and he said this explicitly, claiming on the one hand that I could still play with only one leg because I was so strong and, on the other, that he'd like to see me train more because, in his opinion, the intensity of my preparation during the week was no more than thirty percent. He was partly right – and the subject would come up again in a much more dramatic way in his second spell – but it needs to be explained here.

In every game, I took a lot of kicks. Hits from behind on my ankles of varying degrees of violence – and the tightening of sanctions on this sort of foul play didn't improve the situation much – studs down the shins, bruising blows to the thighs; in short, the normal assortment of fouls that a valued number 10 receives. I never complained about it too much, at least as long as the treatment I got remained within certain limits. Ever since I was a young kid, I'd heard my coaches repeat, 'You're the best, this is the price.' To absorb these kicks, though, I needed time: two days, to be precise, and if one of these is usually the free one – let's say Monday – then I always dedicated the Tuesday to massages and work without the ball in the gym, going back onto the pitch on Wednesday. From then on, I trained at seventy percent, not thirty. Many said 'Play how you train.' Batistuta, for example, when he was in good shape, even took rondos seriously. That wasn't the case for me, because these were two profoundly different situations. The game was too special an event, different every time, albeit always very intense, to be able to be replicated during the week.

Be that as it may, Spalletti came to Rome because he was convinced that the team, reorganised in a particular way, only needed the quality that it already had in order to win. Judging from the approach he took with me, it was clear that I was a big part of this view. The work in the first year began with a 4-2-3-1 system (he was one of the first to use it in Italy) that saw me behind a single striker – rotating here were Montella, Shabani Nonda and, a couple of times, Cassano (by then he was close to leaving: in fact, he would go to Madrid in January).

In December, due to a series of injuries, Spalletti asked me to try being the centre forward. This happened in Genova, against Sampdoria: the game finished 1-1 and the feelings were all positive, both because I scored our goal with a touch inside the six yard box (can you be more of a striker than this...) and because my vertical movements pulled the Doriani centre backs out, creating space for Perrotta and Tommasi to make runs into deep. After that draw, Roma put together eleven wins in a row, and I scored a lot of goals in the first eight, proving that I was enjoying the new role. Unfortunately the tenth game in that sequence was Roma-Empoli, and you already know what happened then. From there until the end of the season, Spalletti got by, first with Montella and then, after losing him to injury too, came up with a team without attackers. We finished fifth, climbing up to second place after the sentences following Calciopoli.

Winning the World Cup changed a lot. I continued to get a kicking, but there was more respect. Playing as a centre forward – even though it had been a tactical move – led to me spending more time in the opposition penalty area, and that's a free zone for ankles, defenders are more careful. A good life, compared to the heavy kicks from before. And it's a good life also because the dressing room was a good place to be, the atmosphere was always positive, and the way we were playing the game was fun. By moving me up front – by then a stable solution – Spalletti gave me back the joy for goals that I had had as a kid: in Serie A I'd always played as an attacking midfielder, or as a winger under Zeman, and I learned to derive greater satisfaction from an assist than from a goal. But I was born a forward, and so the fact that I no longer found any of my teammates between me and the goal brought me back to my footballing childhood. And I liked it. Oh yes, I liked it.

The result was a great season for me personally, with the completely unexpected award of the European Golden Boot. I scored 26 goals, one more than Ruud van Nistelrooy, and – in addition to the Brazilian Afonso Alves, who played in Holland – I saw Diego Milito, Ronaldinho and Didier Drogba, not exactly fresh-faced youngsters, behind me in the standings. The league season was anomalous, given the absence of Juve, demoted to Serie B, and the points deductions for Milan, Fiorentina and Lazio. We finished runners-up, but we were a long way behind Inter.

That year, however, Roma played magnificently in terms of our intensity and ability to score. Just think of the November triple-header of Milan, Catania and Sampdoria. We hadn't won in the red and black half of San Siro for 19 years, yet we dominated that game. I scored immediately with a fine volley on the turn, and after Cristian Brocchi equalised later on,

I scored the winning goal at the end of a move that perfectly represented what Spalletti's first Roma side was about. Max Tonetto won the ball very high up the pitch because he had had the courage to press the opponent there. He passed it to Aquilani who, instead of adjusting himself, played a first-time rabona that left everyone stunned except Mancini, precisely on time after his run down the left. His perfect cross was for your favourite striker – he's called Francesco – who ruthlessly headed it past Dida.

In the 'team goals' category, this one was the best of the year, and I was pleased that the central element in this move was Alberto Aquilani, because now I have an excuse to talk about him. Alberto is another Roman who, like me and De Rossi, dreamed of becoming a Giallorossi player as a child, and to achieve it, he made his way through the club's youth teams. He had a decent career – Liverpool, Juve, Milan, Sporting Lisbon, and the national team – but his potential was even greater. Unlike Cassano, however, he has nothing to blame himself for, only the physical fragility that kept him off the pitch for very long periods. A real misfortune, because he had everything: technique, vision, a good shot, even leadership. On the few occasions when we managed to play together, the all-Roman and Romanista triangle composed of Alberto and Daniele in the middle of the pitch and me further forward, in the area, produced exceptional football. Come on, find me a trio of 'locals and fans' who have done better in modern football…

Aquilani's rabona ended up on the front page of Spanish sports papers, because it was said that Alberto – after Cassano – might also receive a call from Real. The problem, unfortunately frequent in his career, was that a few days later in training, he wrecked his knee: six months out, just when he was at his best. I was truly sorry, because beyond being good on the pitch, Alberto was a teammate who progressed in the way I like: he was the captain of the Primavera, spent a formative year in Trieste, and then came back thinking first of all about proving his worth by putting himself at the service of the team and only then about asking for something. Yes, he deserved a lot more.

I mentioned a triple-header of games. The second was one of the biggest wins of those years: 7-0 at home to Catania. A massacre that can partly be explained by their difficulty with reading my movements in the centre of the attack. Furthermore, Mascara, in the first half, and Baiocco, in the final minutes, were both sent off, transforming the final result into a disaster for the poor Catanesi. In these circumstances, which were quite tense, Spalletti had the idea at the end of the game of going down the stairs that lead to the corridor to the dressing rooms and stopping there to shake the hand of every Catania player. I don't know what his real intentions were, I've never asked him about it, but they certainly took it very badly, thinking he was making fun of them. A few minutes later I saw Antonino Pulvirenti and Pietro Lo Monaco – Catania's president and general director – coming down the corridor as furious as caged beasts. And if there's one thing that Spalletti loves to do it's argue (I think he had a wild time), alone or in tandem with his long-term collaborator Daniele Baldini. The words that flew – only words, fortunately – were not to be repeated in schools. 'Wash your mouth out' is the (repeatable) expression that was most used by both pairs. The problem was that from then on, every game against them became a battle, and the following season, Catania-Roma would be a very important match...

But let's go in order, because the triple-header isn't finished. Samp are missing. When I'm asked what the best goal of my career is, I always waver between two options: the first is the chip in the San Siro over Júlio César in 2005, the second the diagonal left-footed volley at the Marassi in that November of 2006. The merit of the second goal, executed with perfect technique and coordination, obviously comes from the fact that I scored it with my 'weak' foot. It was the goal that made it 4-1. Roma were running but Inter were flying, and would soon be out of reach.

In that season, there was also an incident that caused me a lot of embarrassment, a bit of shame and lots of vitriolic criticism from the usual people who just can't stand me. In the first game of the second half of the season, we were playing in Livorno after being in Parma in midweek for the Coppa Italia. An ugly, tense game, and we went behind. I managed to equalise when there wasn't too long to go until the end, and in injury time, disaster struck when Fabio Galante was fighting for the ball with me with the help of his elbow.

There was no malice, but he caught me fully. I believe that if the referee, Giovanni Ayroldi, had whistled, nothing would have happened, because

Fabio is a friend. I just told him to be more careful. What made me lose my calm was the fact that Ayroldi didn't intervene: I shoved Galante away forcefully, without using my elbow, but the red card came anyway because what I did was blatant. So it was me who was sent off, having done (almost) nothing, while he, who started it all, stayed on the pitch.

Thankfully injury time was almost up. I was furious as I left the pitch, and as Vito tried to lead me away from the flashpoint I pushed him away too, sending him tumbling. Leaving the stadium, I was already imagining the comments of the next day, and I predicted all of them: I'm an immature person capable of mistreating even those who are fond of me.

Since it's clear that I was behaving badly, I'd like to explain why. We have to go back to the previous Wednesday, to the hotel in Parma where we were staying before the cup tie, when Vito informed me that my cousin Angelo – you've already met him, he's someone I'm very attached to – had been in a traffic accident and broken a leg. 'It sucks but it's nothing tragic. His mobile doesn't have signal in the hospital he's been admitted to, though. He said he'll call you.'

At the time I didn't suspect a thing, partly because I'd heard from Mum and she confirmed that there was no need to worry. The game came, which I didn't play in, by the way, because Spalletti had decided to rotate the team, and afterwards, on leaving the dressing room, Vito took me by the arm. I immediately sensed that something was wrong. 'This morning I hid the truth to keep you calm before the game, but now I have to tell you. Angelo is in a coma. They operated on his skull yesterday evening. He had a head-on collision on the Ostiense, we don't know how it happened. He was taken to hospital in Ostia, but Dr Brozzi immediately arranged to transfer him to San Camillo.'

To say that I got angry would be an understatement. The truth was that I was first very harsh with Vito and then, on the phone, my mother. I understood all the precautions of the situation, but hiding Angelo's true well-being from me wasn't an option. There's no match that comes before your best friend being in a coma. Back in Rome I raced straight to San Camillo, to the intensive care unit. The doctors allowed my aunt, Angelo's girlfriend and me in. Three minutes, not a second more. Absolute silence, even tears were forbidden. I saw him, and my blood ran cold. Angelo was unrecognisable. He had a tube of oxygen in his mouth and his face was swollen as if something inside him had exploded. My aunt was about to cry. I hugged her to turn her towards my chest and stifle her sobs. Three minutes was too long. After a bit, I motioned to the nurse to open the door. The doctor who had operated on Angelo was waiting for us outside: 'We did what we could, now it's up to him. I won't give you any guarantees, but a little hope instead. He can pull through.' It wasn't much, but for a month we'd have to make it enough because that's how long he would stay in intensive care.

Regardless of how privileged the job is, a footballer is a worker like any other, so he must be able to manage his emotions, especially negative ones, like anyone else too. The footballer has a mitigating factor though: when carrying out his job, which is almost unrivalled in its competitiveness, physical contact is continuous. And staying calm after having an elbow thrown in your face is a lot more difficult than when having a regular discussion in an office. That afternoon in Livorno, I was a different Francesco, troubled beyond measure, upset even, by the risk that a very dear friend of mine was in danger. And here it's not so much that I want you to understand me – Angelo's accident isn't an excuse – but rather to understand Vito's natural ability to interpret how situations will affect me and to intervene. The moment that the referee showed me the red card, I could have reacted in any way at all, even in the most extreme way, because the fury at an unjust sending off was piled on top of a deep anxiety. Vito realised at once that this time the anger was different from usual – potentially dangerous – and essentially put himself between me and the rest of the world, even taking the push that sent him to the ground. That afternoon he went directly to the press room to give reassurances that it was nothing and to explain the reason for my state of mind to everyone, obviously begging them not to write about it. Finally, the ugly side of this story is that after seeing the incident on TV, I was so ashamed of myself that I didn't even find the courage to apologise to him and never touched on the subject again. And so I do it here, now. Forgive me, my friend.

With Spalletti, we were starting to win trophies again, and that hadn't happened for six years, not since the Supercoppa in 2001. At the end of his second season we brought home the Coppa Italia thanks to an extraordinary first leg, 6-2 against an Inter side that won the *scudetto* by a large margin.

Part of the explanation for such a marked success was in our mentalities: Inter weren't in the right place mentally that day, they had spent a couple of weeks celebrating and they clearly weren't able to switch themselves back on. We, on the other hand, had given up in the league at a certain point – when we were too far behind – to focus on the cup. The meeting of these two such different psychological conditions led us to victory.

It took me just fifty seconds to beat Toldo for the first goal – a right-footed shot from a cross from the byline – and after a quarter of an hour we were 3-0 up. This didn't mean that we took our foot off the accelerator: the previous summer, in the Supercoppa, Inter had come back precisely from 0-3 down to beat us 4-3 in extra time, provoking one of the most thunderous (though justified) rages that I remember. A shameful defeat, fortunately unforgettable, in the sense that we remembered it when Crespo made it 3-1 and then 5-2.

There was a second leg in the final, so 6-2 would be a good guarantee. The last goal was born out of, among other things, a type of free kick that I'd enjoyed taking for some time with a new technique, similar to the Brazilian 'three toes' style: the difference was that at the moment of impact, I kept the outside of my foot hard rather than soft. The ball changed direction, but still had a lot of pace. Toldo couldn't read the trajectory well, and the quickest to reach his parry was Panucci, who completed his brace that day.

Christian was a special player above all because he's a special person: he knows how to be respected. In the dressing room he was one of those who stood out, and was sometimes even a little dictatorial. In short, he was both resolute and a great footballer, which gave him the charisma he needed to lead. Such character often led him to be temperamental. Once, in Udine, he got into a row on the pitch with Doni, who was a good and kind person but transformed during arguments. The disagreement hadn't ended even by the end of the game. On the contrary, the two went on in increasingly scathing tones until we had to send ourselves down to ten men in order to separate them. Doni would have butchered him. When he lost his head he could be really scary, but this didn't mean that Christian took a step back.

A week later we went up to San Siro for the second leg of the final, and after a sleepy first half, Inter, at the start of the second half, hit us with a one-two from Crespo and Cruz that suddenly reopened the tie. It was a difficult situation, one in which we seriously risked caving in: a quarter of an hour from the end, Recoba found himself with a big chance, partly due to a slip from Doni. And he missed. Had he put that in for 3-0, it would have been over.

In the time remaining, which wasn't short, Inter, carried on the wave of their enthusiasm, would surely have found a fourth goal against us, and we would have been so down as to be frightening. Instead, our escape from danger had the power to slightly rebalance the two teams' psychological states, and a few minutes from the end, by which point we'd retaken control, my ball into the centre of the box was turned into the net by Perrotta.

It was over, and it didn't seem real to me. We'd brought 12,000 fans to San Siro and they were all there, behind the goal where Simone had just scored, singing and bouncing up and down, calling to us to the stand with arms outstretched, as if by stretching hard they could touch us. The game practically ended with that goal, the wait for the 90th minute was a formality of smiles, hugs, slaps and jokes. Inter themselves had lost the desire to keep trying. Suddenly it was time for everyone to go on holiday. The party on the pitch was big and wonderful, I saw the excitement in Daniele's eyes at his first victory in 'his' shirt, and not even Spalletti held back: he'd just won his first trophy with Roma and was realising that it was a different kind of happiness. This was acknowledged conclusively at Fiumicino: in the middle of the night, 20,000 people felt they had to come and welcome us back.

In those days, the jibes about the Coppa Italia were wasted – those who didn't win it called it an umbrella stand to diminish its importance. I know it's not the Champions League, guys, but let me celebrate it with the 20,000 friends who came to pick us up at the airport…

That was the night between 17 and 18 May 2007. About five weeks before, on 11 April, we'd been given another type of welcome. Fierce in its intentions, melancholy in its effect. Very melancholy. Upon returning from Manchester, where we had lost 7-1 to United in the Champions League quarter-finals, we found piles of greengrocers' crates in front of Trigoria filled with carrots. Rabbit food. Now, 7-1 is a humiliating scoreline, far from the Italian habits of the time, when you often took your foot off the accelerator at 3-0 (it's not like this anymore, you keep playing until the end, like in the rest of Europe). But we hadn't withered with fear at Old Trafford. We weren't cowards. We lost so badly because Manchester United were a very strong side, because they had one of those nights where every shot found the corner, and because our win in the first leg – 2-1 at the Olimpico – had deceived us. But it was a Champions League quarter-final: we reached it and we played in it. You can tell us that we were mediocre, if it makes you feel better. But not cowards.

It had been a nice journey in Europe, until the disaster at Old Trafford. Second in the group behind Valencia (and ahead of Shakhtar Donetsk and Olympiacos), in the Round of 16 we had knocked out Lyon with Spalletti's best ever game in charge. It was a masterpiece, remembered today for Mancini's amazing goal – a sequence of stepovers that dazed Anthony Réveillère – and which deserves to be kept in every fan's video library.

I had already scored myself, a millimetre-perfect header since I didn't have a man on me in the middle of the box, and before that a legitimate goal by De Rossi had been ruled out. Nobody can say better than me that it was valid: it was my push on Cris that was penalised, but it really was an innocent touch. In short, Roma were totally dominant on a pitch that hadn't seen a defeat for a long time. It was our peak, but less than a month later, the carrots arrived...

The party for the Coppa Italia didn't go on as long as the one for the *scudetto*, but it still coloured the city in yellow and red for a long time. Those were sweet days. The season was almost over, and the last objective was a personal one: in the game at the Olimpico against Messina, who had been mathematically down for a long time, I had to score the two goals I needed to win the European Golden Boot. I cared about it a lot, but I felt just as sure of doing it because the task was easy and because I had reached the end of the season in spectacular form. So, taking advantage of the fact that the training retreat before the final game was optional – essentially we'd already passed our own finish line – on Saturday evening we players went to dinner at Checco so that we could be together once more. Nothing that wasn't allowed. But what happened would turn out to be a trailer for Spalletti's second spell, which was such a bitter one for me.

At Roma we had always been mad about cards, but particularly that year: *scopa* and *briscola* tournaments, challenges, rivalries, in short, the classic menu of the era before smartphones and before everyone showed up to a training retreat with a laptop. A season finale of *scopa* was in the air because not all of the annual 'rankings' had been decided: so, at the end of dinner, I proposed to those who would be sleeping at Trigoria that we settle the final scores. The gang accepted almost unanimously: at midnight we were all in my room, and the tournament began. The general atmosphere, very relaxed, made us forget the time, so, when someone knocked on the door, we suddenly realised that it was 5.30am. Turning pale, the others tried to find somewhere to hide.

'Who is it?'

'Don't try to be clever, Francesco.'

I slowly opened the door, finding Spalletti with his finger pointing at his watch.

'Do you know what time it is?'

'Boss, we'll win tomorrow anyway, I'll take care of it.'

But Spalletti didn't let himself be duped. He moved me gently aside with one hand and entered, and immediately saw that Alberto Aquilani, Stefano Okaka and Aleandro Rosi were behind the bed, who – having been caught – came out of their hiding spot with their gazes lowered, and he guessed from the muffled laughter that more had taken refuge in the bathroom. He took a final tally. There were twelve of us. I tried again to sweeten him up, guaranteeing him the Golden Boot, but that expression, caught halfway between surprise and disgust, didn't leave his face.

'Does this seem normal to you, the night before a game?'

He didn't wait for an answer, and went back to his room with the grimace of a teacher struggling with a school of dunces. The next day – or more accurately, the same day – we beat Messina 4-3 at the end of a relaxed, fun game. I missed my fifth penalty of the season – it was easily the year in which I missed the most of those – but even so I scored the two goals that, taking me to a total of 26, won me the top goalscorer award for Serie A and the Golden Boot for the best goalscorer in Europe.

All's well that ends well? Not quite. The incident of the *scopa* game didn't end there. I know that Spalletti talked about it with Rosella, soliciting some form of punishment. Perhaps his phobia about cards, which would play a part in the controversy related to my retirement, was born in that exact moment.

The following season began with another trophy being lifted in San Siro, which is always very satisfying: the Supercoppa Italiana was ours at the end of the now usual contest with Inter (in the post-Calciopoli era, we were like Federer and Nadal; we competed for everything). We put in another very solid performance; the squad had lost Cristian Chivu – who went to Inter – but the framework built by Spalletti still worked perfectly, especially at the beginning of the season, when he could enjoy the fruits of his light pre-season preparation.

I played despite a flexor contracture, because I cared too much. We dominated the first part of the game but without scoring. Inter came close to a goal a couple of times on the counter-attack, but the game was even, and eventually it was resolved by a penalty. I forced it a bit, in the sense that I touched the ball past Nicolás Burdisso, who stretched out his leg as I was trying to get past: a naïve foul, strange for a South American defender, as usually they're the best at making contact without anyone noticing. The blow immediately made me 'feel' the flexor. I would have had to take the penalty very carefully. I had time to collect my thoughts, and then I realised that it wasn't serious: I signalled to Daniele, and I stood aside to watch him take it. I was calm. Just a year before, he had scored from the spot in the World Cup final; not that it was an absolute guarantee, but it helped me to think positively. In fact, he scored it, and a quarter of an hour later, it was my turn to receive the cup and lift it to the sky.

I have several regrets from Spalletti's third season – 2007/08 – because unlike the previous year, that season we fought for the title until the final day. But Inter were still strong. In the period when they were less so, some refereeing decisions went their way, letting them get away from us, and so we were always missing something. Take the head-to-head game at San Siro on matchday 25: we completely dominated it, went ahead thanks to a guided finish from me, and nearly got the knockout goal several times. We should have been at least two goals ahead when the referee Roberto Rosetti overdid the cards, giving Philippe Mexès a second yellow for a minor indiscretion – a push, but nothing serious. And we should have been at least two goals ahead when, in the final minutes, Javier Zanetti – someone who never scores! – fired a shot across goal that slid into the corner. Crazy to equalise like that. I was right there with him, and when I saw the ball on Zanetti's right foot I didn't dive in for a tackle to avoid committing a foul, convinced that a free kick from the edge of the box would be much more dangerous than that shot. But when fate intervenes, you don't have a chance.

I didn't finish that season, because on matchday 34 I suffered the second serious injury of my career: in the home game against Livorno – who weren't exactly lucky opponents, considering my sending off the year before – the cruciate ligament in my right knee tore. I was already in pain, but the shooting window that opened up in front of me had been too delicious to resist: I shot, and as soon as I put my foot on the ground I felt that something was wrong. At least I might have scored. But no, Amelia's save was outstanding, and while leaving the field I would have gone over to compliment him... if I could have got up off the stretcher.

At that moment, we were four points behind Inter, who played the next day; we just couldn't afford not to win. The longed-for goal arrived in the second half from Mirko Vučinić, one of the strongest strikers I ever played with. Mirko has many gifts: technique, speed, acceleration, and he makes himself well-liked by being generous and kind. To be a champion, he only needed the last piece: determination. He was too relaxed, almost lackadaisical at points. He didn't always chomp at the bit. That day he did, but it wasn't enough: a few minutes from the end, a spectacular free kick by Alino Diamanti made it 1-1, which was a catastrophe for us. Livorno would be relegated, finishing last, but their sting in the tail kept us three points behind Inter, who went six points clear again the following day by winning at Torino.

I left the scene, cursing what I thought had been a godsend. The previous week, in Udine, I almost got into another mess of my own making: the referee Nicola Rizzoli hadn't been quick enough to get out of the way after a pass put me in a position where I was almost certain to take a shot, and to avoid hitting him with the ball I had to contort myself, sending it way over. It was a very tense moment. Udinese had just gone ahead and the earth was starting to crumble under our feet. So, having lost the opportunity, I turned to Rizzoli with a loud '*vaffa*' – 'fuck off!' – repeated a moment later in response to his startled expression. Yellow card, which I was fine with. More than fine, actually, because when the caution appeared, I exploded with a third '*vaffa*' towards the referee. He, though, partly because he felt guilty and partly because he understood my sense of anger – which was aimed at the circumstances and not him personally – didn't pull out the red as the rules dictated. In short, he forgave me.

With eleven against eleven, we ended up winning 3-1, and the controversy over the lack of a sending off filled the newspapers all week. Rizzoli had a bad few days because he would be criticised and then suspended. Years later, it was discovered that there had been a phone call about his resignation at that time, and that would have been real stupidity given what he was destined for: Rizzoli refereed the 2014 World Cup final in the Maracanã. The paradox that concerns me is that if he'd sent me off that day in Udine, the resulting suspension would probably have saved me from rupturing my cruciate. And who knows how things would have turned out then: Inter were exhausted, in the final games they lost the derby and drew at home with Siena, turning up for the last game, at Parma, just a single point ahead of us.

The fixture list wasn't our friend, given that we had to play in Catania against a side – remember the 7-0 and the fighting over Spalletti's handshakes – who openly hated us. Also, if they didn't get at least a point, they wouldn't stay up. Despite the unfavourable atmosphere – and I'm using all the euphemisms I'm capable of – we quickly took the lead through Vučinić, overtaking Inter in the in-game standings. The dream lasted for more than an hour before, in the downpour in Parma, Zlatan Ibrahimović entered the fray; he had been on the bench just in case, despite being injured, and he resolved it like the superstar he is. Once we found out about the Nerazzurri's 2-0 lead, psychologically we came down with a crash. Catania equalised, and we had to settle for another second place. Once again, at the end of the season, there was the consolation of the

Coppa Italia, which we won in a single-game final at the Olimpico – against Inter, of course. I lifted the cup in slip-ons, as a non-playing captain. After the operation on my knee, my comeback was scheduled for the summer training camp.

In fact, such a quick recovery was wishful thinking. I actually returned to the pitch in August 2008, in time to miss the penalty that would have given us another Supercoppa and which instead became José Mourinho's first title at Inter. But there was no continuity to speak of until at least the New Year: I played one game, missed three, played a little bit, then had another month on the sidelines; in short, genuine despair. The pathologies were different, not all connected to the knee, but it was clear that my body had lost a little bit of its legendary (in the sense that all doctors always talked about it in fabled tones) capacity for rapid healing. At thirty-two years old, however, it took me as long as it took others, and if I returned too soon then the risk of a relapse was very high. Welcome back to Earth, Francesco. Too bad that the team were taking my seesawing very badly, and early on we were hovering above the relegation zone. After about ten games we started to get ourselves back above the waterline, but by then it was too late to meet any of our objectives.

Of that disastrous season, I remember thirteen goals – a pittance for a recent Golden Boot winner – assorted tensions, even a fight with Daniele Conti, which needed to be cleared up because Bruno is a father to both of us, and an atmosphere in the dressing room that was starting to deteriorate. Every group always finds a way to make fun of the coach: a physical detail, a saying that he often repeats, his gait, a tic. It's something independent of any level of esteem, or reverential awe, or any professional aspect. Just as schoolchildren make fun of their teacher, so the dressing room smiles at their coach. In his absence, obviously. Though we're mostly talking about innocent things, it was important that they didn't leak out because, out of context, they might sometimes seem unkind.

That year, many people suspected that someone was passing on the jokes to Spalletti, because we felt him gradually distancing himself from us. Suspicions fell on Daniele Baldini: precisely because the teasing was harmless, we were never worried about hiding it, even when he was around. The doubt will remain with me forever, I guess. What's certain is that Spalletti's fourth season was his worst, and he made it quite clear that he felt he had already reached the highest point of our arc and feared that the team wouldn't be able to raise its level further. Especially in a lean period for us, when it was difficult to get help from the transfer market.

Spalletti started a fifth season, 2009/10, but the air around him quickly darkened. Two defeats in the first two games, the first in Genova and the second at the Olimpico against Juve, and he decided to resign. It was a choice that shows great decency, because the club didn't have the financial strength to sack him, but given what came out later – his regret at my failure to intervene – perhaps it was also a provocation. In any case, for two days after his resignation, he covered up his tracks completely: no one was able to talk to him, there was even a thread of concern going around. Then, when training resumed – the international break thinned out the days – Pradè came into the dressing room to officially inform us that Spalletti was no longer our coach and that announcements about his successor would follow. With that said, he left, and a few seconds later, Luciano entered.

It was an impressive departure. I saw many in my time and I never liked them – even in the case of full-blown enemies like Carlos Bianchi – because I felt disarmed when faced with sadness. But Spalletti floored us without saying a word. Or rather, he floored us precisely because of that. He came into the general silence, looked at the ground for a very long time, then suddenly left, as if his emotions had prevented him from remaining with us for a second longer. A couple of minutes passed, when we looked at each other, perplexed, and then Spalletti came back into the dressing room. This time he tried to keep his gaze up. Two or three times he seemed on the verge of starting to speak, but the tears pushed the words back down his throat. He ended up doing the round of goodbyes by shaking everyone's hand, but without saying a word. I was the last one, the captain, and I got a very strong hug, one of those bone-breaking ones. A hug that I reciprocated with the same intensity, because my eyes were watery too. Of all the farewells that I witnessed, this was the one in which I felt myself the most personally involved.

17.

Faces of Dreamed *Scudetti*

THE SUMMONS CAME IN THE MIDDLE OF THE AFTERNOON. Rosella Sensi was awaiting the elders of the squad at Villa Pacelli. Accompanying me were Daniele De Rossi, David Pizarro and Simone Perrotta, and we found Bruno Conti and Daniele Pradè already there, sitting next to the president. After Luciano Spalletti's resignation, they told us that they were undecided between Roberto Mancini and Claudio Ranieri, and would like our opinion. Without even having to discuss it among ourselves, we all 'vote' for Mancini, who recently won *scudetti* with Inter and had a more international profile. It would be a high-calibre choice, he was universally respected. The directors thanked us. We left the building on the Via Aurelia convinced that the club had been weighing up both coaches and that our direction had helped to tip the scales. I went home, played with Cristian for a while, and at dinner time I turned on the TV: 'Roma have officially appointed Claudio Ranieri as the new coach. The coach from Testaccio has signed a two-year contract.' I was stunned for a long moment, then a feeling of irritation started to come over me: *What had they wanted my opinion for?*

I called Bruno Conti, but before I could open my mouth, he ploughed straight in: 'You players are crazy. Don't you read the newspapers? We don't have a euro to spend, the club is for sale, and you choose a coach famous for having the most expensive players on the market bought for him… Ranieri hasn't asked us for anyone, so, right now, he's the perfect solution for us.'

I had nothing against him, but in that case, why had we been involved? 'Because the club is in a situation that requires utmost responsibility from everyone. We wanted your input, you're key parts of this club. We thought you'd understood. It nearly gave us a heart attack when you named Mancini…'

It was pointless continuing, but however you look at it, in the end, Bruno was right. Today, I still have to laugh when I think back to certain polemical statements later made by Spalletti when he said that we'd gone to the airport to welcome Ranieri… *Yeah, sure.* The dressing room was so enthusiastic about his arrival that just a few hours earlier it had suggested a different name.

In retrospect (though actually I already admitted this at the end of that season), I'm happy to acknowledge that working with Ranieri was a great experience, and I would have missed out on something by not doing so. Claudio is above all a decent person, a trait that in this mad world now sounds like a weakness, but actually is a strong point because it 'forced' the other honest figures in the dressing room – and in those years there were many of these at Roma – to give everything to help him. Plus, he's Roman, and this is another wildcard that he knew how best to play: he understood our jokes immediately and made his own in turn, keeping the right distance but in a tongue-in-cheek and relaxed atmosphere. We really needed that when he arrived because the team was still struggling to get going again. We won a couple of games, then slowed down again. Then I injured the knee that had been operated on the year before; it happened in the game against Napoli – two goals against my friend Morgan De Sanctis, the second was a shot across goal worth remembering – and was out for a month. On my return, we were 14 points behind Mourinho's Inter, and obviously there were a lot of teams between us and them. Before the paranoia of the relegation zone returned, though, we manage to restart the car. For real this time.

The 2009/10 season was an unlucky one for me. I was in and out of the starting line-up because I always had one problem or another. But up front, Vučinić was now a star, Júlio Baptista gave us a hand, and importantly Luca Toni arrived in January from Bayern, a really priceless addition. I was very close to Luca following our World Cup experience. I called him 'Cammellone' (Camel) because of his height, and I admired him as a person because he has a good character and isn't desperate to stand out, like me. On the pitch, he made his presence felt because his eye for goal made you win games – that's obvious – but he also managed to make himself useful even when you were behind and struggling. All you had to do was launch it up to him to get a minute's breather: he knew how to hold the ball up and was shrewd enough to keep his marker at bay. I called him a 'defender in attack' because he knew how to use all the means that are typical of defensive stoppers to his advantage. Toni was one of the key figures in our long comeback – just think of the 2-1 goal at Inter that, seven games from the end, brought us back to one point behind. We passed them on matchday 33, when we beat Atalanta the day after Inter's draw in Florence, then they overtook us again on matchday 35, the mind-blowing home defeat to Samp that I already talked about in the chapter on Cassano (don't make me suffer that again). Between these two games came the most controversial derby of the many I played in – and it was little to do with Lazio. It's worth summarising it again.

That afternoon – 18 April 2010 – Roma entered the pitch as the new league leaders, while Lazio were just above the relegation zone: there were 31 points between us, a vast chasm, which, as anyone who knows the mystique of the derby is aware, shows how well-laid the trap was for us. It was sprung precisely on time: Gianluca Rocchi started the game, and our minds went completely blank. It was an awful first half. We should all have been substituted. But while that's just an expression, the reality awaited us in the dressing room. Perhaps the most shocking half-time decision I remember.

'Francesco and Daniele are coming off.' Ranieri's voice, which isn't loud but very terse, has the power of creating absolute silence. It had an incredible effect: when you come back in from the first half, normally there's a loud hubbub, someone might be celebrating, a couple are angry with a teammate, someone's swearing because he's taken a blow and is in pain, someone's running to the bathroom because he's bursting, and so on, and if the coach has something to say, he waits for the adrenaline coursing round to diminish a bit. This time, however, the boss communicated his choice to us immediately, and it was met by icy silence. I felt everyone's gaze turning towards us: the two Romans were being substituted, those who insisted most on the importance of winning the derby. Ranieri was taking an unprecedented risk. Neither of us moved a muscle, paralysed at first by surprise, then by disappointment. It seemed that life in that dressing room froze for ten seconds, everyone was as still as a statue. You see scenes like these in the cinema every so often, in sci-fi films. But after a while – since there was no reaction on our part – things started to come to life again: teammates took off their sweaty shirts to put on a new one, those who had a bandage on rewrapped it, those who were dying of thirst drank, and Daniele and I were suddenly like two aliens, sitting on the bench up against the wall, helpless spectators of what would happen from here on in.

We took a shower when the others were going back onto the pitch, and there, finally, we opened our mouths to tell each other angrily that Ranieri was crazy, because if he didn't turn the result around, he'd always be labelled as the idiot who took off Totti and De Rossi at half time in the derby. Anger gnawed at us, it's pointless denying it, to the extent that we were both reluctant to go back out to see how things turned out. As we got dressed again, we did everything very slowly, making almost any excuse to delay.

In the meantime, Lazio had been awarded the penalty that would have decided the game, but Júlio Sérgio saved Floccari's attempt. Shortly after, it was our turn from the spot, and Vučinić made no mistake, making it 1-1. That still wasn't enough yet, but half the job was done. And with the title at stake, in the end, De Rossi and I hurried to run and see Vučinić's second goal, a wonderful free kick, and watch Ranieri's triumph without resentment.

He'd had balls, there's not much to argue with there. In the first half, we'd all played badly, but his judgement – that the Romans were feeling that game too much – turned out to be correct. And that's not all. Later on, Rosella told me that she came down to the corridor outside the dressing room at half time and, once she'd heard the news that we were being subbed, that she saw Ranieri as he came out of the room.

'Don't say anything to me,' he warned her, in a polite but firm tone.

'I'm the president,' she pointed out, but she got no other response than a finger to the lips.

Naturally, Rosella would never have asked for us to be put back into the team, and if we'd lost she wouldn't have touched Ranieri despite his refusal to listen to her: she too is a decent person, and the coach knew that. The fact remains that Claudio acted with great character on all fronts in defence of a chance at the *scudetto*, which he'd been chasing for his entire career and which seemed to be on the verge of materialising after the victory in the derby. I suffered for me and I suffered for him in the next game with Samp that cost us the title. And not just that.

To make you understand the affection I have for Ranieri, I don't believe I ever cheered for a foreign team as much as for his Leicester side a few years later: a little message before every game and, on the day of his triumph, came his recognition: 'Thanks, Francesco, you brought me luck.' There, at least.

That season also saw the worst foul I ever committed, the kick from behind on Mario Balotelli in the Coppa Italia final. It wasn't a sudden frenzy. Already very annoyed about my exclusion – Ranieri explained to me that he wanted to save me for the last two league games, but a final is a final – I watched a very tough match, in which Balotelli was even less bearable than usual, unfold from the bench.

Mario was a strong player, but no one had given him a sporting education. He was somewhat similar to Cassano, if you like, but with a difference that I attribute a little to the older Inter players: I tried every way I could to explain how to act on the pitch to Antonio, and he understood many things while maintaining his rebellious nature, but with Mario, his reference points at Inter must soon have got tired of this. Or maybe certain behaviour was inspired by Mino Raiola, given that another of his famous clients, Zlatan Ibrahimović, behaves in the same way. Shouting 'I'm the best' from the rooftops isn't part of my character, but I understand that we're not all the same: if you do, though, prove it before proclaiming it, and do it continuously, not just when you feel like it. Furthermore, a champion respects his teammates and his opponents: he doesn't complain to the former about a misplaced pass, and he doesn't mock the latter after a successful piece of skill.

There had already been some previous with Balotelli. That evening he insulted the Romans again. De Rossi was so close to hitting him that he was held back by his own teammates. I told the people sitting beside me on the bench, 'If I come on, I'll break him,' and my hands were really itching.

Ranieri threw me on at the start of the second half. We were a goal down – Diego Milito scored at the end of the first half – I tried to organise a comeback but it wasn't happening, this time Inter were stronger. This obviously added to the frustration. So, three minutes from the end, I was no longer seeing straight. I was hanging around on one touchline with Balotelli, and while the ball was out of play, he murmured something like 'When will you get me?' to me, framed as an insult. It was the last straw. When the game resumed, he set off with the ball at his feet towards the byline. I chased after him, determined not just to kick him but to really hurt him. He got into a space that opened up between Taddei and Marco Motta – they should have been dealing with him, I had no business being there – and I gave him a horrible kick from behind. I didn't even know where the ball was. I was aiming for the ankle, and he crumpled to the ground, screaming in pain. It was a horrible foul.

I walked over, stretched out a hand, then withdrew it because, judging by the strength of the kick, he wouldn't be getting up for at least a minute. And I knew I didn't have that much time. I didn't even wait for Rizzoli's red card, it was totally inevitable, so I headed towards the dressing room. I passed Maicon, who gave me a pat on the back. There was mutual respect between us, of course, but looking at it more closely, there was a general lack of reaction from the Interisti, and this is the worst sentence for Balotelli: my kick wasn't a foul, it was an assault, and it should have brought his teammates over to pound me, with words and shoves, and mine to defend me. In short, what happened as the final whistle blew for another challenge, by Taddei on Muntari, that reiterated how tense the atmosphere was that evening. Conversely, my bad foul didn't provoke any reaction. I left with the feeling that even his own teammates wanted to beat him, while the sound of applause had come down from the stands in the Olimpico.

Years later, I was visiting the national team's training camp to greet some old friends when Balotelli approached me. I realised that we'd never cleared the air since that challenge, and I felt a little embarrassed: I could at least have called him. Holding my hand out, I wanted to say something to him, but he didn't give me a chance: he embraced me, smiling, and said 'How are you, Francesco?' in a friendly tone and stopped to chat for a few minutes. A different person. Later on, messages arrive through social media, conversations from a distance, all very pleasant and never forced. The youngsters who are coming into Serie A now don't have the tact of my generation, when we were embarrassed even to take a shower with the 'grown-ups', and it was exaggerated modesty in the other sense. But if they aren't flashes in the pan and their careers last longer, then, after a while, they understand. The law out there is always the same: respect, demonstrate, then speak. And this law will never change, because it's a fair one.

The following season, 2010/11, we started so badly that, despite beating an Inter side fresh from the treble – Vučinić scored in the 92nd minute – we were second last after six games. The performances then stabilised and we climbed back up the table, but without ever seeing the light at the top. Things went better in the Champions League because we got through the group stage, getting the satisfaction of beating Bayern at the Olimpico after coming back from two goals down, and the penalty for 3-2 is a beautiful memory (including because their goalkeeper, Thomas Kraft, nearly reached it).

But in February, we lost at home in the first leg of our Round of 16 tie against Shakhtar and set off on a dismal run in the league. In Genova, against Genoa, we even went 3-0 up and ended up losing 4-3. An embarrassment, and Ranieri didn't hide from it. He resigned and, for the last time, the small group of veterans was called together by Rosella Sensi for a consultation on the name of the next coach. I say 'the last time' because Vincenzo Montella, suggested by both the directors and us players, was the last Roma coach under the Sensis. The sale of the club was now imminent, and the first thing that the new owners would make clear is that the coach would be exclusively chosen by them.

Montella, then. He was already part of the club, as he coached the Giovanissimi, as well as a former teammate and, above all, a friend, which meant things worked in the opposite way to how many might think. A friend on the bench implies greater intensity in training and maximum attention given to your behaviour because, even from an unconscious point of view, you want to avoid someone being able to say 'You're taking advantage of him.' Also, who can a former teammate trust in his first job if not those who used to play with him?

Vincenzo immediately showed himself to be a capable person because he had clear ideas, and while he remained his usual touchy self, he knew how to deal with the players. He restored me to my forward role – Ranieri had moved me further back to make room for Marco Borriello – and I started scoring a lot again, but Roma finished sixth because at the end of the campaign, won by Milan, those at the top started running away from us. We all hoped that Vincenzo would stay. The dressing room believed he had earned a new deal. But the club had been sold, and the new owners wanted to send a signal of discontinuity. Who was the best coach around then? Many would answer Pep Guardiola, but the new American owners brought in Luis Enrique, who was his successor in charge of Barcelona's B-team. At the time I didn't know if it was a good thing, but it was certainly an idea.

Specifically, the person who hired the Spanish coach was Franco Baldini, the director who – between one break and another – had been part of Roma's history for the previous twenty years. Baldini was sporting director in the days of Franco Sensi and general director when the American owners arrived, and he was also the consultant who James Pallotta listened to the most. Our relationship has always been sincere but complicated at the same time, especially after the departure of Capello, with whom he was very close. In the summer of 2011, he wasn't yet officially working for Roma because he was running down his contract with the English FA, but it was an open secret that he would be the new director.

One day when we were having lunch with the physios at Checco, Vito passed me the phone. It was Baldini. He wanted to talk to me.

'Hi Fra', so, you're back...' I said in an easy-going tone because I thought it was time to reconnect, forgetting the uneasiness of the past. He too, initially, replied in an affable manner. But when the discussion moved into specifics, he dropped a bombshell.

'Look, Francesco, if it were up to me, I'd sell you.'

Like that. Plain and simple. I was speechless. I didn't understand if it was a joke or if he was being serious. He repeated it, then I responded spontaneously.

'Find me a team, then, fine by me.'

'I can't. Every coach I contact starts negotiations with the same question: "Totti's staying, right?" Everyone wants you, so I'm not selling you.'

The phone call ended there, and it can't be said that the relationship restarted on a different basis: Baldini considered me the evil of Roma because, in his opinion, I had too much of an effect on the atmosphere. But the coaches, before accepting the club, wanted to be assured that I'd be there, and that seemed normal to me too. To give Baldini the benefit of the doubt, I came to think that he might have said this to me to make me connect with Luis Enrique immediately. It would make sense: though the relationship with him remained as cold as before, I knew that the coach had insisted on me staying, and so I'd be right behind him.

A few days later – we were already on our pre-season training camp at Brunico – the second blow arrived: in an interview with *La Repubblica*, Baldini accused me of laziness. This wasn't the kind of public criticism you expect from your directors. Journalists tried to intercept me in the morning, before training started, but I hadn't seen anything at that point so I decided not to make any comments just then. When I read (and reread) the interview, which actually wasn't as shocking as it was made out to me to be, I still got angry. But I decided not to respond. I didn't want the new era to get off to a controversial start. I did let off steam with Mauro Baldissoni and Walter Sabatini, directors who had only recently arrived themselves but whom I saw every day. But I ended it there, annoyed and rueful.

Luis Enrique moved into a house in Parioli and went to and from

Trigoria by bicycle every day. That's 40 kilometres there and 40 kilometres back, 400 a week: enough to suggest a fanaticism with athleticism, and Baldini's words about my laziness obviously resonated in my head during the early days of our work. Those who subject their body to such a demanding everyday life don't find it easy to have a good opinion of those who have a reputation for conserving energy. In fact, the first signal that Luis Enrique sent me wasn't a positive one: I didn't play in the first leg of the Europa League qualifying round against Slovan Bratislava, which we lost 1-0. In the second leg, we soon took the lead with a goal from Perrotta, but with a quarter of an hour to go, he took me off for Okaka. *What? We're doing well, the job isn't done yet, and you're taking me off?* The change was whistled by the whole stadium, and as often happens in such circumstances, a few minutes from the end, Slovan equalised, knocking us out. We were out of Europe before the season had even begun.

People were almost clambering over the fences they were that angry. At that moment, there weren't a lot of optimistic thoughts in my head. Was Luis Enrique going to play me in dribs and drabs because he thought I was lazy too? And yes, I should have been the one who was feeling hurt: several years before, in the Camp Nou against Barcelona, we had said all sorts of things to each other, and in the end he'd drawn blood with a kick to my calf.

Actually, all of these fears were swept away very quickly by the behaviour of a decent coach and above all a decent man. Many fell in love with Luis Enrique, starting with me and Daniele, because he brought new ideas and explained them with the passion of a prophet. The first thing to say is that he revolutionised everything: the tactical principles of the years before were ignored as he set up a 4-3-3 with the famous *salida lavolpiana* (named after Ricardo La Volpe, the Argentine coach who came up with it): the two full backs pushed up at the same time and the two centre backs moved to the sides to allow a midfielder to drop back, thus switching from a four-man defence to a three-man one. As such, Luis Enrique demanded that our moves always start from the back. No more long throws but many, many short passes. We struggled a bit in the early stages, in which there were often only two players in defence, and there was a clamour from our fans because the ball often went backwards. But it was necessary work to improve our passing and, therefore, our possession.

The season was a long rollercoaster ride: we lost the first game 2-1 at home to Cagliari, then we drew with Inter in San Siro; we had to wait until the fourth game for our first win. The team played flashes of excellent football but never managed to pick up speed, because after every good result, there inexorably came a misstep. One problem was that the signings who arrived from La Liga, who had seemed very strong in the summer, didn't manage to break through at the Olimpico. José Ángel looked like Maldini during the pre-season training camp in Brunico, but in the league he just didn't show up, while Bojan, who Luis Enrique had coached in Barcelona's youth teams, was a different player compared to the one we admired on TV. But he was a really great guy: he suffered from jeers and criticisms, and we suffered with him, because it's sad to live with the fears and frustrations of a bewildered twenty-one-year-old.

Off the pitch, Luis Enrique tried everything to get us into gear: the retreats before home games had already been done away with by Spalletti, and he cancelled the ones for away games too; if the place and time allowed it, we left by bus from Trigoria on the Sunday morning. He was always on our side, whatever happened. He massacred us in training – it has to be said – but the strength and conditioning trainer and the mental coach, the men on his staff, were nice guys: as a result, we would curse them during every exercise, because they were all very tough, but at least with a smile on our faces. Then there were the gestures and rituals that increased team spirit: we'd been used to all screaming together in the dressing room since Spalletti's time, and the Spaniard wanted us to move this to the middle of the pitch, a proposal that daunted us a little. Here we found a compromise: a yell in front of the bench, before kick off. In short, Luis Enrique truly was a revolution. He just wasn't understood.

People jeered at the intermittent performances, while the press criticised the league position that never got very high. More and more frequently, Luis would angrily utter '*Puta madre*' – holy shit. But it was just an issue of inexperience: he didn't want to give the impression of not feeling confident, so he didn't change his methods even if both De Rossi and I implored him, once we'd gone ahead, to give us a bit of defensive cover. There was nothing you could do. We always played in the same way, the result was an optical illusion. The more we reminded him that Rome is a difficult place, where results have been lacking for longer than we'd care to think, the more he replied that victories would only come when his game plan was best interpreted by each of us. It was a dead end.

Luis Enrique really did treat everyone the same, and proof of this came on that famous afternoon in Bergamo when he decided to leave De Rossi out against Atalanta because he was a minute late to the team meeting before the game. I wasn't there, as I had to serve a one-match ban. I was having lunch at home when a text arrived from Daniele: 'You want to know the latest? I'm going to sit in the stands as punishment.' The 12.45 meeting lasted a quarter of an hour and preceded the bus' departure for the stadium: in it, the boss would give us the line-up and show us the final video on the opposition's set piece routines. It's right to arrive on time out of respect for your teammates and because at that point timings are really tight, but one minute, come on... It should be emphasised that Daniele was furious (his second message was frank: 'I'm so angry, you've no idea!'), but not with the coach. Because he recognised his right and duty to treat everyone the same way. And someone who behaved like this thrilled him.

One morning in May, on the main pitch at Trigoria, the first team staff were facing the Roma TV journalists in an end-of-season practice match. We players were all in the stands, making fun of the various protagonists in the friendly, but after just three minutes Luis Enrique – who often trained with us, so he was in good shape – strained a calf muscle and went back into the dressing room. I let a few minutes go by and then I headed off too, to see how he was. I found him sitting there, staring into space. He sensed my presence, raised his eyes. He smiled with infinite slowness.

'Captain, it's over.'

'Over? Because of a strain?' I realised where he was going with this, but I wanted to delay the moment as much as possible. Because I'd be sorry.

'My story with Roma is over. I'm getting old, look, I've got injured after three minutes. I'm getting old, and that's the thought that this wonderful and impossible city is giving me. I can't do it anymore. I've decided to leave.'

I felt a piercing pain. It was the one that often caught me in my career when faced with a departure, but this time it was a little stronger because

Luis Enrique left something with me. The memory of a real person. I embraced him, and we both had watery eyes.

'Training you has been a great joy, captain. Don't say anything to the others yet, they must find out from me, tomorrow. It's the last favour I ask of you.'

I went home without going back up to the stands, because I wouldn't have known how to explain my sad face. The next day, Luis Enrique called us together in the middle of the pitch and communicated his decision to us in a very low and pained voice. Almost all of us were moved, and many implored him to reconsider, assuring him that, usually, the second season is a joke compared to the first. Bitter chuckles, someone felt the need to hug him. If I could have given him a little of my ability to live in this city I'd have done it straight away. It can't be said that it was a good season: seventh in the league, so we didn't qualify for Europe, and we were knocked out in the quarter-finals of the Coppa Italia and even the qualifying round of the Europa League. Yet we all felt that, by losing Luis Enrique, we were burning up an asset that would have given its yield the following year.

A few days later, I encountered Baldini in the pool at Trigoria. He asked me who I would prefer on the bench for the following season between Vincenzo Montella and Zdenek Zeman. It was the first time he'd tackled a serious topic with me since the controversy about laziness the previous summer. The choice between the two exes was the big ongoing debate in Rome. Both were coming off excellent seasons: Montella had led Catania to a superb eleventh place in Serie A, while Zeman had won the Serie B title with Pescara. It didn't take me long to say Vincenzo, and I know that many will be surprised here, because my affection for Il Boemo is well-known. I'll say it again: no one touches Zeman when I'm around. In the summer of 2012, however, I was about to turn thirty-six years old, and since I knew him, I had no illusions about the possibility that he'd change his approach, despite the fact that I wasn't the only seasoned member of the squad. The idea of going back to repetitions and ladder drills scared me. Montella had a much fresher knowledge of the group, thanks to his experience the year before, and in Catania he had confirmed the good tactical skills he had demonstrated to us.

He would have been the best choice.

Instead, Zeman returned. I understood the club's choice because the people's vote was almost plebiscitary: 90 fans out of 100 wanted him, and it was a pressure that was difficult to ignore. Roma supporters especially loved his personality, of being rebellious and controversial, of giving the very clear impression that he was fighting for you and only for you, burning his bridges behind him so as to never be tempted by retreat. These were feelings that he had always communicated to me too, and which cemented a uniquely affectionate relationship.

But managing a dressing room like ours was a different matter. A personalised approach was needed and instead he was the usual hammer, with everything and everyone. On one of his first days, I plucked up my courage with both hands and told him, 'Boss, are you really sure that repetitions and ladder drills are still indispensable for me?' He had never stopped calling me Stella, but any favouritism from him ended there. 'Don't you want to do them, Stella? Don't do them. But then you don't play.' *Never mind.*

The problem was that we were no longer as young as we used to be, and the charm of the harsh but fair teacher no longer stuck. Zeman perceived this, and increased his vigilance on those who stopped to talk to doctors or physios, leaving out those who didn't train at 100%. It wasn't a situation that could last. The performances of the team – which was certainly not worthy of the title, but of Europe, yes – went through scary ups and downs. Suffice to say that, on matchday 2, we won at Inter, a good 3-1 win against one of the favourites, while on matchday 3 we lost 3-2 at home to Bologna despite being 2-0 up after 70 minutes. Stuff to test the walls of the locker room.

Going forward the team was well-armed – as always with Zeman, goals weren't a problem – but we often ended up shooting ourselves in the foot because the defensive side nullified the attacking performance. It was a problem of lacking cover, and I talked about this with the coach many times, imploring him to change something, because if we didn't, we'd all be running into a brick wall. Useless, words in the wind. In fact, since my commitment was still at its peak, he often singled me out in training – 'Stella runs more than anyone, this isn't normal' – implying that many of the younger players weren't fully applying themselves. And when the team wasn't running smoothly, these comparisons had deadly effects: if it was already a widespread belief that I was his big supporter – and as we've seen, I would have preferred Montella – certain phrases convinced even the dressing room that this was the case.

The ship was heading for the rocks at full speed. We lost badly at Juve. We lost the derby. The trend was always a rollercoaster, but the team couldn't withstand the big matches. Zeman dropped De Rossi, who was guilty of not playing directly like Panagiotis Tachtsidis, telling me that he was playing against him. This was absolutely ridiculous nonsense. Daniele is a pure man who always put the good of Roma above all else. Then he dropped Miralem Pjanić, and we lost a top-class midfielder. Finally, and by that point the ground was disappearing from under his feet, came the disaster at home to Cagliari: 4-2 to them, and their second goal was a grotesque own goal by our keeper Mauro Goicoechea. Maarten Stekelenburg had been on the bench for some time, and he retook his place in goal the following Sunday when Zeman was no longer there.

For those who were very fond of him, like me, it was the end of a really painful journey. It had been clear how it would end for a long time, and yet no one – him first of all – did anything about it. He was kicked out the night after the defeat to Cagliari. The next day he left us without big speeches, admitting to some mistakes but ultimately nothing major. It was February 2013. The club didn't want to tie themselves down to the future and so promoted Aurelio Andreazzoli, who had been part of the first team technical staff for years. It was a good choice, because at that point of the season, starting down a new path would have been counter-productive.

That same evening, Andreazzoli called me to ask me to get to Trigoria an hour before the others the next day: 'I need to talk to you.' What he gave me, asking me for the support that he'd obviously get, was a very personal speech: at sixty years old, his big chance has arrived, and he wanted to try to give it a go in the face of all the newspapers that called him a 'ferryman'. I liked this determination, and I also liked the way he redesigned the team. The results came quickly. After a defeat at Samp, a result of the rapid restructuring, we hosted leaders Juventus at the Olimpico. We were ninth and some way back, and if the game wasn't a classic, the prediction would have been that it would be one-sided. Yet that evening, our pride of being Roma, stimulated obviously by our most heartfelt opponent, worked like a miracle: we played a memorable match, particularly those players who had got their places back like De Rossi and Stekelenburg, and in the 58th minute a perfect ball for the inside of my right foot arrived just outside the penalty area. A torpedo came out that gave Buffon no chance and flew into the top corner.

Let's pause here. It was the last goal I'd score against Gigi from open play. Two seasons later, I'd beat him once more, but it was a penalty that in the end didn't affect a highly controversial game. This one from 2013, however, was a goal from open play that was the crucial one to secure a 1-0 win, a goal that mattered and that forced one of my closest friends – incidentally, the best goalkeeper in the world and the poster boy of the club I always stood against – into surrender, in a sporting sense. In short, there was a real tangle of emotions in that powerful right-footed shot that flew just under the crossbar. At the end of the game, Gigi and I hugged each other as always, and maybe I'd somehow have liked to have known that that would be the last great goal I'd score against him, because then I'd have celebrated it differently; maybe I'd have asked him to have dinner together, he could go back home the next day – it was Saturday, after all. We were both old men. Certain moments should be prolonged and not cut short like this, '*Ciao, ciao*, say hi to the family.' My last great goal against Buffon (and against Juve). Happiness. Pride. Even a tinge of sadness. Our sporting stories were heading towards their end.

Andreazzoli's Roma worked quite well, partly because such prestigious victories turn the retrorockets on and, for a while, you can make the most of a big boost. We climbed from ninth place up to fifth, and in the Coppa Italia we reaffirmed our superiority over Inter by winning 3-2 in the second leg of the semi-final in April. We'd won the first leg 2-1 at home in January, when Zeman was still in charge. There was a certain surprise in the Roman air about what Andreazzoli was doing, and the word 'ferryman' no longer appeared in every article as it did before, when apparently it was obligatory. Not that it's an insult, but people should think about the meaning of the words they use, perhaps asking themselves if they aren't running the risk of hurting a person. Not a professional, a person. The ferryman is the one who transports the team from a failure to a new start, two situations handled by others. But why deny him the possibility, halfway through the journey, of turning the rudder and steering the ship towards the open sea? Especially if he found himself able to handle it without crashing it on the rocks, despite the low tide?

If Andreazzoli had won the Coppa Italia, he'd probably have been kept on: in the end, it's always results that decide everything. You can talk all you want about the principles of the game and their application, but if they don't make you win, the fans will abandon you. In the most delicate moment of his adventure, the coach made a couple of mistakes in his decisions, above all that of reintroducing Mattia Destro – back from a long convalescence – for Pablo Osvaldo, who had been rattling goals in during the spring. It ended badly, and the goal from Senad Lulić gave Lazio not only the cup but also the qualification for the Europa League that was at stake. Osvaldo, furious at his exclusion, went too far by calling Andreazzoli a Laziale on social media. The boss thanked us and returned to the assistants' ranks, aware that what he'd done hadn't been enough. It was nice to see him return to Serie A in charge of Empoli in 2017.

Rudi Garcia was the third coach appointed by the American owners after Luis Enrique and Zeman. In the spring, a rumour spread in Trigoria that contact had been made with Max Allegri, tired of a Milan that was continuing to downsize year after year: the story was absolutely true, but he preferred to stay in Milan, so Sabatini turned to the French coach who had won Ligue 1 a couple of years earlier with Lille, discovering and enhancing the great talent of Eden Hazard. The public grumbled, because after recent disappointments they feared another gamble, and I was perplexed myself: the years were going by and the dream of winning another *scudetto*, while still alive, seemed less and less possible. For this to happen, we needed a specialist on the bench and some reliable signings in the transfer market: in fact, I couldn't help thinking that my only title was linked to the arrival of Capello as our coach and Batistuta as our great goalscorer. In that sense, I confess that I knew nothing of Garcia other than about his success in France, which obviously can't be compared to Serie A in terms of difficulty. I was hesitant. Then I was informed about his first inspection of the sports complex during which Sabatini and Massimo Tarantino, the new head of the youth sector, told him that I was finished and that I should give up as soon as possible. These weren't pleasant things to hear. The atmosphere in Trigoria was becoming oppressive. On the first day of pre-season training, I shook the boss' hand for the first time, uncertain about what to expect both for myself and for the team's prospects.

The first mists to clear were those related to him as a person. Rudi Garcia is a delightful guy, very good at managing the group. He was also smart, because by setting up a very light preparation – lots of ball work and little long-distance running – he surrounded himself with smiles: summer footballers are always happy to work without too much intensity, because it's hot and it's difficult. What would happen when things caught up with us – as De Rossi and I feared – wasn't part of the group's concerns just then. Then, Garcia and his assistants – Fred and Claude, very likeable guys – came up with new, fun and competitive exercises with the ball, and we'd put up the next coffee as the stakes. The general atmosphere was pleasant and most importantly calm, and this was perceived by the fans, many of whom were still furious with us for the derby defeat in the Coppa Italia. Garcia was good with them too because he knew how to use words well. He took time to find the best ones. He expressed his pride and joy at being part of Roma like no one before him. He was a professional communicator. And the public started to calm down, to listen to him, even to wait for his press conferences, because there was always a joke or an idea that led you to take pride. After the victory in the derby, the first major success under his management, his phrase 'We've put the church back in the centre of the village' had a multiplier effect on both the fans and our self-confidence, because it was the best illustration of the club's role in the city. Rome belongs to Roma. In all my years, this was my favourite metaphor by far, the one that made me feel most proud of being the Giallorossi captain.

I must say that the club also worked at its best that year, because the summer transfer market brought some high-level players to Trigoria: Morgan De Sanctis in goal, Medhi Benatia in defence, Kevin Strootman in midfield, and Adem Ljajić and Gervinho in attack, with the fundamental addition of Radja Nainggolan in January. I worked 'against' the sales because I was sorry that Osvaldo's future was in doubt, as he was an excellent striker. I left him a penalty in the friendly against Bursaspor. The move was a message to the fans, who had been booing him since Andreazzoli's first game, at Sampdoria, when, without saying anything to me, he picked up the ball after winning a spot kick and took it regardless of the fact that I'd been Roma's penalty taker for almost twenty years. He even missed it, which ended up turning people against him. The 'theft' made me angry at the time, but we later cleared things up between ourselves. The 'gifted' penalty against the Turks was intended to be a kind of public rehabilitation, but it ended up making little difference. While the signings were of good quality, there were also the painful sales of Osvaldo himself, of Marquinhos, and of Erik Lamela, who begged me to help him to stay because he was very happy at Roma. On the first Sunday, we won 2-0 at Livorno with an opening goal from De Rossi, who thus ensured he would stay too: without a 'loud' performance from him, the negotiations Sabatini had begun with Chelsea would have continued.

In any case, Garcia's start was astonishing: ten straight victories, a new record for opening wins. We played without a nominal centre forward, so the reference point up front was me once again because my movement, which pulled centre backs out of position, opened space up for the quick forward runs of Gervinho, whose signing was expressly requested by the coach, who had had him at Lille. I scored less than usual – I was 37 by then, don't forget – but as an attacking playmaker, I felt like I was the key man in the team again. Garcia himself, when he was asked about my physical condition, replied with surprising simplicity: 'Totti is the one who's in the best shape.' It was also thanks to his management, that is, to personalised training – which doesn't mean mild, but rather was aimed at what I had to do on the pitch – and to an intelligent use of my resources: I didn't always play, in agreement with him I calmly took a place on the bench, reserving myself for the most important games. There were two of those in that initial streak, the derby in the fourth game and Inter away in the seventh, and these were two individual performances worthy of my best years. I worked on the wings against Lazio, often changing position, and set up Federico Balzaretti's goal to make it 1-0 as if I were a right winger; then I contributed to the destruction of Inter with a great goal and a penalty, and they went into half time 3-0 down and never re-emerged. All too good to last, unfortunately.

I got injured on matchday 8, against Napoli. A strange injury, the gluteus tendon detached from the muscle. I could only rest and wait for it to find the best place to reattach itself. It's a natural process that Professor Mariani – obviously consulted immediately – ruled out being able to accelerate through surgery: 'If I operate on you, you'll probably have to retire.' There was nothing else to do but wait, and it was a long and painful wait because I returned for the first time in mid-December, after less than two months, but the leg wasn't feeling as it should. I held out until mid-February, but then I had to stop for another month until an X-ray confirmed that the tendon had reattached itself six centimetres below its previous position. In the meantime, though, the fight for top spot had ended.

A few details: the first ten consecutive wins only gave us a five-point advantage over Juve and Napoli. Too few to last once the tank was empty, because that's what happened, as I'd feared since July: once the physical vibrancy had been used up – and also once they were deprived of their captain (I say this without arrogance but also without false modesty) – Roma visibly slowed down by drawing too much before the abrupt 3-0 defeat to Juventus. This was the Juve side that got 102 points, a title liberally celebrated as having been won at the Olimpico with a goal from Osvaldo, signed in January from Southampton: he was a sort of nemesis for us, accentuated by the fact that that was his only goal in black and white. You couldn't make it up. The final outcome of the season, however, was more than positive: we finished in second place again after three years of not even being in Europe (we only saw the qualifying round under Luis Enrique), an airtight relationship bound the team and the technical staff, and the Olimpico public had made their peace with us after the anger of previous seasons. There was enough to plan for the 2014/15 season with confidence and ambition.

In the meantime, Rudi Garcia had fallen in love. I'll tell you this story because it's a very good illustration of how difficult it is to work in Rome, a city in which rumours and hearsay from the media never cease, not even at night. Give it a try: find a photo of a coach who has just arrived in Rome and compare it with one of the same coach a few months later. In the first you'll see a man in top shape, in the second a guy who's aged prematurely, his hair whitened and his shoulders hunched.

So, we were talking about Garcia's engagement. I practically followed it live, because Rudi often ate with us 'seniors', and when he caught a glimpse of Francesca, a good-looking girl from Roma TV, at the buffet, he invariably remained frozen with his fork in mid-air. 'How elegant she is, what a beautiful smile.'

We made fun of him, though without going too far because you need a little distance between coach and players, but with a lot of affection and – let's be honest – emotional involvement too. In a world that people think is tied to unbridled sex, Garcia exhibited all the symptoms of a high school crush, and I liked how he didn't hide it; it was a sign of confidence. Rudi was divorced and single, nothing stood in the way of him courting Francesca, and when the two got together we were all happy. A story like that, of course, quickly got into the public domain, so they posted their famous selfie at the Colosseum on social media, making their relationship official. Pure romance, but as soon as the team began to struggle, the chatter in the media became incessant: 'Now the coach doesn't care', 'She's the one who's picking the team', 'Forget about people who distract you', and so on. It's the great limitation of Rome, and probably not only Rome: as soon as something stops working, the reason for that is sought outside the technical context, within the private lives of those involved. Either you win or you're a lazy nighthawk. It's a ridiculous way of thinking, but unfortunately very widespread.

The 2014/15 season revolved around some very specific matches. In the league, we started at full speed like Juve and we both arrived at our head-to-head game on matchday 6 with maximum points. We were playing at the Juventus Stadium, Gianluca Rocchi was the referee, the match was full of contentious decisions and, honestly, I believe Roma came out of it damaged. We lost 3-2, two penalties were awarded to them and one to us – as I said before, this was the very last goal I scored against Buffon – and the decisive goal was scored by Leonardo Bonucci while Arturo Vidal was offside, active for us and passive for them, and we've not stopped arguing about it since. Garcia made his violin gesture to suggest the referee had been intimidated psychologically, but in the end it wasn't this game that set the course for the season because a few weeks later, thanks to Juve's defeat in Genova, we were level again. Like the previous year, the duel essentially lasted the first half of the season, which finished with five points separating us. From then on, we began to get lost in a series of draws that ended up suffocating us: we finished this season in second place too – and that's always a good result – but without having reduced the gap to Juventus at all: 17 points, like the previous season. But we both collected 15 points fewer. In fact, we were only one point ahead of Lazio, who didn't overtake us simply because we picked up four points in the derbies.

In Garcia's second season there was European football too, and it was a very promising journey that one October evening turned into total depression. But let's go in order. The first game in the Champions League group was a dream because we beat CSKA Moscow 5-1 in an Olimpico that was going crazy. The second game saw us travel to Manchester, to City's patch, and since we were unbeaten in the league and playing great, Garcia was convinced that we could win there too. After going behind after just a few minutes from a penalty, Roma reorganised themselves and came out of it in style. Partly thanks to me. Halfway through the first half, Nainggolan turned a ball out of defence towards me first-time, there was some nice open space in front of me and I was feeling very calm as I ran into it because I'd seen that the keeper was coming out and that his defenders were out of the game. The ball needed a touch underneath it, soft and surprising, to get just far enough over Hart's outstretched body; it was on the outside of my right foot, and despite my age it was child's play. As I ran, I repeated where I wanted to put it to myself twice and placed it right there, in the far corner, a real touch of class. We held onto the draw while dominating the game and only taking risks at the end, which I followed from the bench because Garcia introduced the freshness of Juan Iturbe for the last twenty minutes. Two games, four points, and awaiting me in the dressing room was the surprise of compliments from UEFA officials and then from everyone, because at the age of 38 years and 3 days, I'd become the oldest goalscorer in the history of the Champions

League. By the way, this was a record I extended almost two months later in Moscow, scoring the goal that temporarily gave us the lead over CSKA.

There's a big difference between the records you set as a youngster and those that you set as an older player. Both say that you're a special type of player, but if the former raise expectations around you because you're talented·and have your whole life ahead of you, the latter always contain a hint of regret. How many times have I heard it repeated, in an unnecessarily harsh tone, that I would have hoarded Ballons d'Or by going to Real Madrid... But it was precisely in order not to have regrets that I kept playing at an age at which the majority of my peers were already sitting behind a desk at a coaching course. Goals like the one in Manchester told me that I was still capable of influencing games – you should have read the headlines in the English newspapers the next morning – and as long as there was still an ounce of energy in me, I wanted to dream of another *scudetto*, or that Champions League that would complete that most sought-after of trebles.

The match that defined the season, and made Garcia's experience in Rome a negative one, was the third group game. Pep Guardiola's Bayern Munich arrived at the Olimpico, and the city was filled with an impressive winning fever. Everyone was convinced that we'd do it. The Germans had maximum points. They'd won the competition two years previously, and on that occasion they hadn't been coached by the great Pep. Many considered them the real favourites for the Champions League: yet there was no fan who we passed outside Trigoria who didn't make the sign of victory with their fingers, there was no friend who didn't ask for a disproportionate number of tickets 'because it will be a historic evening', there was no pundit on the radio, on the TV or in the newspapers that wasn't talking about Roma's big chance. A collective hallucination? In retrospect, evidently yes, but I admit that I too was confident before the game because the team was functioning and all the signs were positive. We didn't even start badly, but... with their first shot, Robben scored, and from then on the game quickly became a nightmare. Everyone scored: Götze, Lewandowski, Robben again, Müller, Ribéry, Shaqiri, practically every shot ended up in the net like that other unreal night at Old Trafford. The final score of 7-1 was the worst defeat of my life, the worst because it happened at the Olimpico, while the other European beatings all happened away. I went off at the end of the first half when it was 0-5, when there was no longer any hope in that game. It needed people who could run a lot to plug the leaks.

The public didn't even whistle, there was so much pain. Indeed, they heartened us because they immediately realised the risk of the psychological backlash: it wouldn't be easy to 'forget' such a thrashing. At the end of the game, Guardiola looked for me to tell me that he was sorry for humiliating us but that you don't stop in the Champions League, and I knew he was right. Our paths had crossed for a few months in Rome in the autumn of 2002, in Capello's era, but since he didn't play much, he returned to Brescia in January. I remember a playmaker who by then was old, not very dynamic on the pitch but highly skilled in keeping the ball moving, and as a person he was on a different level compared to normal footballers. He felt he was passing through and was fairly solitary, but since he had become the most famous coach in the world by that evening, we spent five minutes talking about families, about Mazzone and about old teammates. It didn't cure the pain of the 7-1, but it was nice all the same.

The beating from Bayern marked a before and after in Garcia's experience in Rome. It demoralised him to the extent that it made him lose much of his self-confidence. Instead of dismissing the game as a hiccup, he mulled over it for months, thus sowing confusion in a tactical setup that had found its balance. Garcia isn't a coach with a rigid scheme, he gives its interpreters the right amount of freedom, he creates situations in a game where you can choose from several solutions: his added value is in the calm that he exudes, but when he was the first to lose it, it became complicated to follow him. Francesca herself stopped coming to Trigoria, in search of a respite from the social media bombardment that judged her to be the cause of the problem, and the January transfer window was the icing on the cake: Gervinho needed to be replaced, as he was at the African Cup of Nations, but the striker who arrived, Seydou Doumbia, was absent for the same reason. There was also Victor Ibarbo, signed from Cagliari like Nainggolan, but signings like Ninja don't happen every year, and this one didn't even come close.

Garcia was on his knees by the end of the season, and even in the summer, some strange discussions could be heard, as if his position was unstable despite two consecutive second-place finishes. The transfer window was a significant one: Wojciech Szczęsny, Edin Džeko, Mo Salah and Antonio Rüdiger arrived without any big names leaving. On paper, it seemed to me to be the strongest Roma side for many years, and in the league, in the face of Juve facing a serious crisis at the outset (they lost four of their first ten games), we started quite well, going top and mainly battling with Inter. The problem was that I got injured on 26 September against Carpi, ten minutes after coming on and setting up a goal for Salah. As everyone was celebrating his goal, I called for a doctor because I felt a stabbing pain in the usual tendon. So I spent the Monday of my 39th birthday at Villa Stuart, trying to learn the seriousness of the injury. I ended up being ruled out until the New Year, and by the time I returned – at the end of the match against Milan – the situation had deteriorated irremediably. Amid much torment, Garcia got through the Champions League group, less difficult compared to the previous season, was fifth in the league, seven points behind Napoli, and was sensationally knocked out of the Coppa Italia by Spezia. The rumours about his dismissal were now a clamour, but the club decided to give him another chance after the New Year, I think more than anything else because they wanted to choose the new coach calmly in the spring.

These were downhearted days, because it was perfectly clear that a decision had been made and the sentence only postponed. Garcia had surrendered. He no longer had the mental or physical energy to govern the situation. He was awaiting the sentence like a liberation. At the Christmas dinner, organised at a restaurant on the Tiburtina, I saw a clear illustration of the separation between the club and the coach because his assistants hadn't been invited – only the squad and the coach – and Rudi suddenly found himself alone. I observed him with sideways glances, trying not to let him see, because the sight made an impression on me: he had the gaze of a hunted animal, his eyes jumped constantly from one tablemate to another, as if the last blow, the fatal one, could arrive from anyone.

After the home draw with Milan on 9 January, his dismissal was made official: the team were given two days off, and when we returned, at ten in the morning on the Tuesday, we found Garcia waiting to say his goodbyes.

'We loved each other, you gave me so much joy. Thank you, everyone, and work hard, because you can play much better than you've shown under me...'

The kisses and hugs contained an element of haste. At noon, Luciano Spalletti returned to Trigoria.

18.

The Second Tragic Spalletti

I WAS GLAD SPALLETTI WAS BACK. AT THE END OF HIS FIRST spell, he'd let slip some resentful phrases, including towards me, but every time we met again afterwards – in Florence, for example – there were kisses and hugs. During his long tenure at Roma, he became friends with Claudio, the owner of La Villetta restaurant, which as you know is my favourite refuge. So, in later years, when he informed him that I was having dinner there, the boss would send him a shirtless photo – one of his favourite antics – to show me that he hadn't put on a pound of fat. I often met Daniele Baldini, Spalletti's long-time collaborator, in the other restaurant I frequent, Checco dello Scapicollo, and in Garcia's final months, when the Frenchman's position on the bench had become unstable, there was always the same phrase: 'Come on Francesco, you're the one who can bring us back to Roma...' It was all a laugh and a joke, but at the same time the sign of good feelings, of a desire to work together again.

I also spoke about this to Ilary, saying that I was lucky. It was the opposite situation to the one with Zeman: they both knew me well, but while Il Boemo is unwavering in his athletic principles, Spalletti is a more flexible man; he knew what my body needed to perform at its best and would certainly find a good way to help me manage my exit from the stage. Because by then that was what was being talked about: I had set myself the goal of playing in Serie A at 40, then I would quit. In other words, finish the current season and play one more. When we met each other again for the first team meeting – not many of his old side were still there – Spalletti shook my hand and asked how Mum and Dad were, who at the time he knew well, given that he lived in Axa. A measured approach. Strangely, however, he didn't ask anything about the injury that had kept me inactive for three months, and from which I had returned just the previous Saturday. Something smelled fishy to me, and I also talked about it with Ilary. It was too early to start worrying, but I had been expecting a different connection. Warmer, more involved.

The evening before Roma-Verona, the start of 'his' campaign, Spalletti called us together to dictate a few rules of conduct. 'I found out that on the last night before a game, the one before you played Milan, some of you were up late playing cards. I don't want you playing cards, as your internal rules dictate.' I felt called into question. I was the most passionate card player in the group, bordering on compulsive. I didn't stay up late, but I played plenty of cards on training retreats.

'Actually, those rules weren't signed by everyone...' I tried to defend myself.

Spalletti replied bluntly: 'Don't bust my balls, Checco.' He used the informal diminutive, the one my friends call me by, to send both me and the dressing room a message of total closure. I didn't reply. It was the first disagreement, and he won it.

The second was semi-private. I say 'semi' because from the beginning of his second spell, Spalletti made sure that two witnesses were present at each of our discussions, clearly one on each side, given that Vito was always there; he added a staff member or someone from the press office. Not a great sign. Before Juve-Roma, his second game, we had a confrontation because I'd misplaced a few passes in training, he came down hard on me, and eventually I told him where to go. I explained to him that it was taking me longer than expected to get back to 100% and that it didn't help to see him talking to everyone except me when I was still the captain. He responded with unusual harshness, doing nothing to allay the fears of an almost forty-year-old.

'Last time I allowed you everything, Francesco, not anymore. You have to run like the others, even if your name is Totti' was the gist of his speech, which annoyed me a lot, given that I had never demanded favouritism. The following evening, I greeted Buffon in the dressing rooms at the Juventus Stadium. He gave me a broad smile and asked 'How's it going with the Doberman?', only to immediately become serious when he saw my face.

After a while, my teammates realised that Spalletti had taken aim at me, because the frequent reproaches in training were those that a coach normally makes to youngsters who are getting big-headed. There was something off-key in making them to the captain, and at breakfast someone asked me what I had done to him. At home, I got the same doubts from Ilary, who, when faced with my stories, always played devil's advocate. 'Are you sure you haven't disrespected him in some way? A word or a gesture that he could have misinterpreted?' I examined my conscience several times, I swear, because disbelief still prevailed over anger. Until some of his highly controversial responses to journalists' questions made it clear that he was still convinced about the role I had played – or rather, about my 'failure to come to his rescue', given that he accused me of not having said anything – at the end of his previous spell with Roma in 2009.

The difficult relationship with Spalletti was compounded by a recovery from physical problems that had never been so slow and arduous. I finally played a bit against Frosinone, then he sent me to warm up at the end of the first half in Reggio Emilia against Sassuolo and forgot about me so completely that after half an hour I started having a kickabout with a ball boy of Cristian's age, I asked him what position he played, and so on; in short, it was a nice moment. The game was quite easy; once all the changes had been made, I went back to the bench, played a joke on Pjanić, it ended 2-0, and everything seemed to have turned out for the best. Or so I thought. Not at all. That evening, the images of the kickabout with the kid were already doing the rounds on TV, and someone commented that I hadn't been showing much investment in the fate of the team. The next day, I read about my substantial indifference in various newspapers. Useless malice written – look closely – by journalists who were normally closest to the club. If I was grimacing, why was I grimacing? If I was joking, why was I joking? For the first time, I suspected that my retirement wasn't something only Spalletti had taken to heart.

But the team was doing very well. After the defeat in Turin, a series of eight wins brought us back to third place, which offers a spot in the Champions League qualifying round, while we paid the price for being drawn against Real Madrid in the Champions League and went out in the Round of 16. The fact that relations between us had deteriorated didn't stop me from seeing that Spalletti was still a great coach: I was sure I'd know how to make myself useful to a team that was in such form, but I wasn't given the opportunity.

I was so depressed that, ahead of the trip to Carpi in mid-February, I did something that I'd never done before: I called in sick. Or rather, since I felt a little discomfort in my tendon, I said that I couldn't manage it so that I could stay in Rome. I thought there was no difference between the bench and the sofa, as I'd only be watching either way, and then, when I began to think about it with a cooler head, I realised that it was the beginning of the end. I no longer believed in myself. That was what it had come to.

Those were bitter days in which Ilary was extraordinary, because she encouraged me without compromising her position: in her opinion, I should retire at the end of the season. My time had come. And it was an opinion that weighed heavily, because I was sure that she was being dispassionate.

The following Saturday, 20 February, the eve of the home game against Palermo, was a date that had been set for some time for Donatella Scarnati from *Rai* to interview me about the decade since the World Cup win. We recorded at lunchtime in the presence of a press officer, who also authorised Donatella to ask me a few questions about my situation at Roma. At the same time – though I only discovered this later – Spalletti was saying in the press conference that the following evening, I'd be in the starting line-up for the first time since he returned.

In the interview, which has been listened to again and again – it's still easy to find it on the web today – I said I'd expected different treatment from him: above all, I'd have liked certain things that I'd read in the newspapers to have been said to my face. Nothing more. I didn't ask to play. I didn't criticise him. On the contrary, I recognised his value for Roma both then and in the future. I asked for more respect and clarity from the club, that's true, because my contract expired at the end of the season and I still wanted to play. Whether there or elsewhere, because I wasn't lacking offers from abroad. Respect meant letting me know the truth. My side of it is that in the summer, I spoke with President Pallotta in Boston, who told me: 'You decide.' I saw him again in Rome in December, at the Hotel de Russie, and he asked me what I intended to do as a director. I replied that I wanted to play for another year, and he seemed surprised. A few days after the interview with *Rai*, Pallotta was back in Rome, and he suggested that he'd listen to Spalletti's opinion. 'I don't think he wants anything to do with it,' I replied, and that's how we said goodbye, still on excellent terms, but with the problem still on the table.

But let's take a step back, to the moment when the aftermath of the interview provoked the first major crisis with the coach. It happened on Sunday morning at breakfast because, as often happens, the written word causes more of a stir than those spoken on TV. On Saturday evening, *Tg1* had headlined with my attack on the boss, and frankly I didn't see it as that – I said I'd expected different treatment, but an attack? The next morning's newspapers made matters worse. I ate alone in a corner, away from the table where Spalletti and the staff were, where Vito was also sitting. He was the one who came over to me to pass on the summons: 'He wants to talk to you about the interview.' We went to a meeting room. The coach had the press review in his hand. He waved it around as if it were a cudgel.

'What should I do now?' he asked three times, his tone increasingly impatient.

'Boss, have you listened to the interview? Vito's recorded it...'

'I don't give a shit about the interview, what matters is what's written here, in the papers.'

'Look, I only spoke well of you. It's the club I asked for more respect from.' I addressed him formally; as I recalled, it was the first time: a clear signal of the chill that had descended over us. We went on for a long time, me clarifying and him reiterating his irritation. I thought I'd get a hefty fine for that interview. I didn't imagine the slap in the face that was about to arrive.

'Enough, it's pointless going on. You just don't get it. You were wrong. Now you're going home.'

It was the most humiliating of punishments. Kicked out of Trigoria. Me. Kicked out of my home. I was shaking with anger. After a long silence, I honed the most cutting words that came to me at that moment.

'Alright, I accept your punishment. We'll see if it's me or you that suffers the consequences.'

'Are you threatening me?'

'You know the people in Rome are on my side. I've only spoken well of you, yet you want to kick me out. Face up to your responsibilities.'

'You're like the others now, you're not irreplaceable anymore.'

'Coward, now that you don't need me anymore you're fucking me over, eh? You came back here on a mission, carry it out!'

We said all sorts of things to each other. By the end, nothing had been left unsaid. I left exhausted. A quarter of an hour later I rang the doorbell at home and my wife was bewildered. I was feeling really down, the lowest point I can remember. I didn't want to see anyone, and if I could have taken a plane to go to a different continent, I'd have done it the same day. The match against Palermo was that evening, but I ruled out the idea of going to the Olimpico. I wouldn't have been able to stand everyone's gazes being fixed on me.

And it was then, at that precise moment, that Ilary – supported by Vito, who agreed with her – took control of the situation: 'We'll all go to the stadium: us, friends, relatives, everyone. You've got nothing to hide or to be forgiven for, quite the contrary. You have to show your face precisely for this reason, so that people know whose conscience is clear.' As soon as I tried to protest, she was resolute: 'Look, if we don't go to the stadium tonight, I'm dumping you. I can't bear the thought that you would bow to injustices.' It was driven by love, but it was quite the threat. 'OK, call everyone and organise it, tonight we're going to the Olimpico.'

Before the game, I stopped by the dressing room, where the atmosphere was a bit dispirited. An arm-wrestling contest between the coach and captain inevitably ends up destabilising the squad. I bumped into Spalletti, who seemed surprised. He asked me what I was doing there. I responded that a captain should always come to see his teammates, and it ended there – neither he nor I wanted to rekindle the fire. I guess the fight had taken something out of him, too.

While I was going back upstairs to our seats, Angelo called to tell me that Spalletti's name had been jeered while the teams were being announced. There was an anxious journey from the dressing room to the stand because a thousand thoughts were coming to mind, and above all I wondered what to expect once I came out into the open, where everyone could see me.

There was only applause. A standing ovation, even, a roar as soon as I appeared in the stands and the camera that transmits onto the big screen fixed itself on me. Do you remember what I said at the beginning of the book, about the doubts about what I could ever have done to deserve such affection from so many people? Yeah. I had goosebumps from emotion and gratitude. Ilary was right, and before I could tell her she sent me a text, because it wasn't easy to hear each other in that noise. I've never deleted it. She said: 'This is the greatest satisfaction you could ever have.' I sent her a kiss of gratitude.

Roma won easily, 5-0, with braces from Džeko and Salah. The people sang, and they whistled Spalletti every time the camera focused on him. In the following month, I played a few minutes against Fiorentina in addition to the final minutes at the Bernabéu: not many at all, and that was a shame, because by then I was back at 100% again, a new diet had made me lose four kilos and I was as toned as a young man. I had to wait until 11 April to get back onto the pitch for Roma-Bologna, and in a certain sense we were nearing the finale because those two months off the pitch had affected my mental resistance: put bluntly, by then I was convincing myself that Spalletti was right, that my time was up and that I'd stopped being important. My self-esteem had dropped below the danger level. So I was surprised when the coach, when we were 1-0 down at the end of the first half, asked me to warm up so that he could put me on as soon as the game restarted. The few minutes I'd been granted until that point had come when the result was already secure, as if it was only in this way that he could risk using me. Humiliating, thinking about it. This time, however,

I came on in the 46th minute with a result to recover. It was the chance that I had been looking for.

One of the magical things about football is how easily it comes back to you, even if you haven't practised for a long time. No pieces of skill had disappeared: they were all there, waiting for me to need them once again. Of course, there are some players who make a mistake with the first couple of bits of skill and get inhibited, convinced they're no longer capable of doing them. Not in my case: the first ball that I touched was a first-time through ball that cut the centre of Bologna's defence in two and freed Salah to score and make it 1-1. Simple. I didn't even think about that move: it was instinct, happy to welcome me back. We didn't score any more goals and it finished like that, but I knew that my forty-five minutes – which suddenly seemed like a lot to me – were of a good standard. I could almost see it 'graphically', with my self-confidence indicator changing its direction and starting to rise again. It hadn't taken much.

The quality of my performance was also testified by the fact that the media started talking about me in a certain way again, and I knew that this, for the purposes of internal balance, wasn't a good thing. The next round in the race for second place – Napoli didn't miss a beat – took us to Bergamo, and the day before, I sensed something shifting. In hotels before away games, Spalletti invariably ended up occupying a room adjacent to mine, to the extent that one time I asked him if it was really a coincidence, and in response he said: 'I want to monitor you better.' One of the logistics staff also confirmed this to me; the boss always tried to place himself between me, Nainggolan and Pjanić – we were an inseparable trio who spent time together before going to sleep. His problem was the usual one, our games of cards, which in his view took away energy and focus.

Since he returned, knowing his phobia (and mindful of his first speech), we had stopped. Really. Everyone instead carried a computer or a tablet around with them, and we entertained ourselves with those while waiting for sleep. Our computer games were endless. That Saturday evening in Bergamo, Mire, Radja and I were together in my room – Texas Buraco was on the screen – when, around 23.30, dressed in a black tracksuit, Spalletti sneaked up to my door and sat on the ground outside, leaning his back against the wall, waiting, practically invisible because the corridor was poorly lit. In his attempt to surprise us, however, he hadn't considered the physiotherapy room, which was always open and was next to mine. Shortly before midnight, De Rossi, who often needed a massage to sleep the night before games, emerged from it. In the semi-darkness, he didn't believe his eyes. 'Boss, is that you? What are you doing?' Spalletti replied in a low voice: 'Nothing, nothing, I know you'll just tell your friends now...' Daniele feigned ignorance – 'Tell them what? I'm minding my own business' – went back to his room and immediately sent a WhatsApp message to Pjanić: 'Look out for the boss hiding outside the door.' It was 0.15, a quarter of an hour after the cut-off time: not that serious, but Radja and Mire still considered the idea of escaping out of the window and letting themselves fall to the ground. But we were on the second floor. It was too high.

We didn't know what to do, other than to laugh while trying not to make a noise, because the situation was objectively comical, but making ourselves heard wouldn't have been smart. In the end, I half-opened the door, just wide enough to see Spalletti's outstretched legs. Radja went out, pretending to trip over them, 'Oh my God, who is it? Boss, what the hell...', Pjanić followed him and I... closed the door behind them. But I was in time to hear Spalletti's sarcastic voice: 'Don't get smart, I know what you were doing in Francesco's room, you were playing cards', and Mire immediately said: 'What cards? No, we were on the computer!' 'We'll work this out tomorrow' was the last, threatening sentence I heard.

The next morning, at breakfast, he didn't say good morning to us. Marco Domenichini, one of his staff, arrived as the vanguard: 'What were you doing playing cards?' *Oh come on...* 'No, no cards. Computer.' It sounds like I'm talking about children, but that wasn't the end of it because in the pre-match meeting, the one in which we were told about a starting line-up that didn't include Pjanić (the punishment was obvious), Spalletti reiterated that games of cards were forbidden and that someone, the previous night, had made a mockery of this ban. I no longer had the strength to reply.

The game was crazy. We went 2-0 up quite smoothly through Digne and Nainggolan, but D'Alessandro and a brace from Borriello turned things around: 3-2 to Atalanta. Spalletti turned towards us – Mire and

I were sat close to each other – and said, 'This shit's on you now, I'm revealing everything in the press conference.' Ten minutes from the end, he threw me on for Daniele, and soon I scored the goal to make it 3-3 with a good shot from the edge of the box. Perotti did well to bring the ball into the area, as did Florenzi to turn it back towards me on the slide, but the right-footed shot that beat Sportiello bore my trademark, and two minutes later Džeko nearly made the most of a pass from me that would have made it a phantasmagoric 4-3.

Sent off for protesting a minute from the end, Spalletti was waiting for us outside the dressing room, visibly wired. When the last of us had entered, he closed the door behind him, slamming it, and started yelling. My locker was the furthest from the entrance. I was next to De Rossi and Florenzi, bent over the boots that I was taking off. I didn't notice the sudden silence. When I raised my head, I found Spalletti's face a centimetre from mine. He was waiting for me. 'Enough, you're a pain in the arse, you still expect to lead and instead you should be gone, you ignore my bans to play cards – you're finished!' All shouted at full volume. It was the last argument between me and Spalletti, in the sense that I also lost my temper. It took four people to separate us because otherwise we would have taken out a lot of righteous anger on each other. From then on, we were done. Having recovered his calm, he went into the press room to say that even though I'd scored, the merit of the comeback belonged to the team – and that was absolutely fine, but everyone noticed the desire to belittle me.

I came out of the dressing room, warning the directors, 'I'm talking now', and immediately a safety cordon was set up around me. In reality, I did without the controversy because, as always, I thought it would harm Roma. The next day, at the request of the staff who still found him worked up, I went to Spalletti with Radja and Mire to apologise. Not for having played cards – he kept repeating that like a broken record – but for having stayed up late on the Saturday. He claimed it was one o'clock while it had actually been a quarter past midnight, but ultimately he was still right because the cut-off point was midnight. Better to shut it down so that the matter was closed.

But a certain dynamic had been set in motion, and it was hard not to see the hand of a great director at work. The assist against Bologna, the equaliser against Atalanta, what might the next step be? Perhaps a brace to turn a result around?

Three evenings later, the last midweek round of the season was scheduled. Torino arrived at the Olimpico, and after 86 minutes we were 2-1 down: Džeko and Pjanić had already come on, Spalletti threw me on as the final change, but there was really very little time left. I came on for a set piece, a free kick well inside their half on the right-hand side, which Kostas Manōlas flicked on, and I, racing in from the left, managed to turn it into the net. Under the Curva Sud. I went crazy.

My previous goal at the Olimpico had also been my last one anywhere until the goal in Bergamo three days earlier: it had been on matchday 4 in September, 2-2 against Sassuolo. I'd scored it at the opposite end, the one that made it 1-1, a mistake by their keeper who had kicked it towards Pjanić, who intercepted the ball and gave it to me immediately. I was alone, and I hadn't struck it well. Incomparable to this one against Torino, which gave me back the old thrill of running under the *curva*, leaping over a couple of advertising boards. Stuff that, on account of not playing, also makes you wonder: 'If I score, will I make it over, or might I trip and make the whole stadium laugh at me?' Instead it was like swimming, as soon as you're thrown in the water you remember how to do it. Just then, the *curva* had a magnetic appeal, because the recovery of the result coupled with the fact that I'd scored made me go crazy.

With three minutes left, the referee Gianpaolo Calvarese gifted us a penalty; there just wasn't a handball by Nikola Maksimović after Diego Perotti crossed it. It was customary that it was left to me, and it was a doubly heavy responsibility because it affected both the team – we needed the win to keep the teams behind at a distance – and my personal story: if I could also score the goal that completed the comeback in the four minutes (plus injury time) that had been permitted to me, the achievement would be among my biggest.

Since we've spoken a lot about cards, it was the most classic of all-ins. The pitch was heavy because it had rained. I decided on the usual penalty with the inside of my right foot, but I didn't connect with it well, it was neither angled enough nor hard enough. At least it was low, though:

Daniele Padelli touched it without being able to save it, and it ended in glory. The teammates who hugged me were literally fanatical, the fans in the *curva* were crying, and while leaving the pitch even Spalletti couldn't do less than give me a conspiratorial pat on the head. It was simply an incredible conclusion.

As I've already said several times, the love of the people was the wind that pushed me on throughout my career. An irrational and powerful feeling, certainly explainable in its roots – a Roman and Romanista captain, and a talented one at that – but not in its wild intensity. Of course, in the 25 years that passed between my debut in Serie A and my last game, there were some moments when this affection slipped lightly off me and others in which I felt it roar on my skin, burning and absolute. This was one of the times I felt it the most because it came, to borrow the formula of marriage vows, not in good times but in bad.

After the brace against Torino, I played the final minutes against Napoli – a key game to get closer to them and try to overtake them in extremis – and I started the move that led to Nainggolan's goal to make it 1-0 in the 89th minute. The following week I came on in Genova and, after a few minutes, made it 2-2 with a great free kick, and Stephan El Shaarawy added the winning goal late on. Another week later and in my half hour – Spalletti was giving me more game time – against Chievo, I created a first-time assist for Pjanić that was so beautiful it prompted him not to celebrate at all: he turned the ball into the net and immediately pointed at me to the people, indicating that the goal was entirely the merit of my pass.

The fans were celebrating because, even if Napoli didn't drop any more points and finished above us, forcing us to play in the Champions League qualifying round, Spalletti's Roma seemed to be reborn. But if before, within this rebirth, many had been worried about my lack of use, and therefore about an extraordinary story that was ending sombrely, the previous few weeks had seen my full participation in the team's successes. And I felt the relief of a child when Mum and Dad stop arguing. The public that year suffered for me and with me, without even being able to take it up too much with the coach because he was still doing his job well. Now that I'd recovered the role of a partial protagonist – partially because I knew I couldn't expect ninety minutes on a Sunday at my age –

the people's happiness was no longer overshadowed. No one felt guilty with their conscience anymore for having celebrated a victory in which the captain didn't take part. As it should be, but the irrational can't always be controlled.

As I write this book, now that the giant dust cloud of those days has settled, I'm sure of one thing. I should have retired on the evening of Roma-Torino: I was only given four minutes, but I made that enough to turn the game around with a brace, I ran beneath the Curva Sud, the team won, and my teammates carried me in triumph. It would have been the perfect ending, both Ilary and Vito said so, and they have the same sort of sensibility about these things. To tell the truth, the thought crossed my mind, on that evening of explosive joy, but it immediately dissolved because at that moment I wouldn't have known how to introduce it, how to say it, how to do it. I should have improvised, and perhaps that would have been the best choice because people have always appreciated my spontaneity above all else.

Before the season was over, I had a conversation with Mauro Baldissoni, our general director, and I sensed that my brilliant ending had changed something in the club's perception. There was no longer hostility about a renewal. In fact, in June, Pallotta returned to Rome with the contract prepared. I just had to sign it. It was a moment of great doubt, because I had numerous offers from abroad – from China and Japan to the American league and Abu Dhabi – and Ilary would have been in favour: 'I'll take a year off from television,' she said to convince me, 'and you'll live peacefully with your break from competitive football. Don't look at the end of this season, because it was a miracle. Next year will be worse, don't delude yourself.' I knew that she was right, but there was something that she couldn't understand. I'd stopped considering myself a player, and then, suddenly, I felt like I was one once again. An intoxicating sensation, almost a second debut, instead of the obvious thought of only having postponed the sunset. In those days, I even dreamed of being able to play at least a few games from the start again. I was beside myself with the joy of feeling alive again. And I signed.

The last season basically began and ended with the interview that Ilary gave to *La Gazzetta dello Sport* on the occasion of my 40th birthday, in which she defined Spalletti as a 'little man'. Only those who have a distorted relationship with their own partner might think that I could or should have done something to stop that interview. Ilary is a woman with a strong personality, she suffered while living with my bitterness, she fought to keep it from becoming depression, she tried as much as possible to explain it to our children, especially to Cristian – he's the oldest – and on many occasions she faced the conversation about the beginning and the end of everything and about the fact that this champion father of whom she was so proud was simply fading. When she thought it appropriate to give her opinion, she did. And the evening before that interview came out – we were at dinner at home, Angelo was there too – everyone burst out laughing in my face as the spiciest comments were disclosed to me. 'Are you mad? This will cause such a mess, it'll kill me...'

In fact, the next day, Spalletti told me that this sort of situation isn't normal: either I'd fix it by talking to my wife or he would. But there was little to fix. Ilary certainly isn't the type of person who, twenty-four hours after expressing an opinion, will take it back. But the coach also showed a sense of humour, doing an about-turn to wish me a happy birthday by giving me a model of the DeLorean – the car from *Back to the Future* – and my wife a single by Mia Martini, promising that he loved her song *Piccolo uomo*. I invited Spalletti to the party at her insistence as well, taking care that I should never be the one at fault. That day, there was something surreal about the conversation with him at Trigoria.

'Francesco, do you really want me to come to your party?'

'Boss, see for yourself. I invited you...'

'If I come, your friends will end up beating me up.'

'And if they beat you up, they must have a good reason...'

All of this, make no mistake, was said in a much lighter tone than the heated confrontations of the previous season. In any case, on the Sunday before in Turin, I scored the 250th goal of my career in Serie A with a penalty. My last goal. From then on, I was a bit-part player, five minutes here, three there, a few full games in the Europa League, where we went out in the last 16. At the start of the season, Ilary had said to me: 'This is the final final Francesco, and since a year flies by, start preparing yourself now, because then you'll have to put an end to it.' It wasn't easy. In June, when signing my last renewal, Pallotta told me that he was dreaming of a Kobe Bryant-type season for me, a long goodbye, city by city, perhaps organising some side events. I'd explained to him that Italy isn't America, but I actually liked the idea: it was a pity not to have tried to put it into practice. After that, the only time the club talked about my retirement was five games from the end, before Roma-Lazio, when I was asked if I wanted to say anything in the press conference about my last derby. By then the realisation had dawned on me, it was obvious, so much so that I'd even completely given up in training in February, but it was in this way that I officially found out that I had to retire.

I imagine saying 'It's over' to someone like me isn't the easiest thing in the world. Later, at the end of June, when Ilary and I went to London to meet Pallotta and set down the terms for our new working relationship – before leaving, Rosella Sensi had prepared a director's contract for me, which obviously had to be worked out with the new ownership on the day of my retirement – we found Franco Baldini there too. What we said to each other was like the final page in a crime novel. The killer's revelation. And then the way to start afresh.

'It was me, Francesco.'

'To do what, Franco?'

'To make you give up.'

'...'

'I wanted and supported Spalletti because I knew that he thought like me. Years ago, I told you that I wanted to sell you but that every coach I contacted asked me to guarantee you would be here.'

'I remember.'

'Spalletti didn't ask me for that, quite the contrary. After all, we all know that your presence has been a burden for Roma in these last seasons.'

'And the millions made on my shirt sales? And the cachet of friendlies, which changed depending on whether I was there or not?'

'That's true. But you'll see that, from next season, Roma, freed from such a hulking presence, for which there is of course profound gratitude too, will open a new chapter in its history. A happy chapter, and you'll be there regardless.'

'I'd like to be vice-president. Not because I particularly care about the post, but I'd like to be the highest in rank at Trigoria.'

'You don't need it, Francesco.'

'Why?'

'You are Totti, and you always will be. The people listen to you, believe you, love you. We directors are seen as annoying pen pushers, you're the real Roma. And it's by still being Totti that you can start making yourself useful again.'

19.

I Was Hoping I'd Die Before This

THE LAST GAME OF MY CAREER WAS TOO BIG A CONCEPT TO be able to rationalise. Trying not to think about it, I kept it there, in the background, for a good month. But it kept getting closer.

Four games from the end, Spalletti inflicted the final humiliation on me. I'd have loved to have been on the pitch to say goodbye to the San Siro, a legendary stadium that always treated me with respect and admiration. I knew that the Milan fans had also prepared a choreography for me – and this was a huge honour, usually if you have respect for a historic opponent, you just applaud him – and when El Sharaawy made it 3-1 to us with ten minutes to go, I imagined that the last substitute would be me. Instead, in the 84th minute, Spalletti called Bruno Peres and brought him on for Džeko. 'I feared their counter-attacks,' the coach would answer in response to the outraged questions of many journalists. As if that weren't enough, in those last irrelevant minutes, we also won a penalty. Daniele took it, but if I'd been on the pitch it would have been mine: finishing at the San Siro with the last goal of my career, just think, what a great story.

We were still aiming for second place, and an automatic qualification spot for the Champions League, and on matchday 36 we beat Juve 3-1 at the Olimpico, postponing their title party and keeping Napoli, who weren't dropping a single point, at a distance. I came on in the 93rd minute, a nice minute that let me say goodbye to Buffon on the pitch. It was a small thing, but at that time such things seemed important to me. The following week we struggled slightly to a win in Verona, and then there was only the home game with Genoa remaining. Roma needed to pick up three points to get automatic qualification for the Champions League, which would be an excellent accomplishment. Yet nobody in the city was talking about it: Roma-Genoa would see the Olimpico sold out for a completely different reason.

I also realised that it was a special week because of the fact that Spalletti was looking for a confrontation. He behaved with me as he did during his first spell in charge, when we got on well with each other. But he had to deal with my frostiness. The atmosphere of the last year and a half couldn't be forgotten.

'Francesco, let's find a nice way for you to play this last game.'

'What do you have in mind, boss?'

'You tell me. Do you want to play from the start?'

'Hmm, I don't like it… If we don't win, then it's my fault.'

'Come off it.'

'Boss, do as you always have this year. Think about the good of the team, protect it from me. If we're winning 4-0 in the last minute, then I can come on and say goodbye to everyone.'

'Ah, I knew there wouldn't be any reasoning with you…'

I was resentful. It was natural. But I listened to him, for a good hour, because he asked me what I intended to do, and I realised that none of it would matter to him because he'd already decided to leave. Vito maintains that great champions need someone to tell them 'It's over', because otherwise they'd go on forever: we don't realise the passage of time. Spalletti was that someone for me, but he ended up paying for the way he did it in terms of stress. He's said so himself on TV: if he could go back, he wouldn't accept his second go at Roma. We ended our long discussion by agreeing I would play a role in the second half. Time would also tell, depending on how the game was going: I was 40 years and 8 months old, I hadn't been training with the necessary attention since February, and I couldn't let myself forget that Roma were playing for quite a lot on Sunday.

It was a complicated week. For one thing, I needed to find all the tickets that were being asked of me: I'd always got hold of a lot, and in normal situations friends and acquaintances were satisfied with two or three tickets. This time, however, they needed them in packs, ten or fifteen each, because nobody wanted to miss my farewell, and those who were close to me – in the sense that they could get to me – were literally besieged with requests. I didn't want to think too much about it, about Sunday, but it was impossible. Everyone I met said to me, 'I can't believe it, you can't retire', which was obviously a courtesy, but it sprinkled salt on an open wound. Because in those days, the most intimate, most profound part of me still didn't want to retire.

Ilary, who knew this, tried to keep me busy with the preparations for the ceremony – would it be right to call it that? It's not like it was a party… – and the day's logistics. As the good friend he is, Walter Veltroni sent me the sketch of a letter full of poetry and memories, but it seemed too demanding. 'You have to write it yourself, I can help you,' Ilary judged, and we set ourselves down on our big bed to put my most meaningful thoughts together. Every now and then I got stuck, because I had a lump in my throat. 'Hey, don't cry!' she pleaded with her usual conviction. I didn't cry. Or I cried just a bit, trying to make sure she didn't notice. I had an allergy. A cold. A bug in my eye. The last letter I'd written was to her, a message of love ahead of our marriage. I told her that I was moved by that memory, and maybe she believed me.

But would I be able to read this letter in front of 80,000 people? Doubt suddenly came over me because, after all, I was used to playing football in front of such a crowd, not talking. Of course, there had been several occasions when I needed to say something in public, but not to *this* public. What if I couldn't carry on? Ilary had an idea. 'If you get stuck, the kids will come forward. A kind of passing of the baton, like in a relay race.' Cristian immediately waved his hand vigorously: don't even think about it. Chanel, on the other hand, was more than willing. Eager. If it were up to her, she'd read it all for me herself. We also set down the salient aspects of the afternoon with Vito. There were times when it seemed I was organising someone else's retirement, and then there were others when I had to force myself to calm the growing anxiety. But I couldn't concentrate on anything for more than five minutes: a TV show, a phone call, the computer. I tried to distract myself by looking on YouTube to see how the great modern English players – Beckham, Gerrard, Terry – had said goodbye. I watched all of those videos, partly in search of inspiration. I felt no pain for what was about to happen. An accurate way of defining the emotional state in which I found myself is melancholic.

Saturday evening. We had dinner at home, in the kitchen, and I noticed that Cristian and Chanel, instead of being in pyjamas as usual at this time, were dressed to go out. They also seemed to be agitated. Isabel's nanny was still around, another oddity that I didn't question. I had a sick feeling in my stomach that was so big it oppressed me. After eating, I sat down on the sofa to watch a game, but everyone was still awake and lively at half time. 'Hey? Why aren't you going to sleep?' Before getting an answer, I noticed a movement on the surveillance monitor of the external courtyard out of the corner of my eye. A moped had arrived. *That's rare, at this hour.* I told Ilary, who as always played it down: 'They'll go to the neighbours.' *Hmm.* I stayed in front of the screen, and within a few minutes a second moped had arrived, then a third. Eventually there were around ten. 'Ilary, call security, this is a gang!' She went over to where she'd left her phone (where I couldn't see her) and came back two minutes later with a mocking expression on her face, 'There's a party next door, don't worry. *Mamma,* how stressed you are!' There was a moment of silence, as I wasn't sure how to respond. She didn't let it slide: 'Listen, let's all go and get some ice cream at EUR, maybe that'll calm you down a bit, eh?' Cristian stifled a laugh. I was retiring the next day, and here they were, taking me for a ride.

We got on our mopeds. Cristian got on with me because he was afraid of riding with his mother. I always told him that Ilary doesn't know how to carry him. The gate opened to the external courtyard… and the convoy that I'd seen on the surveillance monitor was waiting there for us. Horns, applause, laughs, joy. All our closest friends were lined up with their helmets in hand. I looked at Ilary. 'You wouldn't have slept tonight. Let's go for a ride through Rome,' she said to me. Surprise. Happiness. Excitement. Just a few minutes before, I'd been feeling down. I love this woman.

It was a warm evening at the end of May, the time of year in which the majesty of Rome reaches its peak. I totally indulged myself. I led the group along the Cristoforo Colombo, heading towards Testaccio, because I'd learned that the fans had put a sticker on the street sign in Piazza Santa Maria Liberatrice, and I couldn't not get a picture taken under the new text, 'Piazza Francesco Totti, eighth king of Rome'. Wonderful. From there we continued on the Lungotevere, and when we'd drawn level with the centre we dived right in – I'd developed such a strong desire to see Piazza Navona after so many years that I was jumping out of my skin. Magnificent. We went around it two or three times, I couldn't get enough of it, but we had to go because some people had recognised me (even though I had a helmet on, who knows how they do it) and at that time of the evening – it must have been eleven – there was still a reasonable crowd. We travelled down Via del Corso, another street I hadn't been to for some time, and we went to have an ice cream on the Pincio terrace, above the Piazza del Popolo. Our friends brought it to me and Ilary so that we could sit there out of the way for a bit, on a bench, looking at the illuminated rooftops of Rome, and it was a perfect moment.

I told everyone about the letter that I'd prepared. They were enthusiastic about the idea of hearing it at the Olimpico. Then there were other stops, other sudden starts at red lights because people in their cars had recognised me, other views, other beautiful things, and it was all great. By the time we returned home it was four in the morning, and at no point in the night had I felt at a loss, thinking about the fact that I'd be retiring from football the following day. Indeed, it seemed to me that I was reliving the night of the *scudetto*. I was even tired. I fell asleep immediately, like a little angel.

Sunday morning. I went to Trigoria for breakfast, as always, but I was reminded that it was a special occasion by the groups of kids on the street and outside the sports centre's gates. The match was a very important one, but their chants weren't the usual incitements to victory. This time they were all about me. At Trigoria, I lingered, trying not to let myself be noticed, for a long time on the looks that my teammates were giving me. They were sad but at the same time excited at the idea of the spectacle of a full stadium, so rare nowadays. Everyone was expecting an afternoon of many tears, but of sweet, positive, affectionate ones. 'Think what a day it'll be,' some of them said to me. 'Your farewell to football, and it's happening at the Olimpico: imagine what bad luck it would have been if the last game had been away.' I hadn't thought about it, but it was true.

We played at six. After our meal came the technical meeting. I followed the brief video analysis of Genoa's set pieces absent-mindedly. The tension was mounting. Since I woke up, it had been a whole series of 'the last time I do this', 'the last time I do that', but now that the time for getting the bus to the stadium was approaching – another last time, and a big one – I couldn't sit still. Before the meeting, Mum called: 'I'm not coming, I can't do it. Enjoy the evening, I'll be crying in front of the TV.' *I stayed in Rome all my life for you, Mum. Above all, for you. If people's affection is overflowing out of every pore tonight, as I imagine, it will also be because of you.*

Vito called me when I was getting dressed after my shower. 'There are a couple of people who'd like a photo.' *I'm coming, I'm coming, but quickly, before the bus leaves. Selfies today too, huh? Maybe it could have been avoided...* I went out into the square, where there was a bus. An unstoppable anger rose inside me. 'Hey, there must be fifty people in there! Do I have to take a photo with everyone? You're crazy!' Vito didn't answer. He just smiled. Inside the bus, the occupants jumped to their feet at the same moment, they'd been crouched down on their seats to avoid being seen. Ilary appeared at the front, on the exit steps, and a quick glance at the scene was enough to understand that all the people I cared about were inside. They sang, they jumped around and they showed off their 'strip', a white T-shirt with the words '6 unico'. A brilliant quote. I didn't know what to say. 'You almost got the number right,' Vito tells me, 'there are forty-eight in there. Poor things, look at how sweaty they are: they've been waiting for you out here in the sun since lunchtime.' A kiss and a hug for everyone, for Angelo, for Giancarlo and Giancarlo, for Bambino, for Silvia and Melory. My most important support had arrived. It was up to me to take the next step myself.

On the way to the stadium, I turned off the camera pointing at me for a future documentary. De Rossi and Florenzi were sat behind me, and as soon as I got distracted they started pulling faces, damn them. They were taking advantage of it while they could because when it came to it, they'd break down. Daniele had said to me: 'I'll come and give you the team's gift, but don't remotely think about making me say something. I won't even be able to look you in the face because of the emotion. It's only fair that you know.' Arriving at the stadium, I thought I'd developed a fever because a long cold shiver ran down my back, even though it was boiling hot. I never had such a fragmented journey from the bus to the dressing room: everyone stopped me, both people who know me and people I'd never seen. I had the impression that someone had 'sold' a few seats in the front row because even certain areas that were off-limits to non-employees were full of unknown yet visibly excited faces. When photographers asked me for a preliminary lap of the pitch to take some nice farewell pictures, I gladly said yes: the dressing room was too crowded.

The game was strange. Their young forward Pietro Pellegri scored immediately. Luckily Džeko equalised just as quickly. Roma dominated, creating chances, but without getting the breakthrough. We went in at half time at 1-1, while Napoli were already winning 2-0 at Samp. We already knew it before, but this was confirmation: there was no other option. If we wanted to finish second, we had to win. On returning to the dressing room, Spalletti asked me to start warming up.

It was during that warm-up that I clearly perceived a different noise than usual in the Olimpico. A kind of long rumble, like a very powerful engine coming from far away, which was slowly increasing in decibels and which, when it arrived, would have a deafening effect. During the lap of the pitch before kick-off, I'd seen that people had displayed flags and banners dedicated to me everywhere, a prologue to what – I imagined – would happen after the 90th minute. Then, however, the pathos of the game took a sort of planned shore leave: people knew I would come on in the second half, so they could focus on Roma's fate until that happened. Seeing me jog down the touchline brought everyone's attention back to why they were there. At the cost of sounding egocentric, I have to say that, at that moment, the perception was all-consuming. In fact, it was almost paralysing, because when Spalletti called me to put me on in place of Salah – incidentally, the exit from Roma of a champion for whom, the following year, there would be talk of the Ballon d'Or – my legs were shaking. If we'd been in Brescia in March instead of in Rome at the end of May, I'm sure that in the attempt to take off my tracksuit bottoms quickly, they would have got caught around my boots like on that afternoon in

1993. It would have been the perfect closing of the circle between my first game in Serie A and number 619, the one that Tagliavento invited me to enter by signalling for me to come on. It was the ninth minute of the second half. This time, Spalletti gave me plenty of minutes, and crucially he put me on while the result was still in the balance.

Physically I was down, I knew it, and that was confirmed on the pitch. Consequently, I played without taking many touches, making the most of my technique: I freed Kevin Strootman for a shot from distance that went just wide and then, in the middle of the area, made a run and called for an easy cutback from Džeko. I was about to hit it with my right foot when De Rossi, who was in a frenzy that day, came in left-footed with a strike that was three times more powerful than mine would have been. I even had to jump out of the way, otherwise it could have hit me: it was the goal that made it 2-1, and it seemed to dispel the shadows from our pitch.

But a few minutes later, Darko Lazović, taking advantage of a misjudgement from Szczęsny, brought the scores level again at 2-2, and in the following counter-attack, it was Lazović again who hit the post. Panic. The public were there for me, but for the day to be fully successful, victory was essential. From thirty metres out, I put a ball on the head of El Shaarawy, but he sent it over. By then we were camped in the Genoa half, and the prize came in the 90th minute: a flick-on from Džeko and a great volley from Perotti from close range: 3-2, and everyone went crazy. Diego jumped a couple of advertising boards and ran under the Curva Sud. I was among the last to join him, partly because I climbed over everything slowly – I didn't want to hurt myself at that point. My worries were almost over. Almost. The referee signalled five minutes of injury time, and in the meantime gave Perotti a yellow card for excessive celebration.

Five minutes. It was then that I felt the avalanche come down on me. As long as Roma were chasing a result, my mind had been focused on something else. Now that the result had been achieved, and the mission was to 'waste' five minutes, the situation suddenly appeared to me in all its enormity. And in its paradox. I had to *waste* the last five minutes of my career. I, who, if I could, would have played another five thousand minutes. The thought tormented me until I found myself, who knows how, by the corner flag, ready to battle with Diego Laxalt in front of me. I kicked the ball, and seconds later the referee blew his whistle three times. It was over. A couple of Genoa players came over to be the first to hug me, Laxalt did so afterwards, as if it was only in that moment that it occurred to him that he was part of a scene that was bigger than him.

It was over. I felt a huge hole widening inside me, like a chasm that takes your breath away. I briefly celebrated with my teammates because ultimately we'd achieved our objective, and this was a great thing. But then I was in a hurry to get to the dressing room. I'd promised this to myself again and again: *If you feel you're losing emotional control, trust in the schedule you've memorised.* So at that point, I had to disappear and get changed while the others stayed on the pitch, the president came down from the stands, and the scenography could be set up.

The first very hard moment was this one. In the empty dressing room, where the noises of the stadium were a distant hum, there was me, Vito and our five kit men. They were crucial people, burdened by me for their entire lives, indeed for longer than that because before them it was their fathers, a reaffirmation of this extraordinary family story that is Roma. Think of Giuseppe Giannini, whose father was a youth team coach. Think of Daniele De Rossi, whose father is the Primavera coach. Think of Bruno Conti and the relations with his son Daniele I told you about. The five kit men started to cry their eyes out, and I had to start shouting – with my voice broken by the first tears – 'Don't try it', 'If we start like this we'll be here all night', and any similar nonsense that came into my head to stem the tide. They turned around to avoid looking at me, I turned around to avoid looking at them, and Vito later told me that he almost fainted at that precise moment when, with my back to him, I took off my shirt. He knew that that was the last Roma shirt that I would take off, the last one soaked in my sweat, and he felt the earth fall away beneath his feet. A knife to the heart. I faltered a moment later, while taking off my boots. I hurried things up and left the dressing room. I sat on the steps outside, and I waited for the moment to enter the stage. Many minutes passed, about twenty minutes, there are photos that show me staring into the void. Actually, I was thinking: not about the future, but about the past. I thought and I relived victories, defeats, injuries. The deprivation was unbearable. Mutilating.

When they told me that it was time – everything was ready and the stadium was waiting for me – I headed towards the Distinti Sud exit, thinking about how nice it would be if Pallotta was waiting for me with a new contract in his hand, ready to say that it was all a big joke. But it was nonsense that flashed through my mind in a few moments. I knew all too well that it was over, that this was it. I came out into the light, and the roar of the Olimpico was like the one for the *scudetto*. Everyone was on their feet, applauding. Music from *Gladiator* floated through the air.

I've rewatched the videos of those minutes many times. I continue to do so even today, and every time gifts me with a new detail, a banner that I hadn't noticed, a face that makes me feel some very intense emotions. What happened at the Olimpico that afternoon was unprecedented, because thousands and thousands of people were crying as if a very dear relative had died, interpreting my retirement from football as a farewell to an important part of their lives. Without insincerity, I knew it would be a special ceremony, somewhere between a graduation party and a day of mourning. But not this. The amount of affection and gratitude that poured over me was so huge that it brought me back to the same old question: Did I do enough to deserve this? I can only answer in one way: I love these people, from the bottom of my heart, and everything I did had only one purpose, to hear them roar with joy and pride at the moment when Roma scored a goal. I'm a simple and helpful person, I almost never say no, and sometimes I suffer because of how much the people's passion ultimately denies me the pleasure of enjoying my city. But I'd do it all again, without the slightest doubt, just so that I could feel what it was like to receive such exorbitant love once again. The most famous banner from that day, 'I was hoping I'd die before this', is very funny, but it also makes you think: while it's just for fun, and has that typically Roman sense of humour, whoever wrote it put the pain he felt at my retirement above that for his own death… I still can't believe it.

Pallotta was the first to meet me. He hugged me and spoke in English in my ear for a long time. I hardly understood anything, but it was the tone that mattered, and it was affectionate and respectful. The public whistled it and I was sincerely sorry for that, just as I was sorry that there were whistles when I went to greet the other directors. It was over, even those who loved me needed to understand that. The second very hard moment came when Ilary and our children arrived on the pitch. It was a condition that I'd set: I only wanted my family next to me during the lap around the stadium. But when the kids ran towards me, the defences that I'd built up to keep me from getting emotional came crashing down. We held each other for a long time, a very long time. You can see that I needed a little release, because after those tears I felt quite refreshed. I picked up Isabel in my arms and we started the lap.

Everyone was crying. Some composedly, some shaking with sobs, many couples were crying in each other's arms, and there were even those who turned around because they couldn't look at me, couldn't find the strength. It wasn't just an unforgettable moment. It was much more than that.

I slowly passed under the Curva Nord. Every now and then I bowed down because it was the only way for me to pay homage to such excessive affection. *I love you. I love you all, each one of you.* When I arrived under the Tribuna Tevere, I stopped, leaning against an advertising board, and I looked – because I knew they were there – for the old fans from the Curva Sud, those who a quarter of a century earlier had first initiated me and immediately chosen me as their favourite, supporting me and defending me. They were memories that burned at that moment. I was getting emotional again, and Vito had to come and lead me away, as usual with both gentleness and decisiveness, because otherwise I would have remained in the eye of that storm of emotions for who knows how long.

Every so often I brushed Cristian's blond hair with one hand, as if looking for the energy of youth. I needed a lot of that for the most tiring lap of the pitch – or rather, running track – of my career. Which became an Everest once I was in front of the Curva Sud.

The plan was to kick a ball into it, but there had been a crazier one, if fate had given me the opportunity: if, on that final Sunday, I'd been able to take a penalty – with the result already secured – I would have kicked it directly into the stand, a kind of ultimate gift to my people. The result being secured already was a condition that I'd promised to the very few who knew, in fact I'd have liked to do it anyway... as soon as we were a goal up. OK, right, let's not exaggerate. In any case, there was no penalty, and the ball I had to give to the *curva* was the one Vito was handing me, together with a marker pen. I wrote 'I'll miss you' on it, signed it and, before kicking it far away, I looked at it for a long time, reluctant to part with it.

Everything seemed symbolic to me, and the final kick had a powerful significance. Then I decided. I turned slightly to set myself, then sent it with the outside of my right foot into the *curva*, towards the highest rows. I saw a good melee where it landed, and for a moment I wondered who would take it home. (I soon found out, just a couple of days later, because the guy who managed to capture it came to Trigoria to let me know, also showing me the video – taken on his mobile – in which you can see the ball being kicked and flying closer and closer until it hits the smartphone. Yes, I hit it, making him drop it, and the screen broke too, but from what the guy told me, he wasn't worried about getting a refund: 'I've already been offered €100,000 for that ball, but I wouldn't give it away even for €10 million.' Come on now, it's not like it's a relic.)

Back under the main stand, I found the team lined up. De Rossi was the last in the line. He came forward to bring me the gift and, as promised, was noticeably looking at the ground because he didn't have the strength to look me in the eyes. He managed to give Cristian a pat but then, when he handed me the salver signed by all the members of the team, I hugged him and he dissolved. He went back to his place, and I started the thanks by going to the other end of the line. Where Spalletti was waiting for me. I didn't waste time and shook his hand without letting our eyes meet. During my lap, the TV cameras had focused on him a couple of times, and the stadium had whistled him angrily. I know that he later had a heated discussion with a journalist from Sky, thinking that he was the one who was picking the camera shots. I began to go up the line from Federico Fazio, stopping to hug Emerson Palmieri because he was on crutches, and I told him, 'Take care of yourself.' He's a good guy, I wanted him to come back strong. I also hugged Bogdan Lobonț, old Lobonț, my rehabilitation partner, an exceptional guy. Many were crying, Alisson said 'Thank you' to me, and his face was red as a pepper. Not even a tough guy like Manōlas held back the tears. I arrived at the far end, where the teammates who were closest to me for various reasons were waiting. Radja Nainggolan isn't the sort for tissues, but he wasn't hiding his emotions. The tears were flowing for Florenzi. De Rossi, well... he'd already told me. He still couldn't look at me. How much you and I mean to each other, Daniele.

I was handed a microphone, while the chant went up from the Olimpico, 'One captain, there's only one captain,' which is the chant I'm most fond of. The one that, at a certain point in every game, reminded me of my role, of its privileges and its responsibilities, wherever I played, whether in Italy or in Europe.

I read the letter I prepared with Ilary, often stopping myself, though not out of emotion but rather to give it a rhythm. By then I was quite detached, as I had to be, given the fervour of the subjects I'd written about.

There was one subject in particular that I wanted to express: the fear of what would happen now that I could no longer work with my feet. I'd been forgiven for everything, thanks to them. I'd got to know incredible people, thanks to them. I went through twenty-five wonderful years, thanks to them, because I went into the dressing room at Roma as a boy and I left it that day as a man. I reminded everyone that being born a Roman and a Romanista is a privilege and that captaining my people for so many years had been an immense honour. By this point, the tears were less intense, and while the big screen continued to focus on very drained fans, I saw salty tear trails already drying on their cheeks in some of the close-ups.

It was time to rationalise what had happened, for everyone. To remember our glory one last time – and the reference to the day of all days, the *scudetto*, was a must – and to start thinking about what was to come. In the air that the Olimpico breathed that day, there was, very noticeably, the lives of all of us who were there. Real, profound lives, and the humanity they contain. Everything that unites us is the child of our humanity.

Speaking of children: many would have liked it if, once I'd taken off my captain's armband, I'd then put it around Cristian's arm. I never gave it a second thought. I didn't want to put either burdens or pressure on him. He enjoys football a lot and he's good at it too, but it will be him, at the right moment and based on the skill he's developed, to decide what he does with his life. And I find this freedom to be the greatest gift a father can give to his children. The armband thus ended up on the arm of Mattia Almaviva, the captain of the Esordienti, class of 2006, the year of my world title. He tied it tightly around his arm, wrapping it around it twice, because he was terrified of the idea of it slipping off. I know that today, when he plays on the various pitches around the city, many point at him: 'He's the one who received the armband from Totti.' I hope I didn't create a problem for him, but being a captain means he had already started developing his personality. The fundamental quality, if you want to wear the captain's armband.

The rest was my teammates throwing me in the air – and I put up with it, because that type of celebration always scared me – the last shower with them, billions of photos on and off the pitch, because everyone had a relative who 'absolutely can't miss this chance', and comments about what had just happened at the Olimpico while we were returning to Trigoria, where I had left the car. I was very calm by then. I'd been afraid of this day, I'd feared that something would happen that might ruin it, but instead everything went smoothly. I felt good, but empty. My apprehension concerned what came next. My life had been running in the same way for twenty-five years. It wouldn't be easy to find new rhythms, new things that would excite me. But I decided I'd think about that tomorrow. At that point, I just wanted to go home.

Ilary, however, had a different idea: 'Let's go to Claudio's, this isn't an evening to spend on the sofa.'

'OK, but we should have warned him. He'll have closed now.'

'Let's try anyway.'

We arrived at the Piramide, and from a distance I could see that the sign was off, just like the lights in the restaurant. A little bad humour came over me. A phone call would have been enough.

'Let's get a better look, come on.' Thinking back to the night tour around Rome of the previous night, I sensed that something had been secretly organised here as well. But it was only right to give Ilary the satisfaction, so I pretended I hadn't realised. 'We'll go if you really want, but it all looks closed to me.' We approached La Villetta cautiously; everything was dark and silent inside. She tried the door handle, which 'strangely' went down. It was the signal. The lights went on, people came out from under the tables, there were more friends and relatives there than there had been in the bus at Trigoria, 150 people with the same

T-shirt, the now proverbial '6 unico'. It was a wonderful evening, full of songs and even dancing, because at one point Claudio cleared the tables, and it didn't seem real to be getting on them: we laughed, we joked, we talked more about the afternoon at the Olimpico, we toasted a thousand things, and above all everything was kept at full volume next to me to stop silence and solitude from making me think. And from making me sad.

We returned home at half past two, with Cristian and Chanel overcome by tiredness. The gate slid on its tracks, and Ilary immediately noticed the lights were on in the kitchen. *What's happened?* I let her get out before I parked the car in the garage, and when I entered the house – two minutes later – I couldn't have been more worried. Isabel was struggling to breathe. *What do we do?* Ilary called her mother, who lived next door to us, and together they left for the emergency room at the Bambino Gesù. I put the other two to bed and sat down on the sofa, waiting for news. The anguish was such that suddenly I'd forgotten everything, the day, the previous months, my career: Isabel's emergency prevailed over everything, or rather the spotlight shifting to her removed it from all of my stories, which had gone on for long enough. I just wanted her to be OK, that was the only thing I asked for, and the sigh of relief when Ilary told me, with a text message, that she was reacting well to treatment must have been heard all over Italy. Two more messages and the picture cleared: the doctor said that it was a laryngospasm – an enlargement of the vocal cords that makes breathing difficult – caused by some allergy or virus. When he realised that it was my daughter and therefore that she'd spent the afternoon rolling around on the grass at the Olimpico, he said that she definitely picked it up there. Nothing that some antibiotics couldn't cure.

Of course, there was no connection – if not precisely her presence on the pitch – between my retirement and the shock that Isabel had. Once I was calmer, though, I couldn't help but think that real life had immediately sent me a signal that the party was over: Francesco, you've enjoyed yourself enough. At seven in the morning, Ilary returned with Isabel, who was sleeping peacefully. The longest day of my life was finally over.

After a three-month holiday, during which there was the meeting in London with Pallotta and Baldini that I've already told you about, I started work again, trying to learn tricks of the trade from Monchi, the new sporting director, a Spaniard who did great things at Sevilla and from the very start showed grace and pleasure in sharing his work with me. In recent years, Roma have become a very solid club, no longer exposed to the financial turmoil that has become so normal in the football world, and when I tour the world to represent them – such as at the Champions League draw – there is a general feeling of respect. For the club, and of course for me. Once my apprenticeship is over, I think the best role for me will be in the technical area, in contact with the coach and the team, because I'm well aware of what they need to perform at their best. And then, let me also say that I can quickly recognise who the stars are, or at least, before others can. All I need to see is a control, a shot or a dribble to know how much football someone has inside them. If his talent crosses a certain threshold, it somehow manages to communicate with mine. It's a kind of magic.

I'm very determined to make a mark in this new career too, but the old one will never be forgotten, in part because it's largely recorded, and all I need is a remote control to arrange a nice journey back in time. But I need to take Cristian to a good eye doctor. The other evening, he caught me on the sofa while I was watching an old goal compilation, from the first Zeman era, and he asked me if I was crying. What an idea. A trivial allergy. I'd got a cold. And then a bug had flown in my eye.

Acknowledgements

WHEN PAOLO CONDÒ SUGGESTED THAT WE WRITE THE story of my life together, I said yes straight away because I knew about and admired the depth of the human narrative in his interviews. At that point, however, I had to provide him with all the 'raw material' in my possession – forty years of memories – as well as what was preserved in the memories of those who accompanied me along this extraordinary journey. I asked my mum Fiorella and dad Enzo for help to reconstruct my childhood years. My brother Riccardo and cousin Angelo were invaluable in reviving the most entertaining incidents from our youth. Invaluable friends like the two Giancarlos – Pantano and Ciccacci – brought back moments that I hadn't forgotten, but which had been lying dormant in my head under a veil of dust. I smiled many times when remembering particular stories; I reconnected the younger part of me with the present one, Francesco the father. I think Cristian and Chanel – and, one day, young Isabel – will laugh a lot at some of the exploits of their young dad.

The recovery work, naturally, became easier – and more pleasant – from the chapter in which I meet Ilary, the woman who changed my life even without being a huge football expert. In fact, precisely for this reason. Her love and her extraordinary perception have always allowed her to read my moods as a person and not as a personality, and as a result to give me the right advice at the most delicate times. Without her support,

I wouldn't have been able to withstand the long goodbye to my playing career, and the way that she knew how to tell the children – without making them sad – why their father, after many happy and carefree years, was often coming home feeling down was incredible. Ilary really is my secret, and I thank her sister Silvia for having favoured our first meeting at the time, and for the care with which she managed me during the period when I had to dedicate time to working on the book despite having many commitments as a director at Roma.

Vito Scala has long since crossed the boundaries of my sporting life: he's the friend I wish everyone had, loyal, precious, able to make you think with a courageous 'no' rather than throwing you into a comfortable 'yes'. We met when I was little more than a child, and we've been together throughout my entire career as a footballer, both for Roma and for Italy. Many 'playing' memories are his; listening to them again, at times I was touched. And the photos: Luciano Rossi and his son Fabio took thousands of me, and with such high-quality material, choosing a selection was a long job but not a difficult one.

Paolo knows Rome well but he isn't a Roman, so he needed some help to fully understand some aspects of my world: Alessio Nannini, a journalist born and raised in the Quadraro and Capannelle districts, and who is used to working with him, gave him a good explanation of the environments of youth football and the expectations that accompanied me from when I was just a kid. They were his, too, given that he supports Roma. I then pointed Paolo and Alessio in the direction of various 'custodians' of my secrets, from Claudio – the owner of the restaurant La Villetta – to Vincent Candela, from Daniele Pradè to Giorgio Perinetti, from Rosella Sensi to Marcello Lippi. I thank each of them for their willingness to remember, and for their pleasure in doing so as well. I felt very flattered by how determined Rizzoli were in having my story. They made me feel really important, and they gave the task of making the book a reality to the best members of their team. Massimo Turchetta – the director – man-marked me until I signed the contract; Andrea Canzanella – the editor – worked meticulously on the text, improving it in numerous places (even Paolo admitted this, albeit through gritted teeth); Luisa Colicchio – PR – oversaw the book's fine-tuning and the launch. I spoke with them many times, and I realised one thing: it wasn't just work. By the end, it was them who were thanking me...

www.decoubertin.co.uk